THE PICKERING MASTERS

SELECTED WORKS OF ROBERT OWEN

Volume 1. *Early Writings*

SELECTED WORKS OF
ROBERT OWEN

EDITED BY
GREGORY CLAEYS

VOLUME
1

EARLY WRITINGS

Routledge
Taylor & Francis Group
LONDON AND NEW YORK

First published 1993 by Pickering & Chatto (Publishers) Limited

Published 2016 by Routledge
2 Park Square, Milton Park, Abingdon, Oxon OX14 4RN
605 Third Avenue, New York, NY 10017

Routledge is an imprint of the Taylor & Francis Group, an informa business

British Library Cataloguing in Publication Data

Owen, Robert

Works of Robert Owen. – (Pickering Masters Series)

I. Title II. Claeys, Gregory III. Series

335.0092

ISBN 13: 978-1-851-96088-0 (set)
ISBN 13: 978-1-138-64637-7 (hbk)

Typeset by Waveney Typesetters
Norwich

VOLUME 1

CONTENTS

VOLUME 2

CONTENTS

VOLUME 3

CONTENTS

VOLUME 4

CONTENTS

These volumes are dedicated to my wife,
Christine Lattek,
upon whom they have entailed
more practical infant education
than might otherwise have been the case;
and to
Christopher and Daniel,
born 21 May 1993.

ACKNOWLEDGEMENTS

These volumes, and especially Owen's *Life* (vol. 4) would have been impossible to annotate adequately without the efforts of many already hard-pressed librarians throughout Britain. I have relied particularly heavily on the resources of the Mitchell Library, Glasgow (with special thanks to Anne Escott); the Central Library, Manchester (with special thanks to David Taylor); and the National Library of Wales (with special thanks to Geraint Phillips). I am very grateful, in addition, to the Co-operative Union Library, Manchester; the Goldsmiths' Library, University of London, especially for help in supplying many of the texts in vol. 2; the libraries of University College, London, and Royal Holloway, University of London; The British Library, and especially Alastair Lunn; The Oriental and India Office Collections, British Library; The Library, Westminster Abbey; The Army Records Society, National Army Museum; The Library, Friends House, London; The Guildhall Library, London; The Library of the German Historical Institute, London; Southwark Council Local Studies Library; Lambeth Palace Library, London; Kensington Palace Library; The Royal Archives, Windsor Castle; The Library of the Bank of England; The Foreign and Commonwealth Office Library; the libraries of Wadham College, Oxford, and Queens' College, Cambridge; The Lindsay Institute, Clydesdale District Council, Lanark; Blair Castle Library; Edinburgh University Library; Glasgow University Library; Ewart Library, Dumfries: West Lothian District Council Library Services; Central Library, Paisley; Edinburgh University Library; The Signet Library, Edinburgh; The General Register Office for Scotland; The Scottish Record Office; Central Library, Newcastle upon Tyne; Central Library, Gateshead; Harrogate Library; District Central Library, Blackburn; Castle Gates Library, Shrewsbury; Central Library, Reading; Grantham Library; Central Library, Leeds; Salford Local History Library; John Rylands University Library, Manchester; Stockport Central Library; Central Library, Derby; Bedfordshire County Record Office; Northamptonshire County Record Office; Lincolnshire Archives; Princeton University Library; The Workingmen's Institute, New Harmony, Indiana; University of Michigan Library; The Texas State Library, Austin; Madame Tussaud's; to the History of Ideas Unit and Historical Division of the Research School of the Social Sciences, The Australian National University, for a Visiting Fellowship; The Robert Owen Association of Japan, and especially Chushichi Tsuzuki; Westminister Cathedral Library; Jim Arnold and Lorna Davidson, New

Lanark Conservation; Newtown Library, Powys County Council; John Davidson, The Robert Owen Memorial Museum, Newtown; Dr Williams's Library, London; The Public Record Office, Kew; the Staatsbibliothek zu Berlin; the Bibliothèque Nationale, Paris; to David Craig for assistance in preparing the text; to John Hampson for help with proofreading; and finally to Yoshio Nagai, Shigeru Goto, and Naobumi Hijikata, John Hatton Davidson, John Cookson, David S. Scarth, Geoffrey Alderman, David McLaren for bibliographical assistance, and to John Corina, in particular, for generously sharing with me his vast knowledge of Owen's life.

INTRODUCTION

1. *Owen's Life*

The eighty-seven adventurous years of Robert Owen's life can be divided into two phases, each as extraordinary as they are extraordinarily different from each other. In his first four decades, Owen rose from obscure origins and small fortune, through great effort and ingenuity, to become one of the classic success stories of his age. Moreover, he was a pioneer in a field, cotton-spinning, which helped greatly to propel Britain towards industrial supremacy. By 1817, at the age of forty-six, Owen could boast a substantial fortune. His name opened palace gates and ministerial doors throughout Europe. He enjoyed wide respect as a successful entrepreneur and a philanthropist to boot. But during the second half of his life, Owen's passion for benevolence led him to expend his fortune, to defy respectable public opinion, and to herald a 'new moral world' of economic and social justice, security and equality, in which poverty would be abolished for all time. With comparable energy as he had mustered getting rich, he became a prophet, socialist, co-operator, secularist, feminist, and trade union organiser. At his death, he was widely regarded as among the most influential opponents of unrestricted *laissez-faire* in an age still reluctant to concede the limits of the doctrine. His name remains synonymous with all that the industrial revolution threatened and promised.

Owen was born in Newtown, Montgomeryshire, North Wales, on 14 May 1771, the next but youngest in a family of seven. His father, a saddler and ironmonger as well as the local postmaster, seems to have started well in life, but lost an estate worth £500 per annum through, he believed, his lawyer being bribed by an opponent. Owen's mother came from a farming family. A good sportsman, dancer, and budding clarinettist, the young Robert was a precocious child, devouring books at the rate of one a day, and becoming the schoolmaster's assistant. Pious in the extreme – it was a habit of mind which never entirely left him – he wrote youthful sermons and was known as 'the little parson'. But at the age of ten, Owen reached a great turning point in his life in concluding that 'there must be something fundamentally wrong in all religions, as they had been taught up to that period'.[a] Scepticism did not undermine his industriousness, however.

[a] Robert Owen, *The Life of Robert Owen*, vol. 1 (1857), p. 4 (*infra*, vol. 4, p. 54). All books cited in this edition were published in London unless otherwise noted.

Apprenticed to a Lincolnshire cloth merchant named James McGuffog from 1781–4, Owen still read five hours daily (including the Stoic, Seneca, whose advocacy of benevolence to all doubtless had some influence on his youthful views). But he also learned much about the clothing trade, and showed clear signs of initiative and promise. After three years, he joined a London retailer, here on his feet twelve or more hours daily, until a better offer arose in Manchester, at that time still a town of about 45,000, but poised to become the great industrial metropolis it would be by 1820.[a] Becoming curious about the new machinery being applied to cotton-spinning, Owen borrowed £100 from his brother William and entered into a partnership with a machine-maker constructing 'mules' for making thread. This was a success, with forty employees soon at work, and Owen's half was soon bought out by another eager investor, leaving him, in 1789–90, with the promise of six machines, though he finally received only three.

Opportunities now abounded for Owen. He seems to have made a striking impression on all around him; and his old master, McGuffog, offered him half of the profits in his shop. But Owen decided to spin thread instead, for the profits were considerable, with demand well outstripping supply. He was doing well when a large manufacturer, Drinkwater, advertised for a manager for his mill of five hundred employees.[b] A naive and inexperienced youth of twenty-one, Owen was hired nonetheless, though failure was widely predicted.[c] He spent six weeks scrutinising the factory, and quickly saw ways of refining the manufacturing process. Soon the quality of his thread was recognised as the best in the country, and he assumed the management of another mill of Drinkwater's in Cheshire employing several hundred workers.[d] Though he was still awkward socially, and spoke an accented Welsh English, Owen had a natural flair for dealing with all sorts of people, especially his employees. For some reason he also took a special interest in the morals and condition of his workforce, and the question of poor relief generally.[e] At the time, it was commonly believed that only religious conviction and draconian laws could

[a] On the general industrial context, see for example R. Lloyd-Jones and M. J. Lewis, *Manchester in the Age of the Factory* (Croom Helm, 1988). The economic ideas of the manufacturers are dealt with on pp. 131–54. For the origins of the factory system, see especially the late R.S. Fitton's *The Arkwrights. Spinners of Fortune* (Manchester: Manchester University Press, 1989).

[b] The best account of these events is W. H. Chaloner, 'Robert Owen, Peter Drinkwater and the Early Factory System in Manchester, 1788–1800', *Bulletin of the John Rylands Library*, vol. 37 (1954), pp. 79–102. On Owen's activities at this time, see also E. M. Fraser, 'Robert Owen in Manchester, 1787–1800', *Memoirs and Proceedings of the Manchester Literary and Philosophical Society*, vol. 82 (1937–8), pp. 29–41.

[c] Owen's autobiography errs by a year here, putting the date in spring 1791 instead of April 1792 (*Life*, vol. 1, 1857, p. 27).

[d] *New Moral World*, vol. 1, no. 42 (15 August 1835), p. 332.

[e] On the treatment of the poor in Manchester during this period, see G.B. Hindle, *Provision for the Relief of the Poor in Manchester 1754–1826* (Manchester: Chetham Society, 1975).

restrain the natural anarchy and sloth of the poor. But Owen suspected, and experience within a few short years at Manchester seemingly confirmed, that substantial differences in the moral behaviour of individuals, rich and poor alike, resulted primarily from their upbringing and environment. (His earlier loss of religious faith was clearly important in this respect).

Soon the order and discipline in Drinkwater's factory were the admiration of other cotton-spinning masters throughout Manchester. Drinkwater offered him a partnership with his own sons, which he accepted. He was solicited to join the prestigious Manchester Literary and Philosophical Society, which admitted him on 1 November 1793, and here he mingled with prominent local physicians, scientists, and fellow manufacturers. For an autodidact in illustrious company, he was precocious here, too, reading several papers, two of which, 'On the Origin of Opinions with a View to the Improvement of the Social Virtues' and 'Thoughts on the Connection Between Universal Happiness and Practical Mechanics', now lost, indicate that he had already thought much about moral reform. Owen was not, however, politically minded. He affirmed his loyalty to king and constitution during the great debates about reform in the early 1790s, declaring that he was 'fully confident that a Constitution, thus formed, will not fail to redress every real grievance, and effect every necessary improvement'.[a] But he also signed a petition supporting efforts to make peace with France in early 1795.[b] There was an air of independence, in fact, in much of what he did. When a powerful manufacturer, Samuel Oldknow, became Drinkwater's son-in-law and demanded greater control over his assets, Owen, in an impulsive if honourable move, voluntarily renounced his agreed partnership. But he soon attracted new partners, opened a new mill, and prospered. On a business visit to Glasgow, he met Caroline Dale, the daughter of a well-known Scottish manufacturer, David Dale, and they were married on 30 September 1799 at Dale's palatial house on Charlotte Street, Glasgow.[c] Dale and Richard Arkwright had built a mill south of Glasgow at New Lanark, in 1785, and commenced cotton-spinning the following year at a beautiful location on the banks of the Clyde which greatly impressed Owen on his first visit there (arranged as a pretext to meet Dale while courting his daughter), on 15 June 1798.[d] At the mill, Dale, who also had a philanthropic bent, had tried to

[a] *Manchester Herald*, 29 December 1792, p. 3. Other signatories included William Kennedy, Thomas Percival, Thomas Barnes, Thomas Henry, John Atkinson, James McConnel, Richard Moulson, and John Kennedy.

[b] *The Boroughreeve and Constables of Manchester* [broadside], 26 January 1795. This belies the oft-repeated view that Owen's politics were simply 'conservative' in this period. See for example Ralph Miliband, 'The Politics of Robert Owen', *Journal of the History of Ideas*, vol. 15 (1954), pp. 233–45.

[c] On Owen as a father, see Robert Dale Owen, *Threading My Way. An Autobiography* (New York, 1874), pp. 57–116. He gained £3000 by the marriage, thereby doubling his capital.

[d] On Dale, see David McLaren, *David Dale of New Lanark* (2nd edn, Milngavie: Heatherbank Press, 1992).

improve his workers' living standards and conditions, and, by the mid-1790s, had achieved considerable respect for his efforts.[a] Acquiring the factory with several partners in 1799, Owen moved there to take the post of manager of the New Lanark Twist Company on 1 January 1800. He had a ninth share in the proceeds, though when Dale died in 1806, he formed a new partnership which gave him about forty per cent of the profits, averaging about twelve and a half per cent per annum. Eventually he would share in some £300,000/$1.5 million (at contemporary prices) from its operations.[b]

But Owen was already thinking about more than profits. He sought at New Lanark 'to introduce principles in the conduct of the people, which I had successfully commenced with the workpeople in Mr Drinkwater's factory; and to change the conditions of the people'.[c] His approach here was not 'socialist'. Not only was the word not coined until the late 1820s,[d] Owen did not advocate profit-sharing at the mills. Nor did he dream of eliminating 'competition', which he would come to see as the chief cause of poverty. Indeed, he would later write that 'but small justice' had been done to the New Lanark population 'compared with that to which all humanity is justly entitled'.[e] Instead he sought to eradicate vice with minimal punishment, and without invoking eternal damnation, and to improve living and working conditions for his labourers. Initially, however, his ideas met with considerable resistance. The workforce naturally resented a foreigner living in their midst. Most were in Owen's eyes idle, intemperate, and dishonest to the point of regarding the mill as public property. He could have prosecuted several for theft. But Owen chose instead to treat them as victims of circumstances, and to adopt a more forgiving if also 'firm' and 'determined' approach to reform their habits.[f]

Some eighteen hundred people were settled at New Lanark, including about five hundred pauper children sent by parishes to gain respectable employment. (By 1820 about twenty-five hundred would reside there.) Despite Dale's educational efforts, life at the mill was far from idyllic. The working day remained

---

[a] On his educational schemes, see David McLaren, *David Dale of New Lanark* (2nd edn, Milngavie: Heatherbank Press, 1992), pp. 55–74.

[b] Robert Owen, *The New Existence of Man Upon the Earth* (1854), pt 5, appendix, p. xliii. On the business side of the New Lanark years, where Owen's own account must be treated with some caution, see Peter Gorb, 'Robert Owen as a Businessman', *Bulletin of the Business Historical Society*, vol. 25 (1951), pp. 127–48, A. J. Robertson, 'Robert Owen, Cotton Spinner: New Lanark, 1800–1825', in Sidney Pollard and John Salt, eds, *Robert Owen. Prophet of the Poor* (Macmillan, 1971), pp. 145–65, and especially John Butt. 'Robert Owen as a Businessman', in John Butt, ed., *Robert Owen. Aspects of His Life and Work* (New York: Humanities Press, 1971), pp. 168–214.

[c] Robert Owen, *Life*, vol. 1 (1857), pp. 56–7.

[d] 'Owenite' was used as early as 1821 (*The Economist*, vol. 2, no. 39, 20 October 1821, p. 212). Owen protested against its use to describe his system (*The Sun*, no. 9801, 21 January 1824, p. 2). 'Socialist' first appears in print in the *London Co-operative Magazine*, vol. 2, no. 11 (November 1827), p. 509n.

[e] *Robert Owen's Millenial Gazette*, no. 9 (15 October 1856), p. 8.

[f] Robert Owen, *A New View of Society* (1857 edn), in *Life*, vol. 1, p. 283 (*infra*, vol. 1, p. 51).

long, goods in the company store were shoddy and expensive, and the housing was inadequate.[a] Owen set out to change all this.[b] He brought in superior goods at lower prices, reducing the cost of living by some twenty-five per cent. When an American cotton embargo halted production for four months, Owen continued to pay full wages. The risk cost him £7000, but it won him 'the confidence and the hearts of the whole people'.[c] Within six years of arriving, Owen's efforts were relatively unhindered. His next ambition was to improve performance in the workplace. This he effected in part by using a 'silent monitor', a painted piece of wood which reflected with different colours the achievements of each worker, from black denoting poor performance to white connoting excellence. Slowly black gave way to white in the workshop. In 1816, he reduced the working day from eleven and three quarter hours to ten and three quarter hours. That year, he opened his school, the Institute for the Formation of Character. Paid for entirely out of profits from the store, it combined dancing, singing, and military exercises. (Owen taught military tactics himself, and the workers marched to the mills to a fife and drum.)[d] At the Institute, Owen, who could rightly later claim to be a pioneer in the field of infant education[e], sought in particular to exclude punishment, to make learning interesting to young minds, and to encourage the children to see their own happiness as contingent on that of others. Several visitors commented that he was much loved by the children, and had gone far towards extinguishing a 'government by fear'.[f] But fear played some role in his efforts to combat social indiscipline in the village itself. He fined all who had illegitimate children, the proceeds going into a sick fund. Pilfering, absenteeism and sloth were reduced by a firmer system of checks on stock and output. One-sixtieth of wages was automatically set aside for sickness, injury and old age. Internal order was also encouraged by reorganising the village into groups of houses called 'neighbourhood divisions'. Annually, the heads of households in each division chose a 'principal'. These elected twelve 'jurors' to sit monthly for one year, hearing and judging cases respecting the internal order of the community.[g]

The experiment was a marvellous success. Sometimes referred to as 'the

---

[a] Nonetheless Owen sometimes exaggerated his own achievements in relation to Dale, who already had a reputation as a philanthropist. For an account of Dale's management, see *Monthly Magazine*, vol. 2 (July 1796), pp. 458–60. At this time, Dale's school at the mills had 16 teachers and 507 pupils.

[b] On his early acts, see *Robert Owen at New Lanark* (Manchester, 1839).

[c] Robert Owen, *Life*, vol. 1 (1857), p. 64 (*infra*, vol. 4, p. 116).

[d] There is a good account of Owen's educational views in Harold Silver, *The Concept of Popular Education* (Macgibbon and Kee, 1965), pp. 67–200. The best contemporary view is Robert Dale Owen, *An Outline of the System of Education at New Lanark* (1824).

[e] See *New Moral World*, vol. 1, no. 3 (15 November 1834), p. 22.

[f] James Smith, *Notes Taken During an Excursion in Scotland* (Liverpool, 1824), p. 57.

[g] The original regulations are reprinted in Robert Owen, *The New Existence of Man Upon the Earth* (1854), pt 5, pp. ix–xi.

happy valley', within fifteen years New Lanark was renowned throughout Europe, and became a mandatory visit for touring foreign nobility, philanthropists, and the merely curious.[a] Despite the isolated location, over twenty thousand visitors arrived between 1815–25, sometimes as many as seventy a day. Owen's accomplishment was considerable: he had seemingly combined astonishing profits with wages which, while lower than in some factories, had a higher purchasing power in the village itself, as well as, as all conceded, a morally improved workforce. So well behaved were Owen's workers, indeed, that he could not be blamed for concluding in 1812 that 'any character might be formed by applying the proper means'.[b]

Owen planned to introduce public kitchens and dining rooms to reduce his employees' expenses still further.[c] His partners, however, grew alarmed at the potential expense of more improvements. Owen, in turn, was now tired of associates 'merely trained to buy cheap and sell dear'. In 1813, he formed a new partnership composed of the Baptist physician and philanthropist Joseph Fox; a former fishmonger and future Lord Mayor of London, Michael Gibbs; the exceedingly pious Quaker philanthropist William Allen; two other Quakers, Joseph Foster and John Walker; and the philosopher Jeremy Bentham. The latter was much too busy to concern himself with the management of New Lanark, though it was the sole investment in which he made any profit. (Owen did take up a vaguely defined utilitarianism in exchange, though he drew collectivist conclusions from it which were foreign to Bentham.) Amongst the other partners, William Allen usually held sway. Like Owen, Allen desired moral reform, but he could not accept that any but Christian means could attain it. At the outset, he prayed that 'the divine blessing attend the undertaking', and ensured, by pushing the point with Joseph Fox against Owen, that the articles of partnership included provision for religious education in the school, with no books to be placed in the library without being approved by a general meeting of the partners. Thus he hoped that the partners would 'be kept humble and cautious'. In several respects, however, Owen was neither. Within months, Allen recorded having 'painful conversation' on the subject of Owen's religious opinions, and in turn he firmly resolved to combat the latter's 'infidel plans'.[d] When the local Presbytery wrote to Allen and the other

[a] *Spirit of the Times*, no. 3 (24 March 1849), p. 21.

[b] *A Statement Regarding the New Lanark Establishment* (1812), p. 4 (*infra*, vol. 1, p. 14). For the industrial context generally, see especially Sidney Pollard, *The Genesis of Modern Management. A Study of the Industrial Revolution in Great Britain* (Edward Arnold, 1965), and for the cotton industry, Thomas Ellison, *The Cotton Trade of Great Britain* (1886). A good contemporary account is William Radcliffe, *Origins of the New System of Manufactures, Commonly Called 'Power-Loom Weaving'* (Stockport, 1828).

[c] For details of these plans, which Owen regarded as crucial to the growth of a more communal consciousness at New Lanark, see *infra*, vol. 1, pp. 58–9.

[d] William Allen, *The Life of William Allen* (3 vols, 1846), vol. 1, pp. 209, 215. Owen later reprinted several letters from Walker. See Robert Owen, *The New Existence of Man Upon the Earth*

partners, after a futile attempt to embarrass Owen by exaggerating the number of illegitimate births in the community (which was actually remarkably low), they mustered quickly to investigate, with Allen apparently leading the charge.[a] Owen hence later termed him 'a bigoted persecutor of my opinions during our partnership'.[b] But John Walker, at least, was much friendlier, and Owen acknowledged that he had learned much from their conversations, which he rarely admitted of anyone else.[c] The source of Owen's quarrels with William Allen was his essentially secular view of education, which at this time, heartened by the reception of a speech he had given at a dinner in honour of the educational reformer Joseph Lancaster, Owen first presented to the world in the form of *A New View of Society; or, Essays on the Principle of the Formation of the Human Character* (1813–14).[d] With the agreement of members of the goverment, who presumably found Owen's strong opposition to political reform useful,[e] he had two hundred copies distributed to organisations and institutions, bound with blank pages for comments. Claiming that he was 'making a greater sacrifice than perhaps any other person in the kingdom', he solicited the assistance of Samuel Whitbread and other social reformers.[f] As the evangelical movement gathered steam, a number expressed some sympathy, for the need to improve the morals of the poor was once again topical among the well-to-do. Still perhaps his best-known work, *A New View of Society* demanded a system of national education to prevent idleness, poverty and crime among the 'lower orders', and recommended restrictions on 'gin

(1854), pt 5, appendix, pp. lxviii-lxx. His sons, Charles (b. 1798) and Henry (b. 1807) acquired New Lanark after Owen's retirement, and managed the mills until their sale in 1881 to the Birkmyres (in 1903, Gourock) Ropeworks. Charles Walker was censured by the Edinburgh Quaker meeting for non-attendance and for allowing 'a system of education partly inconsistent with the Society' (William Marwick, 'Quakers in Victorian Scotland', *Journal of the Friends Historical Society*, vol. 52, 1969, p. 73). This may indicate an effort to continue some of Owen's principles. Charles resigned from the Society in 1841, and Henry in 1845.

[a] *Robert Owen at New Lanark* (Manchester, 1839), pp. 10–13. On this dispute, see *Wooler's British Gazette*, vol. 6, no. 246 (14 September 1823), p. 115.

[b] Robert Owen, *The New Existence of Man Upon the Earth*, pt 5 (1854), p. 6. For Allen's view of the partnership, see William Allen, *The Life of William Allen* (3 vols, 1846), vol. 1, pp. 181–3, 215, 244–8, 344–53. Allen tried to end the partnership in 1823 because the school education was insufficiently Christian (*ibid.*, vol. 2, p. 366). Walker seems to have agreed (*ibid.*, vol. 1, p. 182). Owen later reprinted some of the correspondence between Allen and himself. See Robert Owen, *The New Existence of Man Upon the Earth* (1854), pt 5, appendix, pp. i–ix, xv–lxvii.

[c] Robert Owen, *Life*, vol. 1 (1857), pp. 89, 94 (*infra*, vol. 4, pp. 142, 146–7). On Walker, see Robert Dale Owen, *Threading My Way* (1874), pp. 102–4. The John Walker who opposed Owen at the August 1817 meetings was not his partner, but the pioneer vaccinator John Walker (1759–1830), another wayward Quaker whose religious views (he was a friend of Paine's) were in fact not far from Owen's.

[d] There is some evidence that Owen approached Liverpool as early as 1810 with a draft 'Bill For the Formation of Character Among the Poor and Working Classes' to establish a national school system (Liverpool Papers, British Library Add. MS. 38, 361, ff. 47–51).

[e] See the passage deleted from later editions of *A New View of Society* and reproduced *infra* (vol. 1, p. 53).

[f] Owen to Whitbread, 21 March 1813, Bedfordshire County Record Office.

shops and pot houses' by raising duties until the price exceeded what most could pay. The state lottery and gambling should be curtailed, Owen suggested, and the penal system reformed, the monopolistic position of the Church of England ended, and statistics on the value and demand for labour throughout the country collected. Some have seen this variegated plan as a form of 'tentative state socialism'.[a] A few contemporary critics, such as William Hazlitt, linked it to the utopian tradition of Godwin, More, Plato and Harrington, and derisorily dismissed all such schemes as 'superannuated ... dead and buried'.[b] But other proposals for poor law reform in this period, such as Charles Weston's, were far more comprehensive, calling for the creation of a 'Board of Industry' to employ the poor, and considerable regulation of trade and the labour throughout the country.[c] Owen in fact denied advocating 'that the British government should now give direct employment to all its working population'. Instead, education would lead the poor 'to find employment sufficient to support themselves, except in cases of great sudden depression in the demand for, and consequent depreciation in the value of, labour'. To ensure the primacy of private enterprise, public labour on roads, docks, and ship-building would be paid less than the average local wage.[d] Given the fact that there is nothing socialistic in these proposals, it is hardly the case, as Leslie Stephen erroneously assumed, that Owen's 'essential views' are encapsulated here.[e]

At this time Owen evidently spoke freely about his environmentalist conception of character, which he felt eliminated not only any idea of Original Sin, but, when properly understood, all blame, anger and aggression. But he did not yet, at least too deliberately, offend the religious, for his acquaintances included Bishops and Archbishops as well as political economists and members of the nobility. (His wife Caroline also continued to hold strong Calvinist beliefs, and some visitors staying at New Lanark were brought a Bible unasked.)[f] In 1812–13, in fact, Owen stressed that the 'first grand step' in getting his plans adopted was to enlist the support of the Church.[g] But his secularist views, and even more his anti-clericism, were probably hardening throughout

---

[a] *Palgrave's Dictionary of Economics* (3 vols, Macmillan, 1926), vol. 2, p. 48.

[b] *The Examiner*, no. 449 (4 August 1816), p. 493.

[c] See Charles Weston, *Remarks on the Poor Laws and the State of the Poor* (1802), pp. 141–60.

[d] Robert Owen, *New View of Society* (1857 edn), in *Life*, vol. 1, pp. 311–13, 324–5 (*infra*, vol. 1, pp. 80–82, 93); *Palgrave's Dictionary of Political Economy*, (Macmillan, 1926), vol. 2, p. 48; *The Complete Works of William Hazlitt*, vol. 7 (Dent, 1932), p. 98; Charles Weston, *Remarks on the Poor Laws and the State of the Poor* (1802), pp. 141–60.

[e] *Dictionary of National Biography* (63 vols, Smith, Elder & Co., 1885–1900), vol. 14, p. 1345.

[f] John Griscom, *A Year in Europe* (2 vols, 1823), vol. 2, p. 383. Caroline Owen reputedly belonged to a sect, perhaps her father's, which had no established ministers and allowed anyone to preach. She did not attend the local kirk. She longed, however, for Owen's conversion from deism to Christianity, and even young Robert Dale Owen made an effort to convert his father, before succumbing for many years to scepticism himself (Robert Dale Owen, *Threading My Way*, 1874, pp. 76–7, 84).

[g] Robert Owen, *Life*, vol. 1 (1857), p. 80 (*infra*, vol. 1, p. 91).

this period. Between 1813–18, Owen made about fifty visits to the political thinker and religious sceptic William Godwin, whose *Enquiry Concerning Political Justice* (1793) had caused a great stir during the revolutionary debates a generation earlier. Godwin was also convinced that the innate elements in character were relatively unimportant, though his individualist approach to reform probably made him less sympathetic to the legislative thrust of Owen's plans. In addition, Godwin was almost permanently in financial difficulty, and could no longer afford to antagonise public opinion even if he wanted to.[a] Owen was still cautious about associating with plebeian secularists, however, refusing for example to attend Richard Carlile's blasphemy trial, when requested, on the grounds that 'for a short time I must continue to neglect the few for the many, that all may derive permanent benefit'.[b] Most who met him in this period, thus, seem to have taken Owen to be an enthusiastic but essentially benign and respectable philanthropist who held strong views on educational innovation and the condition of the labouring classes.

In an era when well-meaning philanthropists were legion, Owen might have remained no more than this. But circumstances forced him to insist that the experimental improvements of New Lanark should be extended to the nation at large. The events of 1815–16 underpinned this conclusion. As post-war unemployment rose sharply, wages fell, in some cases by fifty percent in a year, and social disorder threatened. In 1816, Owen announced that 'the chief object' of his existence would be to make 'universal' the results of his experiments with the character of the labouring classes.[c] Crucially, he now also insisted that the new manufacturing process be 'gradually diminished', for it had become, he claimed, 'our weakness and our danger'. Pleading for self-sufficiency, Owen stressed that Britain already depended 'far too much on a foreign demand for our manufactures', which he saw as far worse than relying on 'other countries for a limited supply of grain'. Eventually other manufacturing competitors would arise, and Britain would find her capacity to grow food limited by the division of labour she had forced on the world market.[d] By 1816 Owen was thus much more clamorous about the harmful social and psychological effects of the manufacturing system. He was evidently beginning to feel that irreconcilable differences lay between the imperatives of moral improvement and actual social and economic developments.

---

[a] For the contemporary linkage of Godwin to Owen, see for example Jasper Beatson, *An Examination of Mr. Owen's Plans* (Glasgow, 1823), p. 40.

[b] *The Reasoner*, no. 160 (20 June 1849), p. 382.

[c] *An Address to the Inhabitants of New Lanark* (1816), p. 17 (*infra*, vol. 1, p. 118).

[d] Robert Owen to Sidmouth, 16 March 1815, reprinted in *Bulletin of the Society for the Study of Labour History*, vol. 28 (1974), pp. 13–15, and introduced by Fred Donnelly. In the same year, Owen wrote that 'It is highly probable … that the export trade of this country has attained its utmost height, and that by the competition of other states, possessing equal or greater local advantages, it will now gradually diminish' (*Life*, 1A, 1858, p. 39) (*infra*, vol. 1, pp. 104–5).

Owen's doubts first surfaced in the *Observations on the Effects of the Manufacturing System* (1815). Here he identified for the first time 'immediate pecuniary gain, to which on the great scale every other [principle] is made to give way' as the 'governing principle of trade, manufactures, and commerce'. 'Buying cheap and selling dear', the 'spirit of competition', were now villified as the moral cause of the excesses of industrialisation.[a] Greed had always been a generic element in commerce, but the hasty scramble for wealth which machinery induced seemed to Owen to have thrust aside every traditional restraint that had previously prevented great inhumanity. The factory system, in fact, actually bred 'a new character in its inhabitants ... formed upon a principle quite unfavourable to individual or general happiness'. Not only had a general lust for wealth and luxury corrupted ever larger numbers of people, and fostered a 'disposition which strongly impels its possessors to sacrifice the best feelings of human nature to this love of accumulation'. Greed enticed the smaller manufacturers in particular to drive their workers harder, 'reducing them by successive changes, as the spirit of competition increased and the ease of acquiring wealth diminished, to a state ... infinitely more degraded and miserable than they were before the introduction of those manufactories'. The new system brought two main results. Morally, a prolonged struggle to 'buy cheap and sell dear' engendered 'strong powers of deception ... destructive of that open, honest sincerity, without which man cannot make others happy, nor enjoy happiness himself'.[b] Social bonds were further loosened by the 'dissension, jealousy, and want of fellow-feeling' which poverty produced.[c] Economically, the living and working conditions of the labouring classes were worsening steadily. And the introduction of machinery, Owen now concluded, underpinned this process. At first, steam power had reduced the price of manufactured goods and increased demand for them. But by 1815, 'mechanical power was much cheaper than human labour', and wages had plummeted in some trades to below even the subsistence level.[d] Owen conceded, however, that curtailing machinery was impossible in the short term, for any manufacturer who did, another would simply step in to fill the gap. Indeed, the point was not to limit mechanisation, which was 'one of the necessary stages in the progress of what is called civilisation', but to introduce it 'only in aid of, and not in competition with, human labour', and thus to reduce the hours of work required to secure a decent living.[e] And technical innovation, Owen later stressed, was possible 'in every department', so that each community might

[a] Robert Owen, *Life*, 1A (1858), pp. 38–9 (*infra*, vol. 1, pp. 104–5).
[b] Robert Owen, *Life*, 1A (1858), pp. 39–45 (*infra*, vol. 1, pp. 105–11).
[c] *Evening Mail*, 30 May 1817.
[d] Robert Owen, *Life*, 1A (1858), pp. 54–5 (*infra*, vol. 1, pp. 110–11).
[e] *Manchester and Salford Advertiser*, vol. 8, no. 428 (25 February 1837), p. 2; Robert Owen, *Life*, 1A (1858), pp. 55, 60, 64, 216 (*infra*, vol. 1, pp. 137, 142–3, 253).

have 'a full supply of the best machinery'.[a] (This contradicts David Ricardo's charge that Owen opposed all machinery, which was obviously calculated to bracket him with the Luddites).[b]

Owen the benevolent manufacturer, the 'prince of the cotton-spinners', as some had termed him,[c] was now rapidly becoming Owen the socialist, a Lycurgan legislator for the industrial age. He now had no shortage of evidence that children as young as five were trained to crawl under and between incessantly-moving machinery, and worked up to sixteen hours daily in hot and dangerous conditions, breathing air dense with pestiferous fibres. Much of his time was now spent in London attempting, with the assistance of the elder Sir Robert Peel, himself a cotton lord, to get a bill regulating the employment of children approved by a Select Committee of Parliament. This sought to prohibit employment before the age of ten; to reduce hours of labour to ten and a half per day (in 1818, he proposed ten hours); and to require a minimal education to begin work. These regulations he wished to apply to all manufactories.[d] Owen met the committee five times, first embarking on a tour of the factory districts with his eldest son. Conditions were worse than he had feared. As many as a quarter of the children he saw suffered from work-related injuries or deformities, which were well documented by some of the physicians Owen had first met at the Manchester Literary and Philosophical Society. His first substantial economic tract, *Observations on the Cotton Trade and on the Late Duties on the Importation of Cotton Wool* (1803), had argued against new duties on raw cotton imports passed by Parliament, holding that these would undermine Britain's advantage over growing foreign competition. But Owen, outraged, now declared, 'perish the cotton trade, perish even the political superiority of our country (if it depend on the cotton trade), rather than they shall be upheld

---

[a] Robert Owen, *The Revolution in the Mind and Practice of the Human Race* (1849), p. 45; *Lloyd's Weekly London Newspaper*, no. 240 (27 June 1847), p. 5. See also *The Revolution in the Mind and Practice of the Human Race* (1849), *Supplement*, p. 59, and 'The Social System, (*New Harmony Gazette*, vol. 2, no. 21, 21 February 1827, p. 161), (*infra*, vol. 2, p. 85).

[b] In the third edn (1821) of his *The Principles of Political Economy and Taxation*, first published in 1817, Ricardo acknowledged that he now believed that 'the substitution of machinery for human labour is often very injurious to the interests of the class of labourers' (ch. 31; ed. D. Winch, J. M. Dent, 1978, p. 264). A debt to Owen here seems evident, though Ricardo was also influenced by John Barton's *Observations on the Circumstances Which Influence the Condition of the Labouring Classes* (1817). Barton was acquainted with Owen's proposals, but dismissed them as incapable of adding to the demand for labour (*An Inquiry into the Causes of the Progressive Depreciation of Agricultural Labour*, 1820, p. 77).

[c] See Robert Owen, *Life*, vol. 1 (1857), p. 163 (*infra*, vol. 4, p. 218).

[d] On this phase, see especially J. T. Ward, 'Owen as Factory Reformer', in John Butt, *Robert Owen, Aspects of His Life and Work* (New York: Humanities Press, 1971), pp. 99–134, which helps correct lapses of memory in Owen's own account. For Owen's evidence, see *Report of the Select Committee on the State of Children Employed in the Manufacturies of the United Kingdom*, vol. 3, pp. 238–42. His proposed bill, with comments by its opponents, and the final Act passed, are reprinted in Owen's *Life*, vol. 1A (1858), pp. 21–32.

by the sacrifice of everything valuable in life by those who are the means of supporting them'.[a]

This was not a popular stance to adopt. Though some observers stepped forward to assist Owen, most of his fellow manufacturers, such as Arkwright and Strutt, objected strenuously to any restriction beyond the twelve hours per day limit for workhouse apprentices established by Peel's 1802 Act.[b] Some even countered that workers were dissolute in proportion to their free time, and could thus be glad of long hours of supervised labour which instilled orderliness and discipline. His opponents succeeded easily in blocking Owen's efforts. At public meetings called to examine the distressed state of the labouring population, critics rejected Owen's view that while taxes to assist the poor had swollen, wealth had been growing much faster. When another parliamentary Select Committee met to consider poor law reform, it refused to his deep disappointment even to take his evidence.[c] (An 1823 Committee investigating Irish poverty did listen to him). A few largely unenforcable restrictions, relating only to cotton mills, were passed in an 1819 Act; adequate inspection of factories would wait until 1833.

By late 1816, Owen was becoming increasingly frustrated. He was proud to have acquaintances among the rich, famous, and powerful: it showed how far a poor boy from Wales had risen through sheer effort. But, while still too prone to misinterpret well-mannered sympathetic platitudes for real acquiescence with his principles, he was beginning to see the limits of his reputation. It dawned on Owen in 1816–17 that a new solution to the problem of poverty was required which would be more far-reaching than any other ever proposed. The more entrenched his opponents became, the more radical were Owen's proposals. He was not a man to become angry; his whole philosophy prevented it, and he was never recorded as even raising his voice against an opponent during any of the many debates he held. So what would have been anger in other men took another form: Owen's principles hardened, and he became adamant that more fundamental changes still were required. The Whigs, Malthusians, and political economists in particular, he would later say, had starved millions by their inhumanity, at a time when both surplus land and capital existed.[d] Sympathy had to prevail before matters worsened.

---

[a] Robert Owen, *Life*, 1A (1858), pp. 3–9, 8–17. On Owen as an entrepreneur see also W. H. Chaloner, 'Robert Owen, Peter Drinkwater and the Early Factory System in Manchester, 1788–1800', *Bulletin of the John Rylands Library*, vol. 37 (1954), pp. 79–102.

[b] See *Reasons in Favour of Sir Robert Peel's Bill, for Ameliorating the Condition of Children* (1819), *Answers to Certain Objections Made to Sir Robert Peel's Bill*, 1819), and *An Inquiry into the Principle and Tendency of the Bill Now Pending in Parliament, for Imposing Certain Restrictions on Cotton Factories* (1818).

[c] Its report, which included a review of Owen's system, was published in *The Times*, no. 10117 (9 April 1817), p. 3. Owen's intended evidence was reprinted in the *New Moral World*, vol. 2, no. 85 (11 June 1836), pp. 257–60.

[d] Robert Owen, *Life*, vol. 1 (1857), p. 128 (*infra*, vol. 4, p. 182).

The pace of Owen's conversion thus quickened in 1816 and 1817. At Manchester, he had become concerned with improving the health, sanitation and education of the labouring classes. At New Lanark, he had gone far towards accomplishing this for his own workforce. *A New View of Society* had suggested that the unemployed might build roads or engage in other public works projects. But in seeking substantial reform on a nationwide scale, Owen was stymied at every turn. In 1816, he first turned towards a quite different solution, suggesting that 'in due time communities shall be formed' for the entire unemployed population which, besides providing work, would instill an improved character defined by 'temperance and simplicity of manners'.[a] The experiment at New Lanark was to be the germ from which would spring model industrial townships to combat both the growing immorality fostered by the factory system and the more immediately pressing issues of unemployment and hunger. Moreover, Owen was persuaded increasingly that labour, rather than capital, essentially created wealth. In these communities, therefore, economic justice could also be attained. Not only the poor, moreover, but 'every class in society' who wished to join would soon be able to escape 'intemperance, disease, and suffering'.[b] These 'villages of union' of 500 to 1500 people united by 'mutual and combined interest', would be situated in the countryside, but would have some machinery of their own. (Early illustrations show this steaming away in the background.)[c] Thus they could be largely self-sufficient. Ideally, he thought, communities should be constructed in the form of a large quadrangle, with public buildings in the centre. Persons of a particular political or religious persuasion might want to associate with others of their ilk, and Owen designed a table showing 140 combinations of such views.[d] Each community could start with as little as £60,000, which the government would, he hoped, provide, though if private capital were necessary a five per cent return was thought likely. Having lived with, indeed thrived upon, competition for much of his life, Owen now probably became aware of more paternalist approaches to national economic management. If he had not known of them earlier, he probably became acquainted with the ideas of Adam Ferguson and Fletcher of Saltoun, and of Sir James Steuart's proposals for substantial direction of the economy.[e]

---

[a] Robert Owen, *An Address Delivered to the Inhabitants of New Lanark* (1816), p. 39 (*infra*, vol. 1, p. 129).

[b] Robert Owen, *Life*, 1A (1858), p. 125 (*infra*, vol. 1, p. 211).

[c] See *infra*, vol. 1, p. 130.

[d] Robert Owen, *Life*, 1A (1858), pp. 130–1 (*infra*, vol. 1, pp. 216–17).

[e] The only economist with whom Owen had much sympathetic contact in this period was his friend Professor James Mylne, who taught political economy at the University of Glasgow. But Mylne's *Plan of a Course of Lectures on Political Economy* (Glasgow, 1804) does not reveal any particular antipathy to *laissez-faire*. Mylne was also a friend of Frances Wright, an American Owenite and feminist. A student of Adam Smith, Adam Ferguson (1723–1816) was much more sceptical about the benefits of the division of labour than his teacher. Andrew Fletcher of Saltoun

Owen refined 'The Plan', as it was now increasingly called, throughout what was to become, for him, the momentous summer of 1817. He began bombarding the newspapers with letters about his proposals, and when they were printed, bought thousands of copies and flooded the country with them, spending some £4000 in two months and on one occasion delaying the departure of the London mail coaches by twenty minutes. (Indeed, he may well have invented the press 'blitz'.) His ideas about how to solve the problem of poverty had clearly shifted quite dramatically. In July, he discussed 'the principle of united labour and expenditure' as applied to a 'community of mutual and combined interests'. He did not yet call the system one of a 'community of goods', but his description of work incentives and the need to avoid disputes over property indicates that this was among his goals. But he still sought as broad an appeal as possible. Considering what might happen when communities offered their wares in competition with the rest of society, for example, Owen's solution aimed to placate every opinion. Communities might produce only 'to the amount of their own immediate wants; and constituted as they will be, they can have no motives to produce an unnecessary surplus'. In the long run, however, when the 'true interests' of society were clarified, they would be permitted 'gradually to supersede the others; inasmuch as the latter are wretchedly degrading, and directly opposed to the improvement and well-being of those employed either in agriculture or manufactures, and consequently are equally hostile to the welfare and happiness of all the higher classes'.[a]

Owen's determination to publicise these conclusions to the entire nation reached a peak in two remarkable public meetings which he called in August 1817. On 14 August, he addressed an audience of many hundreds at the City of London Tavern. Prominent members of the clergy and government were present, as well as political economists and many of the leaders of London plebian radicalism. The reform movement had only just begun to recover from the débâcle of the 1790s, when it had been squashed by repressive legislation which drove thousands to emigrate to America. The radicals thus attended only to oppose what they saw as a paternalistic, oppressive plan to 'turn the country into a workhouse' or 'pauper barracks' and 'rear up a community of slaves' (in the words of Robert Wedderburn, himself the son of a slave).[b] Owen's plans not only omitted any demand for parliamentary reform and reduced taxation. Rumours abounded that the government was

(1655–1716) was the author of a mildly utopian plan for reorganising the government (*An Account of a Conversation Containing a Right Regulation of Governments for the Common Good of Mankind*, 1704). Sir James Steuart (1712–80) favoured a much more regulatory approach to trade and manufactures. See his *Inquiry into the Principles of Political Economy* (2 vols, 1767).

[a] Robert Owen, *Life*, 1A (1858), pp. 74–5.

[b] *Black Dwarf*, vol. 1, no. 30 (20 August 1817), p. 469.

manipulating him in order to deflect working-class attention from political reform, and that Owen himself actually wished, as W.T. Sherwin had suggested in the spring, to deprive the working classes of their political rights.[a] At the August 14 meeting, the radical leader Henry Hunt thus moved to amend Owen's proposals so as to portray excessive taxation as the root of pauperism.[b] The liberal political economists present, though their aims were very different, had a similar desire to see Owen defeated. Their star was rising fast, for they had gone far towards convincing the Liverpool government of the case for free trade.[c] They were not about to be challenged by an overly enthusiastic and misguided philanthropist. (Ricardo would later state that he was 'completely at war with Mr Owen'.)[d] Their representative, Major Robert Torrens, thus complained at length that Malthus's population doctrines had long since invalidated all but the harshest regimes of poor relief.[e]

After the first meeting, Owen had a week to prepare his counterattack. He faced a most unfortunate alliance between groups who rarely saw eye to eye. The reformers he assailed in a letter to the newspapers, dismissing their schemes as promising only 'one general scene of anarchy and dreadful confusion'.[f] At the second meeting, on 21 August, he reiterated the fundamentals of the Plan. He now tried to meet his radical critics directly by insisting that reducing governmental expenditure by lowering taxes would only add those who lived from public spending to the ranks of the unemployed (with this the economists largely agreed). Instead, he sought to persuade them that increasing mechanisation was a far more fundamental source of distress. Even if 'every shilling of your national debt and taxes [were] removed tomorrow, and were the Government wholly unpaid for its services, – in a few years either this or some other country must suffer more than you now experience', he told his audience. For while mechanism might potentially be 'the greatest of blessings to humanity', it was instead 'its greatest curse', and this the economists in particular refused to concede. Owen then condemned rival plans for poor relief, especially all variations upon what he termed 'the separate individualized cottage system'. He also

---

[a] *Republican*, vol. 2 (14 January 1820), p. 10; *Sherwin's Political Register*, vol. 1, no. 4 (26 April 1817), p. 62; no. 19 (9 August 1817), pp. 297–8.

[b] *The Reformists' Register*, NS. no. 5 (23 August 1817), p. 144.

[c] See generally Boyd Hilton, *Corn, Cash, Commerce: The Economic Policies of the Tory Governments, 1815–1830* (Oxford: Oxford University Press, 1977), and Barry Gordon, *Political Economy in Parliament, 1819–1823* (Macmillan, 1976).

[d] *Wooler's British Gazette*, vol. 1, no. 51 (19 December 1819), p. 412.

[e] Torrens also attacked Owen in *The Philanthropist*, vol. 10 (1817), pp. 514–18. He described the meeting in a letter to Francis Place, calling Owen 'an interesting enthusiast in whose brain a copulation between vanity and benevolence has engendered madness' (British Library Add. MS. 37949 ff. 50–2).

[f] *The Reformists' Register*, NS. no. 5 (23 August 1817), p. 154.

suggested that future co-operative communities of the wealthy could employ those of the poor and working classes.[a]

This was all controversial enough. Most astonishing of all, however, Owen for a few minutes then rounded on all teachers of religion as having made man 'a weak, imbecile animal; a furious bigot and fanatic; or a miserable hypocrite'. His audience, Owen later recalled, was 'thunderstruck'. A few clergymen hissed. But 'the loudest cheers' then erupted in praise of what the *Observer* politely described as Owen's condemnation of the 'vices of existing religious establishments'.[b] (Sympathisers would later complain that it was clear 'to every liberal mind, that Mr Owen meant no more than universal toleration amongst the people'.)[c] Nonetheless this support was insufficient to win over his audience. Though some radicals, like John Gale Jones, soon remarked that there must be something in it if the Plan was – as it soon appeared to be – also opposed by the government, Owen's proposals were dismissed as impracticable at the end of the meeting 'by a great majority' present, on a vote introduced by the London radical Robert Waithman.[d] Claiming that he had been misunderstood, Owen dispensed tens of thousands of copies of newspapers with reports of these proceedings, though this was somewhat counterproductive, since his critics' views were also detailed.

In conjunction with this attack, Owen made another surprising move. These meetings were a turning point in his career not merely because of the substance of his thought, but a prophetic gloss which he now imposed on his ideas, and which was clearly linked to his attack on all existing religions. Irritated by opposition from those blinded by selfishness, and deeply imbued with a sense of impending social and economic catastrophe, in August 1817 Owen suddenly began to speak with the tongue of the visionary. We do not know quite why this happened as it did. He had long been exposed to evangelicals and religious reformers of all types without assuming their language and style. Now, perhaps, in the heat of the summer, and amidst the tremendous excitement of his one man crusade to save humanity, something snapped in Owen, and he underwent a quasi-religious conversion from philanthropist

[a] Robert Owen, *Life*, 1A (1858), pp. 109–17; *Reformists' Register*, no. 5 (23 August 1817), p. 158; *Sherwin's Political Register*, vol. 1, no. 19 (9 August 1817), p. 296. For accounts of this meeting and the various reactions to Owen, see for example *Champion*, no. 242 (24 August 1817), pp. 265–7, and *Independent Whig*, no. 608 (24 August 1817), pp. 116–19. Major John Cartwright was one of Owen's chief opponents here, though another veteran radical, John Gale Jones, was more sympathetic to his ideas. On radical opposition to Owen's view of machinery, see for example *Manchester Observer*, vol. 1, no. 48 (28 November 1818), p. 380.

[b] Robert Owen, *Life*, vol. 1A (1858), p. 115 (*infra*, vol. 1, p. 199); *Observer*, no. 1333 (17 August 1817), p. 4; no. 1334 (24 August 1817), p. 4.

[c] *Manchester Observer*, no. 42 (17 October 1818), p. 335.

[d] *Independent Whig*, no. 608 (24 August 1817), pp. 120–2. See Robert Owen, *Life*, vol. 1A (1858), p. 162 (*infra*, vol. 4, p. 216). It was later also asserted that Owen's views on property led him to oppose Christianity, because the right of private property was frequently connected to religion. See *New Moral World*, vol. 7, no. 70 (22 February 1840), p. 1116.

to prophet. Or perhaps he coolly calculated, with the eyes of the public on him as never before, that enveloping his Plan in theological guise would be the most effective means of selling it to an increasingly evangelized population. (He would soon assert, however, that it was 'no part of my plans to form a sect'.)[a] It may have been the mere fact of his apparent popularity, to which he often thereafter adverted, which imbued him with such a strong sense of the messianic. Whatever the cause, Owen now clearly envisioned both a secular apocalypse, '*the crisis*'; and, in his mind's eye, the 'new moral world' or 'millennial world' which would succeed it, where laws, commerce, religion, war, and self-interest would disappear.[b] He had already suggested in 1813, but now began loudly to proclaim, following Paul's sermon to the Corinthians verse by verse, that charity was both the core of all religious teaching, and the greatest good any individual could attain.[c] Owen's world was thus transformed by this revelation (for such it was, after a fashion). Since all existing religions were false, Owen had to invent his own. No longer a mere poor law reformer, he now became a prophet, 'a kind of atheistic messiah', critics would assert, a secular evangelist for the new 'religion of charity' which for some was the heart of the 'social system', and which would have considerable appeal to his followers in the late 1830s and early 1840s.[d] Owen's object, thus, was no longer solely 'the relief of the poor', but now, far more importantly, 'the emancipation of mankind'. Unfortunately, this messianic strain fuelled his already strong sense of self-rectitude. Owen's willingness to compromise, never very great, shrank. He did not reason with associates; he pontificated at them. Pride and dogmatism were Owen's great weaknesses, combined with a tendency to think that the character of men could be recut as easily as cloth, and the world governed like the New Lanark mills. The events of 1817 did nothing to weaken these propensities: Daniel had entered the lion's den, and he no longer had need of fear.

[a] *Mirror of Truth*, no. 2 (7 November 1817), p. 40.

[b] Owen's argument that because no two cases were alike, laws were unjust, probably owes something to Godwin. See the latter's *Enquiry Concerning Political Justice* (1793), Bk 7, ch. 4.

[c] Robert Owen, *Life*, vol. 1 (1857), p. 272 (*infra*, vol. 1, p. 41). See Owen's later *Six Lectures on Charity* (1834) for the fullest statement of this type. There were certainly echoes of Godwin's fervent belief in universal benevolence here, though Godwin had backtracked substantially from his stronger formulations of this ideal.

[d] *Westminster Review*, vol. 74 (1860), p. 385. On Owen and millennialism, see J. F. C. Harrison, *Robert Owen and the Owenites in Britain and America* (Routledge and Kegan Paul, 1969), pp. 92–102, and W. H. Oliver, 'Owen in 1817: The Millennialist Movement', in Sidney Pollard and John Salt, eds, *Robert Owen. Prophet of the Poor* (Macmillan, 1971), pp. 166–87. Owen's fullest statement of the 'new religion' comes in two lectures in 1830 (*infra*, vol. 2, pp. 169–201), and in the *Six Lectures on Charity* (1834). There is a balanced tribute to this aspect of Owen's personality in John Watts, *Robert Owen, 'The Visionary'* (Manchester, 1843). On the importance of the split between secular and quasi-religious Owenism, see my *Machinery, Money and the Millennium. From Moral Economy to Socialism, 1815–1860* (Princeton: Princeton University Press, 1987), e.g., pp. 118–19. For evidence that Owen in his prime still adhered to a vague sense of providential government of the world, see for example *The Book of the New Moral World*, pt 3 (1842), p. 65 (*infra*, vol. 3, p. 179). In his dotage, this emerged even more clearly (*Life*, vol. 1, 1857, p. 208; *infra*, vol. 4, p. 155).

In the aftermath of these meetings, it was soon clear, as Owen later recalled, that he had 'in a few minutes' destroyed much of the popularity built over many years. Though some Tories, like Robert Southey,[a] remained sympathetic despite their disagreements over the issue of religion, Owen was now widely damned as an infidel.[b] Respectable booksellers refused to sell his tracts. Clerical broadsides took aim at him. In a new edition of Malthus' *Essay on Population*, he became a key target.[c] William Allen vowed to dissolve the partnership, unless the mills 'be most narrowly and constantly watched, by some one on whom we can thoroughly rely'.[d] Owen had spoken the Truth, and now few wanted to listen. But he had his reasons. Owen sometimes described other groups – notably 'distributors' – as the most active 'demoralizers' of society.[e] But he never renounced the idea that religion was 'the sole cause now of all the disunion, hatred, uncharitableness, and crime, which pervade the population of the earth'. As far as he was concerned, it was the Church which 'governs in all countries in which a national church exists'. And religion not only played a fundamental role in forming character (sometimes he ascribed it primacy), it also cemented the system of social and political oppression, for amongst the chief vices of the priesthood, Owen believed, was its willingness 'to train an order of men to live by the labour of other men'.[f]

Passions cooled while Owen embarked on a tour of experimental educational establishments on the continent, meeting various influential persons. Stopping at the post-war Congress of the great powers at Aix-la-Chapelle in 1818, he distributed a pamphlet written for the occasion to as many leaders as he could.[g] (But he failed to press one into the hands of the Czar, who had no pocket large enough for the bulky octavo, and dismissed Owen so gruffly that he did not try again.) At dinner, he sat next to Metternich's associate Friedrich Gentz, who complained, in response to Owen's remonstrances, that 'we do not want the mass to become wealthy and independent of us. How could we govern them if they were?'[h] But the message was slow to sink in, for

[a] Southey wrote that despite differing with Owen on religion, 'I admire his practical benevolence, I love his enthusiasm, and I go far with him in his earthly views' (*A Letter to William Smith*, 1817, p. 33).

[b] See Robert Owen, *Life*, vol. 1 (1857), pp. 163, 189 (*infra*, vol. 4, pp. 218, 244). For the view that most of Owen's audience would have opposed him regardless of his comments on religion, see the *New Monthly Magazine*, vol. 9 (1 May 1818), p. 313.

[c] Malthus included an attack on Owen in the fifth edn of his *Essay on Population* (1817), pp. 274–86.

[d] William Allen, *The Life of William Allen* (3 vols, 1846), vol. 1, p. 325.

[e] Robert Owen, *The Book of the New Moral World*, pt 2 (1842), p. 22 (*infra*, vol. 3, p. 101).

[f] Robert Owen, *The New Religion* (1830), p. 9 (*infra*, vol. 2, pp. 181–2); Owen, *Second Lecture on the New Religion* (1830), p. 3 (*infra*, vol. 2, p. 193); Owen, *Report of the Discussion between Robert Owen and the Rev. William Legg* (1839), p. 11.

[g] See *infra*, vol. 1, pp. 245–59, and generally Albert Volwiler, 'Robert Owen and the Congress of Aix-la-Chapelle, 1818', *Scottish Historical Review*, vol. 19 (1922), pp. 96–105.

[h] Robert Owen, *Life*, vol. 1 (1857), p. 183 (*infra*, vol. 4, p. 238).

Owen would long continue to court the powerful, and seek to win over the great despots of Europe by the sheer force of ideas, just as he himself had been similarly converted.

Once home, he tried to enlist the assistance of the leading educational reformers Andrew Bell and Joseph Lancaster. Most of the period from 1818–20 he spent in London, usually staying at John Walker's town-house at 49 Bedford Square, writing pamphlets addressed to the working classes and to manufacturers, distributing literature, and rallying support. In the spring of 1818, he reiterated his demands for the regulation of child labour in factories. Renewing a moderate approach, he insisted that 'the natural course of trade, manufactures, and commerce, should not be disturbed', unless 'the well-being of the whole community' was affected. Stating that it was from the working classes that the wealthy derived 'all which they hold', Owen pleaded that if manual labour were fully and correctly employed, the working classes would produce more wealth, even for the higher classes, than under the existing system. Self-interest might thus usher in the new world.[a] He often met with the Duke of Kent, father of the future Queen Victoria, who sympathised with his schemes (he had sent his own physician to verify the results at New Lanark[b]), and assisted him by chairing meetings. When the Duke died suddenly in 1820, Owen thought he could still count on a few influential friends, like the liberal Whig peer Lauderdale. But then Lauderdale sabotaged the discussion of a petition of Owen's in the House of Lords, complaining that the 'New Views' if adopted would level every government in Europe.[c] Some radicals in turn now began to feel that Owen might have something to say,[d] and isolated working class supporters, such as the former London Corresponding Society leader John Bone, actually began to develop his ideas in their own way.[e] A few dissident political economists, while dismissing Owen's grand Plan, also still maintained that some of the accomplishments of New Lanark might be imitated elsewhere.[f] But in the eyes of the public, on the whole, Owen and his faith were now largely anathema.

The support that remained was mostly north of the Tweed. At the invitation of a group of Lanarkshire notables, Owen in 1820 composed one of his most important works, the *Report to the County of Lanark* (1821). Partly in reaction to a great commercial crisis in 1819, this suggested that in order to avoid both fluctuations in the money supply and the payment of unjust wages, labour notes representing hours of work might become a superior form of

[a] Robert Owen, *Life*, vol. 1A (1858), pp. 186–8 (*infra*, vol. 1, pp. 307–10).

[b] See Henry Gray Macnab, *The New Views of* Mr. *Owen of Lanark Impartially Examined* (1819).

[c] See Robert Owen, *Life*, vol. 1 (1857), p. 217 (*infra*, vol. 4, p. 272). For Owen's response see *The Sun*, no. 9893 (28 May 1824), p. 1.

[d] E.g., T. J. Wooler, in *Black Dwarf*, vol. 12, no. 15 (1 June 1824), pp. 446–8.

[e] E.g., *The Age of Civilization*, no. 4 (4 April 1818), pp. 57–66.

[f] See for example *An Essay on the Political Economy of Nations* (1821), p. 257.

exchange medium. Here Owen first proclaimed at length his belief that labour was the foundation of all value, a principle of immense importance to later socialist thought. Acknowledging a debt to the London magistrate Patrick Colquhoun's *Treatise on the Wealth, Power and Resources of the British Empire* (1813), he here prominently advertised the importance of the notions of productive and unproductive labour to any useful social analysis. (He had emphasised in June 1819 that pauperism was caused not merely by lack of employment, but by 'want of a sufficient *productive* employment for those who without it must become poor'.)[a] Another leading novelty in the *Report* lay in Owen's account of the relationship between money and the expansion and contraction of the market. Previously he had argued that mechanisation at a time of reduced demand depressed wages in many industries. Now, denying the market's ability to find a natural equilibrium, Owen stressed the underconsumptionist aspects of productive capacity, and the failure to find 'a market, or means of exchange, co-extensive with the means of production'. And the problem in part, Owen proposed, was that using gold and silver created 'a mere artificial standard' of value which 'retarded the general improvement of society' because it was too dependent on the value and supply of metals. This seemed proven by the fact that after the gold standard had been reintroduced amidst fierce debate in 1819, the resulting deflation and depression had 'plunged the country into poverty, discontent, and danger'.[b]

The *Report* was also noteworthy because it first explicitly stated that Owen sought to begin upon '*the principle of united labour, expenditure, and property, and equal privileges*'. For this reason in particular it is sometimes regarded as marking 'the beginning of modern Socialism'.[c] Owen now condemned the 'principle of individual interest', or the idea 'that man can provide better for himself, and more advantageously for the public, when left to his own individual exertions, opposed to and in competition with his fellows, than when aided by any social arrangement which shall unite his interests individually and generally with society'. The existing divisions within society, he asserted, were 'the most anti-social, impolitic, and irrational, that can be devised'. Against Adam Smith, Owen particularly insisted that further specialisation within production would only harm the working classes. (Later he would develop this critique into a new theory of social organisation.) At present, 'the most minute division of mental power and manual labour in the individuals of the working classes' led private interests to be 'placed perpetually at variance with the public good; and in every nation men are purposely trained from infancy to suppose that their

---

[a] Robert Owen, *Life*, vol. 1A (1858), pp. 125–7, 237 (*infra*, vol. 1, pp. 219–21); Patrick Colquhoun, *A Treatise on the Wealth, Power and Resources of the British Empire* (2nd edn, 1816), pp. 2, 6, 28.

[b] Robert Owen, *Life*, vol. 1A (1858), pp. 265–6 (*infra*, vol. 1, pp. 289–90).

[c] Alexander Cullen, *Adventures in Socialism. New Lanark Establishment and Orbiston Community* (Glasgow: John Smith & Son, 1910), p. 132.

well-being is incompatible with the progress and prosperity of other nations'. The new system, however, would combine 'extensive mental and manual powers in the individuals of the working classes [and] a complete identity of private and public interest'. Nations, too, would soon 'comprehend that their power and happiness cannot attain their full and natural development but through an equal increase of the power and happiness of all other states'.[a] The *Report* also promised that the amount of necessary work in the communities would 'be little more than a recreation, sufficient to keep them in the best health and spirits for rational enjoyment of life'. Not only mechanical but also agricultural inventions would hasten the provision of a surplus, for a Gateshead nurseryman named William Falla had furnished Owen with figures showing that wheat returns could be greatly increased by using spade agriculture to dig more deeply into the soil. To his delight, and to the distress of Owen's critics, the *Report* was adopted by his Lanarkshire associates. He seemed to be appreciated once again.[b]

Most of the ideals which would increasingly be called 'socialism' by the end of the 1820s were now in place in Owen's mind. There remained the problem of how to implement them. He announced himself a candidate for Parliament in 1819, more to air his views than to be elected, and proudly insisted that 'I have no patronage; I expect none; for whoever may be in power, I will not ask a private favour for myself or others'.[c] In May 1822, Owen formed the British and Foreign Philanthropic Society to raise funds, but soon discovered that many of its illustrious members (who included MPs, generals and bankers) had quite limited aims in mind.[d] He journeyed to Ireland in 1822–3 to examine conditions there, speaking for three hours in Dublin to a large meeting which included the Lord Mayor and several aristocrats. At this time, his emphasis was somewhat more upon the agricultural basis of communities (and elsewhere pastoral imagery occasionally loomed large in Owenism).[e] To prospective investors, he promised that the capital required to found any community would be repaid within twelve years. But although he assured his audience that 'this whole arrangement has been devised for the working classes only', Owen in fact extended the implications of his views. Condemning the waste of capital, health and industry which the whims of fashion dictated, he implied that such irrationality could be overcome, and that a new generation might be clothed

---

[a] Robert Owen, *Life*, vol. 1A (1858), pp. 282, 284–5, 289–90, (*infra*, vol. 1, pp. 305, 307–8, 312–13).

[b] For a critical view, see Jasper Beatson, *An Examination of Mr. Owen's Plans* (Glasgow, 1832).

[c] *The Times*, no. 106659 (28 April 1819), p. 2.

[d] For details, see *Proceedings of the First General Meeting of the British and Foreign Philanthropic Society* (1822), and *New Moral World*, vol. 1, no. 40 (1 August 1835), pp. 317–18, no. 41 (8 August 1835), pp. 326–7.

[e] *Proceedings of the First General Meeting of the British and Foreign Philanthropic Society* (1822), p. 46. See J. F. C. Harrison, *Robert Owen and the Owenites in Britain and America* (Routledge and Kegan Paul, 1969), pp. 56–63.

in a simpler costume suitable to the ethos of voluntary restraint he hoped would guide community life.[a] (Members of at least one later community did wear a green tunic of sorts.) Illustrating Colquhoun's statistics about the numbers of the various social classes with a set of different-sized tin cubes, Owen insisted that a large proportion of many useless classes and unproductive occupations could be eliminated by superior economic efficiency.[b] Of the small freeholders, for example, he claimed that many farmed so little land that they could barely support themselves, and were 'also usually deficient in capital, education, and knowledge, and do little more than vegetate upon their farms'. Only one-twentieth of the existing number of shopkeepers could do all of the distributive tasks society required, moreover. If far more of all occupations could be converted into productive labourers, thus, the burden of necessary labour for each could be correspondingly reduced. (Godwin had made a similar point.)[c]

In the second half of the 1820s, Owen's energies focused on the prospect of building a community in America. In 1825, he purchased from a Pietist German émigré sect, the Rappites, a ready-built township set on 20,000 acres at New Harmony in southern Indiana. Unfortunately the establishment soon became an enormous drain on his resources. In a short time, Owen spent about £40,000/$200,000, or four-fifths of his New Lanark fortune (his interest in the mills was finally sold in 1828), in what too rapidly became a fruitless effort to organise the disparate group of eight hundred radicals, freethinkers, backwoodsmen, and scientists who answered his advertisement for members, but who had no desire to be 'governed' like mill hands. Arriving in the young nation, Owen at first excited considerable interest and high hopes with his proposals. In early 1825, he addressed the President, Senate and Supreme Court at the House of Representatives in Washington D.C.[d] Large audiences applauded him from New Orleans to Boston and New York. But having then invited the rational and well-intentioned to join the community, Owen did far too little to regulate the ensuing influx. Though there were many distinguished intellectuals and teachers, few farmers or skilled labourers came. Supplies were expensive, and the community never became self-sufficient. New Harmony was briefly the most vibrant and sophisticated cultural outpost on the American frontier. But centrifugal tendencies tore at the community from the beginning. Most of the colonists were inspired by Owen, but unwilling to

---

[a] John Gray's *Lecture on Human Happiness* (1825) is the classic Owenite statement of this ideal of restraint.

[b] For an account of Owen's use of these cubes, see Owen, *Lectures on the Rational System of Society* (1841), pp. 12–16.

[c] *Wooler's British Gazette*, vol. 4, no. 26 (30 June 1822), p. 207; Robert Owen, *Report of the Proceedings at the Several Public Meetings Held In Dublin* (Dublin, 1823), pp. 29, 35, 68, 70, 80, 160.

[d] See Robert Owen, *Two Discourses on a New System of Society* (1825) (*infra*, vol. 2, pp. 3–37).

submit unquestioningly to his teachings. A few imagined that 'community' meant that Owen's fortune lay at their disposal. By March 1827, New Harmony had divided into four separate groups. Two months later there were ten. Within a year, the experiment was in the final stages of dissolution, with its half-dozen projected imitators elsewhere following close behind. A few new American Owenite colonies were founded during the Fourierist wave of community-building during the 1840s. And the experiment had given Owen himself a real taste of community life, which he now clearly understood as an exercise in spartan frugality, for he reduced his meals to two, and his costs to six cents, per day.[a] (His puritan opposition to changes of fashion in clothes was also especially marked at this time; later he would begin to appreciate the need to furnish the 'merely ornamental'.)[b] But otherwise, Owen's best hope for success in the New World expired with New Harmony.

One further possibility soon presented itself for colonising the frontier, however. In 1828, Owen thought he perceived an opportunity to secure a very substantial land grant from the Mexican government to settle the Texan frontier with the United States. He first paused at Cincinnati for an eight-day long public debate about religion to an audience of a thousand.[c] Then he sailed to Vera Cruz via Jamaica (where, Owen noted, many of the slaves were better-dressed than British workmen),[d] and, accompanied by two Indians who spoke no English, he bounced and jolted across the country in a mule-driven waggon to meet the Mexican President, Guadalupe Victoria.[e] The British Ambassador spoke for an hour and a quarter on his behalf to open negotiations, and Owen thought he was promised full jurisdiction over a strip of neutral territory one hundred and fifty miles wide and some fifteen hundred miles long along the entire length of the U.S. border. The sole proviso, he believed, was that the Mexican Congress formally permit freedom of religious belief throughout the republic. This, however, was apparently defeated 'by the great exertions of the Catholic priesthood', and the scheme came to nothing, though on the way back Owen seized the opportunity to read his 'Twelve Fundamental Propositions' to General Santa Anna.[f]

---

[a] Robert Owen, *Address Delivered by Robert Owen, at a Public Meeting, Held at the Franklin Institute in the City of Philadelphia* (Philadelphia, 1827), p. 24.

[b] See Robert Owen, 'Proposals for a Change of System', *The Crisis*, vol. 3, no. 23 (1 February 1834), p. 184 (*infra*, vol. 2, p. 249). The influence of John Gray on Owen's concession to ornamentality is probable. See my *Machinery, Money and the Millennium*, pp. 110–29.

[c] For an account of these debates, including an illustration, see Frances Trollope, *Domestic Manners of the Americans* (2 vols, 1832), vol. 1, pp. 205–12.

[d] See *Robert Owen's Opening Speech, and His Reply to the Rev. Alexander Campbell* (Cincinnati, 1829), pp. 189–90.

[e] See *infra*, vol. 4, pp. 306–14, for Owen's account of this expedition.

[f] Robert Owen, *The Problem of the Age Solved. Manifesto of Robert Owen to the Civilized World* (New York, 1847), p. 4; *New Moral World*, vol. 1, no. 48 (26 September 1835), pp. 377–9; no. 49 (3 October 1835), pp. 386–8. See Wilbert H. Timmons, 'Robert Owen's Texas Project', *Southwestern Historical Quarterly*, vol. 52 (1949), pp. 286–93.

Returning to Britain, Owen found that a consumer co-operative society indebted to his ideas had been started in Edinburgh by an inspired tanner named Abram Combe. The co-operative made goods available more cheaply to its members, and hoped to acquire land for a settlement. Even more impressively, a community modelled on Owen's ideals, at Orbiston, south of Glasgow, had subsequently been attempted by Combe, who was also fuelled by a healthy dose of semi-secular millenarianism.[a] Orbiston brought together three hundred people for several years before failing to produce quickly enough to satisfy its creditors. The first Owenite martyr, Combe himself died at Orbiston after a heroic act of over-exertion at spade agriculture. At the same time, an urban community eventually aiming to relocate to the country had also been begun in London by George Mudie, the printer and editor of the first important Owenite journal, the *Economist*. But he then made the pilgrimage to Orbiston, and with its collapse lost everything he had invested.

Also active in Owen's absence was the largely working-class London Co-operative Society, which, by 1827, aimed to amass capital to buy land by setting up a co-operative shop. Coincidentally, and especially from 1828, when a successful store opened in Brighton, a large consumer co-operation movement mushroomed which was often inspired by Owen's work, even if its chief aim (the distribution of profits among members) was more limited than his.[b] By 1830, some three hundred co-operative societies were advertising the benefits of collective enterprise. On his return from America, Owen tried to push the new movement in his own direction, and, when he failed, sought to frustrate measures with which he disagreed. Lacking capital, experience, and adequate legal protection, the movement in any case virtually collapsed, and was only revived some fifteen years later.

The middle and late 1820s also saw the publication of several major works inspired by Owen's ideas, notably in the field of co-operative economics. Chief amongst these were the Irish landowner William Thompson's *An Inquiry into the Principles of the Distribution of Wealth Most Conducive to Human Happiness* (1824) and *Labor Rewarded* (1827); and the newspaper editor John Gray's *Lecture on Human Happiness* (1825) and *The Social System* (1831).[c] Both writers differed from Owen on many points. Gray in particular popularised a non-communitarian ideal of socialism in which co-operative labour and exchange ensured an equitable reward for labour, and national economic planning

---

[a] See R. G. Garnett, *Co-operation and the Owenite Socialist Communities in Britain, 1825–45* (Manchester: Manchester University Press, 1972), pp. 65–99, and Alexander Cullen, *Adventures in Socialism: New Lanark Establishment and Orbiston Community* (Glasgow: John Smith & Son, 1910).

[b] On the Brighton shop, see T. W. Mercer, *Co-operation's Prophet. The Life and Letters of Dr. William King of Brighton* (Manchester: Manchester University Press, 1947).

[c] On Thompson, see Richard Pankhurst, *William Thompson (1775–1833): Britain's Pioneer Socialist, Feminist and Co-operator* (1954). On Gray, see Janet Kimball, *The Economic Doctrines of John Gray, 1799–1883* (Washington D.C.: Catholic University of America Press, 1948).

and production assured a rational balance of supply and demand.[a] This was to prove particularly attractive to later socialist Chartist writers like James Bronterre O'Brien and John Francis Bray, for whom economic justice rather than the virtues of community was a priority. Moreover, the majority of those drawn to Owen's ideas in this period were also passionately desirous of political reform, which Owen was not, as he emphasised again during the great debates about reform in 1831–2. Led by William Thompson, most of the working-class co-operators aimed to combine radical and socialist aims. This trend continued during the 1830s, and at the peak of Owenite influence in the 1840s, large numbers of socialists intermingled with the Chartist movement.

But Owenised reformers did often concede crucial facets of Owen's critique of radical doctrines. They agreed that the explosive effects of manufacturing had invalidated at least part of the traditional radical explanation for poverty, which was the overly heavy taxation of a corrupt state establishment. But Owen not merely alleged that the labourer rather than the capitalist created value. He further asserted that any exchange of labour for a wage which did not reflect the full value of the product was unjust. This underscored his basic point that poverty originated in the economic rather than the political system. Owen's 'social' critique of radicalism, in fact, would become the most enduring legacy of his political thought.[b] Its persuasiveness relied strongly upon the example of that great republican utopia, the United States, where poverty became steadily more apparent throughout the 1830s and 1840s despite the exercise of popular sovereignty and a republican form of government. The evidence this furnished for Owen's case gave rise to a tension between 'social' and 'political' reformers which was first notable throughout Europe in 1848, but became increasingly prominent thereafter, and forms one of the major themes of modern social and political thought.

The face of the industrial future was, of course, first apparent in Britain. At the beginning of the 1830s, Owen once again predicted that economic crisis would topple the existing social system. His analysis of this process was now much more sophisticated. The pace of centralisation, he now proclaimed, threatened the entire merchant class. Soon 'the wholesale and retail trade of the kingdom' would 'be absorbed by a few great houses', until 'the whole business shall be taken up by banking bazaars, which will supersede banking, and every more expensive and hazardous mode of representing and distributing throughout society the wealth of the producers'. Expanding free trade at present, Owen insisted, would only 'extend individual competition to such a degree, that the wealth of society would accumulate among a few favoured individuals in two or three favoured countries ... in the same manner that

[a] But Owen did occasionally praise ideas of this sort, probably as a result of reading Gray. See *The Charter of the Rights of Humanity* (1834) (*infra*, vol. 2, p. 256).

[b] See my *Citizens and Saints*, pt 3.

wealth now accumulates in this country in the hands of a few accidentally favoured individuals, to the great injury of the mass of the people'.[a]

The early 1830s also witnessed a new phase in the Owenite movement, when, for a few years, following on the heels of the success of consumer co-operation, Owen considered the creation of 'labour exchanges' as the best means of both escaping the competitive system and raising funds for a community. As early as 1830, Owen announced that 'the working class, as the only practicable, and at the same time peaceable, mode of ameliorating their condition, will be compelled to adopt a system of mutual exchange of labour for labour, and thereby render themselves independent of the non-producing classes'.[b] The exchanges thus went well beyond the aims of many consumer co-operators by involving producers directly. Shoemakers, carpenters, cabinet-makers and other artisans offered their wares to each other using labour notes to reduce distribution costs. To the merry tunes of a band which played every day at Owen's main exchange in London, goods traded 'equitably' on a basis of labour and raw materials costs, with labour evaluated at the supposedly fair mean rate of sixpence per hour. Though Owen reiterated that this means of rewarding labour was only transitional, his goal now was for all producers to hasten into such bazaars, thus annihilating retail competition.[c] The exchanges were very active in 1832–33 in particular, when they involved at least five hundred artisans and perhaps twice as many. Owen closely supervised the largest of them, at Gray's Inn Road, London, through a new organisation, The Association for Removing the Causes of Ignorance and Poverty by Education and Employment. He gave them much publicity in his new journal, *The Crisis* (1832–4), and poured a good bit of his remaining fortune into the enterprise. Another London branch, and one at Birmingham, also opened. Several congresses – at which considerable tension again emerged between Owen and his more radical associates – were called to co-ordinate matters. But, by mid-1834, the exchanges collapsed through an inability to meet demand for a greater variety of products; from complaints of unfairness about the pricing of products, especially foodstuffs; from the greed of Owen's landlord in London; and because labour notes were not widely transferable.[d]

The promise of the exchanges attracted far larger numbers of workers to Owen's efforts and ideals than ever before, however, especially after the 1832

---

[a] *Birmingham Co-operative Herald*, no. 10 (January 1830), pp. 37–8; Robert Owen, *The Addresses of Robert Owen* (1830), p. 19 (*infra*, vol. 2, p. 139); *Manchester Herald*, 9 April 1830, in University of London MS. 578 (Pare Papers), f. 19. The influence of William Thompson's *Inquiry Concerning the Distribution of Wealth* (1824) on this conception is likely, as Owen read the text and commented frequently on it when it was first published.

[b] *Morning Herald*, 15 February 1830, p. 3.

[c] *The Union*, no. 7 (7 January 1832), p. 99.

[d] Robert Owen, *Address to All Classes in the State From the Governor, Directors and Committee of the Association* (1832), pp. 6–7. See W. H. Oliver, 'The Labour Exchange Phase of the Co-operative Movement', *Oxford Economic Papers*, no. 10 (1958), pp. 355–66.

Reform Act failed to extend the vote to most of them. Briefly, in 1833–34, Owen found the role of working-class leader thrust upon him, when thousands of labourers sought to forge the first general union, the short-lived but temporarily powerful Grand National Consolidated Trades' Union. Acknowledging that the unionists' principles were 'correct, their intentions good, and that they were ignorantly and unjustly used by those who employed them', Owen agreed to join the organisation.[a] Especially in London, the Union emerged in part from the co-operative associations, some derived from a single trade, for example the builders. Its members were impressed by Owen's campaign, through the Society for Promoting National Regeneration, for an eight-hour workday, which Owen now termed 'the first step necessary to put society into a rational state'.[b] Clearly appealing, too, was his proclamation that labour was the sole source of wealth, and that only productive labourers, or those who actually furnished articles for consumption, or offered equivalent services, merited a reward, not parasitic capitalists or retailers. Owen proposed an ambitious scheme whereby all trades would affiliate federatively with a Grand National Council, eventually eliminating masters entirely. (Some trade leaders close to Owen also moved towards a 'syndicalist' ideal – as it would later be termed – of a managed national economy controlled by elected union councils, with masters and managers chosen from amongst the workers.) For a time, early in 1834, Owen headed the organisation as Grand Master. This momentum could not be upheld, however, and despite many strikes, the enrolling of many trades in co-operation, and the affiliation of as many as a million members, the Union collapsed.[c] But for a short period, Owen seemed persuaded that the pressure of large numbers might effect social reform quickly and peacefully, through a great union operating democratically.

This remained Owen's sole major effort to rally the massed working classes in this fashion, however. He never again considered retail co-operation as 'the bridge over which society would safely pass out of its present condition', or trades unionism as an appropriate vehicle for raising funds or placing pressure on the government.[d] The experience reinforced suspicions on both sides. His paternalistic style had again grated on many around him. Owen always assumed that his principles were sound no matter what the outcome of any experiment. He insisted that the working classes could not lead themselves, and said so frankly. For his purposes, they would be more pliable if 'the mania

[a] Owen to Henry Brougham (n.d., c. May 1834), Brougham Collection, University College, London, 14065.

[b] *Rights of Industry, Catechism of the Society for Promoting National Regeneration* (Manchester, 1833), 3; British Library Add. MS. 46344 f. 3. The Society's programme is printed in the *Pioneer*, no. 14 (7 December 1833), p. 109.

[c] See generally G. D. H. Cole, *Attempts at General Union, 1818–34. A Study in British Trade Union History* (Macmillan, 1953).

[d] *The Crisis*, vol. 1, no. 29 (22 September 1832), p. 119.

of radicalism' passed. (In fact the Chartist movement was just gathering steam).[a] But such conclusions left Owen seriously short of any means of transforming society quickly. Flirting briefly with an eccentric Tory, James Bernard, Owen made a curious but futile bid to pit farmers against manufacturers. The experience drew virtually no support, and all too clearly revealed Owen's strategic weakness.[b] Then, having ignored efforts to commence an Irish co-operative farm at Ralahine in the early 1830s, he returned with renewed energy to his traditional plan for founding a model community.[c]

On 1 May 1835, a few days before his sixty-fourth birthday, Owen accordingly established a new communitarian organisation, the Association of All Classes of All Nations, later still more awkwardly renamed the Universal Community Society of Rational Religionists, or Rational Society for short. After a slow start, the movement was subsequently given a great impetus by the sharply increasing poverty and unemployment of the late 1830s. Though the unions were no longer involved, working-class support was now crucial. For compared to its reception in 1817, Owen's Plan was now widely perceived as aiming to make 'the poor altogether independent of the rich ... that every producer of wealth should enjoy the produce of his own industry'.[d] To some, Owen's massive new propaganda campaign seemed remarkably successful: by 1839, the *Westminister Review* observed, Owen's antipathy to competition *per se* was seemingly 'the actual creed of a great portion of the working classes'.[e] By 1840, the Rational Society boasted over sixty branches, whose members were styled 'Socialists', with perhaps fifty thousand flocking to weekly lectures. (Among them was the young German merchant Friedrich Engels, who first was instructed in the tenets of socialist political economy by the Manchester lecturer John Watts.) The Society's regular paper, *The New Moral World*, ran for nearly eleven years (1834–45), and achieved a circulation of about 40,000 weekly at its peak (c. 1839–41). The Prime Minister, Melbourne, even presented Owen to the Queen in 1839.[f] Ever energetic, Owen commenced an unprecedented period of literary activity, publishing his most important mature work, *The Book of the New Moral World*, as well as dozens of shorter addresses. He lectured widely in England and Scotland, sometimes six nights a week, to audiences of up to several thousand. He also travelled to Ireland, America, France, Germany and Austria, where he read a tract addressed to Metternich to the prince in person.

---

[a] *New Moral World*, vol. 1, no. 1 (1 November 1834), p. 7.

[b] See my 'A Tory Utopian Revolutionary at Cambridge: the Political Ideas and Schemes of James B. Bernard, 1834–39', *Historical Journal*, vol. 25 (1982), pp. 583–603.

[c] On Ralahine, see R. G. Garnett, *Co-operation and the Owenite Socialist Communities in Britain, 1825–45* (Manchester: Manchester University Press, 1972), pp. 100–129.

[d] *The Halfpenny Magazine of Entertainment and Knowledge*, no. 24 (10 October 1840), p. 187.

[e] See *New Moral World*, vol. 5, no. 26 (20 April 1839), p. 404.

[f] See *Authentic Disclosures of the Introduction of Rob[t] Owen at St. James's Palace* (1840).

As 'Rational Social Father' of his new organisation, which was intended to bear some resemblance to a Dissenting sect despite his earlier dismissal of the idea, Owen retained virtually complete control over its activities until late 1844. Delegates from the branches also met in annual Congresses to help decide policy, but accusations that Owen and his Central Board were dismissive of 'democratic' demands from the members were common. Nonetheless, the Rational Society flourished for some five years. Much of its success was owed to the energies of the branch lecturers or 'Social Missionaries' (many were ex-ministers), some of whom toured widely, expounding upon popular topics like phrenology, mesmerism and the conquests of science. Of the considerable sums raised by the branches, much – at least £22,000 in 1839–40 alone – went towards constructing local 'Halls of Science' where members attended lectures and held soirées. Services were conducted where 'Social Hymns' sang the virtues of community and sociability. Marriages were also performed; the first, in London in 1841, was by Owen himself. Ocasionally children were named. (Primo Communis Flitcroft was the name given to the first child born on the Society's estate.) These activities aroused much interest, and created a distinctive 'social' culture of great value to the movement.[a] Beyond this, the propaganda efforts of the Rational Society gave Owen's ideas an enormous circulation, with millions of pamphlets being distributed between 1839 and 1845 outlining the socialist view of competition, industry and the potential for a just economic system.

Such efforts, directed in the first instance at supplanting the social function of organised religion, predictably prompted a strong reaction from the Church of England and a small army of clergymen of every stripe. Ministers were appalled by Owen's highly liberal views on marriage (whose sacrosanct nature he was forced to defend on numerous occasions),[b] his deist theology, and his frequent challenges to the priesthood to renounce their faith. Egged on by the intolerant Bishop of Exeter, the House of Lords debated the Owenite menace at its peak in 1840.[c] Ministers frequently challenged socialists to theological debates, especially over the question of free will versus necessity, so vital to

[a] See Eileen Yeo, 'Robert Owen and Radical Culture', in Sidney Pollard and John Salt, eds, *Robert Owen. Prophet of the Poor* (Macmillan, 1971), pp. 84–114, and my 'From "Polite Manners" to "Rational Character": the Critique of Culture in Owenite Socialism, 1800–1850', in Frits van Holthoon and Lex Heerma van Voss, eds, *Working Class and Popular Culture in Britain and Holland* (Amsterdam: Stichtung Beheer IISG, 1988), pp. 19–32. The Manchester Hall of Science cost £7000, and had the largest lecture hall in the city.

[b] E.g., *What is Socialism? And What Would Be Its Practical Effects Upon Society? A Correct Report of the Public Discussion Between Robert Owen and* Mr. *John Brindley* (1841), p. 67, or *New Moral World*, vol. 5, no. 28 (4 May 1840), p. 443.

[c] See Henry Phillpotts, *Progress of Socialism. The Bishop of Exeter's Speech in the House of Lords* (1840), and *New Moral World*, vol. 7 (suppl. 8 February 1840, pp. 1073–80, and 15 February 1840). For a fictional account inspired by the Bishop's attack, see Rev. William Gresley, *Charles Lever; or, the Man of the Nineteenth Century* (1841), pp. 106–40.

Owen's system. One of Owen's followers, the later co-operative leader George Jacob Holyoake, was convicted of blasphemy, and served six months in prison. Pressure was applied widely to prevent Socialist branches from meeting. Accusations flew that their members sought community of wives – which was clearly false – as well as of goods.[a] Owen's own moral conduct was thankfully unimpeachable. But some of his disciples apparently drew libertine conclusions from his teachings without much difficulty. And even if they had only 'circumstances' to blame for lapses from propriety, public opinion was less forgiving of sexual peccadilloes. Owen certainly left himself open for misinterpretation, however, declaiming against the swearing in marriage of affection until death 'when perhaps only a week or a day is possible', and impugning 'celibacy' as 'a great crime'. (His publisher's addition of an excerpt from Shelley's *Queen Mab* on free love and the abolition of marriage to Owen's account of the subject served to confirm this dubious reputation.)[b] Public pressure mounted steadily. In the Midlands, some master-manufacturers were persuaded to dismiss those of their workers who were socialists. In several towns, mobs pursued Owenite lecturers, even destroying their meeting halls. Owen's *The Book of the New Moral World* was torched publicly, and plans were also afoot in late April 1840 to set fire to the Manchester 'Social Cathedral'.

In the meantime, however, the Rational Society had acquired land in Hampshire, erected buildings, and in late 1839 commenced a new community called Queenwood on a 533–acre site designed for seven hundred members.[c] Working-class support for the community probably increased after an attempted Chartist uprising in Wales in 1839 ended in failure. Many of the Society's new adherents certainly had Chartist sympathies, and envisioned 'community' as an exercise in democracy as well as social equality. Owen's firm resolution to have no dealings with the Chartists which were not wholly on his terms consequently alienated many Socialists. Moreover, despite limited success in raising funds for Queenwood, Owen's own vision of its creation as a symbol of his ideas also became steadily more grandiose and impractical. Much of the money collected for the community was spent on constructing, in 1842, an impressively large building with lavish fittings. Especially noteworthy was a model kitchen with a conveyor to carry food and dishes to and from the dining-

[a] Even Francis Place claimed that Owen concealed the fact that his plans included 'promiscuous intercourse between the sexes to as great an extent as individuals pleased' (British Library Add. MS. 27791 f. 262).

[b] Robert Owen, *The Book of the New Moral World*, pt 6 (1844), p. 37 (*infra*, vol. 3, p. 324); Robert Owen, *The Marriage System of the New Moral World* (Leeds, 1838), pp. 10, 87–91 (*infra*, vol. 2, pp. 268, 318–22). Owen denied that he sanctioned the inclusion of this quote. See *Report of the Discussion between Robert Owen and the Rev. William Legg* (1839), p. 33.

[c] The most detailed account of the community is R. G. Garnett, *Co-operation and the Owenite Socialist Communities in Britain, 1825–45* (Manchester: Manchester University Press, 1972), pp. 165–213.

room which, its architect exulted, rivalled the amenities of any London hotel. This would have been a great achievement, had Owen been a hotelier. His defence was that the community was intended to be the standard for a superior socialist future where all would enjoy privileges the wealthy monopolised at present, nay even more, for all apartments were eventually to have central heating, cooling, hot and cold water, and artificial light. Its main building thus ought to be 'superior to any palace'.[a] And such, after a fashion, it might have been. But such extravagance removed funds needed for daily operations. By 1844, after over £40,000 had been spent, Queenwood bankrupted the Society. Control over the organisation was seized that summer by a group of chiefly working-class branch delegates to the annual Owenite congress. But without fresh funds, the community was doomed. It was also plagued by many of the problems which had undermined earlier experiments, notably resistance to Owen's sometimes apparently arbitrary rule; the agricultural inexperience of many artisans from the Midland manufacturing towns, which led to the need to hire local labourers; insufficient accommodation for community members; and poor planning in general.

Organised Owenism now ground to a halt. The branches broke up, with some emigrating *en masse* to the United States. Owen himself returned to America several times over the next few years. Though he failed in 1845 to address the Senate again, he bombarded the government with addresses. In 1846, he helped (having met many of the principal negotiators in Mexico nearly twenty years earlier) to ease tensions between Britain and the U.S. over a border dispute in Oregon, crossing the Atlantic four times in fewer than six months in the effort. He announced plans for a variety of new schemes. But his moral capital had also been exhausted by the Queenwood débâcle, and few paid him heed any longer. Those who did tended to adopt part rather than all of his programme. His views on religion were taken up and refashioned into a new ideal called 'secularism' by George Jacob Holyoake. A few Owenites turned to concentrate their efforts on friendly societies. Others entered the again rapidly expanding consumer co-operation movement, which was given a great impetus by the success of the Rochdale Society of Equitable Pioneers, founded by a group of weavers in 1844. Several former Rational Society lecturers renewed their activities in 1848, when revolutions on the continent and a Chartist revival at home raised the possibility of a new alliance between the social and political reformers. Leading social Chartists like Bronterre O'Brien now met with Owenites like the former carpenter and old Orbistonian Alexander Campbell and the journalist Robert Buchanan to try to form a new association, though without success. Owen himself travelled immediately to revolutionary France to popularise his views, spending four months there, and

[a] Robert Owen, *A Development of the Principles and Plans* (1841), p. 48 (*infra*, vol. 2, p. 383).

placarding the walls of Paris with broadsheets.[a] He condemned 'the senseless cry among those called the re-actionists in Paris, for the security of private property and family arrangements, as now existing'. His short-term constitutionalist programme also became more radical. Owen not only suggested that the 'American government, in principle, with some essential modifications in practice, will be a good present model with which to commence'. He also proposed that a new European government be elected by universal suffrage to prepare for the division of Europe into communities. At home, he also became more accommodating to the aims of the parliamentary reformers in England.[b]

Little came of these efforts. But this last great burst of energy, in his seventy-seventh year, must have tired Owen greatly, for he aged quickly after 1848. His last decade was marred for many by his conversion to, as one critic amongst many put it, the 'gross and almost childish superstition' of spiritualist table-rapping in 1853. (But thousands of others were equally attracted to this new idea of the afterlife at the time.)[c] For Owen, the ethereal world was uniformly encouraging; his old friend the Duke of Kent told him that there were no titles in the hereafter.[d] But however egalitarian some of the spirits were, Owen's 'communications' with them seemed to make a mockery of a lifetime of sceptical deism and rationalism. As the world at large showed no propensity to convert *en masse* to socialism, however, this was clearly, in his dotage, Owen's last court of appeal. Nonetheless, he remained active in other ways, dictating – though far too late, for accuracy's sake – the first volume of his autobiography, which was published in September 1857, reprinting earlier works, and attending various reform meetings, where he cut a striking figure in a dark velvet fur cap, gold spectacles, and a full white beard.[e] In October 1858, at the age of eighty-seven, he had to be carried to and from the stage of a National Association for the Advancement of Social Science meeting at Liverpool, though he managed to deliver part of his speech. In November, Owen set off for Newtown, having not revisited it for seventy years, determined, as he put

---

[a] On this stage in his career, see Chushichi Tsuzuki, 'Robert Owen and Revolutionary Politics', in Sidney Pollard and John Salt, eds, *Robert Owen. Prophet of the Poor* (Macmillan, 1971), pp. 13–83, and M. Rubel, 'Robert Owen's Visit to Paris in 1848', *Actualité d'Histoire*, vol. 60 (1960), pp. 1–12. French Owenism is investigated in Henri Desroches, 'Owenisme et Utopies Françaises', *Communautés*, vol. 30 (1971), essentially reproduced as 'Images of Owenism in Nineteenth-Century France', in Sidney Pollard and John Salt, eds, *Robert Owen. Prophet of the Poor* (Macmillan, 1971), pp. 239–84. See also Jacques Gans, 'Les Relations entre socialistes de France et de l'Angleterre au début du XIXe siècle', *Le Mouvement Social*, vol. 46 (1964), pp. 105–18, Jacques Gans, 'Robert Owen à Paris en 1837', *Le Mouvement Social*, vol. 41 (1962), pp. 35–45.

[b] *Northern Star*, no. 573 (October 1848), p. 1; no. 542 (11 March 1848), p. 6.

[c] *Reynold's Newspaper*, no. 183 (12 February 1854), p. 2. For Owen's own account of his acceptance of a spirit world, see Robert Owen, *Address on Spiritual Manifestations* (1855).

[d] See Robert Owen, *Life*, vol. 1 (1857), p. 189 (*infra*, vol. 4, pp. 253–4). Holyoake commented that 'the spirits would hardly dare show their faces to Mr. Owen if they were not friendly to community' (*The Reasoner*, no. 361, 30 March 1853, p. 298).

[e] *The Reasoner*, no. 468 (1855), p. 54.

it, 'to leave his bones where he got them'.[a] He died there, with his son Robert Dale Owen at his side, in a small room (no. 14) at the Bear Hotel, on 17 November 1858. 'A life of labour for all who suffered', as one obituary reflected, was over.[b] He was buried, as he wished, by his parents a few hundred yards away from the hotel in a grave next to, suitably, an abandoned church.[c]

2. *The Basis and Development of Owen's Thought*

It is often presumed, incorrectly, that Owen's ideas were fully formed by 1820.[d] In fact, the evolution of his thinking can be divided into four main phases: the emergence of his early ideas on behaviour and personality, up to about 1815; the period of Owen's rejection of the factory system, commercial competition, and all forms of social organisation besides his own communities, approximately from 1816 to 1820; the stage in which his economic ideas were most substantially refined, during the 1820s; and the maturing of his social system, which remained essentially unchanged after 1830.

Owen's system was founded upon the belief that individuals did not, by and large, *choose* their ideas and character, but rather had these thrust upon them by their surroundings and upbringing. According to the associationist psychology which inspired him, the personality was rooted in certain 'animal propensities' which evolved into natural desires, and in the faculties, also moulded by external stimulae, which received and compared ideas. Guided by 'the all prevailing principle of life, the desire for happiness', which was 'the primary cause' of their actions, individuals reacted to the pattern of stimulae previously enforced upon them. Their personalities were poorly formed when few ideas made an impact upon them, or when these were erroneous. The ways in which individuals received ideas, moreover, were also modified by the 'national character' and laws and customs of their community.[e] 'The character of man is formed for him, and not by him', thus became Owen's recurrent battle cry, repeated numerous times over his long career, and to audiences of many hundreds of thousands in total, whose constantly changing composition accounts for much of the repetitiveness of some of his publications. This simple, but for Owen momentous, principle was at the centre of his writings

[a] *Nonconformist*, no. 682 (24 November 1858), p. 944.
[b] *Glasgow Sentinel*, no. 425 (27 November 1858), p. 4.
[c] The burial as a result was Christian, but his followers tolerated this irony with silent forbearance, only Owen's long-time friend Thomas Allsop refusing to enter the Church.
[d] Several shorter editions of Owen's works stop in 1821, with the *Report to the County of Lanark*.
[e] Robert Owen, *Life*, vol. 1 (1857), pp. 296, 300–1, 314–15 (*infra*, vol. 1, pp. 65, 69–70, 83–4). For an interesting Owenite effort to assess the different influences on personality, see *A Diagram Illustrative of the Formation of the Human Character, Suggested by Mr. Owen's Development of A New View of Society* (1824).

from *A New View of Society* onwards. Christianity and other religions as well as most systems of education and government, he thought, were rooted in the mistaken assumption that individuals possessed a free will, and that all behaviour consequently resulted from free choice and should be rewarded or punished accordingly.

The main context for understanding Owen's constant repetition of this chief principle was the increasingly evangelical atmosphere of late-Georgian and early Victorian England, where a much harsher attitude towards poverty and the supposed immorality of the poor was intimately linked to the Christian fundamentalist emphasis of Wilberforce and others on mankind's fallen nature. To Owen, however, this assumption, so crucial to what we now term 'Victorian morality', merely reinforced poverty and misery. The poor were 'immoral' because their harsh, vicious, and degraded surroundings placed no premium on propriety. Their behaviour would 'improve', in the sense of conforming to the expectations of the higher classes, only when this environment was altered. Attempts to reward or punish them without such changes would thus be fruitless. Correspondingly, if it could be proven that one set of 'circumstances' – Owen's amorphous term for the factors shaping personality – did promote morality, surrounding all with similar stimulae would, almost mechanically, bring similar results. For Owen, this was the grand conclusion of his experiments at Manchester and New Lanark. If only, he never tired of repeating, all realised that behaviour resulted from social factors, then aggression, cruelty and selfishness would give way to kindness, sympathy and charity. Unfortunately, Owen did not usually explain how some individuals, like himself, seemingly broke free from the necessary chain of 'circumstances'. (He usually claimed that his own character had also been formed 'for' him.)[a] It was the rule, not the exception, which interested him. He clearly thought that it was possible to move towards 'controlling circumstances'. But he never conveyed very effectively just what this meant. Critics complained, moreover, about 'the docility, the orderliness, the 'like views and like wants' Owen's system seemed to demand, which many thought 'were results incompatible with the free development of the free man'.[b] They usually contended that Owen underestimated a natural human propensity to folly, obstinacy, irritability, and selfishness. But Owen always retorted that his principles had never been given a fair trial.

The second stage in Owen's thought brought the decision, in the face of widespread opposition to his plans, that the entire society had to be remodelled. By 1817, he condemned as irrational the division of peoples into cities, towns and villages riven by national, class, religious, and marital

[a] Robert Owen, *Life*, vol. 1 (1857), p. xii (*infra*, vol. 4, p. 18).
[b] *The Leader*, no. 452 (20 November 1858), p. 1244.

conflict. Only a uniform system of communities could provide the ideal environment for raising future generations. Though his own ideas on the subject were already well advanced at the time, Owen acknowledged a debt here to the plans of the Quaker social reformer John Bellers, whose proposals for a 'college of industry' he reprinted in 1818; as well as the religious communitarianism of the Shakers, Rappites, and other sects.[a] The utopian tradition had also frequently envisioned model societies of this type.[b] But there was also an economic foundation to this vision. Owen did not merely spin 'duodecimo editions of the New Jerusalem' arbitrarily out of his head, as a dismissive Engels later asserted.[c] The present edition of his works, in particular, demonstrates that he did not believe that socialism was possible before the age of manufacturing, for the machine alone made realistic the promise of a life of greater leisure for the majority. Owen did not see himself as 'utopian', in this sense, but as an analyst of social and economic change who saw more clearly and prophetically than others the profound implications of the new manufacturing system.[d]

There were two main elements in the third stage in Owen's development. Firstly, he concluded between 1816 and 1820 that the root cause of social evil lay not with the doctrine of responsibility alone, but with several related assumptions. Chief amongst these was a misplaced faith in the benefits of a 'competition' of 'individual interests', exemplified in the practice of 'buying cheap and selling dear'.[e] Instead, competition promoted selfishness and produced too many of some types of goods while failing to furnish others in sufficient quantities to meet real human needs. His resolution that only a 'community of mutual and combined interests' would resolve these problems led to the most important break from Owen's previous beliefs. Property, he now decided, had to be held in common, as Bellers had also suggested. Private ownership was the principal cause of 'vanity, pride, luxury, and tyranny, on the one hand; and poverty and degradation, on the other. Hence resulted 'insincerity, deceptions and hatred; traffic, robbery, murder; and a system of law, or artificial justice, covering the grossest injustice'.[f] A more limited form of economic equality, 'co-operation' or profit-sharing, could also promote

[a] See Robert Owen, *Life*, vol. 1A (1858), pp. 143–81.

[b] For some examples, see my edition of *Restoration British Utopias* (Syracuse, N.Y.: Syracuse University Press, 1995).

[c] See Claeys, *Citizens and Saints*, pp. 299–306.

[d] See in particular the *Address of Mr. Robert Owen to the Agriculturalists, Mechanics and Manufacturers, Both Masters and Operatives, of Great Britain and Ireland* (1827) (*infra*, vol. 2, pp. 105–13).

[e] For a more comprehensive account of the development of Owen's economics ideas, see my *Machinery, Money and the Millennium*, ch. 2.

[f] *Robert Owen's Opening Speech, and His Reply to the Rev. Alexander Campbell, in the Recent Discussion in Cincinnati* (Cincinnati, 1829), p. 38; Robert Owen, *Lectures on an Entire New State of Society* (1830), p. 43.

social equality, as the radical John Thelwall had glimpsed in the mid-1790s.[a] It could aid the just exchange of products, as well as the elimination of a large body of middlemen (especially in distribution), and could help to balance supply and demand more efficiently. Economic justice would also release the labouring classes from servitude to others, for no-one had 'A RIGHT TO REQUIRE ANOTHER MAN TO DO FOR HIM, WHAT HE WILL NOT DO FOR THAT MAN'.[b] Only one rule could thus govern all economic relations, and that was that 'no man has a just right to the labour of any other man, *without giving equal labour or value in exchange for it*'.[c] But while co-operation could meet many of these aims, community of goods remained Owen's eventual goal, for only the greater social equality it encouraged could provide a full measure of justice for all. After 1817, he did not retreat from this, and remained inflexible about alternatives. (He was, however, willing to countenance temporary social inequality in interim communities.)[d] The old system and the new were wholly incompatible; like 'oil and water, they must repel each other'.[e] If competition could not be superseded productively, it would eventually destroy the existing social system. First consecutive crises would increasingly centralise wealth. Eventually a few wealthy bankers and manufacturers would be confronted by a poor majority for whom socialism would appear their sole salvation. (This conception anticipated Marx and Engels' later notion of capitalist crisis.)[f] The choice was thus between voluntary conversion to socialism or a bloody revolution led by ill-educated and power-hungry radicals which would degenerate into terror as quickly as the first French revolution had done.

Linked to Owen's analysis of competition, secondly, was an account of the existing scheme of occupational specialisation. Here his proposals marked an even more dramatic departure from existing reform ideals. The future would tolerate no division of labour between worker and capitalist, distributor and producer, idle and industrious. All, instead, would share the same burdens of furnishing useful goods for society as 'productive labourers' (a category which for Owen included working master manufacturers, for example, but not bankers). Adam Smith, in particular, had lauded the tendency of the division of labour

[a] See *The Rights of Nature against the Usurpations of Establishments* (1796), reprinted in *John Thelwall: Political Writings*, ed. G. Claeys (University Park, PA.: Penn State University Press, 1994). Thelwall commented on Owen's plans that they were 'benevolent' and might be 'highly useful to mankind' (*The Champion*, no. 343, 1 August 1819, p. 482).

[b] Robert Owen, *Six Lectures Delivered in Manchester* (Manchester, 1839), p. 69. See also Owen, *The Book of the New Moral World*, pt 5 (1844), p. 64 (*infra*, vol. 3, p. 286).

[c] Robert Owen, *Lectures on the Marriages of the Priesthood of the Old Immoral World* (4th edn, Leeds, 1840), p. 30 (*infra*, vol. 2, p. 280). The debt to Godwin here is probably substantial. See William Godwin, *The Enquirer* (1797), p. 173.

[d] See for example *A Development of the Principles and Plans* (1841), pp. 36, 41 (*infra*, vol. 2, pp. 373, 377).

[e] Robert Owen, *Report of the Proceedings at the Several Public Meetings Held In Dublin* (Dublin, 1823), p. 21.

[f] See my *Machinery, Money and the Millennium*, pp. 166–83.

to increase productivity, while conceding that routinisation stultified the labourer's mind, making him or her incapable of rational political participation or of enjoying a rich social existence. Though the early French socialist Charles Fourier was more detailed about variations of task within the working day, Owen's main point was that with sufficient machinery and the reorganisation of production, no narrow division of labour was necessary. Smith had seemingly assumed that the cost of economic advance was the degradation of the labour force. For Owen this was too high a price to pay for progress. Instead, machinery might help replace much dangerous and monotonous labour, and make possible a new world of justice and equality. With no more than a few hours' necessary daily labour, all could share in the benefits of culture. All would be more virtuous in the new moral environment, too, for rivalry would be unnecessary when machinery aided superfluity. Smith had insisted that butchers did not feed their fellows out of benevolence. Owen thought that people, unhampered by occupational disabilities, might.

Owen may have been aware of earlier criticisms of the dehumanising effects of repetitive work, such as Adam Ferguson's *Essay on the History of Civil Society* (1767).[a] He certainly anticipates much of the assault upon alienation in the writings of the young Marx, whose point of departure was also Adam Smith's treatment of the division of labour.[b] But the sources of his critique are idiosyncratic. His opposition to specialisation owed something to Dissenting concerns with spiritual self-government or 'independence', which Owen occasionally termed his chief aim,[c] where the individual's relation to God was intended to be free from priestly interference.[d] His oft-repeated definition of 'mental liberty' as sincerity of speech is also Nonconformist in origin.[e] Owen was further indebted to a more specifically Quakerish opposition to the separate professions of soldier, lawyer and clergyman. This in turn was partially derived from mid-seventeenth century republicanism. (And Owen occasionally praised the fortitude of the ancient Greeks and Romans, while abhorring classical militarism.)[f] For many republicans, the independence of a free people required opposing standing armies as potential organs of executive tyranny, and relying instead on civic militias. Owen recommended military training for all males at New Lanark, and New Harmony had its own militia.[g] Some republican critics

---

[a] Adam Ferguson, *An Essay on the History of Civil Society* (1767), ed. Duncan Forbes (Edinburgh: Edinburgh University Press, 1966), pp. 180–8.

[b] See Marx's 'Economic and Philosophic Manuscripts' (*Collected Works*, New York: International Publishers, 1975, vol. 3, p. 294).

[c] E.g., *The Charter of the Rights of Humanity* (1834) (*infra*, vol. 2, pp. 253–8).

[d] See *Robert Owen's Opening Speech, and His Reply to the Rev. Alexander Campbell, in the Recent Discussion in Cincinnati* (Cincinnati, 1829), pp. 123–4.

[e] See *infra*, vol. 2, p. 55.

[f] E.g., Robert Owen, *The Book of the New Moral World*, pt 1 (1842 edn), p. 54 (*infra*, vol. 3, p. 62); pt 5, p. 38 (*infra*, vol. 3, p. 268).

[g] Robert Owen, *A New View of Society* (1857 edn), in *Life*, vol. 1, p. 303 (*infra*, vol. 1, p. 72).

of specialisation, like Ferguson, also assumed that intellectual independence was threatened by too narrow a division of labour, as the labourer's mental horizons became hemmed in by a limited occupation. While rejecting the common republican view that personal independence was possible only through property ownership, and that those who were dependent had no right of political involvement, Owen extended such criticisms dramatically. His wish to make everyone 'his own priest, lawyer, physician and soldier, in order that each may be the most independent of others that social arrangements can be made to admit' thus combined elements of both the Nonconformist and the republican ideals of independence. It also demonstrates strikingly how far the language of the individual and that of the social were merged in Owen's ideals.[a] But Owen of course also sought to supersede the division of interest which characterised class society more generally, and 'to merge all individualism in the social'.[b] Here he followed, at least in spirit, proposals for, among others, a system of urban and rural rotation offered as early as More's *Utopia*.

These observations brought the conclusion, by the late 1820s, that the only fair way to distribute labour was to educate all identically and have all share in similar burdens, responsibilities and privileges throughout life. Owen's attitude towards politics, and in particular his wish to solve the problem of political contests once and for all, was a crucial aspect of this proposal. Thus he was hardly simply 'conservative' by contrast to the political radicals who were so often his opponents. Certainly he did not believe that extending the franchise would solve the most pressing social problems. But his objection was to all forms of electoral government. In the short term, Owen preferred to control organisations dedicated to achieving his ends. He conceded, however, that large-scale capital investors in any community should have a substantial say in running it until their capital was repaid. But he by no means deferred to capitalists to the degree that Fourier, for example, recommended.[c] Nor did Owen accept the notion of a hierarchy based upon an industrial meritocracy, as the founder of another socialist school, Henri de Saint-Simon, had advocated.[d] Instead, he suggested in passing in 1816 that 'age shall receive attention and respect' in his new communities, and proposed as early as 1817 that each community might 'ultimately be governed by a committee of its own members, from forty to fifty years of age, or should this number be too numerous, it may

---

[a] *Spirit of the Age*, no. 16 (16 November 1848), p. 244. Owen's political ideas are examined in my *Citizens and Saints*, ch. 2.

[b] *New Moral World*, vol. 13, no. 8 (17 August 1844), p. 57.

[c] *The Utopian Vision of Charles Fourier. Selected Texts on Work, Love, and Passionate Attraction*, eds Jonathan Beecher and Richard Bienvenu (Columbia: University of Missouri Press, 1983), p. 250.

[d] Ghita Ionescu, ed., *The Political Thought of Saint-Simon* (Oxford: Oxford University Press, 1976), p. 193.

be composed of all from forty-five to fifty-five years of age'. Particularly talented individuals could also be added by majority vote. This would 'form a permanent, experienced local government, never opposed to, but always in closest union with, each individual governed'. Each committee 'through its oldest member, might communicate directly with the Government; and the utmost harmony be thus established between the Executive, the Legislature, and the people'.[a] As Owen intimated in 1822, age and experience (the two were often presumed to coincide) were the only just and natural social distinctions. They would thus be the sole basis for social inequalities in the future.[b]

For most of his career, Owen consequently resisted pleas for political reform, especially when mooted by radical working-class leaders. Permitting the working-classes to vote, he insisted, would not eliminate poverty or industrial chaos. After the mid-1820s, he usually argued that the goal of community was to supersede not only democracy as it was usually understood, but also aristocracy, monarchy and every other form of rule. For radical leaders, however, this smacked of elitism but thinly disguised, and Owen's behaviour towards them personally seemed to underscore the point. His own mode of 'government' at Manchester and New Lanark had of course been largely paternalistic, and this, unfortunately, set the stamp on his relations with the working classes for the rest of his life. (Moreover, Owen was not beyond referring to 'the ignorance, vulgarity, and most disgusting assumptions' of the labouring classes, which was hardly calculated to win friends from that quarter).[c] But he continued to protest at least until 1848, and often thereafter, that the struggle for political reform merely obscured the need for more fundamental social, moral and economic changes. In America, in the 1820s, he acknowledged that attaining political liberty might well be 'a necessary step towards the acquirement of real mental liberty'. But he also declared that the American system of government encouraged an aristocracy of priests, lawyers and the wealthy.[d] During the agitation over the Reform Bill in 1831–2, he resisted every suggestion that political reform might aid the co-operative, exchange or community movements. His position was similar throughout the Chartist years until 1848. Owen paid a price for this obstinacy. For while his economic ideas were widely influential, the perfectionist core of Owen's political thought was almost universally ignored. His followers, too, conceded much of Owen's case against traditional radicalism, and also sought 'harmony' of a sort. But most had more

[a] Robert Owen, *Address to the Inhabitants of New Lanark* (1816), p. 39 (*infra*, vol. 1, p. 129); Robert Owen, *New View of Society* (1857 edn), in *Life*, vol. 1, p. 117 (*infra*, vol. 1, p. 201).

[b] Robert Owen, *Permanent Relief for the British Agricultural and Manufacturing Labourers* (?1822), p. 4 (*infra*, vol. 1, p. 346); *New Harmony Gazette*, vol. 2, no. 19 (7 February 1827), p. 146; no. 21 (21 February 1827), p. 161.

[c] Robert Owen, *The Book of the New Moral World*, pt 7 (1844), p. 50 (*infra*, vol. 3, p. 395).

[d] *New Harmony Gazette*, vol. 2, no. 30 (25 April 1827), p. 234; vol. 3, no. 26 (23 April 1828), p. 204.

confidence in the ability of working class Owenites to establish this than Owen himself did, and were not willing to depart as far from traditional political organisation as he was.

By 1829, Owen's perfectionist ideals were formally presented as a 'Universal Code of Laws' for the future organisation of society which established the principle that 'All shall pass through the same general routine of education, and domestic teaching, and employment' as well as government.[a] Society was to be reorganised into eight age-groups, each of which would assume a major social task for a period, then move on to another occupation. Age would thus supplant class as the chief principle of social division. The first 'class' (as Owen termed it), from birth to age 5, would attend school. Those 5 to 10 would assist with domestic labour, supervised in part by those aged 10–15, who would also learn agricultural and industrial skills. From ages 15–20, all would engage in production, also helping to supervise the next youngest age-group. Those 20–25 would supervise all branches of production and education. All aged 25–30 would preserve and distribute wealth. Those 30–40 would govern communities. The most mature, aged 40–60, would conduct 'foreign affairs'. The effect of this scheme, as Owen later put it, was to unite 'in the same individual the producer, and the possessor of wealth, the communicator and the recipient of knowledge, the governor and the governed, to destroy the invidious distinctions that have split up the one great family of man into sections and classes'.[b] This arrangement alone guaranteed fully 'equal rights', which meant 'equal education and condition through life according to age'.[c] Only then could the great problem of the necessity for both dependence and independence be reconciled happily and justly. All, thus, were to be merged in a single model of human social development, with 'the fewest languages, governments, laws, and opposing institutions, prejudices, habits, and manners' possible. (The inevitability of diversity Owen sometimes appeared to concede; its virtues he acknowledged only fleetingly.)[d]

This scheme also required abolishing the traditional family, a theme to which Owen gave increasing prominence from the mid-1820s onwards. In the

[a] Robert Owen, *Robert Owen's Opening Speech* (1829), p. 49.

[b] *New Moral World*, vol. 13, no. 48 (24 May 1845), p. 388.

[c] *New Moral World*, vol. 13, no. 46 (10 May 1845), p. 365.

[d] Robert Owen, *Manifesto of Robert Owen* (Washington D.C., 1844), p. 5; *Spirit of the Age*, vol. 1, no. 11 (7 October 1848), p. 171. Owen occasionally asserted that 'a just equality of the family of man, will not consist in making all alike' (*Robert Owen's Weekly Letters to the Human Race*, 1850, p. 89), and elsewhere conceded that diversity was an element of happiness (*The Book of the New Moral World*, pt 1, 1836, pp. 24–6; *infra*, vol. 3, pp. 40–1). In his *Life*, he even proposed that physical and mental variety constituted the 'very essence' of rational enjoyment (vol. 1, 1857, p. iii) (*infra*, vol. 4, p. 9). On the extreme cosmopolitanism of Owen's vision, see my 'Reciprocal Dependence, Virtue and Progress: Some Sources of Early Socialist Cosmopolitanism and Internationalism in Britain, 1790–1860', in Frits van Holthoon and Marcel van der Linden, eds, *Internationalism in the Labour Movement 1830–1940* (Leiden: E. J. Brill, 1988), pp. 235–58.

existing marriage system, motives of personal gain interfered with true affection. The wife's rights and social roles were severely circumscribed. The difficulty of obtaining a divorce, coupled with a social double standard in the treatment of infidelities, engendered both protracted mutual hostilities and pervasive duplicity. Marriage was a virtually unrivalled source of immorality which was not directly reducible to the commercial or property system. 'There is,' Owen complained, 'perhaps, now more deception expressed in look, manner, and words, all forming languages, between the husbands and wives, made such by the Priesthood of the world, than there is between any other parties throughout the whole of society, not even excepting the present buyers and sellers of goods or money for pecuniary profit.' The contemporary institution of marriage thus fostered prostitution. (Indeed Owen often equated the two, infuriating his critics.)[a] But Owen never contemplated any 'community of wives'. He wanted to raise children collectively in order to foment a stronger sense of communitarian loyalty. Easy divorce would also be introduced (it was over a century before this occurred).[b] Women were to be accorded rights equal to men in every area (which is far from achieved yet in most parts of the world), including an equal voice in governing communities.[c] Owen evidently hoped that birth control would also be practised. For while he initially proclaimed that until 'the whole earth shall become a highly-cultivated garden', there was no need to fear over-population, Owen apparently took Torrens' Malthusian criticisms of his Plan in 1817 to heart. He may have travelled to Paris to learn new methods of birth control, even helping to introduce the vaginal sponge into Britain.[d] Around 1820, he also probably circulated tracts warning of the dangers of overpopulation addressed 'To the Married of the Working People', which induced some working class radicals, ironically, to retort that he was a Malthusian who sought to punish the working classes for

---

[a] Robert Owen, *The Marriage System of the New Moral World* (4th edn, Leeds, 1840), pp. 25–7 (*infra*, vol. 2, pp. 277–9). For discussion see John Saville, 'Robert Owen on the Family and Marriage System of the New Moral World', in M. Cornforth, ed., *Rebels and Their Causes* (Lawrence and Wishart, 1978), pp. 107–21, and generally Barbara Taylor, *Eve and the New Jerusalem. Socialism and Feminism in the Nineteenth Century* (Virago Books, 1983). The mere fact of Owenism's sexual egalitarianism and anti-patriarchalism could be used to argue that its ideas were twice as democratic as those of most contemporary radicals, who often argued that reform should reinstate women in their rightful position in the home. For such a view, see *Weekly True Sun*, no. 315 (8 September 1839), p. 2.

[b] An early discussion of this theme is in 'The Social System', *New Harmony Gazette*, vol. 2, no. 22 (28 February 1827), p. 170 (*infra*, vol. 2, pp. 92–3).

[c] See, for example, Robert Owen, *The Book of the New Moral World*, pt 6 (1844), p. 72 (*infra*, vol. 3, p. 348).

[d] Robert Owen, *Life*, 1A (1858), pp. 74–5 (*infra*, vol. 1, pp. 157–8); *Black Dwarf*, vol. 11, no. 14 (1 October 1823), pp. 499–500; *Report of the Proceedings at the Several Public Meetings Held in Dublin* (Dublin, 1823), p. 130; *Cobbett's Weekly Political Register*, vol. 64 (17 November 1827), p. 499. See Norman Himes, 'The Place of J. S. Mill and Robert Owen in the History of the English Neo-Malthusianism', *Quarterly Journal of Economics*, vol. 42 (1928), pp. 627–40.

bearing children.[a] Despite such criticisms, however, his was an astonishingly radical feminist programme for its time. But it remained such more in principle than practice, for Owen, having intially urged that New Lanark girls be taught sewing, cooking and housework, recommended a similarly traditional division of labour at New Harmony based on 'female nature', and did not markedly depart from such notions in the 1840s.[b]

Feminist measures, of course, were hardly calculated to mollify the sentiments of Owen's (mostly male) radical political critics, and in the 1830s and 1840s their prejudices against him did much to prevent socialism from becoming more popular among the working classes. Slowly, and grudgingly, Owen did apparently take cognizance of their reproaches, at least to the extent of incorporating some of the language of the radical reformers into his Plan, while still maintaining that radical goals could in fact only be attained in community. At the height of the Grand National Consolidated Trades' Union movement of 1833–34, moreover, Owen did defer to a very radical democratic proposal, the election of managers by workers, as well as the possiblity of trades managing their own divisions of industry.[c] But here, as well as in the labour exchanges, he still sought to infuse a modicum of 'harmony' into the deliberative process, for example by urging branches of the National Equitable Labour Exchange to arbitrate internal disputes in a Quakerish fashion, by the 'elders' of each district annually electing a committee of three for such tasks. Vociferous radicalism in the branches of the Rational Society also forced him to tolerate an important measure of traditional democracy there during the late 1830s and early 1840s.[d] But only in 1848, when his following was much diminished, did Owen appear to concede that political reforms might be a useful means of introducing social alterations. Now, at last, he recommended that a congress be elected by universal suffrage, 'under present circumstance and feelings, the least objectionable mode of election', with two delegates from each of the larger European countries, and one from the smaller, establish a constitution to divide Europe into communities.[e]

Nonetheless, other 'political' aspects of his Plan had a more obvious appeal to democrats. His scheme for reorganising the world into communities was broadly federalist in structure, and envisioned a world government where no

---

[a] *The Present Day*, vol. 3, no. 35 (April 1886), p. 78; *Republican*, vol. 11, no. 18 (6 May 1825), p. 556.

[b] Robert Owen, *A New View of Society* (1857 edn), in Owen, *Life*, vol. 1, p. 295 (*infra*, vol. 1, p. 64); Owen, *Life*, vol. 1A (1858), pp. 59–60 (*infra*, vol. 1, p. 142); Owen, *Two Discourses* (1825), p. 33 (*infra*, vol. 2, pp. 34–5). For Owen's proposals on female communitarian employment in the 1840s, see for example *A Development of the Principles* (1841), pp. 46, 69 (*infra*, vol. 2, pp. 380, 398–9). Owenites would later attack the Chartists for failing to propose extending the vote to women. See *New Moral World*, vol. 10, no. 9 (28 August 1841), p. 65.

[c] For details see my *Citizens and Saints*, pp. 194–207.

[d] See for example Robert Owen, *The Book of the New Moral World*, pt 6 (1844), p. 61 (*infra*, vol. 3, p. 340), and generally my *Citizens and Saints*, pp. 247–60.

[e] *Northern Star*, no. 574 (21 October 1848), p. 1; no. 575 (28 October 1848), p. 1.

elections would be necessary. In one of his first statements along these lines, Owen proposed that the youngest individual whose service in the general council of a community was completed might be delegated to a council of ten communities; the second youngest, to the council of a hundred communities; and the eldest to the council of a thousand communities. The oldest members of this council could form another council representing a hundred thousand, a million, or more communities. By this means, further elections were disposed of, no matter how complex administration became. Some national basis would be required for this system in the first instance. Especially after Queenwood seemed lost, Owen became increasingly persuaded that the United States ought to be the 'Central Power' of the union of nations, and even designed a draft 'Provisional treaty of federative union' between Great Britain and America. But this was only intended as a means of commencing community-building. For ultimately, all national boundaries were to disappear inside of a communitarian federation.[a]

Owen's practical politics were also more down to earth. When he offered himself as a candidate for Parliament, his programme included such reforms as a graduated property tax equal to the national expenditure; abolishing all other taxes; free trade; national education and national employment for those who desired them; and liberty of speech, writing, and religious observance. He also promised self-government to British dependencies.[b] Gradually, in fact, Owen evolved a constitutionalist programme which proposed full liberty of conscience and 'the utmost individual freedom of action, compatible with the permanent good of Society'. Thus he sought to parry the charge, particularly pronounced after the mid-1840s, that his system threatened individual freedom even in principle.[c] Criticisms such as this gain in force retrospectively, of course, in light of the authoritarian character of many later forms of socialism. Though Owen abhorred violence, the perfectionist component in his thought, which sought to transcend 'politics' through 'harmony', nonetheless anticipated in several respects the later Marxist ideal of the withering away of the state. Its origins in Owen's thought are thus worth considering briefly. Owen's belief that politics might be superseded had two main sources. Firstly, he

[a] Robert Owen, *Robert Owen's Opening Speech* (1829), pp. 139–40; *Robert Owen's Journal*, vol. 3, no. 54 (8 November 1851), p. 14; no. 71 (6 March 1852), p. 149; *Spirit of the Age*, vol. 1, no. 11 (7 October 1848), p. 171.

[b] Robert Owen, *Robert Owen's Reply to the Question, 'What Would You Do If You Were Prime Minister?'* (?1832), pp. 3, 12 (*infra*, vol. 2, pp. 216, 223). Owen had also run for parliament twice in 1819–20. See F. Podmore, *Robert Owen* (2 vols, 1906), vol. 1, pp. 263–4, for details. In 1858, he proposed that India be governed by a hereditary prince with two legislative houses, with full rights in ten years (*Life*, vol. 1A, 1858, pp. xx–xxi).

[c] Robert Owen, *Robert Owen's Reply to the Question* (?1832), p. 12 (*infra*, vol. 2, p. 223); *Crisis*, vol. 3, no. 27 (1 March 1834), p. 219; *New Moral World*, vol. 10, no. 43 (23 April 1842), p. 337; *Preliminary Charter of the Rational System* (1843), (*infra*, vol. 2, pp. 416–18); Robert Owen, *The Revolution in the Mind and Practice of the Human Race* (1849), p. 60.

greatly respected the remarkably successful approach to social order maintained within the sect of Quakers, whose rigid egalitarianism and moral fervour frequently invoked the respect of even their enemies. He praised them as the most charitable of the Christian denominations.[a] He admired their 'brotherly love – equality – simplicity in language, dress, and all personal externals – kindness and forbearance to all – desire for peace – and patience, under suffering, without resistance', and their refusal to lie.[b] In Quaker meetings, no voting occurred, but a common consensus was sought instead, with greater weight being given to the opinions of 'elders'. Violence and physical coercion were categorically rejected as a means of enforcing order. (By the early 1840s, Owen increasingly extended the idea of non-violence to the animal world as well.)[c] This was thus the main source for Owen's schemes to 'adjust differences' in any future community by recourse to the decisions of elders.[d] Moreover, Owen thought the Quakers' 'plain speaking' came closest to the 'just, open, sincere, benevolent conduct' without which no real virtue or happiness could exist.[e] Thus, said Owen, 'in its original principles', Quakerism was nearer to the Rational System than any religious party', and had 'excluded evil' the longest time.[f] Indeed, *The New Religion* (1830) might be misread as an injunction to join 'the Quaker's broad way'.[g] But William Allen was also a Quaker, and Owen was well aware that many Friends were increasingly prone to self-righteousness, intolerance, pride and selfishness.[h]

A less important but still influential model of social harmony, secondly, was derived from the similar respect accorded to age among those North American Indian tribes known to Owen. This he linked in turn to several personal characteristics (sincerity, for example, which was also a noted Quaker virtue) Owen thought the Indians possessed where their lives had not yet been eroded by civilization. Moreover, Owen believed that Indian tribes had distributed food according to need, first to children, then women, then men, in effect treating wealth as public property.[i] In both cases, different environments seemed to promote different types of personality, and by comparison with the Indians, the 'mere commercial character' and the debased victim of industry were inferior forms of humanity.

---

[a] Robert Owen, *Address Delivered by Robert Owen, at a Public Meeting, Held at the Franklin Institute* (Philadelphia, 1827), p. 9.

[b] Robert Owen, *The New Existence of Man Upon the Earth* (1854), pt 5, p. 13.

[c] E.g., *A Development of the Principles* (1841), p. 40 (*infra*, vol. 2, p. 376).

[d] See, for example, Robert Owen, *The Book of the New Moral World*, pt 6 (1844), pp. 78–82 (*infra*, vol. 3, pp. 352–5).

[e] Robert Owen, *A New View of Society* (1857 edn), in *Life*, vol. 1, p. 288 (*infra*, vol. 1, p. 56).

[f] *New Moral World*, vol. 10, no. 36 (5 March 1842), p. 281; Robert Owen, *Lectures on an Entire New State of Society* (1830), pp. 72–3.

[g] See *infra*, vol. 2, p. 167.

[h] See also *New Moral World*, vol. 10, no. 36 (5 March 1842), p. 201.

[i] *The Sun*, no. 9823 (16 February 1824), p. 1; Robert Owen, *The Book of the New Moral World*, pt 5 (1844), p. 25 (*infra*, vol. 3, p. 259).

Largely formed by the late 1830s, Owen's mature system of thought included a conception of economic and social justice, a plea for social and sexual equality, and a plan for eliminating war, political conflict, and the evils of industrialism and urban life through community life. By and large, however, contemporaries ignored the grand scheme for social reform which Owen proposed, and took up his ideas piecemeal. After his death, Owen's reputation remained fragmented, and today, too, there are many sides to Owen: the 'prince of the cotton spinners' and business genius; the humanitarian social and industrial reformer; the religious sceptic; the co-operator; the socialist; even the spiritualist. His general achievement was usually seen by nineteenth-century contemporaries as having been 'almost the founder of that school of philanthropists to whom the working men of the present day are so uniquely indebted', and as a man whose suitability to his age, in this sense, was 'entire'.[a] No socialist himself, the radical republican Charles Bradlaugh commented that 'society now adopts the view which Robert Owen was the first to popularise, although not the first to enunciate – that man is better or worse according to the conditions surrounding the parents previous to the birth of the child, and those which surround the infant during its childhood, and accompany the boy or girl during youth'.[b] Christian Socialism owed him a considerable debt. The co-operative movement, reborn at Rochdale in 1844, grew strongly after mid-century, even if it never came close to challenging the capitalist system, and reached out to influence French, German and other movements. Industrial co-operation was also incorporated into the ideals of the most important liberal social theorist of this period, John Stuart Mill.[c] The Christian social reformer John Ruskin was certainly much indebted to Owen, and his socialist-humanist approach to political economy was in turn picked up by the chief theorist of the new liberalism of the 1880s, John Hobson, and thence passed on to the founders of the Labour Party. Elements of Owen's ideas also remained in the thought of Marx and Engels even after they had rejected his plea for a peaceful transition to socialism by communitarian example, though his willingness to consider marriage, for example, as a considerable cause of unhappiness in society was largely ignored in their tendency to reduce oppression to class exploitation. William Morris read and 'praised immensely' Owen in 1883.[d] Owen also influenced the neo-Malthusian socialism of A. R. Wallace, and probably helped persuade the latter that there were social as well as natural ways of limiting population.[e] The Fabians, many of whom

[a] *Glasgow Sentinel*, no. 425 (27 November 1858), p. 2; *Daily News*, no. 3905 (19 November 1858), p. 5.

[b] Charles Bradlaugh, *Five Dead Men I Knew When Living* (n.d.), p. 4.

[c] See my 'Justice, Independence and Industrial Democracy: the Development of John Stuart Mill's Views on Socialism', *Journal of Politics*, vol. 49 (1987), pp. 122–147.

[d] Jack Lindsay, *The Life of William Morris* (New York: Taplinger, 1979), p. 256.

[e] Greta Jones, *Social Darwinism and English Thought. The Interaction between Biological and Social Theory* (Harvester Press, 1980), p. 28.

wrote on Owen, acknowledged a debt to his plea for social engineering. And the secularist movement maintained Owen's dictum that 'religions have been and to this day are the strongest causes of repulsive feelings between individuals and nations.'[a]

Today, while his communitarian socialism finds few adherents, Owen's emphases upon feminism and upon 'green' issues, such as the balancing of parks and gardens within urban areas and the benefits of clean air,[b] still strike us as distinctly contemporary. His demands for the humane treatment of the labour force, for release from the shackles of a degrading division of labour, and for a kind education for all children, too, have never grown irrelevant. In these areas, we still recognise that Owen, despite his flaws, was a pioneer whose life was dedicated to serving the cause of the poor. Whether it is the philosopher of New Lanark or the prophet of the new moral world we acclaim as having done this most successfully, this much all who knew him acknowledged.

3. *Additional Reading*

The best biography remains Frank Podmore, *Robert Owen: A Biography* (2 vols, Hutchinson, 1906). Still worth consulting are Lloyd Jones, *The Life, Times, and Labours of Robert Owen* (2 vols, The Labour Association, 1889–90), and G. D. H. Cole, *Robert Owen* (3rd edn, Frank Cass, 1965). The best general account of Owenism is J. F. C. Harrison, *Robert Owen and the Owenites in Britain and America* (Routledge and Kegan Paul, 1969), which also includes an extensive bibliography of primary sources. Specialised studies of Owenite economic thought are Gregory Claeys, *Machinery, Money and the Millennium: From Moral Economy to Socialism, 1815 – 1860* (Princeton: Princeton University Press, 1987), and Noel Thompson, *The People's Science. The Popular Political Economy of Exploitation and Crisis, 1816–34* (Cambridge: Cambridge University Press, 1984). On Owenism and politics, see Gregory Claeys, *Citizens and Saints. Politics and Anti-Politics in Early British Socialism* (Cambridge: Cambridge University Press, 1989). On the feminist component, see Barbara Taylor, *Eve and the New Jerusalem. Socialism and Feminism in the Nineteenth Century* (Virago Books, 1983), and Carol Kolmerten, *Women in Utopia. The Ideology of Gender in the American Owenite Communities* (Bloomington: Indiana University Press, 1990). Owenism's relation to secularism and freethought are treated in two books by Edward Royle, *Victorian Infidels. The Origins of the British Secularist Movement 1791–1866* (Manchester: Manchester University Press, 1974), and *Radicals, Secularists and Republicans. Popular Freethought in*

---

[a] Robert Owen, *Life*, vol. 1 (1857), p. 101 (*infra*, vol. 4, p. 155).

[b] E.g., Robert Owen, *The Book of the New Moral World*, pt 3 (1842), p. 15 (*infra*, vol. 2, pp. 141–2).

Britain, 1866–1915 (Manchester: Manchester University Press, 1980). The millenarian aspects of the subject are studied in J.F.C. Harrison, *The Second Coming: Popular Millenarianism 1780–1850* (Routledge and Kegan Paul, 1979), and W. H. Oliver, *Prophets and Millennialists: The Uses of Biblical Prophecy in England from the 1790s to the 1840s* (Oxford: Oxford University Press, 1978). For background on debates about the poor law, philanthropy and factory reform, see especially David Owen, *English Philanthropy 1660–1960* (Cambridge, MA.: Harvard University Press, 1964), pp. 91–210, and J. R. Poynter, *Society and Pauperism. English Ideas on Poor Relief, 1795–1834* (Routledge and Kegan Paul, 1969). On the British Owenite communities, see R. G. Garnett, *Co-operation and the Owenite Socialist Communities in Britain 1825–45* (Manchester: Manchester University Press, 1972). On New Harmony and American Owenism, see especially A. E. Bestor, *Backwoods Utopias: The Sectarian and Owenite Phases of Communitarian Socialism in America: 1663–1829* (Philadelphia: University of Pennsylvania Press, 1950). Older works include George Lockwood, *The New Harmony Movement* (Marion: Chronicle Co., 1920). A more recent account is Ann Taylor, *Visions of Harmony. A Study in Nineteenth Century Millenarianism* (Oxford: Oxford University Press, 1987). Collected essays on aspects of Owen's life and career are John Butt, ed., *Robert Owen. Prince of the Cotton-Spinners* (Newton Abbot: David and Charles, 1971), Sidney Pollard and John Salt, eds, *Robert Owen. Prophet of the Poor* (Macmillan, 1971), and Chushichi Tsuzuki, ed., *Robert Owen and the World of Co-operation* (Tokyo: Tokyo University Press, 1992). The best collection of Owen's own manuscripts and letters is held at the Co-operative Union Library, Manchester. An excellent collection of published sources by Owen and Owenite writers is in the Goldsmiths' Library, University of London. Bibliographies of Owen's writings include *A Bibliography of Robert Owen, the Socialist* (Aberystwyth, 1914; 2nd edn, 1925); Shigeru Goto's more definitive, *Robert Owen, 1771–1858: A New Bibliographical Study* (2 vols, Osaka, 1932–4), and J. F. C. Harrison, *Robert Owen and the Owenites* (1969), pp. 261–83, which is especially good on the Owenite movement.

4. *Note on the Selection of Texts*

Any incomplete selection of texts must be arbitrary to some degree. I have excluded from this collection tracts relating to Owen's major theological controversies, especially his debate with Alexander Campbell in 1829 (printed as *Robert Owen's Opening Speech, and His Reply to the Rev. Alexander Campbell*, Cincinnati, 1829); many shorter works from the 1830s and 1840s whose themes seemed adequately represented in the texts reprinted; and most of Owen's writings in the 1850s. Major works not reprinted here also include *The Revolution in the Mind and Practice of the Human Race* (1849), and *The New*

Existence of Man upon the Earth (1854–5). Previous collections of Owen's writings include *A New View of Society, & Other Writings*, ed. G. D. H. Cole (Dent, 1927; repr. 1963); *A New View of Society; and, Report to the County of Lanark*, ed. V. A. C. Gatrell (Harmondsworth: Penguin Books, 1970); *A New View of Society and Other Writings*, ed. G. Claeys (Harmondsworth: Penguin Books, 1991).

Wherever possible, the last editions published in Owen's lifetime have been reproduced here. Important variations between editions have been annotated, but not minor or stylistic alterations. Spelling and capitalization have been altered slightly in some texts. The place of publication of all works cited is London unless otherwise noted.

London, 1993 GREGORY CLAEYS

BIBLIOGRAPHY OF THE WRITINGS OF ROBERT OWEN[a]

Additional Statements Respecting Mr Owen's Plan for the Support of the Unemployed Working Classes by Their Own Labour (1819)

An *Address by Robert Owen on His System Delivered at the City of London Tavern, April 12th, 1830* (1830)

Address Dated September 19th, 1817, on 'Measures for the Immediate Relief of the Poor' (1817) (repr. 1854, 1858, 1927, 1977, 1991)

Address Delivered at the City of London Tavern, on Thursday, August 14th (1817) (repr. 1818, 1854, 1927, 1977, 1991)

Address Delivered at the City of London Tavern, on Thursday, August 21st (1817) (repr. 1818, 1854, 1858, 1927, 1977, 1991)

Address Delivered at the Meeting in St. Martin's Hall (1855)

Address Delivered by Robert Owen, of New-Lanark, Wednesday, the 27th of April (New Harmony, 1825) (repr. 1830)

Address Delivered by Robert Owen, at a Public Meeting at the Franklin Institute (Philadelphia, 1827)

An *Address Delivered to the Inhabitants of New Lanark* (1816) (French transl., Paris, 1819). 2nd edn, 1816; 3rd edn, 1817; 4th edn, 1819; another edn, 1841. Repr. 1854, 1857, 1927, 1991

Address of Mr. Owen to the Agriculturalists, Mechanics and Manufacturers, Both Masters and Operatives, of Great Britain and Ireland (Bury, 1827)

Address of Robert Owen, Delivered at the Great Public Meeting, Held at the National Equitable Labour Exchange … on 1st May, 1833 (1833) (repr. 1969)

Address of Robert Owen to the Profession of Arms, from the Commander in Chief to the Private (1857)

The Address of the Spirit of the Late Sir Robert Peel (1835)

Address on Leaving the United States for Europe, June 1st, 1845 (New York, 1845)

Address on Spiritual Manifestations (1855)

[a] Works published or reprinted solely in periodicals are not included here.

Address on the Hopes and Destinies of the Human Species (1836)

Address to All Classes in the State From the Governors, Directors and Committee of the Association [for Removing the Causes of Ignorance and Poverty by Education and Employment] (1832)

Address to Her Royal Highness the Princess Victoria and to Her Majesty the Queen of Great Britain and Ireland (1837)

An *Address to the Agriculturalists, Mechanics, and Manufacturers of Great Britain and Ireland, Both Masters and Operatives* (Bury, 1827)

Address to the Electors of Great Britain and Ireland But Especially to the Electors of the Metropolis of the British Empire and of the World (1857)

An *Address to the Master Manufacturers of Great Britain On the Present Existing Evils in the Manufacturing System* (Bolton, 1819) (repr. 1927)

Address to the Ministers of All Religions (Philadelphia, 1845)

Address to the National Association for the Promotion of Social Science, On Its Second Annual Meeting (1858)

Address to the Operative Manufacturers and Agricultural Labourers in Great Britain and Ireland (1830)

Address to the Socialists, Being the Substance of Two Lectures Delivered in London, Previous to the Congress in May, 1843 (1843)

An *Address to the Socialists on the Present Position of the Rational System of Society* (1841)

Address to the Tories, Whigs, Radicals ... to All Producers of Wealth, and Non-producers in Great Britain and Ireland (1841)

An *Address to the Working Classes* (1819) (repr. 1858, 1927, 1977, 1991)

The Addresses of Robert Owen (1830)

Addresses to the Delegates of the Human Race at the World's Fair (1851)

Adresse à l'Assemblé Nationale de France (Paris, 1848)

Adresse aux Souverains à Aix-la-Chapelle et aux Gouvernements Européens (Paris, 1819)

The Advantages and Disadvantages of Religion (Glasgow, 1830)

'An Attempt to Explain the Cause of the Commercial and Other Difficulties Which Are Now Experienced in the Civilized Parts of the World' in: Richard N. Bacon, *A Report of the Holkham Sheep Shearing* (Norwich, 1821), pp. 118–24

The Book of the New Moral World (parts 1–7, 1836–44) (new edns, 1845, 1849) (abridged French edn, Paris, 1848, repr. 1849, 1852) (German transl., 1840) (Italian transl., 1882)

Calculations Shewing the Facility with Which the Paupers and Unemployed May be

Enabled to Support Themselves Within the Most Desireable Circumstances by Co-operation (1851)

The Catechism of the New Moral World (1835) (2nd edn, Leeds, 1838; new edn, Manchester, 1840)

Catechism of the Rational Society and Proclamation (?1850)

The Coming Millennium (1855)

Debate on the Evidence of Christianity . . . Between Robert Owen . . . and Alexander Campbell (2 vols, Bethany, Va., 1829) (2nd edn, Cincinnati, 1829) (new edn, 1839) (repr. n.d., 1852, 1858, 1870, 1912, 1929)

A Development of the Origins and Effects of Moral Evil (Manchester, 1838)

A Development of the Principles and Plans on Which to Establish Self-Supporting Home Colonies (1841) (2nd edn, 1841)

Dialogue entre La France, Le Monde, et Robert Owen (Paris, 1848)

Dialogue entre les Membres de la Commission Exécutive, les Ambassadeurs d'Angleterre, de Russie, d'Autriche, de Prusse, de Hollande, des Etats-Unis, et Robert Owen (Paris, 1848)

A Dialogue, in Three Parts, Between the Founder of the 'Association of All Classes of All Nations' and a Stranger Desirous of Being Accurately Informed Respecting Its Origin and Objects (Manchester, 1838)

Dialogue sur le Système Social … Entre la France, le Monde, et Robert Owen (Paris, 1848)

A Discourse on a New System of Society (1825)

The Evidences of Christianity; A Debate between Robert Owen, of New Lanark, Scotland, and Alexander Campbell (Cincinnati, 1829)

An Explanation of the Cause of Distress Which Pervades the Civilized Parts of the World, and of the Means Whereby it may be Removed (1823)

Exposition of Mr Owen's Views on the Marriage Question (Coventry, 1838)

A Farewell Address Delivered at the Scientific Institution … on 9th June, 1850 (1850)

First Discourse on a New System of Society (Washington D.C., 1825) (repr. 1970)

A Full Account of the Farewell Festival Given to Robert Owen (1844)

A Further Development of the Plan Contained in the Report to the Committee of the Association for the Relief of the Manufacturing Poor (1817) (repr. 1818, 1823, 1854, 1858, 1927, 1977, 1991)

The Future of the Human Race (1853)

Great Preliminary Meeting on the First Day of the Year 1855 (1855)

Important Public Meeting to Advocate an Entire Change in Forming the Character of Man (1858)

The Inauguration of the Millenium (1855)

Institution of the Intelligent and Well-Disposed of the Industrious Classes (c. 1833)

A Lecture Delivered in the Mechanics' Institute, London (1841)

Lectures on an Entire New State of Society (1830) (new edn, 1841)

Lectures I.–VI., Delivered by Robert Owen, at the Institution of New Lanark, Upon the 13th Chapter of the 1st Epistle to the Corinthians (1833–4)

Lectures on the Marriages of the Priesthood of the Old Immoral World (Leeds, 1835) (2nd edn, Leeds, 1838; 3rd edn, Leeds, 1839; 4th edn, 1840) (French transl., Paris, 1841)

Lectures on the Rational System of Society (1841)

A Letter Addressed to the Potentates of the Earth (1857)

Letter from Mr Owen. To the President and Members of the New York State Convention (Washington D.C., 1846)

Letter Published in the London Newspapers of August 19th, 1817 (1817) (repr. 1818, 1854, 1858, 1927, 1977, 1991)

A Letter to the Archbishop of Canterbury on the Union of Churches and Schools (1818) (repr. 1857)

Letter to the Earl of Lauderdale (c. 1824)

A Letter to the Earl of Liverpool on the Employment of Children in Manufactories (1818) (repr. 1858, 1991)

A Letter to the Moderator of the General Assembly Upon the Late Attack of the Christian Instructor upon Mr Owen (1823)

Letter to the President and Members of the New York State Convention (1846)

A Letter to the Socialists (1841)

Letters on Education (1851)

Letters on Government As It Is and As It Ought To Be (? 1851)

Letters to the Human Race on the Coming Universal Revolution (1850)

Life and Death Society (1857)

The Life of Robert Owen, Written by Himself (2 vols, 1857–8) (repr. Philadelphia, 1866, 1920, 1967, 1971)

Manifesto of Robert Owen (1840)

Manifesto of Robert Owen ... Addressed to All Governments and People Who Desire to Become Civilized (Washington D.C., 1844)

Manifesto of Robert Owen to the Civilized World (New York, 1847)

Memorial of Robert Owen of New Lanark to the Governments of Europe and America (Frankfort upon Main, 1818)

Memorial of Robert Owen to the Mexican Republic (Philadelphia, 1828)

Memorial to the Right Honourable the Lords of her Majesty's Treasury (1858)

The Millenium in Practice (1855)

Mr Owen's Report to the Committee of the Association for the Relief of the Manufacturing and Labouring Poor (1817)

Mr Owen's Sunday Lectures (c. 1830)

Mr Owen's System, as Developed in a Public Lecture (1830)

The New Existence of Man Upon the Earth (1854–55)

New Lanark (1849)

The New Religion (1830)

New State of Society (1817)

A New View of Society; or, Essays on the Principle of the Formation of the Human Character (1813–14) (2nd edn, 1816; 3rd edn, 1817; 4th edn, 1818–19; other edns, New York, 1825; Cincinnati, 1825; Edinburgh, 1826, 1834; Manchester, 1840. Repr. 1857, 1927, 1969, 1991)

New View of Society. Tracts Relative to this Subject (1818)

Notice to All. To New-Form Man and New-Form Society (1857)

Observations on the Cotton Trade of Great Britain (Glasgow, 1803)

Observations on the Cotton Trade, With a View to the Intended Application of the Duty on the Importation of Cotton Wool (1815) (repr. 1854, 1858)

Observations on the Effect of the Manufacturing System (1815) (2nd edn, 1817; 3rd edn, 1818; 4th edn, 1819; another edn, 1841. Repr. 1858, 1927, 1991)

On the Employment of Children in Manufactories (1818)

Oration Containing a Declaration of Mental Independence (New Harmony, 1826)

Outline of the Rational System of Society (1830) (New edns, ? 1836, 1838; Birmingham, 1839; New York, 1839; 1840, 1841, 1842, 1851, 1872) (Welsh transl., 1841) (French transl., Paris, 1837 and 1848)

Papers Sent to the National Association for the Promotion of Social Science (1857)

Peace on Earth – Good Will towards Men: Development of the Plan for the Relief of the Poor, and the Emancipation of Mankind (1817) (repr. 1818, 1854, 1858, 1991)

Permanent Relief for the Agricultural and Manufacturing Labourers (? 1822. Repr. Dublin, 1823)

Preliminary Charter of the Rational System (1843)

The Problem of the Age Solved (New York, 1847)

Proclamation au Peuple francais, aux Militaires et aux Civils de toutes les Classes, de tous les Partis, de toutes les Religions (Paris, 1848)

A Proclamation by Robert Owen (1848)

Proclamation by Robert Owen (1856)

Proclamation (of the World's Convention or Congress of Delegates) (1855)

Reasons for Each Law of the Constitution to Be Introduced into the State of New York (Washington D.C., 1846)

Report of the Meetings of the Congress of the Advanced Minds of the World (1857)

Report of the Proceedings at the Several Public Meetings Held in Dublin (Dublin, 1823) (repr. 1854)

Report to the Committee of the Association for the Relief of the Manufacturing and Labouring Poor (1817) (repr. 1818, 1854, 1857)

Report to the County of Lanark of a Plan for Relieving Public Distress and Removing Discontent (Glasgow, 1821) (another edn, 1832. Repr. 1858, 1927, 1963, 1970, 1991)

The Revolution in the Mind and Practice of the Human Race (1849) (new edn, 1850)

Robert Owen and the Exhibition of 1851 (1851)

Robert Owen on Marriage, Religion, and Private Property (1839)

Robert Owen's Address Delivered at the Meeting in St Martin's Hall (1855)

Robert Owen's Address to the Human Race on his Eighty-Fourth Birthday (1854)

Robert Owen's Address to the Ministers of All Religions (Philadelphia, 1845)

Robert Owen's Congress of Advanced Minds (1857)

Robert Owen's Great Preliminary Meeting on the First Day of the Year, 1855 (1855)

Robert Owen's Journal (1850)

Robert Owen's Letter to the Senate of the 28th Congress (Washington D.C., 1845)

Robert Owen's Millennial Gazette (1856)

Robert Owen's Opening Speech, and His Reply to the Rev. Alexander Campbell (Cincinnati, 1829)

Robert Owen's Rational Quarterly Review (1853)

Robert Owen's Reply to the Question, 'What Would You Do, If You Were the Prime Minister of England?' (Stockport, c. 1832) (2nd edn, 1832)

Robert Owen's Tracts for the World's Fair (1851)

Robert Owen's Weekly Letters to the Human Race (1850)

The Royal Consort's Schools For All Children (1857)

Second Lecture on the New Religion (1830) (repr. 1991)

The Signs of the Times; or, the Approach of the Millenium (1841) (2nd edn, 1841)

Six Lectures on Charity (? 1834) (repr. ?1834, ? 1838, ? 1840)

Six Lectures Delivered in Manchester (Manchester, 1837)

A Sketch of Some of the Errors and Evils Arising From the Past and Present State of Society (1817) (repr. 1818, 1823, 1854, 1858, 1927, 1977, 1991)

'Socialism', *Cyclopedia of Religious Denominations* (c. 1853)

Socialism Misrepresented, and Truly Represented (1848)

Socialism, or the Rational System of Society (1840)

Société fraternelle centrale. *7e et 8e Discours du Citoyen Cabet sur les Elections. Discours de Robert Owen* (Paris, 1848)

Speech by Robert Owen at New Harmony, April 27th, 1825 (n.d.)

Speeches Delivered by Robert Owen at the Breakfast Given in Anticipation of His Departure for America (1844)

A Statement Regarding the New Lanark Establishment (Edinburgh, 1812) (repr. 1973)

Statements, Showing the Power That Ireland Possesses to Create Wealth (1823)

Statements Submitted to the Most Noble Marquis of Normandy, Secretary of State for the Home Department, Relative to the Principles and Objects of the Universal Community Society of Rational Religionists (n.d.)

Summary of Mr Owen's Plan, for the Permanent Relief of the Working Classes (1822)

A Supplement to the Revolution in the Mind and Practice of the Human Race (1849)

Syllabus of Four Morning and Four Evening Courses of Lectures (1841)

Synopsis of a Course of Four Lectures (Birmingham, 1838)

System, as Developed in a Public Lecture … to Take into Consideration the Best Mode of Rationally Educating, Employing, and Uniting the People (1832)

Temple of Free Enquiry. A Report of the Proceedings Consequent on Laying the Foundation Stone of the Manchester Hall of Science (Leeds, 1839)

Temple of Free Enquiry . . . With an Address by Robert Owen (1839)

Ten Lectures on the Evils of Indissoluble Marriage (Leeds, c. 1840)

To Her Majesty, Victoria … and to her Responsible Advisors (1849)

To Lords John Russell and Stanley, Sir Robert Peel, and Messrs. Cobden, and Feargus O'Connor (1849)

To the Electors of Great Britain and Ireland (c. 1841)

To the Electors of Oldham (1852)

To the Electors of the Borough of Marylebone (1846)

To the Electors of the Borough of Marylebone (1847)

To the Inhabitants of Manchester and Salford (? 1852)

To the President of the United States, and to His Cabinet (Washington D.C., 1846)

To the Senate and House of Representatives of the Congress of the United States (1852)

To the Working Classes (1835)

Tract No. 1. To the Inhabitants of Manchester and Salford (n.d.)

Tracts for the World's Fair. No's 1–6 (1851)

Tracts on the Coming Millenium (1855)

The Twelve Fundamental Laws of Human Nature (n.d.)

Two Discourses on a New System of Society (Louisville, 1825) (repr. 1839, 1970)

Two Memorials on Behalf of the Working Classes (Lanark, 1818) (repr. 1854, 1858, 1991)

The Universal Permanent Government, Constitution, and Code of Laws (c. 1848)

The World's Convention of Delegates from the Human Race (1855)

(and John Brindley), *What is Socialism?* (1841)

(and Alexander Campbell), *Debate on the Evidences of Christianity* (2 vols, Bethany, 1829)

(and Rev. William Legg), *Report of the Discussion between Robert Owen, and the Rev. William Legg* (Birmingham, 1839)

(and Rev. J. H. Roebuck), *Public Discussion between Robert Owen ... and the Rev. J. H. Roebuck* (1837)

OBSERVATIONS ON THE COTTON TRADE, OF GREAT BRITAIN[a] AND ON THE LATE DUTIES ON THE IMPORTATION OF COTTON WOOL. 1803[b]

In the year 1765, cotton, as an article of commerce, was scarcely known in this country.

A few years afterwards, Mr Arkwright[c] obtained his patent for working cotton by machinery.

In 1782 the whole produce of the cotton manufacture did not exceed two millions sterling.

In 1801 the import of cotton wool into Britain was forty-two millions of pounds; and the estimated value of the cotton manufacture, fifteen millions sterling; such was the rapid increase of this trade to the end of the year 1801.

From authentic documents it appears, that the import of this article in 1802 has not been less than fifty-four millions of pounds, and the increase in the value of the manufacture has been corresponding.

The following particulars of the trade, it is presumed, will be found accurate:

The raw material, when delivered on board the merchant ships, now costs about four millions sterling.

Upwards of 30,000 tons of shipping, and 2,000 seamen, are employed in

---

[a] A Report presented at a meeting of the Committee of Management of the Board of the Cotton Trade in Glasgow, 2 February 1803. Present: Dugald Bannatine, Chairman (1755–1842), merchant, 107 Nelson Street, also postmaster from 1806; Kirkman Finlay, Deputy Chairman (1772–1842), merchant, MP for Glasgow 1812–18; Francis Garden (d. c. 1814), merchant; Archibald Campbell (1744–1835), manufacturer and JP; Robert Owen, John M'Ilwham, manufacturer at 79 Glassford Street of the firm of James and John Meikleham; Matthew Preston; Archibald Lawson (d. c. 1848), manufacturer of 55 St Andrew's Square; John Lindsay (d. c. 1820) of John Lindsay & Co, cotton-yarn, worsted and thread manufacturers of 180 Salt Market; Andrew Reid, manufacturer of 36 St Andrew's Square.

'Mr Owen having presented a Report, containing "Observations on the Cotton Trade of Great Britain, and on the late Duties on the Importation of Cotton Wool", the same is read, approved of, ordered to be printed and circulated for the trade at large.' (Signed) Dugald Bannatine, Chairman.

[b] Reprinted in *The New Harmony Gazette*, vol. 3, no. 31 (28 May 1828), pp. 244–5, and *The New Existence of Man Upon the Earth* (1854), pt 1, pp. i–iv. The title given in the 1857 reprint (*Life*, vol. 1A, pp. 3–9), is 'Observations on the Cotton Trade, with a View to the Intended Application to Parliament for a Repeal of the Duty on the Importation of Cotton Wool'.

[c] Sir Richard Arkwright (1732–92): inventor of textile machinery.

bringing the cotton wool to this country, and in exporting the goods manufactured from it.

To work the wool into thread, requires a capital in building and machinery, to the amount of *nine millions two hundred and twenty-five thousand pounds*; and those buildings and machinery are chiefly composed of bricks, slates, glass, timber, lead, iron, copper, tin and leather; from most of which, in one shape or other, a considerable duty is collected for the support of the State.

This trade gives employment or support to upwards of 800,000 individuals, and the annual return of the manufacture is nearly as follows:

Cost of cotton in the countries where it grows, insurance, freight, other shipping charges and merchants' profit	£ 4,725,000
The interest at five per cent upon the capital of £9,225,000 sunk in building and machinery, with ten per cent for wear and tear of do.	1,383,750
Wages of spinning, value of materials consumed in the process of spinning the cotton into thread, and spinners' profit	5,100,000
Value of materials consumed in subsequent manufactures, manufacturing wages, interest of capital and profit	9,000,000
	£20,208,750

Of which sum, at least thirteen millions sterling, are paid in wages to the natives of Great Britain.

The above calculations, both with respect to the money and the people employed, are considerably underrated, that no room might be left for any species of exaggeration; and it should be noticed that a great proportion of the materials employed, such as ashes, soap, candles, leather, oil, dye stuffs, etc, etc, pay very considerable sums in duties to government.

But the importance of this manufacture will be more justly appreciated, when we consider, that the thirteen millions paid for manual labour in this trade are annually expended in purchasing the produce of land, and also in buying other articles of necessity, which, by excise duties or other taxes, contribute in a very great degree to put the finances of Great Britain in a situation infinitely superior to those of any other nation in Europe.

From this cause, also, more than from any other, has proceeded the late, otherwise astonishing, increase in the value of landed property, and in the revenues of this country; and should this branch of our manufacture be injured, or lost, it may confidently be predicted that both land and revenue would suffer by its decline, in the same proportion that they have benefited by its success.

It therefore becomes the duty of those immediately interested in the cotton business, as well as of every well-wisher to the landed property, revenues, and general prosperity of the Empire, to enquire what influence the act of Parliament passed last session, laying certain duties upon the importation of cotton wool into Great Britain, may have upon this most important source of our wealth, industry, and prosperity.

Those duties may annually amount to between £250,000 and £300,000 sterling, and divided upon such an extensive trade, may be supposed to be of small moment, and not likely to be of much injury to it. The case, however, is far otherwise. The countries where the cotton grows which is chiefly consumed by the British manufacturer, do not form any part of the British Empire; other nations of Europe, therefore, can import this material as cheap as Britain, (although no duties were to be levied in our own ports,) and some of them, the Dutch, Portuguese, and French, for instance, at a less prime cost. The colonies belonging to the two first of these powers produce the most useful qualities of cotton known in this island, and we have to procure them through the mother countries at an additional expense of from ten to fifteen per cent.

Independent of the universally acknowledged impolicy of imposing a duty upon the importation of a raw material, which is afterwards to go through a multiplied and highly valuable manufacture, and without considering the essential injury which this country will sustain by being prevented from becoming the Emporium in Europe of cotton wool, can it be supposed that, under the circumstances before mentioned, a commercial nation, so well informed of her interest as Great Britain is, should impose a duty on a raw material upon which her prosperity now so greatly depends, and which operates as a bounty to the same amount to the foreign manufacturer, who is afterwards to meet in competition with the British merchant, for the sale of goods manufactured from this material?

On many qualities of this raw material the duty amounts to from ten to twenty per cent on the first cost of cotton.

To prove that this duty is not of small consideration to the trade, it is only necessary to mention that some houses, in an early stage of the manufacture, pay each, in part of it, upwards of £6000 per annum. Is this to be considered but a trifling inducement to a foreign manufacturer, to establish works of an equal extent in situations where the raw material can be imported free of duty? And with such encouragement held out to strangers, will acts of Parliament prevent our artisans from being enticed abroad, and our machinery from being smuggled out of the Kingdom?

But there is another circumstance relative to the cotton trade which calls for the most serious consideration of the legislature of this country, which is, that duties may be levied and restrictions laid upon it without the evil effects of these being immediately discovered: because, whatever encouragement may be given to the foreign manufacturer by restrictions and duties imposed upon the trade in this country, it will require time for him to erect his buildings, construct his machinery, and initiate his work people in the operative parts of the manufacture; but when these are completed, and the produce of them brought to market, the impolicy of these duties and restrictions will be obvious when too late; and then neither the repeal of them, nor even bounties given for encouraging the importation of cotton wool, will repair the loss which must be sustained, first by the British manufacturer, and afterwards, in a far more extensive and serious degree, by the British nation.

Should it be supposed that we have little fear from foreign competition, it may be justly asked what is to become of the produce of the cotton mills now established in France, Prussia, Saxony, and other places upon the Continent, where, it can easily be proved, this manufacture is now in a more perfect state, than it was in this country twenty years ago? It is also well known that some of these Powers are holding out the most flattering inducements to many of our fellow subjects, whom they imagine competent to the task, to go and put these establishments upon an equal footing with the best in Britain; and out of so great a number it cannot be doubted that many individuals will be tempted by these offers.

To show that we ought not to deceive ourselves by under-rating the idea of foreign competition, a letter upon this subject is subjoined, the contents of which well merit our attention; and the most satisfactory proof can be given of its authenticity.

And when our Gallic neighbours shall be capable of imitating, although in an inferior degree, this manufacture, and can produce a sufficiency of it to supply others as well as themselves, (which they soon will do if by duties here we encourage them to proceed,) it is not difficult to foresee, from the specimen which this country has lately experienced of French policy, that the rulers of that nation will form such treaties with the Powers now under their influence or control, as will effectually exclude the British manufacturer from those States.

Under these circumstances, ought not the Legislature of this country to encourage, rather than throw obstacles in the way of the British cotton manufacturer, who has so much at stake in property that cannot be employed for any other purpose, and who does not ask for a bounty to secure it, which if any trade deserves, surely it is his; but to be permitted (as it is the sound policy of Britain that he should be,) to carry on his business under equal advantages with the manufacturers of other countries?

But, to conclude, is it not extraordinary, or rather, is it not strikingly absurd, that the same nation should give a bounty for the encouragement of one manufacture, and at the same time lay an impost directly tending to discourage another, which, owing to many local circumstances, is of twenty times more consequence and value to that nation?

Extract of a letter from a Cotton Manufacturer in France, dated Paris, 25th of December, 1802, relative to a proposition for the introduction into France of Cotton Yarn spun in Great Britain.

Vos echantillons de Cotton ont eté remis au Cn. M—— member du Conseil de l'interieur, chargé specialement par le Ministre de faire un rapport sur ma petition; il l'a fait aussi avantageusement que possible, mais le Ministre qui a 20 petitions faites par des filateurs françois qui demandent la prohibition du Cotton Anglois, prétendant filer aussi bien qu'en Angleterre, et ayant produit aussi de très beau Cotton filé tant en Water Twist que Mule-Jenny, a rejetté ma petition, comme vous le verréz par la lettre ci-incluse de Mr M.

Ce Mr M—— m'a donné communication d'un Mémoire très bien fait par Mr P—— qui a etabli la pompe à feu de Chaillet, et qui est un grand mécanicien, qui a ètabli une filature de Cotton Water Twist.

Son mé-moire porte qu'il achête

Le Cotton fernambourg a	54s. la liv.
Qu'il file en 24, qui donne 2 oz. d'èchêt	7
Tous les frais de filature par livre	15
	76s. la liv.

Ce qui au change de 24 liv. fait 3s. 2d. la livre, poids de mare, ou 3s. la livre poids Anglois. Son mémoire dit que les Anglois ne peuvent pas filer au même prix, et attendû la prohibition

Your samples of yarn have been transmitted to Citizen M——, a member of the Council of the Minister for the home department, specially charged by the latter to make a report on my petition: he has done it in the most favourable manner; but the Minister having twenty memorials from as many French Cotton Spinners, petitioning for the prohibition of English yarn, and pretending to spin it equally well themselves, in support of which they produced very fine samples, both of Mule and Water Twist, he has rejected my petition, as you will observe from the enclosed letter.

Mr M—— has communicated to me a very able memorial, drawn up by Mr P——, the same person who established steam engines at Chaillot, a great mechanic, and himself proprietor of a cotton mill for Water Twist. This memorial states that he buys,

Pernambuco Cotton, at	54s. per lb.
Spun into No 24's with 2 oz. waste	7
All manufacturing expences	15
Together,	76s. per lb.

Which at an average exchange makes 3s. 2d. per lb. *poids de marc*, or 3s. per lb., English weight. He farther maintains that the English are not capable of spinning at such a low rate, and

du Cotton Anglois, (plus cher que le François,) qui est augmentée d'une forte prime, les negocians qui le vendent le font à 7 liv. Il obtient egalement 7 liv. de tout le Cotton qu'il peut filer, et fait l'enorme bénéfice de 3 liv. 4s. par livre de Cotton. Il demontre donc au ministre qu'un bénéfice si ènorme va continuer à faire établer beaucoup de filatûres, & que bientot la France ira en concurrence avec l'Angleterre dans l'art de la filatûre.

Un autre Mémoire présenté par un nommé A——, de Rouen, dit qu'il a perfectionné de petites mecaniques de filature continuë de 48 broches ou spindles seulement; qu'il y en a deja 400 en activité à Rouen et dans les environs, qui filent du cotton parfait; que ces petites mècaniques sont tournées par un homme & le fil furveillé pur un enfant; que le main d'oeuvre de cet homme à 15 sols par jour est bien meilleur marché que la mise-dehors de gros capitaux pour ètablir de grands etablissemens; que ces metiers ne prennent que 40 pouces quarrès de place, et s'établissent dans les chambres des ouvriers à qui il donne du cotton filé en mêche par une mécanique parfaite, et qui doivent lui rendre le même poids soit en fil soit en d'echêt; qu'il a des ordres considerables pour faire ces mécaniques, qui se propagent beaucoup; et qu'il est certain, vû le haut prix de l'escompte, que c'est le meilleur moyen de filer avec économie.

whilst the prohibition of English yarn, and the high premium for what is imported thereof, advances the price at which it is held to 7 livres, he gets the same 7 livres for yarn of his own spinning, and consequently makes the enormous profit of 3 liv. 4s. or about 2s. 8d. sterling per lb.; from which he infers that such alluring prospects will certainly cause the number of cotton mills in the Republic to increase considerably, and will soon enable French cotton spinners to compete with the English in that line.

Another memorial from Rouen, presented by Mr A——, states, that he has brought the small spinning machines to great perfection; that 400 of them, each with 48 spindles, are already going in and about Rouen. They are managed by a single workman, with a child to take care of the thread; the former at 15s. wages per day, or 7½d. sterling; which being so cheap is a great deal more profitable than the laying out considerable sums in extensive establishments. Besides, these spinning machines do not take up more room than 40 square inches, and are consequently well suited for and easily placed in the small apartments of workmen, to whom he gives the cotton already roved, this operation being also done by perfect machinery: he gets back in yarn and waste the weight he delivered. The memorialist farther says, that he has orders to a considerable amount for the making of these machines, which are daily increasing; and seems to be perfectly convinced of their being the best method of spinning cotton with economy, considering the high interest of money.

MR OWEN'S SPEECH AT A PUBLIC DINNER AT WHICH HE PRESIDED, GIVEN TO JOSEPH LANCASTER AT GLASGOW IN 1812[a]

[An imperfect Report of this Speech having appeared at the time in the newspapers, the following copy was published subsequently in the *New Harmony Gazette, Vol. 1, No. 18; Jan. 25th, 1826.*]

GENTLEMEN, –
In rising to address you on this occasion, I feel how very inadequate I am to the task which I wish to perform. The situation is altogether new to me. I am unaccustomed to public speaking; and nothing but a strong sense of duty, added to Mr Lancaster's particular request, should have induced me to accept the chair. I beg, therefore, to entreat the utmost stretch of your indulgence to what I shall attempt to say.

The principal object of this meeting is, to promote the cause of giving a good and proper education to those who would otherwise receive a bad and improper one. By education I now mean, the instruction, of all kinds, which we receive from our earliest infancy until our characters are generally fixed and established.

It is, however, necessary, that the *value* of this object should be considered, as well as the means of putting it into execution.

Much has been said and written in relation to education; but few persons are yet aware of its real importance in society; and certainly it has not acquired that prominent rank in our estimation which it deserves; for, when duly investigated, it will be found to be, *so far at least as depends on our operations*, the primary source of all the good and evil, misery and happiness, which exist in the world.

In proof of which, let us in imagination cast our eyes over the surface of the

[a] Reprinted in *The New Harmony Gazette*, vol. 1, no. 18 (25 January 1826), pp. 137–8, *The New Existence of Man Upon the Earth* (1854), pt 2, pp. i–iii, Owen, *Life*, vol. 1 (1857), pp. 249–54 and the *Rational Quarterly Review*, no. 1 (February 1853), pp. 40–4.

earth, and observe the different appearances, bodily and mental, which the inhabitants of the various regions present.

From whence do these general bodily and mental differences proceed? Are they inherent in our nature, or do they arise from the respective soils on which we are born?

Evidently from neither. They are wholly and solely the effects of that education which I have described. Man becomes a wild ferocious savage, a cannibal, or a highly civilised and benevolent being, according to the circumstances in which he may be placed from his birth.

It is an important point, then, for us to consider, whether we have any influence over these circumstances; if we can command any of them; and if we can, to what extent.

Let us, then, suppose, that, wishing, to try the experiment, we were to convey a number of infants, so soon as they were born, from this country into distant regions, deliver them to the natives of those countries, and allow them to remain among them. Can we suppose the result to be uncertain? No, they would become, one and all, like unto those natives, whatever their characters might be.

In the same manner, were an exchange of any given number of children to be made at their birth, between the Society of Friends, of which our worthy guest, Joseph Lancaster, is a member, and the loose fraternity which inhabit St Giles' in London, the children of the former would grow up like the members of the latter, prepared for every degree of crime, while those of the latter would become the same temperate good moral characters as the former.

If such were to be the consequences, (and surely no one will doubt them,) then we can materially command those circumstances which influence character; and if we proceed on this principle, keeping it steadily in view, much more may be yet accomplished for the improvement of society, than has been hitherto even attempted.

We now come to the immediate application of the principle.

There are in this city and suburbs many thousand children, who, from their situation, must generally be trained to vicious habits and to poverty, unless you, gentlemen, and our fellow-citizens, step forth to prevent the evil.

I do not hesitate to say, the remedy is now in your power. You possess the means, and I trust you will not withhold them.

The object is no less than to remove gross ignorance and extreme poverty, with their attendant misery, from your population; and to make it rational, well-disposed, and well-behaved.

You may ask – How have we the means now in our power? I reply, our friend here, Joseph Lancaster, has prepared them ready to our hands; his important improvements and discoveries in education, when properly applied, will enable us easily, cheaply, and effectually, to accomplish it.

And it is on this ground, and this alone, we can effect a speedy and radical improvement in society; for until we begin with that class in the community from whence servants and operatives are usually obtained, it is in vain to expect correct habits and sentiments in any other class. It is from close and minute observation particularly directed to the subject, I state, that the characters of children, in almost every family, are materially influenced through life by those with whom they early associate, and particularly by servants. These impress their sentiments and opinions upon the young mind at a time when an almost indelible impression is made, which is scarcely ever afterwards wholly effaced.

Here is the radical evil; and our first object should be to destroy it.

Give but a rational education, now easily to be accomplished, to all those in the lower walks of life, and the character of the whole community will rise many degrees; and, while none can suffer by this measure, all must be essentially benefited.

But this cannot be effected by individual exertion. It requires our collective force to accomplish it; and fortunately this will be found equal to its attainment.

Let us, then, take every means in our power to interest all those who have any weight or influence in the city, to enter heartily into the support and extension of the Lancastrian system of education for the poor, until every child of that class shall find a place in one of the schools.

There, in a manner peculiar to the system, they must learn the habits of obedience, order, regularity, industry, and constant attention, which are to them of more importance then merely learning to read, write, and account, although we all know and feel the advantages which these have given to each of us.

By attaining this object we shall secure the well-being of the rising generation, and we shall also secure much more.

The schools which will contain the younger children in the day time, will likewise serve for evening and Sunday schools; at which times those who may be past the proper age for the first, and strangers who may come amongst us, may be instructed.

The consequences of such a combined system of discipline and education among the poorer classes will be, as I have previously stated, most beneficial throughout the community; but unless it can be made general, a comparatively small part of the intended good will be attained.

It will be almost in vain to well-educate the few, if they are to spend the greater part of their time among the ignorant and the vicious many. The manners and habits of the latter will continually counteract our good intentions to the former.

What I now recommend is no fanciful theory; it is easily reducible into practice. You now have, or with a little exertion you may have, all the funds which are necessary; there are individuals ready and willing to undertake the task of management; and I think I may engage, with your countenance and assistance, that the whole shall be speedily put into execution.

But we must no longer lose sight of the primary cause of this meeting.

Without our friend here, Joseph Lancaster, this extraordinary man, whom Providence seems to have created for this great and good purpose, all our attempts would have been useless; indeed such a work as the one under consideration, without his aid, would have appeared so impracticable, that it would not have had a beginning.

I therefore refrain from attempting to express to him our feelings in words; this, I am sure, would be impossible:- his health we cannot drink – it would not be in unison with the tenets of the very respectable religious community of which he is a member; but I beg leave to propose that we offer him our sincere thanks and gratitude by general acclamation.

A

STATEMENT

REGARDING

THE NEW LANARK

Establishment.

EDINBURGH:

PRINTED BY JOHN MOIR,

1812.

A STATEMENT REGARDING THE NEW LANARK ESTABLISHMENT 1812[a]

About twenty-six years ago, the late Mr DAVID DALE[b] of Glasgow, whose benevolence and philanthropy are well known, commenced an extensive spinning establishment near the Falls of the Clyde, and he founded it on the combined principles of public and private advantage.

It was continued by him for upwards of thirteen years, when, having no sons to succeed him, and being far advanced in life, he sold it to some English merchants, and myself, who married his eldest daughter.[c]

These gentlemen remained in partnership with me ten years, when some of them resold their interest in it to merchants resident in Glasgow, who still hold these shares.[d] But from the first sale by Mr Dale, until midsummer last, the management of the establishment was under my direction. At the commencement of that period, I arranged the outline of a plan, on a principle on which I had previously acted in a different part of the kingdom for several years; which was intended to unite and bring into action all the local advantages of the situation; to produce the greatest ultimate profits to the proprietors, with the greatest comfort and improvement to the numerous population to whom it afforded employment; that the latter might be a model and example to the manufacturing community, which, without some essential change in the formation of their characters, threatened, and now still more threatens, to

[a] First published at Edinburgh, 1812. Reprinted in 1973.

[b] David Dale (1739–1806): industrialist, philanthropist and Owen's father-in-law. Originally a weaver at Paisley, then a dealer in linen yarn and importer of foreign yarns before becoming a manufacturer, cotton-spinner, banker, dyer and printer.

[c] Owen married Caroline Dale in 1799.

[d] Owen bought New Lanark in 1799 on behalf of the Manchester-based Chorlton Twist Company, with two partners, John Barton and John Atkinson, forming the New Lanark Twist Company. In 1809, he bought the mills from his partners and the following year entered into a new partnership with John Atkinson, Robert Dennistoun, Alexander Campbell of Hallyards, and Colin Campbell, now named the The New Lanark Company (*Life*, vol. 1 (1857), pp. 52, 87 [*infra*, vol. 4, pp. 105–6, 137–49]). The new company had a capital stock of £182,000, divided into 26 shares of £7000 each.

revolutionize and ruin the empire. The plan was founded on the simple and evident principle, that any characters, from the savage to the sage or intelligent benevolent man, might be formed, by applying the proper means, and that these means are to a great extent at the command and under the controul of those who have influence in society; and, although mankind are generally unconscious of these important powers, there are few things admitting of any doubt, which are so easy as this, of full and complete demonstration. This system has been pursued at these works, without a single exception from the principle stated, for 13 years, and the result has been precisely that which was calculated. The population originally brought to the establishment was, with a few exceptions, a collection of the most ignorant and destitute from all parts of Scotland, possessing the usual characteristics of poverty and ignorance. They were generally indolent, and much addicted to theft, drunkenness, and falsehood, with all their concomitant vices, and strongly experiencing the misery which these ever produce. But by means so gradually introduced, as to be almost imperceptible to them, they have been surrounded with those circumstances which were calculated, first to check, and then to remove their inducements to retain these inclinations; and they are now become conspicuously honest, industrious, sober, and orderly; so that an idle individual, one in liquor, or a thief, is scarcely to be seen from the beginning to the end of the year; and they are become almost a new people, and quite ready to receive any fixed character which may be deemed the most advantageous for them to possess.

I was proceeding in preparing the means for accomplishing *this* object, when those gentlemen, who had lately become part proprietors with me of the Establishment, and who rather wished to employ their capital for a more immediate return of profit, objected to this system being pursued, and, alarmed at the events of the times, they would not consent to the temporary expenditure required for carrying it into execution.[a]

I have said, temporary expenditure, because a comparatively small sum to that which had been expended; and a short period of time would have enabled me to complete the great outline of the plan; and in one year more, this latter part alone would have repaid the extra expense, besides giving important permanent advantages to the establishment.

In justice, however, to these gentlemen, it is necessary to state, that they are almost all strangers to the establishment and business; and that during the short period they have been part proprietors with me of the concern, they have not drawn any profits beyond the interest of their capital out of it; for, owing to our foreign political relations, which had created unknown difficulties in the commercial world, it had become necessary to reinvest these in the improvements,

[a] See Owen's *Life*, vol. 1 (1857), pp. 86–94 (*infra*, vol. 4, pp. 138–45).

to place the concern beyond the risk of similar events, and enable it to meet them with success; and, in consequence of the profits being so expended, a permanent saving, exceeding six thousand pounds per annum, has been effected, and a considerable progress has also been made towards the reduction of a still larger annual sum. The contract of the company, however, vested the legal direction of the business in a majority of the shares, and they held a majority, although I possess a greater number of shares than any other individual; and, for the reasons previously stated, they came to a resolution of putting a stop to all those plans which I had in progress for the farther improvement of the community, and ultimate profit to the concern; and which, by the facts they would have established, had the plan been continued, would have soon created a very beneficial change in society, rendering that which now appears inconsistent and uncontroulable among the ignorant, plain, evident, and of easy direction.[a] Under these circumstances, rather than be the active means of destroying a system which promises such important public as well as private advantages, and which had cost me many years close application and study, and much individual expense, I resigned the management; and the other proprietors are now endeavouring to conduct the establishment; but as they do not understand the principles on which it has been formed, and by which it is yet supported, I see the whole in their hands will soon become a manufacturing concern, similar to others in the kingdom; but I fear it will prove too extensive for them to manage with success on any other principles than those on which it has hitherto proceeded, as all its parts have been arranged to form a complete whole. In consequence, I have inquired if they will sell the interest they hold in the business, and have been given to understand, that they are willing to dispose of it on the same terms they purchased about two years ago; and if the system hitherto adopted shall be persevered in, those terms cannot fail to prove highly advantageous to the parties purchasing. I have, therefore, now to consider what is the best practicable plan for carrying these important objects into execution; for my own means are inadequate to so extensive an undertaking. But it may be said, that new schemes are hourly brought forward in all parts of the kingdom, and that ninety-nine of these out of every hundred prove visionary.

This is true; and, in reply to a fact so well known, I have to state, that this establishment has now existed upwards of twenty-six years; that besides the profits which the first proprietor derived from it, during thirteen years from its commencement, but which I have not the means of ascertaining, the latter proprietors have received, over and above five per cent. per annum upon all the capital employed in it, upwards of fifty thousand pounds; besides supporting above two thousand individuals, without any employment, for four months, at

[a] See *infra*, vol. 4, p. 138.

an expense exceeding seven thousand pounds. And in the same period, improvements have been carried on and finished out of the profits, which have now increased the powers of produce at the establishment to five times their original extent, and at an annual reduction of prime cost of nearly sixty thousand pounds, with a great improvement of quality in the material produced; and a considerable progress has also been made towards completing six times the extent, at an annual reduction of prime cost, exceeding eighty-five thousand pounds, which will be the state of the establishment at the end of next year. In the same period, also, an addition has been made to the village, forming part of the establishment, to contain from eleven to twelve hundred more inhabitants, which have been added to its population; and these, with the former occupiers of the houses, have been provided with all manner of public conveniencies and external comforts; and the most ample means were in preparation, and far advanced, to give their children the most beneficial education for their station in the community, and effectually to train them to habits which could not fail to make them valuable members of society. In consequence, likewise, of this system having been adopted and persevered in, the establishment, in a mercantile view, while supported by an adequate capital, is now put beyond the risk of ordinary circumstances; for the produce of it is of the nature of a raw material, applicable to the common purposes of male and female clothing in all ranks of life; it is of course in general demand, and will be always required; and although these improvements have cost upwards of eighty thousand pounds, it can now be produced, covering that expense, as low, – and, in a few months, when the arrangements in progress, which include the daily supply of fuel, food, clothes, and employment, for the whole population, shall be completed, – will be produced lower than it can be at any other establishment: Its success, therefore, becomes as certain as that of any mercantile or manufacturing concern in the kingdom, and so soon as peace shall again take place,[a] very abundant profits may be reasonably expected, while an immediate return of ten per cent. on the capital to be advanced, may be confidently calculated upon. But to those who feel a deep interest in the well-being of their fellow-creatures, it will be considered of far more importance, that the slothful are become diligent, the thief honest, the drunkard sober, the licentious temperate, the wretched and diseased healthy, and comparatively happy; that poors' rates and litigation are banished from the community; and that the rising generation are now acquiring those habits and that knowledge which give the most heartfelt gratification to all who visit them. In consequence the village and works, which have been created at an expense probably of two hundred thousand pounds, have now more the appearance of a national benevolent institution, than of manufacturing works founded by an

[a] War with France, which began in 1793, did not finally end until 1815.

individual; and in fact it has become a national establishment of high interest to the community; for it may now be justly said to be the best model in practice of a charitable institution, which, in lieu of debasing the character of the poor, and impoverishing the rich, directs and enables the former to support themselves in comfort and independence, and, by their industry and good conduct, to add essentially to the national wealth and resources.

If, then, the principles on which this system has been founded, have already effected these beneficial changes, of which all may now satisfy themselves, allow me to say, on the credit of that which has been accomplished, that those parts of it which were in progress, and are to follow, would yet effect far more extensive and important improvements, and give the whole stability.

But it may be necessary to explain more particularly what I mean by those plans which I had in progress, for the further improvement of the community, and ultimate profit to the concern.

They were intended to *increase* the population, diminish its expense, *add* to its domestic comforts, and greatly improve its character. Towards effecting these purposes, a building has been erected, which may be termed the '*New Institution*,' situated in the centre of the establishment, with an inclosed area before it. The objects intended to be accomplished by which are, *first*, To obtain for the children, from the age of two to five, a play-ground, in which they may be easily superintended, and their young minds properly directed, while the time of the parents will be much more usefully occupied, both for themselves and the establishment. This part of the plan arose from observing, that the tempers of children among the lower orders are generally spoiled, and vicious habits strongly formed, previous to the time when they are usually sent to school; and, to create the characters desired, these must be prevented, or as much as possible counteracted. The area is also to afford a place of meeting for the children, from the age of five to ten, previous to and after school hours, and to serve the boys for a drill-ground. It likewise contains conveniences calculated to give the children such habits as will enable the master of police to keep the village in a decent, clean state; and this is no small difficulty to overcome, where other habits have always obtained.

Secondly, To procure a large store-cellar, which was much wanted, and, by this arrangement, has been placed in the most advantageous situation for both the works and village; and it will be found to be of much use to the establishment.

Thirdly, A kitchen upon a large scale, in which food may be prepared of a better quality, and at a much lower rate, than individual families can now obtain it; for, under this arrangement, two or three fires, and half a dozen attendants, will supersede the necessity of several hundred fires, and as many attendants, particularly in summer; and the provisions will be prepared of the most wholesome and nutritious materials, obtained at the cheapest rates, aided by every known conveniency, and the best information which can be collected on the subject. It is obvious, that most of the families among the working class, are unusually destitute of all these advantages.

Fourthly, An eating-room immediately adjoining the kitchen, one hundred and ten feet by forty within, in which those to whom it may be convenient may take all their regular meals. As several of the young persons employed at the works, reside at the county town of Lanark, more than a mile distant, and from which their meals are regularly sent at considerable trouble and expense; and as a still greater number *lodge* in the village, and now inconveniently board themselves, these will all find an immediate benefit from both the kitchen and eating-room, and they afford so many substantial advantages to the general inhabitants of the place, that it is to be feared the space allotted for the eating-room, ample as it may appear, will soon be found too circumscribed.

Fifthly, The eating-room, by an immediate removal of the tables to the ceiling, will afford space in which the younger part of the adults of the establishment may dance three nights in a week during winter, one hour each night; and which, under proper regulations, is expected to contribute essentially to their health. This part of the plan is considered of some importance, because, during the short days of winter, the young people have no means of enjoying exercise in the open air, and this can be obtained as a substitute, at a trifling expense; and this change of motion, from their constant occupations, will be most favourable for their spirits, and a strong source of attachment to the works.

Sixthly, Another room, the whole length of the building, being 140 feet long, 40 wide, and 20 high, which is to be the general education-room and church for the village, and those who attend the works. In this it was intended, that the boys and girls were to be taught to read well, and to understand what they read; to write expeditiously a good legible hand, and to learn correctly; so that they may comprehend and use with facility the fundamental rules of arithmetic. The girls were also to be taught to sew, cut out, and make up useful family garments; and, after becoming perfect in these, they were to attend in rotation in the kitchen and eating-room, to learn to cook cheap and nutritious food, and to clean and keep a house neat and in order. And the boys were to be taught in the drill-ground the manual exercise, and as much of the principles of military tactics as would enable them, with a little previous practice, at any future period of their lives, aided also by the sentiments they would acquire, to render the most effectual defence to their country.

Seventhly, This room was intended to be arranged, not only in the most convenient manner for the several branches of useful education enumerated, but also to serve for a lecture-room and church. The lectures were to be given in winter three nights in the week alternately with dancing, and to be familiar discourses to instruct the population in their domestic economy, particularly in the methods they should adopt in training up their children, and forming their habits from their earliest infancy, in which, at present, they are deplorably ignorant. By these lectures they were also to be taught how to expend their earnings to the most advantage, and to appropriate the surplus, which will arise to them in consequence; to create a well-regulated competency; thus relieving them from the anxious fear of want under any circumstances, or at any period, and giving them that rational independence arising from their own exertions and superior conduct, without which, consistency of character, or domestic comfort, are not to be expected. The church was intended to be a general one, so that no part of the population may be excluded from it, and open occasionally to every sect of Christians in their turn. But the great leading principles of its regular doctrines, were, to inculcate the healing of all religious differences, – a real respect for each other's sentiments, on the ground that every individual, from one cause or other, which in general may be easily explained, must conscientiously deem his own the best, and which, indeed, is the only reason why they are entertained. And, above all, to enforce that most important precept, which, when fully comprehended, will be found alone sufficient to direct all our social intercourse, which is, 'That there is no other way by which mankind can obtain general and continued happiness, than by training every individual from its infancy, to exert itself in promoting, with sincerity, the happiness of every other individual within its circle of action.' And, by adopting the *proper* means, this may be universally taught with ease and with certainty.

And, *lastly*, The plan also included the improvement of the road from the works and village to the old town of Lanark, which is now almost impassable for young children in winter, and in such a state as to prevent in a great measure the population of the latter from being available for the manufacturing purposes of the former, and from deriving any benefit from its institutions, which are calculated to educate the whole of the children in the neighbourhood, as well as the works are to give them employment afterwards.

Beneficial as these arrangements, connected with the *New Institution*, must be to the individuals employed at the works, they will be at least equally advantageous, in a pecuniary view, to the proprietors of the establishment; for the whole expense of these combined operations will not exceed six thousand pounds, three thousand of which have already been expended; and, so far as my former experience enables me to judge of the consequences to arise from them, they cannot save less to the establishment than as many thousand pounds per annum, but probably much more.

First, By the improvement of the road between the old and new towns of Lanark, by shortening and widening it, and forming a good foot-path, making the distance easy and pleasant even for the youngest children from the former, to attend the schools and works at the latter, and which, with the conveniency of the public kitchen and eating-room, will make the population of the old town nearly as available for the objects of the establishment as that of the new is at present; giving a double supply of operatives for the same demand, and of course, constituting a perpetual check against any sudden and great advance of labour, which, in its consequences, is usually as injurious to those employed as to their employers.

Secondly, The kitchen and eating-room will enable the proprietors to support the population of the village, now exceeding 2200 individuals, at 1s 6d. per week less than the expense at which they now feed themselves; which alone will constitute a saving of £8580 per annum, to be divided between the proprietors and population of both towns.

Thirdly, By the arrangements formed for the education of the children, they will be trained regularly for their employment, and all their habits, bodily and mental, formed to carry them to a high state of perfection; and this alone, in its consequences, will be of incalculable advantage to the concern; for to these people are entrusted the care and use of nice and valuable machinery, with a very great variety of materials requisite for the business, with all the varied operations of the manufacture of the establishment through all its processes to the annual value of two hundred thousand pounds, the cost and perfection of which depend essentially on their conduct; and a saving of one penny per lb. on the manufacture is now upwards of £6000 per annum, and in a short period, will be near £8000 per do.; – while hitherto, the works have been supplied with operatives from among strangers from all parts of the country, who have been instructed in the business at an almost incalculable loss and expense to the proprietors, besides keeping the establishment in a comparative state of inferiority.

Advantageous, however, as these arrangements will be to the individuals employed at the works, and to the proprietors of the establishment, they will yet prove of far higher importance in a national view by the principles they will establish, and the consequences which will arise from them. For now, the manufacturing population of this country is feelingly alive to its apparent interests, extremely active, and that activity encreased to the highest pitch by the present state of commerce, requiring all their exertions for their support; but they are also, with partial exceptions, so ignorant as to be easily misdirected, and their numbers exceed the half of the population of the kingdom. Can such a combination of circumstances be contemplated without a conviction, that, if they shall be permitted to continue much longer without an effectual remedy being applied, very fatal consequences must be the result?

The principles on which the arrangements which have been explained have been formed, point out that remedy, and the experience of more than 20 years on an extended scale, prove them to be practically correct; and if they shall be generally adopted, the consequences will be, that not only our manufacturing but our entire population will gradually change its character; and if the means recommended shall be persevered in, it will ultimately become so well instructed, as to distinguish clearly between its true and apparent interests, and to detect the fallacy of those who might attempt to mislead them from the former. Poor's rates, the bane of the lower orders, would cease, foresight and temperance would generally prevail, their industry would be directed by intelligence, and the happiness they would soon experience in consequence, would render them a far more efficient and powerful population for their numbers than has ever yet existed, and with the resources which this country possesses, would make it impenetrable to foreign attack, however formidable it might be. Thus, if this plan had been pursued at these works but for one year longer, a population of from two to three thousand individuals would have been placed in a more happy situation than is to be found in any manufacturing class at present known; and, from the singular success which their superior conduct must give to the establishment in a pecuniary view, permanence would be given to the system. And, that the advantages of such a system being seen upon an extended scale in practice, may not be lost to our country and the world in general. –

I propose, that an association of some of the leading and most patriotic characters in the country, should be formed, either by charter or otherwise, for the purpose of giving such weight and influence to the system, as would ensure its speedy and general adoption; for, as many of the most intelligent and enlightened men in the kingdom, of all sects and parties, who have seen it in practice, as well as several foreigners of the first distinction, who have also minutely inspected it, have, without one exception, given it their unqualified approbation, I consider it now ready to undergo the most severe scrutiny and investigation.

To conclude. I do not hesitate to say, that this experiment is the most important that has ever yet been attempted for the general happiness of society; and that, conscious of the security of the grounds on which I have proceeded, and mean to proceed, I am ready to pledge my life for its ultimate, full, and complete success.

THE END

[*Copy of Original Title to First Edition.*]

A New View of Society;

OR,

ESSAYS

ON THE PRINCIPLE OF THE FORMATION OF THE HUMAN CHARACTER, AND THE APPLICATION OF THE PRINCIPLE TO PRACTICE.

"Any character, from the best to the worst, from the most ignorant to the most enlightened, may be given to any community, even to the world at large, by applying certain means; which are to a great extent at the command and under the controul, or easily made so, of those who possess the government of nations."

BY ONE OF HIS MAJESTY'S JUSTICES OF PEACE FOR THE COUNTY OF LANARK.

London:
PRINTED FOR CADELL AND DAVIES, STRAND;
BY RICHARD TAYLOR AND CO., PRINTERS' COURT, SHOE LANE

1813.

A NEW VIEW OF SOCIETY; OR, ESSAYS ON THE PRINCIPLE OF THE FORMATION OF THE HUMAN CHARACTER, AND THE APPLICATION OF THE PRINCIPLE TO PRACTICE[a]
1813–16

To William Wilberforce,[b] *Esq.*, MP[c]

My Dear Sir –
In contemplating the public characters of the day, no one among them appears to have more nearly adopted in practice the principles which this Essay develops than yourself.

In all the most important questions which have come before the senate since you became a legislator, you have not allowed the mistaken considerations of sect or party to influence your decisions; so far as an unbiased judgement can be formed of them, they appear generally to have been dictated by comprehensive views of human nature, and impartiality to your fellow creatures. The dedication, therefore, of this Essay to you, I consider not as a mere compliment

[a] According to an early note by Owen, the first essay was written in 1812 and published early in 1813. The second essay was printed and published at the end of 1813, and the third and fourth essays printed and circulated at about the same period. They were first printed for sale in July 1816 (note to the third edn of the first essay, 1817, p. 15). The manuscript copy of parts two and three is in the University of London Library. Two edns of the second essay appeared in 1813. The third and fourth essays appeared in 1814. The complete edn: 2nd edn 1816 (which added a subtitle: 'Preparatory to the Development of a Plan for Gradually Ameliorating the Condition of Mankind'); 3rd edn 1817; 4th edn 1818–19; other edns: New York, 1825; Cincinnati, 1825; Edinburgh, 1826; 1834; Manchester, 1837; Manchester and London, 1840. It was also reprinted in part in *Robert Owen's Journal* (1850), and in full in Owen's *Life*, vol. 1 (1857), pp. 253–332. Later reprints include: 1927, 1970, 1972, 1977, 1991. Some accounts also claim that a first edn appeared in 1812 (Owen, *A Lecture Delivered in the Mechanics' Institute*, 1841, pp. 5, 22; Owen, *Life*, vol. 1, 1857, p. 107; *New Moral World*, vol. 7, no. 69, February 1840, p. 1088; Owen. *The New Existence of Man Upon the Earth*, 1854, pt 2, p. xxxvii), published by Longman and Co. (*New Moral World*, vol. 10, no. 25, 18 December 1841, p. 194). One imprint (possibly not published) has been given an 1812 date, probably erroneously, and is entitled *Essays (1–4) on the Formation of the Human Character* (one copy in the Princeton University Library, though not, as reported in the National Union Catalog, the Johns Hopkins University Library). The edn reprinted here is from Owen's *Life*, vol. 1 (1857), pp. 255–332.

[b] William Wilberforce (1759–1833): evangelical philanthropist, MP, founder of the Society for the Suppression of Vice (1802).

[c] Original dedication of the First Essay, which was omitted in subsequent editions.

of the day, but rather as a *duty* which your benevolent exertions and disinterested conduct *demand*.

Yet permit me to say that I have a peculiar personal satisfaction in fulfilling this *duty*. My experience of human nature *as it is now trained*, does not, however, lead me to expect that even *your* mind, without personal inspection, can instantaneously give credit to the *full* extent of the *practical advantages* which are to be derived from an undeviating adherence to the principles displayed in the following pages. And far less is such an effect to be anticipated from the first ebullition of public opinion.

The proposer of a *practice* so *new* and *strange must be content* for a time to be ranked among the *good kind of people*, the speculatists and visionaries of the day, for such it is probable will be the ready exclamations of those who merely skim the surface of all subjects; exclamations, however, in direct contradiction to the fact, that he has not brought the practice into public notice until he patiently for twenty years proved it upon an extensive scale, even to the conviction of inspecting incredulity itself.

And he *is so content*, knowing that the result of the most ample investigation and free discussion will prove to a still greater extent than he will yet state, the beneficial consequences of the introduction of the principles for which he now contends.

With confidence, therefore, that you will experience this conviction, and, when experienced, will lend your aid to introduce its influence into *legislative practice*, I subscribe myself, with much esteem and regard,

My dear Sir,

Your obliged and obedient Servant,

New Lanark Mills — Robert Owen

To the British public[a]

Friends and Countrymen –

I dedicate this Essay to you, because your primary and most essential interests are deeply involved in the subjects of which it treats.

You will find errors described, and remedies proposed; but as those errors are the errors of our forefathers, they call for something like veneration from their successors. You will therefore not attribute them to any of the individuals of the present day; neither will you for your own sakes wish or require them to be prematurely removed. Beneficial changes can alone take place by well-digested and well-arranged plans temperately introduced and perseveringly pursued.

[a] Original dedication of the second essay; it became the second dedication of the four essays in subsequent editions.

It is however an important step gained when the cause of evil is ascertained. The next is to devise a remedy for the evil, which shall create the least possible inconvenience. To discover that remedy, and try its efficacy in practice, have been the employments of my life; and having found what experience proved to be safe in its application, and certain in its effects, I am now anxious you should all partake of its benefits.

But be satisfied, fully and completely satisfied, that the principles of which the New View of Society is founded are true; that no specious error lurks within them, and that no sinister motive now gives rise to their publicity. Let them therefore be investigated to their foundation. Let them be scrutinized with the eye of penetration[a] itself; and let them be compared with every fact which has existed from the earliest knowledge of time, and with all those which now encircle the earth. Let this be done to give you full confidence, beyond the shadow of doubt or suspicion, in the proceedings which are or may be recommended to your attention. For they will bear this test; and such investigation and comparison will fix them so deep in your hearts and affections, that never more but with life will they be removed from your minds, and your children's from the end of time.

Enter therefore fearlessly on the investigation and comparison, startle not at apparent difficulties, but persevere in the spirit and on the principles recommended; you will then speedily overcome those difficulties, your success will be certain, and you will eventually firmly establish the happiness of your fellow creatures.

That your immediate and united exertions in this cause may be the means of commencing a new system of acting, which shall gradually remove those unnecessary evils which afflict the present race of men, is the ardent wish of

Your fellow subject,

THE AUTHOR

To the superintendents of manufactories, and to those individuals generally, who, by giving employment to an aggregated population, may easily adopt the means to form the sentiments and manners of such a population[b]

Like you, I am a manufacturer for pecuniary profit. But having for many years acted on principles the reverse in many respects of those in which you have been instructed, and having found my procedure beneficial to others and to myself, even in a pecuniary point of view, I am anxious to explain such

[a] See e.g., Job 28:10.

[b] This Address was prefixed to the third essay.

valuable principles, that you and those under your influence may equally partake of their advantages.

In two Essays, already published, I have developed some of these principles, and in the following pages you will find still more of them explained, with some detail of their application to practice under the peculiar local circumstances in which I took the direction of the New Lanark Mills and Establishment.

By those details you will find that from the commencement of my management I viewed the population, with the mechanism and every other part of the establishment, as a system composed of many parts, and which it was my duty and interest so to combine, as that every hand, as well as every spring, lever, and wheel, should effectually co-operate to produce the greatest pecuniary gain to the proprietors.

Many of you have long experienced in your manufacturing operations the advantages of substantial, well-contrived, and well-executed machinery.

Experience has also shown you the difference of the results between mechanism which is neat, clean, well-arranged, and always in a high state of repair; and that which is allowed to be dirty, in disorder, without the means of preventing unnecessary friction, and which therefore becomes, and works, much out of repair.

In the first case the whole economy and management are good; every operation proceeds with ease, order, and success. In the last, the reverse must follow, and a scene be presented of counteraction, confusion, and dissatisfaction among all the agents and instruments interested or occupied in the general process, which cannot fail to create great loss.

If, then, due care as to the state of your inanimate machines can produce such beneficial results, what may not be expected if you devote equal attention to your vital machines, which are far more wonderfully constructed?

When you shall acquire a right knowledge of these, of their curious mechanism, of their self-adjusting powers; when the proper mainspring shall be applied to their varied movements – you will become conscious of their real value, and you will readily be induced to turn your thoughts more frequently from your inanimate to your living machines; you will discover that the latter may be easily trained and directed to procure a large increase of pecuniary gain, while you may also derive from them high and substantial gratification.

Will you then continue to expend large sums of money to procure the best devised mechanism of wood, brass, or iron; to retain it in perfect repair; to provide the best substance for the prevention of unnecessary friction, and to save it from falling into premature decay? – Will you also devote years of intense application to understand the connection of the various parts of these lifeless machines, to improve their effective powers, and to calculate with mathematical precision all their minute and combined movements? – And when in these transactions you estimate time by minutes, and the money expended for the chance of increased gain by fractions, will you not afford some of your attention to consider whether a portion of your time and capital would not be more advantageously applied to improve your living machines? From experience which cannot deceive me, I venture to assure you, that your time and money so applied, if directed by a true knowledge of the subject, would return you, not five, ten, or fifteen per cent for your capital so expended, but often fifty, and in many cases a hundred per cent.

I have expended much time and capital upon improvements of the living machinery; and it will soon appear that time and the money so expended in the manufactory at New Lanark, even while such improvements are in progress only, and but half their beneficial effects attained, are now producing a return exceeding fifty per cent, and will shortly create profits equal to cent per cent on the original capital expended in them.

Indeed, after experience of the beneficial effects from due care and attention to the mechanical implements, it became easy to a reflecting mind to conclude at once, that at least equal advantages would arise from the application of similar care and attention to the living instruments. And when it was perceived that inanimate mechanism was greatly improved by being made firm and substantial; that it was the essence of economy to keep it neat, clean, regularly supplied with the best substance to prevent unnecessary friction, and by proper provision for the purpose to preserve it in good repair; it was natural to conclude that the more delicate, complex, living mechanism would be equally improved by being trained to strength and activity and that it would also prove true economy to keep it neat and clean; to treat it with kindness, that its mental movements might not experience too much irritating friction; to endeavour by every means to make it more perfect; to supply it regularly with a sufficient quantity of wholesome food and other necessaries of life, that the body might be preserved in good working condition, and prevented from being out of repair, or falling prematurely to decay.

These anticipations are proved by experience to be just.

Since the general introduction of inanimate mechanism into British manufactories, man, with few exceptions, has been treated as a secondary and inferior machine; and far more attention has been given to perfect the raw materials of wood and metals than those of body and mind. Give but due reflection to the subject, and you will find that man, even as an instrument for the creation of wealth, may be still greatly improved.

But, my friends, a far more interesting and gratifying consideration remains. Adopt the means which ere long shall be rendered obvious to every understanding, and you may not only partially improve those living instruments, but learn how to impart to them such excellence as shall make them infinitely surpass those of the present and all former times.

Here, then, is an object which truly deserved your attention; and, instead of devoting all your faculties to invent improved inanimate mechanism, let your thoughts be, at least in part, directed to discover how to combine the more excellent materials of body and mind which, by a well-devised experient, will be found capable of progressive improvement.

Thus seeing with the clearness of noonday light, thus convinced with the certainty of conviction itself, let us not perpetuate the really unnecessary evils which our present practices inflict on this large proportion of our fellow subjects. Should your pecuniary interests somewhat suffer by adopting the line of conduct now urged, many of you are so wealthy that the expense of founding and continuing at your respective establishments the institutions necessary to improve your animate machines would not be felt. But when you may have ocular demonstration, that, instead of any pecuniary loss, a well-directed attention to form the character and increase the comforts of those who are so entirely at your mercy, will essentially add to your gains, prosperity, and happiness, no reasons, except those founded on ignorance of your self-interest, can in future prevent you from bestowing your chief care on the living machines which you employ. And by so doing you will prevent an accumulation of human misery, of which it is now difficult to form an adequate conception.

That you may be convinced of this most valuable truth, which due reflection will show you is founded on the evidence of unerring facts, is the sincere wish of

THE AUTHOR

To His Royal Highness the Prince Regent[a] *of the British Empire*[b]

Sir –

The following pages are dedicated to Your Royal Highness, not to add to the flattery which through past ages has been addressed to those of our fellow men who have filled elevated situations; but they claim your protection because they proceed from a Subject of the empire over which you preside, and from one who disregards every inferior consideration in order that he may accomplish the greatest practical good to that empire.

Your Royal Highness, and all who govern the nations of the world, must be conscious that those of high rank, as well as those in the inferior stations of life, now experience much misery.

The Essays, of which these pages constitute the Fourth, have been written to show that the true origin of that misery may be traced to the ignorance of

[a] This dedication was the first in the 2nd edn (1816), but was omitted in the 3rd edn (1817).

[b] George (1762–1830), later George IV. Original dedication of the fourth essay; it became the first dedication of the four essays in subsequent editions.

those who have formerly ruled, and of those whom they governed; to make that ignorance known and evident to all; and to sketch the outlines of a practical Plan of Government, founded altogether on a preventive system, and derived from principles directly opposed to the errors of our forefathers. And should the outlines which have been sketched be formed into a legislative system, and adhered to without deviation, the most important benefits may be anticipated, both to the subjects of these realms and to the human race.

Your Royal Highness and those who direct the policy of other nations have been taught that you have duties to execute; but which, with the highest ability and best intentions, under the prevailing systems of error, cannot be performed.

Hence the dissatisfaction of those for whose benefit Governments were or ought to have been first established, and the perplexity and danger of those who govern.

And it is concluded with a confidence equal to certainty itself, that the principles unfolded in these Essays are competent to develop a practice which, without much apparent change, or any public disorder, shall progressively remove the difficulties of those who in future may rule, and the discontent of those who may be governed.

The language now addressed to Your Royal Highness is the result of a patient and extensive experience of human nature; of human nature, not indeed as it is explained in legendary tales of old, but as it now may be read in the living subject – in the words and actions of those among whom we exist.

It is true that many myriads of human beings have been conscientiously deceived; and, it may be said, it is most probable that another may be now added to the number: it is equally true, however, that similar language has been applied to many, and might have been applied to all who have been the instruments of beneficial improvements.

It may be said that the principles herein advocated, may nevertheless, like the former millions which have misled mankind, originate in error; in the wild and perverted fancy of a well-meaning enthusiasm. They have, however, not only been submitted to several of the most intelligent and acute minds of the present day, and who, although urged to the task, have candidly declared they could find no fallacy in the inductions, but they are such as few, if any, will venture to deny, or scruple to declare that they already admit.

And if these principles shall demonstrate themselves to be in unison with every existing fact which can now be examined and compared, they will ere long prove themselves to be of a permanent and substantial value beyond any of the discoveries which have previously been made.

Great, however, as the advantages may prove, the introduction of principles and practices so new, without being well understood, may create a momentary ferment.

To prevent the possibility of any such evil, the leaders of all the sects and parties in the state are invited to canvass these principles, and to endeavour to prove error in them, or evil in the consequences which might follow from their admission into practice.

The encouragement of such fair discussion and examination of these principles is all that is now solicited from Your Royal Highness.

And should that discussion and examination prove them to be erroneous, they will then be, as they ought to be for the public good, universally condemned. On the contrary, should they bear the test of that investigation to which they are now earnestly submitted, and be found, without a single exception, uniformly consistent with all the known facts of the creation, and consequently true; then, under the auspices of Your Royal Highness's Administration, will mankind naturally look for the establishment of a practical System of Government which can introduce and perpetuate such important public advantages.

That these principles, if true, may give birth to the measures which they immediately recommend; and that Your Royal Highness and the Subjects of these Realms, and the Rulers and Subjects of all other Realms, may in the present age enjoy the advantages of them in practice, is the sincere wish of

Your Royal Highness's faithful Servant,

THE AUTHOR

FIRST ESSAY

Any general character, from the best to the worst, from the most ignorant to the most enlightened, may be given to any community, even to the world at large, by the application of proper means; which means are to a great extent at the command and under the control of those who have influence in the affairs of men.

According to the last returns under the Population Act, the poor and working classes of Great Britain and Ireland have been found to exceed fifteen millions of persons, or nearly three-fourths of the population of the British Islands.

The characters of these persons are now permitted to be very generally formed without proper guidance or direction, and, in many cases, under circumstances which directly impel them to a course of extreme vice and misery; thus rendering them the worst and most dangerous subjects in the empire; while the far greater part of the remainder of the community are educated upon the most mistaken principles of human nature, such, indeed, as cannot fail to produce a general conduct throughout society, totally unworthy of the character of rational beings.

The first thus unhappily situated are the poor and the uneducated profligate among the working classes, who are now trained to commit crimes, for the commission of which they are afterwards punished.

The second is the remaining mass of the population, who are now instructed to believe, or at least to acknowledge, that certain principles are unerringly true, and to act as though they were grossly false; thus filling the world with folly and inconsistency, and making society, throughout all its ramifications, a scene of insincerity and counteraction.

In this state the world has continued to the present time; its evils have been and are continually increasing; they cry aloud for efficient corrective measures, which if we longer delay, general disorder must ensue.

'But,' say those who have not deeply investigated the subject, 'attempts to apply remedies have been often made, yet all of them have failed. The evil is now of a magnitude not to be controlled; the torrent is already too strong to be stemmed; and we can only wait with fear or calm resignation to see it carry destruction in its course by confounding all distinctions of right and wrong.'

Such is the language now held, and such are the general feelings on this most important subject.

These, however, if longer suffered to continue, must lead to the most lamentable consequences. Rather than pursue such a course, the character of legislators would be infinitely raised, if, forgetting the petty and humiliating contentions of sects and parties, they would thoroughly investigate the subject, and endeavour to arrest and overcome these mighty evils.

The chief object of these Essays is to assist and forward investigations of such vital importance to the well-being of this country, and of society in general.

The view of the subject which is about to be given has arisen from extensive experience for upwards of twenty years, during which period its truth and importance have been proved by multiplied experiments. That the writer may not be charged with precipitation or presumption, he has had the principle and its consequences examined, scrutinized, and fully canvassed, by some of the most learned, intelligent, and competent characters of the present day: who, on every principle of duty as well as of interest, if they had discovered error in either, would have exposed it – but who, on the contrary, have fairly acknowledged their incontrovertible truth and practical importance.

Assured, therefore, that his principles are true, he proceeds with confidence, and courts the most ample and free discussion of the subject; courts it for the sake of humanity – for the sake of his fellow creatures – millions of whom experience sufferings which, were they to be unfolded, would compel those who govern the world to exclaim – 'Can these things exist and we have no knowledge of them?' But they do exist – and even the heart-rending statements which are made known to the public during the discussions upon negro-slavery, do not exhibit more afflicting scenes than those which, in various parts of the world, daily arise from the injustice of society towards itself; from the inattention of mankind to the circumstances which incessantly surround them; and from the want of a correct knowledge of human nature in those who govern and control the affairs of men.

If these circumstances did not exist to an extent almost incredible, it would be unnecessary now to contend for a principle regarding Man, which scarcely requires more than to be fairly stated to make it self-evident.

This principle is, that '*Any general character, from the best to the worst, from the most ignorant to the most enlightened, may be given to any community, even to the world at large, by the application of proper means; which means are to a great extent at the command and under the control of those who have influence in the affairs of men.*'

The principle as now stated is a broad one, and, if it should be found to be true, cannot fail to give a new character to legislative proceedings, and such a character as will be most favourable to the well-being of society.

That this principle is true to the utmost limit of the terms, is evident from the experience of all past ages, and from every existing fact.

Shall misery, then, most complicated and extensive, be experienced, from the prince to the peasant, throughout all the nations of the world, and shall its cause and the means of its prevention be known, and yet these means withheld? The undertaking is replete with difficulties which can only be overcome by those who have influence in society: who, by foreseeing its important practical benefits, may be induced to contend against those difficulties; and who, when its advantages are clearly seen and strongly felt, will not suffer individual considerations to be put in competition with their attainment. It is true their ease and comfort may be for a time sacrificed to those prejudices; but, if they persevere, the principles on which this knowledge is founded must ultimately universally prevail.

In preparing the way for the introduction of these principles, it cannot now be necessary to enter into the detail of acts to prove that children can be trained to acquire '*any language, sentiments, belief, or any bodily habits and manners, not contrary to human nature*'.[a]

For that this has been done, the history of every nation of which we have records, abundantly confirms; and that this is, and may be again done, the facts which exist around us and throughout all the countries in the world, prove to demonstration.

Possessing, then, the knowledge of a power so important, which when understood is capable of being wielded with the certainty of a law of nature, and which would gradually remove the evils which now chiefly afflict mankind, shall we permit it to remain dormant and useless, and suffer the plagues of society perpetually to exist and increase?

No: the time is now arrived when the public mind of this country, and the general state of the world, call imperatively for the introduction of this all-pervading principle, not only in theory, but into practice.

Nor can any human power now impede its rapid progress. Silence will not retard its course, and opposition will give increased celerity to its movements. The commencement of the work will, in fact, ensure its accomplishment; henceforth all the irritating angry passions, arising from ignorance of the true cause of bodily and mental character, will gradually subside, and be replaced by the most frank and conciliating confidence and goodwill.

Nor will it be possible hereafter for comparatively a few individuals unintentionally to occasion the rest of mankind to be surrounded by circumstances which inevitably form such characters as they afterwards deem it a duty and a right to punish even to death; and that, too, while they themselves have been the instruments of forming those characters. Such proceedings not only create innumerable evils to the directing few, but essentially retard them and the great mass of society from attaining the enjoyment of a high degree of positive happiness. Instead of punishing crimes after they have permitted the human character to be formed so as to commit them, they will adopt the only means which can be adopted to prevent the existence of those crimes; means by which they may be most easily prevented.

[a] The 1st edn adds: 'even to make them, to a great extent, either imbecile or energetic characters'.

Happily for poor traduced and degraded human nature, the principle for which we now contend will speedily divest it of all the ridiculous and absurd mystery with which it has been hitherto enveloped by the ignorance of preceding times: and all the complicated and counteracting motives for good conduct, which have been multiplied almost to infinity, will be reduced to one single principle of action, which, by its evident operation and sufficiency, shall render this intricate system unnecessary, and ultimately supersede it in all parts of the earth. That principle is *the happiness of self, clearly understood and uniformly practised; which can only be attained by conduct that must promote the happiness of the community*.

For that Power which governs and pervades the universe has evidently so formed man, that he must progressively pass from a state of ignorance to intelligence, the limits of which it is not for man himself to define; and in that progress to discover, that his individual happiness can be increased and extended only in proportion as he actively endeavours to increase and extend the happiness of all around him. The principle admits neither of exclusion nor of limitation; and such appears evidently the state of the public mind, that it will now seize and cherish this principle as the most precious boon which it has yet been allowed to attain.[a] The errors of all opposing motives will appear in their true light, and the ignorance whence they arose will become so glaring, that even the most unenlightened will speedily reject them.

For this state of matters, and for all the gradual changes contemplated, the extraordinary events of the present times have essentially contributed to prepare the way.

Even the late Ruler of France,[b] although immediately influenced by the most mistaken principles of ambition, has contributed to this happy result, by shaking to its foundation that mass of superstition and bigotry, which on the continent of Europe had been accumulating for ages, until it had so overpowered and depressed the human intellect, that to attempt improvement without its removal would have been most unavailing. And in the next place, by carrying the mistaken selfish principles in which mankind have been hitherto educated to the extreme in practice, he has rendered their error manifest, and left no doubt of the fallacy of the source whence they originated.

These transactions, in which millions have been immolated, or consigned to poverty and bereft of friends, will be preserved in the records of time, and impress future ages with a just estimation of the principles now about to be introduced into practice; and will thus prove perpetually useful to all suceeding generations.

For the direful effects of Napoleon's government have created the most

[a] 1st edn: 'which Providence has yet allowed it to acquire'.

[b] Napoleon Bonaparte (1769–1821).

deep-rooted disgust at notions which could produce a belief that such conduct was glorious, or calculated to increase the happiness of even the individual by whom it was pursued.[a]

And the late discoveries and proceedings of the Rev Dr Bell and Mr Joseph Lancaster[b] have also been preparing the way, in a manner the most opposite, but yet not less effectual, by directing the public attention to the beneficial effects, on the young and unresisting mind, of even the limited education which their systems embrace.

They have already effected enough to prove that all which is now in contemplation respecting the training of youth may be accomplished without fear of disappointment. And by so doing, as the consequences of their improvements cannot be confined within the British Isles, they will for ever be ranked among the most important benefactors of the human race. But henceforward to contend for any new exclusive system will be in vain: the public mind is already too well informed, and has too far passed the possibility of retrogression, much longer to permit the continuance of any such evil.

For it is now obvious that such a system must be destructive of the happiness of the excluded, by their seeing others enjoy what they are not permitted to possess; and also that it tends, by creating opposition from the justly injured feelings of the excluded, in proportion to the extent of the exclusion, to diminish the happiness even of the privileged: the former therefore can have no rational motive for its continuance.

If, however, owing to the irrational principles by which the world has been hitherto governed, individuals, or sects, or parties, shall yet by their plans of exclusion attempt to retard the amelioration of society, and prevent the introduction into PRACTICE of that truly just spirit which knows no exclusion,

---

[a] The 1st edn adds:

Had not Providence in its superior wisdom intended that these gigantic and otherwise uncontroulable measures of Napoleon's should in their consequences produce a general good far to outweigh their partial and temporary evils, can ignorance itself suppose that they would have been permitted?

May we not, therefore, be allowed to hope that those capable of pursuing a principle of error to its utmost bound, finding it by experience to be a mere phantom, unproductive of the happiness which it promised, may, by the same overruling Power, be directed to adopt the principle which can alone give the human mind that high and solid gratification of which it is in search; and they may thus put a stop to the present murderous devastations of war, and direct the energies of their mind to form, in the true spirit of confidence which these principles cannot fail to generate, a bond of peace and amity which shall in some measure tend to compensate the inhabitants of these countries for the extreme of sufferings which they have now for so many years endured.

[b] Andrew Bell (1753–1832): founder of the Madras System of education, which used senior pupils to instruct those younger; also of a scheme of national education with schools supervised by parochial clergy; Joseph Lancaster (1778–1838) emphasised a similar 'monitorial' system of instruction. The Royal Lancastrian Society (founded 1809) became the basis for the British and Foreign School Society (1814), whose non-denominational emphasis became part of the later foundation of the state educational system.

such facts shall yet be brought forward as cannot fail to render all their efforts vain.

It will therefore be the essence of wisdom in the privileged class to co-operate sincerely and cordially with those who desire not to touch one iota of the supposed advantages which they now possess; and whose first and last wish is to increase the particular happiness of those classes, as well as the general happiness of society. A very little reflection on the part of the privileged will ensure this line of conduct; whence, without domestic revolution – without war or bloodshed – nay, without prematurely disturbing any thing which exists, the world will be prepared to receive principles which are alone calculated to build up a system of happiness, and to destroy those irritable feelings which have so long afflicted society – solely because society has hitherto been ignorant of the true means by which the most useful and valuable character may be formed.

This ignorance being removed, experience will soon teach us how to form character, individually and generally, so as to give the greatest sum of happiness to the individual and to mankind.

These principles require only to be known in order to establish themselves; the outline of our future proceedings then becomes clear and defined, nor will they permit us henceforth to wander from the right path. They direct that the governing powers of all countries should establish rational plans for the education and general formation of the characters of their subjects. *These plans must be devised to train children from their earliest infancy in good habits of every description (which will of course prevent them from acquiring those of falsehood and deception). They must afterwards be rationally educated, and their labour be usefully directed. Such habits and education will impress them with an active and ardent desire to promote the happiness of every individual, and that without the* shadow of exceptions *for sect, or party, or country, or climate. They will also ensure, with the fewest possible exceptions, health, strength, and vigour of body; for the happiness of man can be erected only on the foundations of health of body and peace of mind.*

And that health of body and peace of mind may be preserved sound and entire, through youth and manhood, to old age, it becomes equally necessary that the irresistible propensities which form a part of his nature,[a] and which now produce the endless and ever multiplying evils with which humanity is afflicted, should be so directed as to increase and not to counteract his happiness.

The knowledge however thus introduced will make it evident to the understanding, that by far the greater part of the misery with which man is encircled *may* be easily dissipated and removed; and that with mathematical precision he *may* be surrounded with those circumstances which must gradually increase his happiness.

[a] The 1st edn adds: 'and which are evidently designed by Providence'.

Hereafter, when the public at large shall be satisfied that these principles *can* and *will* withstand the ordeal through which they must inevitably pass; when they shall prove themselves true to the clear comprehension and certain conviction of the unenlightened as well as the learned; and when, by the irresistible power of truth, detached from falsehood, they shall establish themselves in the mind, no more to be removed but by the entire annihilation of human intellect; then the consequent practice which they direct shall be explained, and rendered easy of adoption.

In the meantime, let no one anticipate evil, even in the slightest degree, from these principles; they are not innoxious only, but pregnant with consequences to be wished and desired beyond all others by *every* individual in society.

Some of the best intentioned among the various classes in society may still say, 'All this is *very delightful and very beautiful in theory*, but *visionaries* alone expect to see it *realized*.' To this remark only one reply *can* or *ought* to be made; that *these principles have been carried most successfully into practice*.

(The beneficial effects of this practice have been experienced for many years among a population of between two and three thousand at New Lanark, in Scotland; at Munich, in Bavaria; and in the Pauper Colonies, at Fredericksoord.)[a]

The present Essays, therefore, are not brought forward as mere matter of speculation, to amuse the idle visionary who *thinks* in his closet, and never *acts* in the world; but to create universal activity, pervade society with a knowledge of its true interests, and direct the public mind to the most important object to which it can be directed – to a national proceeding for rationally forming the character of that immense mass of population which is now allowed to be so formed as to fill the world with crimes.

Shall questions of merely local and temporary interest, whose ultimate results are calculated only to withdraw pecuniary profits from one set of individuals and give them to others, engage day after day the attention of politicians and ministers; call forth petitions and delegates from the widely spread agricultural and commercial interests of the empire – and shall the well-being of millions of the poor, half-naked, half-famished, untaught, and untrained, hourly increasing to a most alarming extent in these islands, not call forth *one* petition, *one* delegate, or *one* rational effective legislative measure?

No! for such has been our education, that we hesitate not to devote years and expend millions in the *detection* and *punishment* of crimes, and in the attainment of objects whose ultimate results are, in comparison with this,

[a] The 1st–4th edns referred only to New Lanark. Benjamin Thompson, Count Rumford (1753–1814) operated a military-style workhouse in Munich from 1789 until the late 1790s. It is described in his *An Account of an Establishment for the Poor in Munich* (1799). Fredericks-oord was a Dutch pauper settlement on the land, described in *The Philanthropist*, no. 1 (1829), pp. 67–76.

insignificancy itself: and yet we have not moved one step in the true path to *prevent* crimes, and to diminish the innumerable evils with which mankind are now afflicted.

Are these false principles of conduct in those who govern the world to influence mankind permanently? And if not, *how* and *when* is the change to commence?

These important considerations shall form the subject of the next Essay.

SECOND ESSAY

The Principles of the Former Essay continued, and applied in part to Practice

It is not unreasonable to hope that *hostility* may *cease*, even where *perfect agreement cannot be established*. If we cannot *reconcile all opinions*, let us endeavour to unite all hearts. – MR VANSITTART'S LETTER TO THE REV. DR HERBERT MARSH[a]

General principles only were developed in the First Essay. In this an attempt will be made to show the advantages which may be derived from the adoption of those principles into practice, and to explain the mode by which the practice may, without inconvenience, be generally introduced.

Some of the most important benefits to be derived from the introduction of those principles into practice are, that they will create the most cogent reasons to induce each man 'to have charity for *all* men'. No feeling short of this can indeed find place in any mind which has been taught clearly to understand that children in all parts of the earth have been, are, and everlastingly will be, impressed with habits and sentiments similar to those of their parents and instructors; modified, however, by the circumstances in which they have been, are, or may be placed, and by the peculiar organizations of each individual. Yet not one of these causes of character is at the command, or in any manner under the control of infants, who (whatever absurdity we may have been taught to the contrary), cannot possibly be accountable for the sentiments and manners which may be given to them. And here lies the fundamental error of society; and from hence have proceeded, and do proceed, most of the miseries of mankind.

Children are, without exception, passive and wonderfully contrived compounds; which, by an accurate previous and subsequent attention, *founded on a correct knowledge of the subject*, may be formed collectively to have any human character. And although these compounds, like all the other works of nature,[b] possess endless varieties, yet they partake of that plastic quality, which, by perseverance under judicious management, may be ultimately moulded into the very image of rational wishes and desires.

In the next place these principles cannot fail to create feelings which,

[a] Nicholas Vansittart, *Letter to the Rev. Marsh* (1811), p. 10. This pamphlet argued for greater co-operation between Anglicans and Dissenters in furthering the cause of religious freedom.

[b] 1st edn: 'of the Great Directing Power of the Universe'.

without force or the production of any counteracting motive, will irresistibly lead those who possess them to make due allowance for the difference of sentiments and manners, not only among their friends and countrymen, but also among the inhabitants of every region of the earth, even including their enemies. With this insight into the formation of character, there is no conceivable foundation for private displeasure or public enmity. Say, if it be within the sphere of possibility that children can be trained to attain *that* knowledge, and at the same time to acquire feelings of enmity towards a single human creature? The child who from infancy has been rationally instructed in these principles, will readily discover and trace *whence* the opinions and habits of his associates have arisen, and *why* they possess them. At the same age he will have acquired reason sufficient to exhibit to him forcibly the irrationality of being angry with an individual for possessing qualities which, as a passive being during the formation of those qualities, he had not the means of preventing. Such are the impressions these principles will make on the mind of every child so taught; and, instead of generating anger or displeasure, they will produce commiseration and pity for those individuals who possess either habits or sentiments which appear to him to be destructive of their own comfort, pleasure, or happiness; and will produce on his part a desire to remove those causes of distress, and his own feelings of commiseration and pity may be also removed. The pleasure which he cannot avoid experiencing by this mode of conduct will likewise stimulate him to the most active endeavours to withdraw those circumstances which surround any part of mankind with causes of misery, and to replace them with others which have a tendency to increase happiness. He will then also strongly entertain the desire 'to do good to *all* men', and even to those who think themselves his enemies.

Thus *shortly*, *directly*, and *certainly* may mankind be taught the essence, and to attain the ultimate object, of all former *moral* and *religious* instruction.

These Essays, however, are intended to explain that which is *true*, and not to attack that which is *false*. For to explain that which is true may permanently improve, without creating even temporary evil; whereas to attack that which is false, is often productive of very fatal consequences. The former convinces the judgement when the mind possesses full and deliberate powers of judging; the latter instantly arouses irritation, and renders the judgement unfit for its office, and useless. But why should we *ever* irritate? Do not these principles make it so obvious as to place it beyond any doubt, that even the present irrational ideas and practices prevalent throughout the world are not to be charged as either a fault or a culpable error of the existing generation? The immediate cause of them was the partial ignorance of our forefathers, who, although they acquire some vague disjointed knowledge of the principles on which character is formed, could not discover the connected chain of those principles, and consequently knew not how to apply them to practice. They taught their children that which they had themselves been taught, that which they had acquired, and in so doing they acted like their forefathers; who retained the established customs of former generations until better and superior were discovered and made evident to them.

The present race of men have also instructed their children as they had been previously instructed, and are equally unblameable for any defects which their systems contain. And however erroneous or injurious that instruction and those systems may now be proved to be, the principles on which these Essays are founded will be misunderstood, and their spirit will be wholly misconceived, if either irritation or the slightest degree of ill will shall be generated against those who even tenaciously adhere to the worst parts of that instruction, and support the most pernicious of those systems. For such individuals, sects, or parties have been trained from infancy to consider it their duty and interest so to act, and in so acting they merely continue the customs of their predecessors. Let truth unaccompanied with *error* be placed before them; give them time to examine it and to see that it is in unison with all previously ascertained truths; and conviction and acknowledgement of it will follow of course. It is weakness itself to require assent *before* conviction; and *afterwards* it will not be withheld. To endeavour to force conclusions without making the subject clear to the understanding, is most unjustifiable and irrational, and must prove useless or injurious to the mental faculties.

In the spirit thus described we therefore proceed in the investigation of the subject.

The facts which by the invention of printing have gradually accumulated now show the errors of the systems of our forefathers so distinctly, that they must be, when pointed out, evident to all classes of the community, and render it absolutely necessary that new legislative measures be immediately adopted to prevent the confusion which must arise from even the most ignorant being competent to detect the absurdity and glaring injustice of many of those laws by which they are now governed.

Such are those laws which enact punishments for a very great variety of actions designated crimes; while those from whom such actions proceed are regularly trained to acquire no other knowledge than that which compels them to conclude that those actions are the best they could perform.

How much longer shall we continue to allow generation after generation to be taught crime from their infancy, and, when so taught, hunt them like beasts of the forest, until they are entangled beyond escape in the toils and nets of the law? when, if the circumstances of those poor unpitied sufferers had been reversed with those who are even surrounded with the pomp and dignity of justice, these latter would have been at the bar of the culprit, and the former would have been in the judgement seat.

Had the present Judges of these realms been born and educated among the poor and profligate of St Giles's or some similar situation, it is not certain, inasmuch as they possess native energies and abilities, that ere this they would have been at the head of their *then* profession and, in consequence of that superiority and proficiency, would have already suffered imprisonment, transportation, or death? Can we for a moment hesitate to decide, that if some of those men whom the laws dispensed by the present Judges have doomed to suffer capital punishments, had been born, trained, and circumstanced, as these Judges were born, trained, and circumstanced, that some of those who had so suffered would have been the identical individuals who would have passed the same awful sentences on the present highly esteemed dignitaries of the law?

If we open our eyes and attentively notice events, we shall observe these facts to multiply before us. Is the evil then of so small magnitude as to be totally disregarded and passed by as the ordinary occurrences of the day, and as not deserving of one reflection? And shall we be longer told 'that the convenient time to attend to inquiries of this nature is not yet come: that other matters of far weightier import engage our attention, and it must remain over till a season of more leisure?'

To those who may be inclined to think and speak thus, I would say – 'Let feelings of humanity or strict justice induce you to devote a few hours to visit some of the public prisons of the metropolis, and patiently inquire, with kind commiserating solicitude, of their various inhabitants, the events of their lives and the lives of their various connections. Then will tales unfold that *must* arrest attention, that will disclose sufferings, misery, and injustice, upon which, for obvious reasons, I will not now dwell, but which previously, I am persuaded, you could not suppose it possible to exist in any civilized state, far less that they should be permitted for centuries to increase around the very fountain of British jurisprudence.' The true cause, however, of this conduct, so contrary to the general humanity of the natives of these Islands, is, that a practical remedy for the evil, on clearly defined and sound principles had not yet been suggested. But the principles developed in this 'New View of the Society', *will point out a remedy which is almost simplicity itself, possessing no more practical difficulties than many of the common employments of life; and such as are readily overcome by men of very ordinary practical talents.*

That such a remedy is easily practicable, may be collected from the account of the following very partial experiment.

In the year 1784 the late Mr Dale, of Glasgow, founded a manufactory for spinning of cotton, near the falls of the Clyde, in the county of Lanark, in Scotland; and about that period cotton mills were first introduced into the northern part of the kingdom.

It was the power which could be obtained from the falls of water that induced Mr Dale to erect his mills in this situation; for in other respects it was not well chosen. The country around was uncultivated; the inhabitants were poor and few in number; and the roads in the neighbourhood were so bad, that the Falls, now so celebrated, were then unknown to strangers.

It was therefore necessary to collect a new population to supply the infant establishment with labourers. This, however, was no light task; for all the regularly trained Scotch peasantry disdained the idea of working early and late, day after day, within cotton mills. Two modes then only remained of obtaining these labourers; the one, to procure children from the various public charities of the country; and the other, to induce families to settle around the works.

To accommodate the first, a large house was erected, which ultimately contained about 500 children, who were procured chiefly from workhouses and charities in Edinburgh. These children were to be fed, clothed, and educated; and these duties Mr Dale performed with the unwearied benevolence which it is well known he possessed.

To obtain the second, a village was built; and the houses were let at a low rent to such families as could be induced to accept employment in the mills; but such was the general dislike to that occupation at the time, that, with a few exceptions, only persons destitute of friends, employment, and character, were found willing to try the experiment; and of these a sufficient number to supply a constant increase of the manufactory could not be obtained. It was therefore deemed a favour on the part even of such individuals to reside at the village, and, when taught the business, they grew so valuable to the establishment, that they became agents not to be governed contrary to their own inclinations.

Mr Dale's principal avocations were at a distance from the works, which he seldom visited more than once for a few hours in three or four months; he was therefore under the necessity of committing the management of the establishment to various servants with more or less power.

Those who have a practical knowledge of mankind will readily anticipate the character which a population so collected and constituted would acquire. It is therefore scarcely necessary to state, that the community by degrees was formed under these circumstances into a very wretched society: every man did that which was right in his own eyes, and vice and immorality prevailed to a monstrous extent. The population lived in idleness, in poverty, in almost every kind of crime; consequently, in debt, out of health, and in misery. Yet to make matters still worse – although the cause proceeded from the best possible motive, a conscientious adherence to principle – the whole was under a strong sectarian influence, which gave a marked and decided preference to one set of religious opinions over all others, and the professors of the favoured opinions were the privileged of the community.

The boarding-house containing the children presented a very different scene. The benevolent proprietor spared no expense to give comfort to the poor children. The rooms provided for them were spacious, always clean, and well ventilated; the food was abundant, and of the best quality; the clothes were neat and useful; a surgeon was kept in constant pay, to direct how to prevent or cure disease; and the best instructors which the country afforded were appointed to teach such branches of education as were deemed likely to be useful to children in their situation. Kind and well-disposed persons were appointed to superintend all their proceedings. Nothing, in short, at first sight seemed wanting to render it a most complete charity.

But to defray the expense of these well-devised arrangements, and to support the establishment generally, it was absolutely necessary that the children should be employed within the mills from six o'clock in the morning till seven in the evening, summer and winter; and after these hours their education commenced. The directors of the public charities, from mistaken economy, would not consent to send the children under their care to cotton mills, unless the children are received by the proprietors at the ages of six, seven and eight. And Mr Dale was under the necessity of accepting them at those ages, or of stopping the manufactory which he had commenced.

It is not to be supposed that children so young could remain, with the intervals of meals only, from six in the morning until seven in the evening, in constant employment, on their feet, within cotton mills, and afterwards acquire much proficiency in education. And so it proved; for many of them became dwarfs in body and mind, and some of them were deformed. Their labour through the day and their education at night became so irksome, that numbers of them continually ran away, and almost all looked forward with impatience and anxiety to the expiration of their apprenticeship of seven, eight, and nine years, which generally expired when they were from thirteen to fifteen years old. At this period of life, unaccustomed to provide for themselves, and unacquainted with the world, they usually went to Edinburgh or Glasgow, where boys and girls were soon assailed by the innumerable temptations which all large towns present, and to which many of them fell sacrifices.

Thus Mr Dale's arrangements, and his kind solicitude for the comfort and happiness of these children, were rendered in their ultimate effect almost nugatory. They were hired by him and sent to be employed, and without their labour he could not support them; but, while under his care, he did all that any individual, circumstanced as he was, could do for his fellow creatures. The error proceeded from the children being sent from the workhouses at an age much too young for employment. They ought to have been detained four years longer, and educated; and then some of the evils which followed would have been prevented.

If such be a true picture, not overcharged, of parish apprentices to our manufacturing system, under the best and most humane regulations, in what colours must it be exhibited under the worst?

Mr Dale was advancing in years: he had no son to succeed him; and, finding the consequences just described to be the result of all his strenuous exertions for the improvement and happiness of his fellow creatures, it is not surprising that he became disposed to retire from the cares of the establishment. He accordingly sold it to some English merchants and manufacturers; one of whom, under the circumstances just narrated, undertook the management of the concern, and fixed his residence in the midst of the population. This individual had been previously in the management of large establishments, employing a number of workpeople, in the neighbourhood of Manchester, and, in every case, by the steady application of certain general principles, he succeeded in reforming the habits of those under his care, and who always, among their associates in similar employment, appeared conspicuous for their good conduct. With this previous success in remodelling English character, but ignorant of the local ideas, manners, and customs, of those now committed to his management, the stranger commenced his task.

At that time the lower classes of Scotland, like those of other countries, had strong prejudices against strangers having any authority over them, and particularly against the English, few of whom had then settled in Scotland, and not one in the neighbourhood of the scenes under description. It is also well known that even the Scotch peasantry and working classes possess the habit of making observations and reasoning thereon with great acuteness; and in the present case those employed naturally concluded that the new purchasers intended merely to make the utmost profit by the establishment, from the abuses of which many of themselves were then deriving support. The persons employed at these works were therefore strongly prejudiced against the new director of the establishment – prejudiced, because he was a stranger, and from England – because he succeeded Mr Dale, under whose proprietorship they acted almost as they liked – because his religious creed was not theirs – and because they concluded that the works would be governed by new laws and regulations, calculated to squeeze, as they often termed it, the greatest sum of gain out of their labour.

In consequence, from the day he arrived amongst them every means which ingenuity could devise was set to work to counteract the plan which he attempted to introduce; and for two years it was a regular attack and defence of prejudices and malpractices between the manager and the population of the place, without the former being able to make much progress, or to convince the latter of the sincerity of his good intentions for their welfare. He, however, did not lose his patience, his temper, or his confidence in the certain success of the principles on which he founded his conduct.

These principles ultimately prevailed: the population could not continue to resist a firm well-directed kindness, administering justice to all. They therefore slowly and cautiously began to give him some portion of their confidence; and as this increased, he was enabled more and more to develop his plans for their amelioration. It may with truth be said, that at this period they possessed almost all the vices and very few of the virtues of a social community. Theft and the receipt of stolen goods was their trade, idleness and drunkenness their habit, falsehood and deception their garb, dissensions, civil and religious, their daily practice; they united only in a zealous systematic opposition to their employers.

Here then was a fair field on which to try the efficacy in practice of principles supposed capable of altering any characters. The manager formed his plans accordingly. He spent some time in finding out the full extent of the evil against which he had to contend, and in tracing the true causes which had produced and were continuing those effects. He found that all was distrust, disorder, and disunion; and he wished to introduce confidence, regularity, and harmony. He therefore began to bring forward his various expedients to withdraw the unfavourable circumstances by which they had hitherto been surrounded, and to replace them by others calculated to produce a more happy result. He soon discovered that theft was extended through almost all the ramifications of the community, and the receipt of stolen goods through all the country around. To remedy this evil, not one legal punishment was inflicted, not one individual imprisoned, even for an hour; but checks and other regulations of prevention were introduced; a short plain explanation of the immediate benefits they would derive from a different conduct was inculcated by those instructed for the purpose, who had the best powers of reasoning among themselves. They were at the same time instructed how to direct their industry in legal and useful occupations, by which, without danger or disgrace, they could really earn more than they had previously obtained by dishonest practices. Thus the difficulty of committing the crime was increased, the detection afterwards rendered more easy, the habit of honest industry formed, and the pleasure of good conduct experienced.

Drunkenness was attacked in the same manner; it was discountenanced on every occasion by those who had charge of any department: its destructive and pernicious effects were frequently stated by his own more prudent comrades, at the proper moment when the individual was soberly suffering from the effects of his previous excess; pot- and public-houses were gradually removed from the immediate vicinity of their dwellings; the health and comfort of temperance were made familiar to them; by degrees drunkenness disappeared, and many who were habitual bacchanalians are now conspicuous for undeviating sobriety.

Falsehood and deception met with a similar fate: they were held in disgrace; their practical evils were shortly explained; and every countenance was given to truth and open conduct. The pleasure and substantial advantages derived from the latter soon overcame the impolicy, error, and consequent misery, which the former mode of acting had created.

Dissensions and quarrels were undermined by analagous expedients. When they could not be readily adjusted between the parties themselves, they were stated to the manager; and as in such cases both disputants were usually more or less in the wrong, that wrong was in as few words as possible explained, forgiveness and friendship recommended, and one simple and easily remembered precept inculcated, as the most valuable rule for their whole conduct, and the advantages of which they would experience every moment of their lives; viz. – 'That in future they should endeavour to use the same active exertions to make each other happy and comfortable, as they had hitherto done to make each other miserable; and by carrying this short memorandum in their mind, and applying it on all occasions, they would soon render that place a paradise, which, from the most mistaken principle of action, they now made the abode of misery.' The experiment was tried: the parties enjoyed the gratification of this new mode of conduct; references rapidly subsided; and now serious differences are scarcely known.

Considerable jealousies also existed on account of one religious sect possessing a decided preference over the others. This was corrected by discontinuing that preference, and by giving a uniform encouragement to those who conducted themselves well among all the various religious persuasions; by recommending the same consideration to be shown to the conscientious opinions of each sect, on the ground that all must believe the particular doctrines which they had been taught, and consequently that all were in that respect upon an equal footing, nor was it possible yet to say which was right or wrong. It was likewise inculcated that all should attend to the essence of religion, and not act as the world was now taught and trained to do; that is, to overlook the substance and essence of religion, and devote their talents, time, and money, to that which is far worse than its shadow, sectarianism; another term for something very injurious to society, and very absurd, which one or other well-meaning enthusiast has added to *true religion*, which, without these defects, would soon form those characters which every wise and good man is anxious to see.

Such statements and conduct arrested sectarian animosity and ignorant intolerance; each retains full liberty of conscience, and in consequence each partakes of the sincere friendship of many sects instead of one. They act with cordiality together in the same departments and pursuits, and associate as though the whole community were not of different sectarian persuasions; and not one evil ensues.

The same principles were applied to correct the irregular intercourse of the sexes: such conduct was discountenanced and held in disgrace; fines were levied upon both parties for the use of the support fund of the community. (This fund arose from each individual contributing one sixtieth part of their wages, which, under their management, was applied to support the sick, and injured by accident, and the aged.) But because they had once unfortunately offended against the established laws and customs of society, they were not forced to become vicious, abandoned, and miserable; the door was left open for them to return to the comforts of kind friends and respected acquaintances; and, beyond any previous expectation, the evil became greatly diminished.

The system of receiving apprentices from public charities was abolished; permanent settlers with large families were encouraged, and comfortable houses were built for their accommodation.

The practice of employing children in the mills, of six, seven and eight years of age, was discontinued, and their parents advised to allow them to acquire health and education until they were ten years old. (It may be remarked, that even this age is too early to keep them at constant employment in manufactories, from six in the morning to seven in the evening. Far better would it be for the children, their parents, and for society, that the first should not commence employment until they attain the age of twelve, when their education might be finished, and their bodies would be more competent to undergo the fatigue and exertions required of them. When parents can be trained to afford this additional time to their children without inconvenience, they will, of course, adopt the practice now recommended.)

The children were taught reading, writing, and arithmetic, during five years, that is, from five to ten, in the village school, without expense to their parents. All the modern improvements in education have been adopted, or are in process of adoption. (To avoid the inconveniences which must ever arise from the introduction of a particular creed into a school, the children are taught to read in such books as inculcate those precepts of the Christian religion, which are common to all denominations.)[a] They may therefore be taught and well-trained before they engage in any regular employment. Another important consideration is, that all their instruction is rendered a pleasure and delight to them; they are much more anxious for the hour of school-time to arrive than to end; they therefore make a rapid progress; and it may be safely asserted, that if they shall not be trained to form such characters as may be most desired, the fault will not proceed from the children; the cause will be in the want of a true knowledge of human nature in those who have the management of them and their parents.

During the period that these changes were going forward, attention was given to the domestic arrangements of the community.

Their houses were rendered more comfortable, their streets were improved, the best provisions were purchased, and sold to them at low rates, yet covering the original expense, and under such regulations as taught them how to proportion their expenditure to their income. Fuel and clothes were obtained for them in the same manner; and no advantage was attempted to be taken of them, or means used to deceive them.

In consequence, their animosity and opposition to the stranger subsided, their full confidence was obtained, and they became satisfied that no evil was intended them; they were convinced that a real desire existed to increase their happiness upon those grounds alone on which it could be permanently increased. All difficulties in the way of future improvement vanished. They were

---

[a] The 1st edn adds:

and on Sunday the school is opened for the express purpose of teaching the catechisms, psalms, etc of the established church to those children whose parents are of that persuasion, while the remainder attend their respective places of worship.

taught to be rational, and they acted rationally. Thus both parties experienced the incalculable advantages of the system which had been adopted. Those employed became industrious, temperate, healthy, faithful to their employers, and kind to each other; while the proprietors were deriving services from their attachment, almost without inspection, far beyond those which could be obtained by any other means than those of mutual confidence and kindness. Such was the effect of these principles on the adults; on those whose previous habits had been as ill-formed as habits could be; and certainly the application of the principles to practice was made under the most unfavourable circumstances. (It may be supposed that this community was separated from other society; but the supposition would be erroneous, for it had daily and hourly communication with a population exceeding its own number. The royal borough of Lanark is only one mile distant from the works; many individuals came daily from the former to be employed at the latter; and a general intercourse is constantly maintained between the old and new towns.)

I have thus given a detailed account of this experiment, although a partial application of the principles is of far less importance than a clear and accurate account of the principles themselves, in order that they may be so well understood as to be easily rendered applicable to practice in any community and under any circumstances. Without this, particular facts may indeed amuse or astonish, but they would not contain that substantial value which the principles will be found to possess. But if the relation of the narrative shall forward this object, the experiment cannot fail to prove the certain means of renovating the moral and religious principles of the world, by showing whence arise the various opinions, manners, vices, and virtues of mankind, and how the best of the worst of them may, with mathematical precision, be taught to the rising generation.

Let it not, therefore, be longer said that evil or injurious actions cannot be prevented, or that the most rational habits in the rising generation cannot be universally formed. In those characters which now exhibit crime, the fault is obviously not in the individual, but the defects proceed from the system in which the individual was trained. Withdraw those circumstances which tend to create crime in the human character, and crime will not be created. Replace them with such as are calculated to form habits of order, regularity, temperance, industry; and these qualities will be formed. Adopt measures of fair equity and justice, and you will readily acquire the full and complete confidence of the lower orders. Proceed systematically on principles of undeviating persevering kindness, yet retaining and using, with the least possible severity, the means of restraining crime from immediately injuring society; and by degrees even the crimes now existing in the adults will also gradually disappear: for the worst formed disposition, short of incurable insanity, will not long resist a firm, determined, well-directed, persevering kindness. Such a proceeding, whenever practised, will be found the most powerful and effective corrector of crime, and of all injurious and improper habits.

The experiment narrated shows that this is not hypothesis and theory.[a] The principles may be with confidence stated to be universal, and applicable to all times, persons, and circumstances. And the most obvious application of them would be to adopt rational means to remove the temptation to commit crimes, and increase the difficulties of committing them; while, at the same time, a proper direction should be given to the active powers of the individual; and a due share provided of uninjurious amusements and recreation. Care must also be taken to remove the causes of jealousy, dissensions, and irritation; to introduce sentiments calculated to create union and confidence among all the members of the community; and the whole should be directed by a persevering kindness, sufficiently evident to prove that a sincere desire exists to increase, and not to diminish, happiness.

These principles, applied to the community at New Lanark, at first under many of the most discouraging circumstances, but persevered in for sixteen years, effected a complete change in the general character of the village, containing upwards of 2,000 inhabitants, and into which, also, there was a constant influx of newcomers. But as the promulgation of new miracles is not for present times, it is not pretended that under such circumstances one and all are become wise and good; or, that they are free from error. But it may be truly stated, that they now constitute a very improved society; that their worst habits are gone, and that their minor ones will soon disappear under a continuance of the application of the same principles; that during the period mentioned, scarcely a legal punishment has been inflicted, or an application been made for parish funds by any individual among them. Drunkenness is not seen in their streets; and the children are taught and trained in the institution for forming their character without any punishment. The community exhibits the general appearance of industry, temperance, comfort, health, and happiness. These are and ever will be the sure and certain effects of the adoption of the principles explained; and these principles, applied with judgement, will effectually reform the most vicious community existing, and train the younger part of it to any character which may be desired; and that, too, much more easily on an extended than on a limited scale. To apply these principles, however, successfully to practice, both a comprehensive and a minute view must be taken of the existing state of the society on which they are intended to operate. The causes of the most prevalent evils must be accurately traced, and those means which appear the most easy and simple should be immediately applied to remove them.

In this progress the smallest alteration, adequate to produce any good effect, should be made at one time; indeed, if possible, the change should be so gradual as to be almost imperceptible, yet always making a permanent advance

[a] The 1st edn adds: 'the whole has been done, and may be again done'.

in the desired improvements. By this procedure the most rapid practical progress will be obtained, because the inclination to resistance will be removed, and time will be given for reason to weaken the force of long-established injurious prejudices. The removal of the first evil will prepare the way for the removal of the second; and this facility will increase, not in an arithmetical, but in a geometrical proportion;[a] until the directors of the system will themselves be gratified beyond expression with the beneficial magnitude of their own proceedings.

Nor while these principles shall be acted upon can there be any retrogression in this good work; for the permanence of the amelioration will be equal to its extent.

What then remains to prevent such a system from being immediately adopted into national practice? Nothing, surely, but a general destitution of the knowledge of the practice. For with the certain means of preventing crimes, can it be supposed that British legislators, as soon as these means shall be made evident, will longer withhold them from their fellow subjects? No: I am persuaded that neither prince, ministers, parliament, nor any party in church or state, will avow inclination to act on principles of such flagrant injustice. Have they not on many occasions evinced a sincere and ardent desire to ameliorate the condition of the subjects of the empire, when practicable means of amelioration were explained to them, which could be adopted without risking the safety of the state?[b]

For some time to come there can be but one practicable, and therefore one rational reform, which without danger can be attempted in these realms; a reform in which all men and all parties may join – that is, a reform in the training and in the management of the poor, the ignorant, the untaught and untrained, or ill-taught and ill-trained, among the whole mass of British population; and a plain, simple, practicable plan which would not contain the

---

[a] Malthus had claimed that population increased in a geometrical, and food supplies in an arithmetical, ratio.

[b] The 1st–4th edns add:

> They have, it is true, refused one measure called a reform, and most wise have they been in persevering in that refusal. But, have the advocates for that measure, well-intentioned and patriotic as many of them are, shown one good practical effect to be derived from it in the present state of ignorance in which the mass of the British population is now allowed to be trained? On the contrary, can any rational being attentively observe the scenes exhibited during every general election, and wish for those scenes to be extended? That, indeed, would be to wish any thing but a reform of the manners, habits and principles of our abused and deluded fellow subjects. Nor is it easy to say which most deserve our pity and commiseration; those who, with some pretensions to knowledge, adopt every low art to deceive, – to engender the most pernicious habits, – nay, to foster crime which they afterwards enact laws to punish, – or those whose welfare and substantial comforts are sacrificed in such proceedings.
>
> Away then with this abuse of terms! It would not, it could not be reform; but if now adopted it would soon terminate in dire anarchy and confusion.

least danger to any individual, or to any part of society, may be devised for that purpose.

That plan is a national, well-digested, unexclusive system for the formation of character and general amelioration of the lower orders. On the experience of a life devoted to the subject, I hesitate not to say, that the members of any community may by degrees be trained to live *without idleness, without poverty, without crime, and without punishment*; for each of these is the effect of error in the various systems prevalent throughout the world. *They are all necessary consequences of ignorance.*

Train any population rationally, and they will be rational. Furnish honest and useful employments to those so trained, and such employments they will greatly prefer to dishonest or injurious occupations. It is beyond all calculation the interest of every government to provide that training and that employment; and to provide both is easily practicable.

The first, as before stated, is to be obtained by a national system for the formation of character; the second, by governments preparing a reserve of employment for the surplus working classes, when the general demand for labour throughout the country is not equal to the full occupation of the whole: that employment to be on useful national objects from which the public may derive advantage equal to the expense which those works may require.

The national plan for the formation of character should *include* all the modern improvements of education, without regard to the system of any one individual; and should not *exclude* the child of any one subject in the empire. Anything short of this would be an act of intolerance and injustice to the excluded, and of injury to society, so glaring and manifest, that I shall be deceived in the character of my countrymen if any of those who have influence in church and state should now be found willing to attempt it. Is it not indeed strikingly evident even to common observers, that any further effort to enforce religious exclusion would involve the certain and speedy destruction of the present church establishment, and would even endanger our civil institutions.

It may be said, however, that ministers and parliament have many other important subjects under discussion. This is evidently true; but will they not have high national concerns always to engage their attention? And can any question be brought forward of deeper interest to the community than that which affects the formation of character and the well-being of every individual within the empire? A question, too, which, when understood, will be found to offer the means of amelioration to the revenues of these kingdoms, far beyond any practical plan now likely to be devised. Yet, important as are considerations of revenue, they must appear secondary when put in competition with the lives, liberty, and comfort of our fellow subjects, which are now hourly sacrificed for want of an *effective legislative measure to prevent crime*. And is an act of such vital importance to the well-being of all to be longer delayed? *Shall yet another year pass in which crime shall be forced on the infant, who in ten, twenty,* or thirty years hence shall suffer DEATH for being taught that crime? Surely it is impossible. Should it be so delayed, *the individuals of the present parliament, the legislators of this day*,[a] ought in strict and impartial justice to be amenable to the laws for not adopting the means in their power to prevent the crime; rather than the poor, untrained, and unprotected culprit, whose previous years, if he had language to describe them, would exhibit a life of unceasing wretchedness, arising *solely* from the errors of society.

Much might be added on these momentous subjects, even to make them evident to the capacities of children: but for obvious reasons the outlines are merely sketched; and it is hoped these outlines will be sufficient to induce the well-disposed of all parties cordially to unite in this vital measure for the preservation of everything dear to society.

In the next Essay an account will be given of the plans which are in progress at New Lanark for the further comfort and improvement of its inhabitants; and a general *practical* system be described, by which the same advantages may be gradually introduced among the poor and working classes throughout the United Kingdom.

[a] The 1st edn adds in a note:

Particularly the administration; and members for the commercial and manufacturing districts in which crime abounds, such as Middlesex, Yorkshire, Lancashire, Warwickshire, Nottinghamshire, Derbyshire, etc; and London, Liverpool, Glasgow, etc, etc.

THIRD ESSAY

The Principles of the Former Essays applied to a Particular Situation

Truth must ultimately prevail over error

At the conclusion of the Second Essay, a promise was made that an account should be given of the plans which were in progress at New Lanark for the further improvement of its inhabitants; and that a practical system should be sketched, by which equal advantages might be generally introduced among the poor and working classes throughout the United Kingdom.

This account became necessary, in order to exhibit even a limited view of the principles on which the plans of the author are founded, and to recommend them generally to practice.

That which has been hitherto done for the community at New Lanark, as described in the Second Essay, has chiefly consisted in *withdrawing some of those circumstances which tended to generate, continue, or increase early bad habits; that is to say, undoing that which society had from ignorance permitted to be done.*

To effect this, however, was a far more difficult task than to train up a child from infancy in the way he should go; for that is the most easy process for the formation of character; while to unlearn and to change long acquired habits is a proceeding directly opposed to the most tenacious feelings of human nature.

Nevertheless, the proper application steadily pursued did effect beneficial changes on these old habits, even beyond the most sanguine expectations of the party by whom the task was undertaken.

The principles were driven from the study of human nature itself and they could not fail of success.

Still, however, very little, comparatively speaking, had been done for them. They had not been taught the most valuable domestic and social habits: such as the most economical method of preparing food; how to arrange their dwellings with neatness, and to keep them always clean and in order; but, what was of infinitely more importance, they had not been instructed how to train their children to form them into valuable members of the community, or to know that principles existed, which, when properly applied to practice from infancy, would ensure from man to man, without chance of failure, a just, open, sincere, and benevolent conduct.

It was in this stage of the progress of improvement, that it became necessary to form arrangements for surrounding them with circumstances which should gradually prepare the individuals to receive and firmly retain those domestic and social acquirements and habits. For this purpose a building, which may be termed the 'new institution', was erected in the centre of the establishment, with an enclosed area before it. The area is intended for a playground for the children of the villagers, from the time they can walk alone until they enter the school.

It must be evident to those who have been in the practice of observing children with attention, that much of good or evil is taught to or acquired by a child at a very early period of its life; that much of temper or disposition is correctly or incorrectly formed before he attains his second year; and that many durable impressions are made at the termination of the first twelve or even six months of his existence. The children, therefore, of the uninstructed and ill-instructed, suffer material injury in the formation of their characters during these and the subsequent years of childhood and of youth.

It was to prevent, or as much as possible to counteract, these primary evils, to which the poor and working classes are exposed when infants, that the area became part of the New Institution.

Into this playground the children are to be received as soon as they can freely walk alone; to be superintended by persons instructed to take charge of them.

As the happiness of man chiefly, if not altogether, depends on his own sentiments and habits, as well as those of the individuals around him; and as any sentiments and habits may be given to all infants, it becomes of primary importance that those alone should be given to them which can contribute to their happiness. Each child, therefore, on his entrance into the playground, is to be told in language which he can understand, that 'he is never to injure his playfellows; but that, on the contrary, he is to contribute all in his power to make them happy.' This simple precept, when comprehended in all its bearings, and the habits which will arise from its early adoption into practice, *if no counteracting principle be forced upon the young mind*, will effectually supersede all the errors which have hitherto kept the world in ignorance and misery. So simple a precept, too, will be easily taught, and as easily acquired; for the chief employment of the superintendents will be to prevent any deviation from it in practice. The older children, when they shall have experienced the endless advantages from acting on this principle, will, by their example, soon enforce the practice of it on the young strangers: and the happiness, which the little groups will enjoy from this rational conduct, will ensure its speedy and general and willing adoption. The habit also which they will acquire at this early period of life by continually acting on the principle, will fix it firmly; it will become easy and familiar to them, or, as it is often termed, natural.

Thus, by merely attending to the evidence of our senses respecting human nature, and disregarding the wild, inconsistent, and absurd theories in which man has been hitherto trained in all parts of the earth, we shall accomplish with ease and certainty the supposed Herculean labour of forming a rational character in man, and that, too, chiefly before the child commences the ordinary course of education.

The character thus early formed will be as durable as it will be advantageous to the individual and to the community; for by the constitution of our nature, when once the mind fully understands that which is true, the impression of that truth cannot be erased except by mental disease or death; while error must be relinquished at every period of life, whenever it can be made manifest to the mind in which it has been received. This part of the arrangement, therefore, will effect the following purposes:

The child will be removed, so far as is at present practicable, from the erroneous treatment of the yet untrained and untaught parents.

The parents will be relieved from the loss of time and from the care and anxiety which are now occasioned by attendance on their children from the period when they can go alone to that at which they enter the school.

The child will be placed in a situation of safety, where, with its future schoolfellows and companions, it will acquire the best habits and principles, while at mealtimes and at night it will return to the caresses of its parents; and the affections of each are likely to be increased by the separation.

The area is also to be a place of meeting for the children from five to ten years of age, previous to and after school-hours, and to serve for a drill-ground, the object of which will be hereafter explained; and a shade will be formed, under which in stormy weather the children may retire for shelter.

These are the important purposes to which a playground attached to a school may be applied.[a]

---

[a] The 1st edn adds:

> The building called the New Institution contains three principal apartments, besides extensive store-cellars, which were conveniently contained by a rapid slope of the ground on which the building is erected.
>
> It is about 150 feet long and 45 feet wide, and in front appears to contain three stories, while on the opposite side, where the store cellars are seen, it has the appearance of four: there are however but two above the cellars, for both the upper rows of windows belong to the second, which is the highest story.
>
> The first apartment to the left of the front entrance is intended for a public kitchen for the community; the second, which adjoins the first, and includes about two-thirds of the length of the building, is to be appropriated for an eating and exercise room; while the upper apartment is contrived, without any division or separation, to serve the purposes of a school-room, lecture-room, and church. The public kitchen and eating-room, under the management intended, will be the means of giving many substantial advantages to the community; for it is known to those who practically understand the subject, that food may be prepared of a better quality and much cheaper in large than in small quantities.
>
> The inhabitants of the village, and those who attend the works from the old town of Lanark, will enjoy these benefits; and those who partake of their meals at the public tables will have an opportunity of meeting their friends and acquaintances; their frequent meetings will soon create a general interest in each other's welfare, and teach them to associate together with order and regularity, and assist in leading them by degrees to acquire that rational, manly, and benevolent character which the several parts of the New

Those who have derived a knowledge of human nature from observation know that man in every situation requires relaxation from his constant and regular occupations, whatever they be: and that if he shall not be provided with or permitted to enjoy innocent and uninjurious amusements, he must and will partake of those which he can obtain, to give him temporary relief from his exertions, although the means of gaining that relief should be most pernicious. For man, irrationally instructed, is ever influenced far more by immediate feelings than by remote considerations.

Those, then, who desire to give mankind the character which it would be for the happiness of all that they should possess, will not fail to make careful provision for their amusement and recreation.

The Sabbath was originally so intended. It was instituted to be a day of universal enjoyment and happiness to the human race. It is frequently made, however, from the opposite extremes of error, either a day of superstitious gloom and tyranny over the mind, or of the most destructive intemperance and licentiousness. The one of these has been the cause of the other; the latter the certain and natural consequence of the former. Relieve the human mind from useless and superstitious restraints; train it on those principles which facts, ascertained from the first knowledge of time to this day, demonstrate to be the only principles which are true; and intemperance and licentiousness will not exist; for such conduct in itself is neither the immediate nor the future interest of man; and he is ever governed by one or other of these considerations, according to the habits which have been given to him from infancy.

The Sabbath, in many parts of Scotland, is not a day of innocent and cheerful recreation to the labouring man; nor can those who are confined all the week to sedentary occupations, freely partake, without censure, of the air and exercise to which nature invites them, and which their health demands.

The errors of the times of superstition and bigotry still hold some sway, and compel those who wish to preserve a regard to their respectability in society, to an overstrained demeanour; and this demeanour sometimes degenerates into hypocrisy, and is often the cause of great inconsistency. It is destructive of every open, honest, generous, and manly feeling. It disgusts many, and drives them to the opposite extreme. It is sometimes the cause of insanity. It is founded on ignorance, and defeats its own object.

While erroneous customs prevail in any country, it would evince an ignorance of human nature in any individual to offend against them, until he has convinced the community of their error.

Institution are intended to create, and which, when created, cannot fail to add more to their happiness than can be supposed by those who are yet unacquainted with the principles on which these proceedings are founded.

The eating-room, by a proper distribution of the tables, may be converted into a room for regulated exercise or dancing.

To counteract, in some degree, the inconvenience which arose from the misapplication of the Sabbath, it became necessary to introduce on the other days of the week some innocent amusement and recreation for those whose labours were unceasing, and in winter almost uniform. In summer, the inhabitants of the village of New Lanark have their gardens and potato grounds to cultivate; they have walks laid out to give them health and the habit of being gratified with the ever-changing scenes of nature – for those scenes afford not only the most economical, but also the most innocent pleasures which man can enjoy; and all men may be easily trained to enjoy them.

In winter the community are deprived of these healthy occupations and amusements; they are employed ten hours and three-quarters[a] every day in the week, except Sunday, and generally every individual continues during that time at the same work: and experience has shown that the average health and spirits of the community are several degrees lower in winter than in summer; and this in part may be fairly attributed to that cause.

These considerations suggested the necessity of rooms for[b] innocent amusements and rational recreation.

Many well-intentioned individuals, unaccustomed to witness the conduct of those among the lower orders who have been rationally treated and trained, may fancy such an assemblage will necessarily become a scene of confusion and disorder; instead of which, however, it proceeds with uniform propriety; it is highly favourable to the health, spirits, and dispositions of the individuals so engaged; and if any irregularity should arise, the cause will be solely owing to the parties who attempt to direct the proceedings being deficient in a practical knowledge of human nature.

It has been and ever will be found far more easy to lead mankind to virtue, or to rational conduct, by providing them with well-regulated innocent amusements and recreations, than by forcing them to submit to useless restraints, which tend only to create disgust, and often to connect such feelings even with that which is excellent in itself, merely because it has been judiciously associated.

Hitherto, indeed, in all ages and in all countries, man seems to have blindly

---

[a] 1st edn: 'thirteen hours' (changed in the 2nd edn).

[b] The 1st edn:

> a room for regulated exercise or dancing: and to obtain the substantial benefits which such exercise is calculated to give, and avoid the evils which some may apprehend from this measure, it is intended that those who wish to partake of or see the exercise, shall return home at seven o'clock in the evening, make themselves clean and neat, and then, under the usual system of order and regularity to which they are trained, to enter the room, the males at one end and the females at the other, where each party will remain until the exercises shall commence, and where they will retire during its cessation, or when finished, previously to their return home in the same manner they came. The company will chiefly consist of parents and the young people of the village, who, it is intended, shall meet three alternate nights in the week, and remain each time about an hour.

conspired against the happiness of man, and to have remained as ignorant of himself as he was of the solar system prior to the days of Copernicus and Galileo.[a]

Many of the learned and wise among our ancestors were conscious of this ignorance, and deeply lamented its effects; and some of them recommended the partial adoption of those principles which can alone relieve the world from the miserable effects of ignorance.

The time, however, for the emancipation of the human mind had not then arrived: the world was not prepared to receive it. The history of humanity shows it to be an undeviating law of nature,[b] that man shall not prematurely break the shell of ignorance; that he must patiently wait until the principle of knowledge has pervaded the whole mass of the interior, to give it life and strength sufficient to bear the light of day.

Those who have duly reflected on the nature and extent of the mental movements of the world for the last half-century, must be conscious that great changes are in progress; that man[c] is about to advance another important step towards that degree of intelligence which his natural powers seem capable of attaining. Observe the transactions of the passing hours; see the whole mass of mind in full motion; behold it momentarily increasing in vigour, and preparing ere long to burst its confinement. But what is to be the nature of this change? A due attention to the facts around us, and to those transmitted by the invention of printing from former ages, will afford a satisfactory reply.

From the earliest ages it has been the practice of the world to act on the supposition that each individual man forms his own character, and that therefore he is accountable for all his sentiments and habits, and consequently merits reward for some and punishment for others. Every system which has been established among men has been founded on these erroneous principles. When, however, they shall be brought to the test of fair examination, they will be found not only unsupported, but in direct opposition to all experience, and to the evidence of our senses.

This is not a slight mistake, which involves only trivial consequences; it is a fundamental error of the highest possible magnitude; it enters into all our proceedings regarding man from his infancy; and it will be found to be the true and sole origin of evil. It generates and perpetuates ignorance, hatred, and revenge, where, without such error, only intelligence, confidence, and kindness, would exist. It has hitherto been the Evil Genius of the world. It severs man from man throughout the various regions of the earth; and makes enemies of those who, but for this gross error, would have enjoyed each other's kind

[a] Nicolaus Copernicus (1473–1543): astronomer.
Galileo (1564–1642): Italian mathematician and astronomer.

[b] 1st edn: 'the Great Ruler of the Universe'.

[c] 1st edn: 'Providence in its infinite wisdom is about to permit man'.

offices and sincere friendship. It is, in short, an error which carries misery in all its consequences.

This error cannot much longer exist; for every day will make it more and more evident *that the character of man is, without a single exception, always formed for him; that it may be, and is, chiefly created by his predecessors; that they give him, or may give him, his ideas and habits, which are the powers that govern and direct his conduct. Man, therefore, never did, nor is it possible he ever can, form his own character*.

The knowledge of this important fact has not been derived from any of the wild and heated speculations of an ardent and ungoverned imagination; on the contrary, it proceeds from a long and patient study of the theory and practice of human nature, under many varied circumstances; it will be found to be a deduction drawn from such a multiplicity of facts, as to afford the most complete demonstration.

Had not mankind been misinstructed from infancy on this subject, making it necessary that they should unlearn what they have been taught, the simple statement of this truth would render it instantly obvious to every rational mind. Men would know that their predecessors might have given them the habits of ferocious cannibalism, or of the highest known benevolence and intelligence; and by the acquirement of this knowledge they would soon learn that, as parents, preceptors, and legislators united, they possess the means of training the rising generations to either of those extremes; that they may with the greatest certainty make them the conscientious worshippers of Juggernaut, or of the most pure spirit, possessing the essence of every excellence which the human imagination can conceive; that they may train the young to become effeminate, deceitful, ignorantly selfish, intemperate, revengeful, murderous – of course ignorant, irrational, and miserable; or to be manly, just, generous, temperate, active, kind, and benevolent – that is intelligent, rational, and happy. The knowledge of these principles having been derived from facts which perpetually exist, they defy ingenuity itself to confute them; nay, the most severe scrutiny will make it evident that they are utterly unassailable.

Is it then wisdom to think and to act in opposition to the facts which hourly exhibit themselves around us, and in direct contradiction to the evidence of our senses? Inquire of the most learned and wise of the present day, ask them to speak with sincerity, and they will tell you that they have long known the principles on which society has been found to be false. Hitherto, however, the tide of public opinion, in all countries, has been directed by a combination of prejudice, bigotry, and fanaticism, derived from the wildest imaginations of ignorance; and the most enlightened men have not dared to expose those errors which to them were offensive, prominent, and glaring.

Happily for man this reign of ignorance rapidly approaches to dissolution; its terrors are already on the wing, and soon they will be compelled to take their flight, never more to return. For now the knowledge of the existing errors is not only possessed by the learned and reflecting, but it is spreading far and wide throughout society; and ere long it will be fully comprehended even by the most ignorant.

Attempts may indeed be made by individuals, who through ignorance mistake their real interests, to retard the progress of this knowledge; but as it will prove itself to be in unison with the evidence of our senses, and therefore true beyond the possibility of disproof, it cannot be impeded, and in its course will overwhelm all opposition.

These principles, however, are not more true in theory than beneficial in practice, whenever they are properly applied. Why, then, should all their substantial advantages be longer withheld from the mass of mankind? Can it, by possibility, be a crime to pursue the only practical means which a rational being can adopt to diminish the misery of man, and increase his happiness?

These questions, of the deepest interest to society, are now brought to the fair test of public experiment. It remains to be proved, whether the character of man shall continue to be formed under the guidance of the most inconsistent notions, the errors of which for centuries past have been manifest to every reflecting rational mind; or whether it shall be moulded under the direction of uniformly consistent principles, derived from the unvarying facts of the creation; principles, the truth of which no sane man will now attempt to deny.

It is then by the full and complete disclosure of these principles, that the destruction of ignorance and misery is to be effected, and the reign of reason, intelligence, and happiness, is to be firmly established.

It was necessary to give this development of the principles advocated, that the remaining parts of the New Institution, yet to be described, may be clearly understood. We now proceed to explain the several purposes intended to be accomplished by the School, Lecture Room, and Church.

It must be evident to those who have any powers of reason yet undestroyed, that man is now taught and trained in a theory and practice directly opposed to each other. Hence the perpetual inconsistencies, follies, and absurdities, which everyone can readily discover in his neighbour, without being conscious that he also possesses similar incongruities. The instruction to be given in the School, Lecture Room, and Church, is intended to counteract and remedy this evil; and to prove the incalculable advantages which society would derive from the introduction of a theory and practice consistent with each other. The uppermost storey of the New Institution is arranged to serve for a School, Lecture Room, and Church. And these are intended to have a direct influence in forming the character of the villagers.

It is comparatively of little avail to give to either young or old 'precept upon precept, and line upon line', *except the means shall be also prepared to train them in good practical habits*. Hence an education for the untaught and ill-taught becomes of the first importance to the welfare of society; and it is this which has influenced all the arrangements connected with the New Institution.

The time the children will remain under the discipline of the playground and school, will afford all the opportunity that can be desired to create, cultivate, and establish, those habits and sentiments which tend to the welfare of the individual and of the community. And in conformity to this plan of proceeding, the precept which was given to the child of two years old, on coming into the playground, 'that he must endeavour to make his companions happy', is to be renewed and enforced on his entrance into the school: and the first duty of the schoolmaster will be to train his pupils to acquire the practice of always acting on this principle. It is a simple rule, the plain and obvious reasons for which children at an early age may be readily taught to comprehend, and as they advance in years, become familarized with its practice, and experience the beneficial effects to themselves, they will better feel and understand all its important consequences to society.

Such then being the foundation on which the practical habits of the children are to be formed, we proceed to explain the superstructure.

In addition to the knowledge of the principle and practice of the abovementioned precept, the boys and girls are to be taught in the school to read well, and to understand what they read; to write expeditiously a good legible hand; and to learn correctly, so that they may comprehend and use with facility the fundamental rules of arithmetic. The girls are also to be taught to sew, cut out, and make up useful family garments; and, after acquiring a sufficient knowledge of these, they are to attend in rotation in the public kitchen and eating rooms, to learn to prepare wholesome food in an economical manner, and to keep a house neat and well arranged.

It was said that the children are to be taught to read well, and to understand what they read.

In many schools, the children of the poor and labouring classes are never taught to understand what they read; the time therefore which is occupied in the mockery of the instruction is lost. In other schools, the children, through the ignorance of their instructors, are taught to believe without reasoning, and thus never to think or to reason correctly. These truly lamentable practices cannot fail to indispose the young mind for plain, simple, and rational instruction.

The books by which it is now the common custom to teach children to read, inform them of anything except that which, at their age, they ought to be taught; hence the inconsistencies and follies of adults. It is full time that this system should be changed. *Can man, when possessing the full vigour of his faculties, form a rational judgement on any subject, until he has first collected all the facts respecting it which are known? Has not this been, and will not this ever remain, the only path by which human knowledge can be obtained?* Then children ought to be instructed on the same principles. They should first be taught the knowledge of facts, commencing with those which are most familiar to the young mind, and gradually proceeding to the most useful and necessary to be known by the respective individuals in the rank of life in which they are likely to be placed; and in all cases the children should have as clear an explanation of each fact as their minds can comprehend, rendering those explanations more detailed as the child acquires strength and capacity of intellect.

As soon as the young mind shall be duly prepared for such instruction, the master should not allow any opportunity to escape, that would enable him to enforce the clear and inseparable connection which exists between the interest and happiness of each individual and the interest and happiness of every other individual. This should be the beginning and end of all instruction; and by degrees it will be so well understood by his pupils, that they will receive the same conviction of its truth, that those familiar with mathematics now entertain of the demonstrations of Euclid.[a] And when thus comprehended, the all prevailing principle of known life, the desire of happiness, will compel them without deviation to pursue it in practice.

It is much to be regretted that the strength and capacity of the minds of children are yet unknown; their faculties have been hitherto estimated by the folly of instruction which has been given to them; while, if they were never taught to acquire error, they would speedily exhibit such powers of mind, as would convince the most incredulous how much the human intellect has been injured by the ignorance of former and present treatment.

It is therefore indeed important that the mind from its birth should receive those ideas only which are consistent with each other, which are in unison with all the known facts of the creation, and which are therefore true. Now, however, from the day they are born, the minds of children are impressed with false notions of themselves and of mankind; and in lieu of being conducted into the plain path leading to health and happiness, the utmost pains are taken to compel them to pursue an opposite direction, in which they can attain only inconsistency and error.

Let the plan which has now been recommended be steadily put in practice from infancy, *without counteraction from the systems of education which now exist*, and characters, even in youth, may be formed, that in true knowledge, and in every good and valuable quality, will not only greatly surpass the wise and learned of the present and preceding times, but will appear, as they really will be, a race of rational or superior beings. It is true, this change cannot be instantaneously established; it cannot be created by magic, or by a miracle; it must be effected gradually – and to accomplish it finally will prove a work of labour and of years. For those who have been misinstructed from infancy, who have now influence and are active in the world, and whose activity is directed by the false notions of their forefathers, will of course endeavour to obstruct the change. Those who have been systematically impressed with early errors,

[a] Euclid (c. 300 BC): Greek mathematician.

and conscientiously think them to be truths, will of necessity, while such errors remain, endeavour to perpetuate them in their children. Some simple but general method, therefore, becomes necessary to counteract as speedily as possible an evil of so formidable a magnitude.

It was this view of the subject which suggested the utility of preparing the means to admit of evening lectures in the New Institution; and it is intended they should be given, during winter, three nights in the week, alternately with dancing.

To the ill-trained and ill-taught these lectures may be made invaluable; and these are now numerous; for the far greater part of the population of the world has been permitted to pass the proper season for instruction without being trained to be rational; and they have acquired only the ideas and habits which proceed from ignorant association and erroneous instruction.

It is intended that the lectures should be familiar discourses, delivered in plain impressive language, to instruct the adult part of the community in the most useful practical parts of knowledge in which they are deficient, particularly in the proper method of training their children to become rational creatures; how to expend the earnings of their own labour to advantage; and how to appropriate the surplus gains which will be left to them, in order to create a fund which will relieve them from the anxious fear of future want, and thus give them, under the many errors of the present system, that rational confidence in their own exertions and good conduct, without which, consistency of character or domestic comfort cannot be obtained, and ought not to be expected. The young people may be also questioned relative to their progress in useful knowledge, and allowed to ask for explanations. In short, these lectures may be made to convey, in an amusing and agreeable manner, highly valuable and substantial information to those who are now the most ignorant in the community; and by similar means, which at a trifling expense may be put into action over the whole kingdom, the most important benefits may be given to the labouring classes, and through them, to the whole mass of society.

For it should be considered that *the far greater part of the population belong to or have risen from the labouring classes; and by them the happiness and comfort of all ranks, not excluding the highest, are very essentially influenced*: because even much more of the character of children in all families is formed by the servants, than is ever supposed by those unaccustomed to trace with attention the human mind from earliest infancy. It is indeed impossible that children in any situation can be correctly trained, until those who surround them from infancy shall be previously well instructed; and the value of good servants may be duly appreciated by those who have experienced the difference between the very good and very bad.

The last part of the intended arrangment of the New Institution remains yet to be described. This is the Church and its doctrines; and they involve considerations of the highest interest and importance; inasmuch as a knowledge of truth on the subject of religion would permanently establish the happiness of man; for it is the inconsistencies alone, proceeding from the want of this knowledge, which have created, and still create, a great proportion of the miseries which exist in the world.

The only certain criterion of truth is, that it is ever consistent with itself; it remains one and the same under every view and comparison of it which can be made; while error will not stand the test of this investigation and comparison, because it ever leads to absurd conclusions.

Those whose minds are equal to the subject will, ere this, have discovered, that the principles in which mankind have been hitherto instructed, and by which they have been governed, will not bear the test of this criterion. Investigate and compare them; they betray absurdity, folly, and weakness; hence the infinity of jarring opinions, dissensions, and miseries, which have hitherto prevailed.

Had any one of the various opposing systems which have governed the world and disunited man from man, been true, without any mixture of error – that system, very speedily after its public promulgation, would have pervaded society, and compelled all men to have acknowledged its truth.

The criterion, however, which has been stated, shows, that they are all, without an exception, in part inconsistent with the works of nature; that is, with the facts which exist around us. Those systems therefore must have contained some fundamental errors; and it is utterly impossible for man to become rational, or enjoy the happiness he is capable of attaining, until those errors are exposed and annihilated.

Each of those systems contains some truth with more error; hence it is that no one of them has gained, or is likely to gain, universality.

The truth which the several systems possess, serves to cover and perpetuate the errors which they contain; but those errors are most obvious to all who have not from infancy been taught to receive them.

Is proof demanded? Ask, in succession, those who are esteemed the most intelligent and enlightened of every sect and party, what is their opinion of every other sect and party throughout the world. Is it not evident that, without one exception, the answer will be, that they all contain errors so clearly in opposition to reason and equity, that he can only feel pity and deep commiseration for the individuals whose minds have been thus perverted and rendered irrational? And this reply they will all make, unconscious that they themselves are of the number whom they commiserate.

The doctrines which have been taught to every known sect, combined with the external circumstances by which they have been surrounded, have been directly calculated, and could not fail, to produce the characters which have existed. And the doctrines in which the inhabitants of the world are now instructed, combined with the external circumstances by which they are surrounded, form the characters which at present pervade society.

The doctrines which have been and now are taught throughout the world, must necessarily create and perpetuate, and they do create and perpetuate, a total want of mental charity among men. They also generate superstitions, bigotry, hypocrisy, hatred, revenge, wars, and all their evil consequences. For it has been and is a fundamental principle in every system hitherto taught, with exceptions more nominal than real, 'That man will possess merit, and receive eternal reward, by believing the doctrines of that peculiar system; that he will be eternally punished if he disbelieves them; that all those innumerable individuals also, who, through time, have been taught to believe other than the tenets of this system, must be doomed to eternal misery.' Yet nature[a] itself, in all its works, is perpetually operating to convince man of such gross absurdities.

Yes, my deluded fellow men, believe me, for your future happiness, that the facts around us, when you shall observe them aright, will make it evident, even to demonstration, that all such doctrines must be erroneous, because THE WILL OF MAN HAS NO POWER WHATEVER OVER HIS OPINIONS; HE MUST, AND EVER DID, AND EVER WILL BELIEVE WHAT HAS BEEN, IS, OR MAY BE IMPRESSED ON HIS MIND BY HIS PREDECESSORS AND THE CIRCUMSTANCES WHICH SURROUND HIM. It becomes therefore the essence of irrationality to suppose that any human being, from the creation to this day, could deserve praise or blame, reward or punishment, for the prepossessions of early education.

It is from these fundamental errors, in all systems which have been hitherto taught to the mass of mankind, that the misery of the human race has to so great an extent proceeded; for, in consequence of them, man has been always instructed from infancy to believe impossibilities – he is still taught to pursue the same insane course, and the result still is misery. Let this source of wretchedness, this most lamentable of all errors, this scourge of the human race, be publicly exposed; and let those just principles be introduced, which prove themselves true by their uniform consistency and the evidence of our senses; hence insincerity, hatred, revenge, and even a wish to injure a fellow creature, will ere long be unknown; and mental charity, heartfelt benevolence, and acts of kindness to one another, will be distinguished characters of human nature.

Shall then misery most complicated and extensive be experienced, from the prince to the peasant, in all nations throughout the world, and shall its cause and prevention be known, and yet withheld? The knowledge of this cause, however, cannot be communicated to mankind without offending against the deep-rooted prejudices of all. The work is therefore replete with difficulties, which can alone be overcome by those who, foreseeing all its important practical advantages, may be induced to contend against them.

[a] 1st edn: 'the Creation'.

Yet, difficult as it may be to establish this grand truth generally throughout society, on account of the dark and gross errors in which the world to this period has been instructed, it will be found, whenever the subject shall undergo a full investigation, that the principles now brought forward cannot, by possibility, injure any class of men, or even a single individual. On the contrary, there is not one member of the great family of the world, from the highest to the lowest, that will not derive the most important benefits from its public promulgation. And when such incalculable, substantial, and permanent advantages are clearly seen and strongly felt, shall individual considerations be for a moment put in competition with its attainment? No! Ease, comfort, the good opinion of part of society, and even life itself, may be sacrificed to those prejudices; and yet the principles on which this knowledge is founded must ultimately and universally prevail.

This high event, of unequalled magnitude in the history of humanity, is thus confidently predicted, because the knowledge whence that confidence proceeds is not derived from any of the uncertain legends of the days of dark and gross ignorance, but from the plain and obvious facts which now exist throughout the world. Due attention to these facts, to these truly revealed works of nature, will soon instruct, or rather compel mankind to discover the universal errors in which they have been trained.

The principle, then, in which the doctrines taught in the New Institution are proposed to be founded, is, that they shall be in unison with universally revealed facts, which cannot but be true.

The following are some of the facts, which, with a view to this part of the undertaking, may be deemed fundamental:

That man is born with a desire to obtain happiness, which desire is the primary cause of all his actions, continues through life, and, in popular language, is called self-interest.

That he is also born with the germs of animal propensities, or the desire to sustain, enjoy, and propagate life; and which desires, as they grow and develop themselves, are termed his natural inclinations.

That he is born likewise with faculties which, in their growth, receive, convey, compare, and become conscious of receiving and comparing ideas.

That the ideas so received, conveyed, compared, and understood, constitute human knowledge, or mind, which acquires strength and maturity with the growth of the individual.

That the desire of happiness in man, the germs of his natural inclinations, and the faculties by which he acquires knowledge, are formed unknown to himself in the womb; and whether perfect or imperfect, they are alone the immediate work of the Creator, and over which the infant and future man have no control.

That these inclinations and faculties are not formed exactly alike in any two individuals; hence the diversity of talents, and the varied impressions called liking and disliking which the same external objects make on different persons, and the lesser varieties which exist among men whose characters have been formed apparently under similar circumstances.

That the knowledge which man receives is derived from the objects around him, and chiefly from the example and instruction of his immediate predecessors.

That this knowledge may be limited or extended, erroneous or true; limited, when the individual receives few, and extended when he receives many ideas; erroneous, when those ideas are inconsistent with the facts which exist around him, and true when they are uniformly consistent with them.

That the misery which he experiences, and the happiness which he enjoys, depend on the kind and degree of knowledge which he receives, and on that which is possessed by those around him.

That when the knowledge which he receives is true and unmixed with error, although it be limited, if the community in which he lives possesses the same kind of degree of knowledge, he will enjoy happiness in proportion to the extent of that knowledge. On the contrary, when the opinions which he receives are erroneous, and the opinions possessed by the community in which he resides are equally erroneous, his misery will be in proportion to the extent of those erroneous opinions.

That when the knowledge which man receives shall be extended to its utmost limit, and true without any mixture of error, then he may and will enjoy all the happiness of which his nature will be capable.

That it consequently becomes of the first and highest importance that man should be taught to distinguish truth from error.

That man has no other means of discovering what is false, except by his faculty of reason, or the power of acquiring and comparing the ideas which he receives.

That when this faculty is properly cultivated or trained from infancy, and the child is rationally instructed to retain no impressions or ideas which by his powers of comparing them appear to be inconsistent, then the individual will acquire real knowledge, or those ideas only which will leave an impression of their consistency or truth on all minds which have not been rendered irrational by an opposite procedure.

That the reasoning faculty may be injured and destroyed during its growth, by reiterated impressions being made upon it of notions not derived from realities, and which it therefore cannot compare with the ideas previously received from the objects around it. And when the mind receives these notions which it cannot comprehend, along with those ideas which it is conscious are true and which yet are inconsistent with such notions, then the reasoning faculties become injured, the individual is taught or forced to believe, and not to think or reason, and partial insanity or defective powers of judging ensue.

That all men are thus erroneously trained at present, and hence the inconsistencies and misery of the world.

That the fundamental errors now impressed from infancy on the minds of all men, and from whence all their other errors proceed, are, that they form their own individual characters, and possess merit or demerit for the peculiar notions impressed on the mind during its early growth, before they have acquired strength and experience to judge of or resist the impression of those notions or opinions, which, on investigation, appear contradictions to facts existing around them, and which are therefore false.

That these false notions have ever produced evil and misery in the world; and that they still disseminate them in every direction.

That the sole cause of their existence hitherto has been man's ignorance of human nature: while their consequences have been all the evil and misery, except those of accidents, disease, and death, with which man has been and is afflicted: and that the evil and misery which arise from accidents, disease, and death, are also greatly increased and extended by man's ignorance of himself.

That, in proportion as man's desire of self-happiness, or his self-love, is directed by true knowledge, those actions will abound which are virtuous and beneficial to man; that in proportion as it is influenced by false notions, or the absence of true knowledge, those actions will prevail which generate crimes, from whence arises an endless variety of misery; and, consequently, that every rational means should be now adopted to detect error, and to increase true knowledge among men.

That when these truths are made evident, every individual will necessarily endeavour to promote the happiness of every other individual within his sphere of action; because he must clearly, and without any doubt, comprehend such conduct to be the essence of self-interest, or the true cause of self-happiness.

Here, then, is a firm foundation on which to erect vital religion, pure and undefiled, and the only one which, without any counteracting evil, can give peace and happiness to man.

It is to bring into practical operation, in forming the character of men, these most important of all truths, that the religious part of the Institution at New Lanark will be chiefly directed, and such are the fundamental principles upon which the Instructor will proceed. They are thus publicly avowed before all men, that they may undergo discussion and the most severe scrutiny and investigation.

Let those, therefore, who are esteemed the most learned and wise, throughout the various states and empires in the world, examine them to their foundation, compare them with every fact which exists, and if the shadow of inconsistency and falsehood be discovered, let it be publicly exposed, that error may not more abound.

But should they withstand this extended ordeal, and prove themselves uniformly consistent with every known fact, and therefore true, then let it be declared, that man may be permitted by man to become rational, and that the misery of the world may be speedily removed.

Having alluded to the chief uses of the playground and exercise rooms, with the School, Lecture Room, and Church, it remains, to complete the account of the New Institution, that the object of the drill exercises mentioned when stating the purposes of the playground, should be explained; and to this we now proceed.

Were all men trained to be rational,[a] the art of war would be rendered useless. While, however, any part of mankind shall be taught that they form their own characters, and shall continue to be trained from infancy to think and act irrationally – that is, to acquire feelings of enmity, and to deem it a duty to engage in war against those who have been instructed to differ from them in sentiments and habits – even the most rational must, for their personal security, learn the means of defence; and every community of such characters, while surrounded by men who have been thus improperly taught, should acquire a knowledge of this destructive art, that they may be enabled to overrule the actions of irrational beings, and maintain peace.

To accomplish these objects to the utmost practical limit, and with the least inconvenience, every male should be instructed how best to defend, when attacked, the community to which he belongs. And these advantages are only to be obtained by providing proper means for the instruction of all boys in the use of arms and the arts of war.

As an example how easily and effectually this might be accomplished over the British Isles, it is intended that the boys trained and educated at the Institution at New Lanark shall be thus instructed; that the person appointed to attend the children in the playground shall be qualified to drill and teach the boys the manual exercise, and that he shall be frequently so employed; that afterwards, firearms, of proportionate weight and size to the age and strength of the boys, shall be provided for them, when also they might be taught to practise and understand the more complicated military movements.

This exercise, properly administered, will greatly contribute to the health and spirits of the boys, give them an erect and proper form, and habits of attention, celerity, and order. They will, however, be taught to consider this exercise, an art, rendered absolutely necessary by the partial insanity of some of their fellow creatures who by the errors of their predecessors, transmitted through preceding generations, have been taught to acquire feelings of enmity, increasing to madness, against those who could not avoid differing from them in sentiments and habits; that this art should never be brought into practice except to restrain the violence of such madmen; and, in these cases, that it should be administered with the least possible severity, and solely to prevent the evil consequences of those rash acts of the insane, and, if possible, to cure them of their disease.

[a] The 1st edn adds: 'hostility would be unknown'.

Thus, in a few years, by foresight and arrangement, may almost the whole expense and inconvenience attending the local military be superseded, and a permanent force created, which in numbers, discipline, and principles, would be superior, beyond all comparison, for the purposes of defence; always ready in case of need, yet without the loss which is now sustained by the community of efficient and valuable labour. The expenditure which would be saved by this simple expedient, would be far more than competent to educate the whole of the poor and labouring classes of these kingdoms.

There is still another arrangement in contemplation for the community at New Lanark, and without which the establishment will remain incomplete.

It is an expedient to enable the individuals, by their own foresight, prudence, and industry, to secure to themselves in old age a comfortable provision and asylum.

Those now employed at the establishment contribute to a fund which supports them when too ill to work, or superannuated. This fund, however, is not calculated to give them more than a bare existence; and it is surely desirable that, after they have spent nearly half a century in unremitting industry, they should, if possible, enjoy a comfortable independence.

To effect this object, it is intended that in the most pleasant situation near the present village, neat and convenient dwellings should be erected, with gardens attached; that they should be surrounded and sheltered by plantations, through which public walks should be formed; and the whole arranged to give the occupiers the most substantial comforts.

That these dwellings, with the privileges of the public walks, etc., shall become the property of those individuals who, without compulsion, shall subscribe each equitable sums monthly, as, in a given number of years will be equal to the purchase, and to create a fund from which, when these individuals become occupiers of their new residences they may receive weekly, monthly, or quarterly payments, sufficient for their support; the expenses of which may be reduced to a very low rate individually, by arrangements which may be easily formed to supply all their wants with little trouble to themselves; and by their previous instruction they will be enabled to afford the small additional subscription which will be required for these purposes.

This part of the arrangement would always present a prospect of rest, comfort, and happiness to those employed; in consequence, their daily occupations would be performed with more spirit and cheerfulness, and their labour would appear comparatively light and easy. Those still engaged in active operations would, of course, frequently visit their former companions and friends, who, after having spent their years of toil, were in the actual enjoyment of this simple retreat; and from this intercourse each party would naturally derive pleasure. The reflections of each would be most gratifying. The old would rejoice that they had been trained in habits of industry, temperance, and foresight, to enable them to receive and enjoy in their declining years every reasonable comfort which the present state of society will admit; the young and middle-aged, that they were pursuing the same course, and that they had not been trained to waste their money, time, and health, in idleness and intemperance. These and many similar reflections could not fail often to arise in their minds; and those who could look forward with confident hopes to such certain comfort and independence would, in part, enjoy by anticipation these advantages. In short, when this part of the arrangement is well considered, it will be found to be the most important to the community and to the proprietors; indeed, the extensively good effects of it will be experienced in such a variety of ways, that to describe them even below the truth would appear an extravagant exaggeration. They will not, however, prove the less true because mankind are yet ignorant of the practice, and of the principles on which it has been founded.

These, then, are the plans which are in progress or intended for the further improvement of the inhabitants of New Lanark. They have uniformly proceeded from the principles which have been developed through these Essays, restrained, however, hitherto, in their operations, by the local sentiments and unfounded notions of the community and neighbourhood, and by the peculiar circumstances of the establishment.

In every measure to be introduced at the place in question, for the comfort and happiness of man, the existing errors of the country were always to be considered; and as the establishment belonged to parties whose views were various, it became also necessary to devise means to create pecuniary gains from each improvement, sufficient to satisfy the spirit of commerce.

All, therefore, which has been done for the happiness of this community, which consists of between two and three thousand individuals, is far short of what might have been easily effected in practice had not mankind been previously trained in error. Hence, in devising these plans, the sole consideration was not, what were the measures dictated by these principles, which would produce the greatest happiness to man; but what could be effected in practice under the present irrational systems by which these proceedings were surrounded.

Imperfect, however, as these proceedings must yet be, in consequence of the formidable obstructions enumerated, they will yet appear, upon a full minute investigation by minds equal to the comprehension of such a system, to combine a greater degree of substantial comfort to the individuals employed in the manufactory, and of pecuniary profit to the proprietors, than has hitherto been found attainable.

But to whom can such arrangements be submitted? Not to the mere commercial character, in whose estimation to forsake the path of immediate individual gain would be to show symptoms of a disordered imagination; for the children of commerce have been trained to direct all their faculties to buy cheap and sell dear; and consequently, those who are the most expert and successful in this wise and noble art, are, in the commercial world, deemed to possess foresight and superior acquirements; while such as attempt to improve the moral habits and increase the comforts of those whom they employ, are termed wild enthusiasts.

Nor yet are they to be submitted to the mere men of the law; for these are necessarily trained to endeavour to make wrong appear right, or to involve both in a maze of intricacies, and to legalize injustice.

[a]Nor to mere political leaders or their partisans; for they are embarrassed by the trammels of party, which mislead their judgement, and often constrain them to sacrifice the real well-being of the community and of themselves, to an apparent but most mistaken self-interest.

Nor to those termed heroes and conquerors, or to their followers; for their minds have been trained to consider the infliction of human misery, and the commission of military murders, a glorious duty, almost beyond reward.

Nor yet to the fashionable or splendid in their appearance; for these are from infancy trained to deceive and to be deceived, to accept shadows for substances, and to live a life of insincerity, and of consequent discontent and misery.

Still less are they to be exclusively submitted to the official expounders and defenders of the various opposing religious systems throughout the world; for many of these are actively engaged in propagating imaginary notions, which cannot fail to vitiate the rational powers of man, and to perpetuate his misery.

These principles, therefore, and the practical systems which they recommend, are not to be submitted to the judgement of those who have been trained under, and continue in, any of these unhappy combinations of circumstances. But they are to be submitted to the dispassionate and patient investigation and decision of those individuals of every rank and class and denomination of society, who have become in some degree conscious of the errors in which they exist; who have felt the thick mental darkness by which they are surrounded; who are ardently desirous of discovering and following truth wherever it may lead; and who can perceive the inseparable connection which exists between individual and general, between private and public good!

It has been said, and it is now repeated, that these principles, thus combined, will prove themselves unerringly true against the most insidious or open attack; and, ere long, they will, by their irresistible truth, pervade society to the utmost bounds of the earth; for 'silence will not retard their progress, and opposition will give increased celerity to their movements'. When they shall have dissipated in some degree, as they speedily will dissipate, the thick darkness in which the human mind has been and is still enveloped, the endless

[a] The 1st edn adds: 'Nor yet are they to be submitted to the mere men of the law; for they are necessarily trained to endeavour to make wrong appear right, or involve both in a maze of intricacies, and to legalize injustice'.

beneficial consequences which must follow the general introduction of them into practice may then be explained in greater detail, and urged upon minds to which they will then appear less questionable.

In the meantime we shall proceed to state, in a Fourth Essay, of what improvements the present state of the British population is susceptible in practice.

FOURTH ESSAY

The Principles of the Former Essays applied to Government

> It is beyond all comparison better to prevent than to punish crime. A system of government therefore which shall prevent ignorance, and consequently crime, will be infinitely superior to one, which, by encouraging the first, creates a necessity for the last, and afterwards inflicts punishment on both.

The end of government is to make the governed and the governors happy.

That government, then, is the best, which in practice produces the greatest happiness to the greatest number; including those who govern, and those who obey.

In a former Essay we said, and it admits of practical demonstration, that by adopting the proper means, man may by degrees be trained to live in any part of the world without poverty, without crime, and without punishment; for all these are the effects of error in the various systems of training and governing – error proceeding from very gross ignorance of human nature.

It is of primary importance to make this ignorance manifest, and to show what are the means which are endowed with that transcendent efficacy.

We have also said that man may be trained to acquire any sentiments and habits, or any character; and no one now, possessing pretensions to the knowledge of human nature, will deny that the government of any independent community may form the individuals of that community into the best, or into the worst characters.

If there be one duty therefore more imperative than another, on the government of every country, it is, that it should adopt, without delay, the proper means to form those sentiments and habits in the people, which shall give the most permanent and substantial advantages to the individuals and to the community.

Survey the acquirements of the earliest ages; trace the progress of those acquirements, through all the subsequent periods, to the present hour; and say if there be anything of real value in them, except that which contributes in practice to increase the happiness of the world.

And yet, with all the parade of learning contained in the myriads of volumes which have been written, and which still daily pour from the press, the knowledge of the first step of the progress which leads to human happiness remains yet unknown or disregarded by the mass of mankind.

The important knowledge to which we allude is, 'That the old collectively may train the young collectively, to be ignorant and miserable, or to be intelligent and happy.' And, on investigation, this will be found to be one of those simple yet grand laws of the universe, which experience discovers and confirms, and which, as soon as men become familiar with it, will no longer admit of denial or dispute. Fortunate will be that government which shall first acquire this knowledge in theory, and adopt it in practice.

To obtain its introduction into our own country first, a mode of procedure is now submitted to the immediate governing powers of the British Empire; and it is so submitted, with an ardent desire that it may undergo the most full and ample discussion, that if it shall, as on investigation it will, be found to be the only consistent and therefore rational, system of conducting human beings, it may be temperately and progressively introduced, instead of those defective national practices by which the state is now governed.

We therefore proceed to explain how this principle may now be introduced into practice, without injury to any part of society. For it is the time and manner of introducing this principle and its consequent practice, which alone constitute any difficulty.

This will appear evident when it is considered that although, from a plain statement of the most simple facts, the truth of the principle cannot fail to prove so obvious that no one will ever attempt openly to attack it; and although its adoption into practice will speedily accumulate benefits of which the world can now form no adequate conception; yet both theory and practice are to be introduced into a society trained and matured under principles that have impressed upon the individuals who compose it the most opposite habits and sentiments; which have been so entwined from infancy in their bodily and mental growth, that the simplicity and irresistible power of truth alone can disentangle them and expose their fallacy. It becomes then necessary, to prevent the evils of a too sudden change, that those who have been thus nursed in ignorance may be progressively removed from the abodes of mental darkness to the intellectual light which this principle cannot fail to produce. The light of true knowledge, therefore, must be first made to dawn on those dwellings of darkness, and afterwards gradually to increase, as it can be borne by the opening faculties of their inhabitants.

To proceed on this plan it becomes necessary to direct our attention to the actual state of the British population, to disclose the cause of those great and leading evils of which all now complain.

It will then be seen that the foundation on which these evils have been erected is ignorance, proceeding from the errors which have been impressed on the minds of the present generation by its predecessors; and chiefly by that *greatest of all errors, the notion that individuals form their own characters*. For while this most inconsistent, and therefore most absurd, of all human conceptions shall continue to be forced upon the young mind, there will remain no foundation whatever on which to build a sincere love and extended charity for man to his fellow creatures.

But destroy this hydra of human calamity, this immolator of every principle of rationality, this monster, which hitherto has effectually guarded every avenue that can lead to true benevolence and active kindness, and human happiness will be speedily established on a rock from whence it shall never more be removed.

This enemy of humanity may now be most easily destroyed. Let it be dragged forth from beneath the dark mysterious veil by which till now it has been hid from the eyes of the world; expose it but for an instant to the clear light of intellectual day; and, as though conscious of its own deformity, it will instantaneously vanish, never to reappear.

As a groundwork, then, of a rational system, let this absurd doctrine, and all the chain of consequences which follow from it, be withdrawn; and let that only be taught as sacred, which can be demonstrated by its never-failing consistency to be true.

This essential object being accomplished (and accomplished it must be before another step can be taken to form man into a rational being), the next is to withdraw those national laws which chiefly emanate from that erroneous doctrine, and which now exist in full vigour, training the population to almost every kind of crime. For these laws are, without chance of failure, adapted to produce a long train of crimes; which crimes are accordingly produced.

Some of the most prominent to which allusion is made, are such as encourage the consumption of ardent spirits, by fostering and extending those receptacles to seduce the ignorant and wretched, called gin-shops and pot-houses; those laws which sanction and legalize gambling among the poor, under the name of a state lottery; those which are insidiously destroying the real strength of the country, under the name of providing for the poor; and those of punishment, which, under the present irrational system of legislation, are supposed to be absolutely necessary to hold society together.

To prove the accuracy of this deduction, millions of facts exist around us, speaking in a language so clearly connected and audible, that it is scarcely credible any man can misunderstand it.

These facts proclaim aloud to the universe, that ignorance generates, fosters, and multiplies sentiments and actions which must produce private and public misery; and that when evils are experienced, instead of withdrawing the *cause* which created them, it invents and applies punishments, which, to a superficial observer, may appear to lessen the evils which afflict society, while, in reality, they greatly increase them.

Intelligence, on the contrary, traces to its source the cause of every evil which exists; adopts the proper measures to remove the *cause*; and then, with the most unerring confidence, rests satisfied that its object will be accomplished.

Thus then intelligence, or in other words plain unsophisticated reason, will consider the various sentiments and actions which now create misery in society, will patiently trace the cause whence those sentiments and actions proceed, and immediately apply the proper remedies to remove them.

And attention, thus directed, discovers that the cause of such sentiments and actions in the British population is the laws which have been enumerated, and others which shall be hereafter noticed.

To withdraw, therefore, the existing evils which afflict society, these unwise laws must be progressively repealed or modified. The British constitution, in its present outline, is admirably adapted to effect these changes, without the evils which always accompany a coerced or ill-prepared change.

As a preliminary step, however, to the commencement of national improvements, it should be declared with a sincerity which shall not admit of any after deviation, that no individual of the present generation should be deprived of the emolument which he now receives, or of that which has been officially or legally promised.

The next step in national reform is to withdraw from the national church those tenets which constitute its weakness and create its danger. Yet still, to prevent the evils of any premature change, let the church in other respects remain as it is; because under the old established forms it may effect the most valuable purposes.

To render it truly a national church, all tests, as they are called, that is, declarations of belief in which all cannot conscientiously join, should be withdrawn: this alteration would tend more perhaps than any other which can be devised, to give stability both to the national church and to the state; and a conduct thus rational would at once terminate all the theological differences which now confound the intellects of men and disseminate universal discord.

The next measure of national improvement should be to repeal or modify those laws which leave the lower orders in ignorance, train them to become intemperate, and produce idleness, gambling, poverty, disease, and murder. The production and consumption of ardent spirits are now legally encouraged; licences to keepers of gin-shops and unnecessary pot-houses are by thousands annually distributed; the laws of the state now direct those licences to be distributed; and yet, perhaps, not one of the authors or guardians of these laws has once reflected how much *each* of those houses daily contributes to public crime, disease, and weakness, or how much they add to the stock of private misery.

Shall we then continue to surround our fellow creatures with a temptation which, as many of them are now trained, we know they are unable to resist – with a temptation, too, which predisposes its victims to proceed gradually from a state of temporary insanity, into which they had been led by the example and instruction of those around them, to one of madness and bodily disease, creating more than infantile weakness, which again produces mental torments and horrors; that silently, yet most effectually, undermine every faculty in man which can contribute to private or public happiness?

Can the British government longer preserve such laws, or countenance a system which trains man to devise and enforce such laws?

(In the year 1736, an act of parliment – stat. 9, Geo. II., c. 23 – was passed, of which the preamble is as follows: 'Whereas the drinking of spirituous liquors or strong waters is become very common, especially among the people of lower and inferior rank, the constant and excessive use of which tends greatly to the destruction of their health, rendering them unfit for useful labour and business, debauching their morals, and inciting them to perpetrate all manner of vices; and the ill consequences of the excessive use of such liquors are not confined to the present generation, but extend to future ages, and tend to the devastation and ruin of this kingdom.' It was therefore enacted, that no person should retail spirits without a licence, for which £50 was to be paid annually, with other provisions to restrain the sale of spirits.

By a report of His Majesty's Justices of the Peace for the county of Middlesex, made in January, 1736, it appeared that there were then within Westminster, Holborn, the Tower, and Finsbury division – exclusive of London and Southwark – 7,044 houses and shops wherein spirituous liquors were publicly sold by retail, of which they had got an account, and that they believed it was far short of the true number.)[a]

Enough surely has been said to exhibit the evil consequences of these laws in their true colours. Let the duties therefore on the production of ardent spirits be gradually increased, until the price shall exceed the means of ordinary consumption. Let the licences be progressively withdrawn from the present occupiers of gin-shops and unnecessary pot-houses; and let the duties on the production and consumption of malt liquor be diminished, that the poor and working classes may be the more readily induced to abandon their destructive habits of dram-drinking, and by degrees to withdraw altogether from this incentive to crime and sure source of misery.

The next improvement should be to discontinue the state lottery.

The law which creates this measure is neither more nor less than a law to legalize gambling, entrap the unwary, and rob the ignorant.

How great must be the error of that system which can induce a state to deceive and injure its subjects, and yet expect that those subjects shall not be necessarily trained to injure and to deceive.

These measures may be thought detrimental to the national revenues.

Those who have reflected on the nature of public revenue, and who possess minds capable of comprehending the subject, know that revenue has but one legitimate source – that it is derived directly or indirectly from the labour of man, and that it may be more or less from any given number of men (other

---

[a] See *Reasons Humbly Offered to the Honourable House of Commons, for the Effectual Suppressing the Excessive Drinking of the Liquor Commonly Called Gin, or Compound Spirits* (?1736).

circumstances being similar), in proportion to their strength, industry, and capacity.

The efficient strength of a state governed by laws founded on an accurate knowledge of human nature, in which the whole population are well trained, will greatly exceed one of equal extent of numbers, in which a large part of the population are improperly trained, and governed by laws founded in ignorance.

Thus were the small states of Greece, while governed by laws comparatively wise, superior in national strength to the extended empire of Persia.

On this plain and obvious principle will the effective power and resources of the British empire be largely increased, by withdrawing those laws which, under the plausible appearance of adding a few, and but a few, millions to the annual revenues of this kingdom, in reality feed on the very vitals of the state. For such laws destroy the energies and capacities of its population, which, so weakened and trained to crime, requires a far greater expenditure to protect and govern it.

Confidently may it be said, that a short experience in practice is alone necessary to make the truth of these positions self-evident even to the most common understandings.

The next measure for the general improvement of the British population should be to revise the laws relative to the poor. For pure and benevolent as, no doubt, were the motives which actuated those with whom the Poor Laws originated, the direct and certain effects of these laws are to injure the poor, and through them, the state, as much almost as they can be injured.

They exhibit the appearance of affording aid to the distressed, while, in reality, they prepare the poor to acquire the worst habits, and to practise every kind of crime. They thus increase the number of the poor and add to their distress. It becomes, therefore, necessary that decisive and effectual measures should be adopted to remove those evils which the existing laws have created.

Benevolence says, that the destitute must not starve; and to this declaration political wisdom readily assents. Yet can that system be right, which compels the industrious, temperate, and comparatively virtuous, to support the ignorant, the idle, and comparatively vicious? Such, however, is the effect of the present British Poor Laws;[a] for they publicly proclaim greater encouragement to idleness, ignorance, extravagance, and intemperance, than to industry and good conduct: and the evils which arise from a system so irrational are hourly experienced, and hourly increasing.

It thus becomes necessary that some counteracting remedy be immediately devised and applied: for, injurious as these laws are, it is obviously impracticable,

[a] System of parish relief by which rates are levied to provide work and support for the poor. Its cost rose from c. £1.9 million in 1785 to £6.9 million in 1817.

in the present state of the British population, to annul at once a system to which so large a portion of the people has been taught to look for support.

These laws should be progressively undermined by a system of an opposite nature, and ultimately rendered altogether nugatory.

The proper system to supersede these laws has been in part already explained, but we proceed to unfold it still more. It may be called 'A System for the Prevention of Crime, and the Formation of Human Character' and, under an established and well-intentioned government it will be found more efficacious in producing public benefit than any of the laws now in existence.

The fundamental principle on which all these Essays proceed is, that 'children collectively may be taught any sentiments and habits' or, in other words, 'trained to acquire any character'.

It is of importance that *this principle should be for ever present in the mind, and that its truth should be established beyond even the shadow of doubt.* To the superficial observer it may appear to be an abstract truth of little value; but to the reflecting and accurate reasoner, it will speedily discover itself to be a power which ultimately must destroy the ignorance and consequent prejudices that have accumulated through all preceding ages.

For, as it is a deduction from all the leading facts in the past history of the world, so it will be found, on the most extensive investigation, to be consistent with every fact which now exists. It is calculated, therefore, to become the foundation of a new system, which, because true and of unparalleled importance, must prove irresistible, will speedily supersede all those which exist, and itself become permanent.

It is necessary, however, prior to the introduction of this system in all its bearings and consequences, that the public mind should be impressed with the deepest conviction of its truth.

For this purpose, let us in imagination survey the various states and empires of the world, and attentively observe man as in these arbitrary divisions of the earth he is known to exist.

Compare the national character of each community with the laws and customs by which they are respectively governed, and, without an exception, the one will be found the archetype of the other.

Where, in former ages, the laws and customs established by Lycurgus formed man into a model for martial exploits, and a perfect instrument for war, he is now trained, by other laws and customs, to be the instrument of a despotism which renders him almost, or altogether, unfit for war. And where the law and custom of Athens trained the young mind to acquire as high a degree of partial rationality as the history of preceding times records, man is now reduced, by a total change of laws and customs, to the lowest state of mental degradation. Also, where, formerly, the superior native American tribes roamed fearlessly through their trackless forests, uniformly exhibiting the hardy, penetrating, elevated, and sincere character, which was at a loss to comprehend how a rational being could desire to possess more than his nature could enjoy; now, on the very same soil, in the same climate, characters are formed under laws and customs so opposite, that all their bodily and mental faculties are individually exerted to obtain, if possible, ten thousand times more than any man can enjoy.

But why proceed to enumerate such endless results as these, of the never-failing influence of training over human nature, when it may be easily rendered self-evident even to the most illiterate, by daily examples around their own dwellings?

No one, it may be supposed, can now be so defective in knowledge as to imagine it is a different human nature, which by its own powers forms itself into a child of ignorance, of poverty, and of habits leading to crime and to punishment; or into a votary of fashion, claiming distinction from its folly and inconsistency; or, to fancy, that it is some undefined, blind, unconscious process of human nature itself, distinct from instruction, that forms the sentiments and habits of the man of commerce, of agriculture, the law, the church, the army, the navy, or of the private and illegal depredator on society: or that it is a different human nature which constitutes the societies of the Jews, of Friends, and of all the various religious denominations which have existed or which now exist. No! Human nature, save the minute differences which are ever found in all the compounds of the creation, is one and the same in all; it is without exception universally plastic, and by judicious training *the infants of any one class in the world may be readily formed into men of any other class, even to believe and declare that conduct to be right and virtuous, and to die in its defence, which their parents had been taught to believe and say was wrong and vicious, and to oppose which, those parents would also have willingly sacrificed their lives*.

Whence then the foundation of your claim, ye advocates for the superiority of the early prepossessions of your sect or party, in opposition to those taught to other men? Ignorance itself, at this day, might almost make it evident that one particle of merit is not due to you, for not possessing those notions and habits which you now the most contemn. Ought you not, and will you not, then, have charity for those who have been taught different sentiments and habits from yourselves? Let all men fairly investigate this subject for themselves; it well merits their most attentive examination. They will then discover that it is from the errors of education, misinstructing the young mind relative to the true cause of early prepossessions, that almost all the evils of life proceed.

Whence then, ye advocates for the merit and demerit of early prepossessions of opinion, do you derive your principles?

Let this system of misery be seen in all its naked deformity! It ought to be exposed; for the instruction which it inculcates at the outset of forming human character is destructive of the genuine charity which can alone train man to be truly benevolent to all other men. The ideas of exclusive right and consequent superiority which men have hitherto been taught to attach to the early sentiments and habits in which they have been instructed, are the chief cause of disunion throughout society; such notions are, indeed, in direct opposition to pure and undefiled religion; nor can they ever exist together. The extent of the misery which they generate cannot, however, be much longer concealed. They are already hastening fast to meet the fate of all errors; for the gross ignorance on which this system of misery has been raised, is exposed to the world on its proper foundation, and, so exposed, it supporters will shrink from the task of defence, and no rational mind will be found to give it support.

Having exhibited the error on which ignorance has erected the systems by which man has been governed, or compelled to become irrational and miserable; and having laid an immovable foundation for a system devoid of that error, which, when fully comprehended and adopted into practice, must train mankind 'to think of and act to others as they would wish others to think of and act to them', we proceed further to explain this *system without error*, and which may be termed a *system without mystery*. As then children collectively may be formed into any characters, by whom ought their characters to be formed?

The kind and degree of misery or happiness experienced by the members of any community, depend on the characters which have been formed in the individuals which constitute the community.

It becomes, then, the highest interest, and consequently the first and most important duty, of every state, to form the individual characters of which the state is composed. And if any characters, from the most ignorant and miserable to the most rational and happy, can be formed, it surely merits the deepest attention of every state to adopt those means by which the formation of the latter may be secured, and that of the former prevented.

It follows that every state, to be well governed, ought to direct its chief attention to the formation of character; and thus the best governed state will be that which shall possess the best national system of education.

Under the guidance of minds competent to its direction, a national system of training and education may be formed, to become the most safe, easy, effectual, and economical instrument of government that can be devised. And it may be made to possess a power equal to the accomplishment of the most grand and beneficial purposes.

It is, however, by instruction only, that the population of the world can be made conscious of the irrational state in which they now exist; and, until that instruction is given, it is premature to introduce a national system of education.

But the time is now arrived when the British Government may with safety adopt a national system of training and education for the poor and uninstructed; and this measure alone, if the plan shall be well devised and executed, will effect the most importantly beneficial changes.

As a preliminary step, however, it is necessary to observe, that to create a well-trained, united, and happy people, this national system should be uniform over the United Kingdom; it should be also founded in the spirit of peace and of rationality, and, for the most obvious reasons, the thought of exclusion to one child in the empire should not for a moment be entertained.

Several plans have been lately proposed for the national education of the poor, but these have not been calculated to effect all that a national system of education of the poor ought to accomplish.

For the authors and supporters of these systems we feel those sentiments which the principles developed throughout these Essays must create in any minds on which they have been early and effectually impressed; and we are desirous of rendering their labours for the community as extensively beneficial as they can be made. To fulfil, however, a great and important public duty, the plans which they have devised must be considered as though they had been produced and published in the days of antiquity.

The plans alluded to are those of the Rev. Dr Bell, Mr Joseph Lancaster, and Mr Whitbread.[a]

The systems of Dr Bell and Mr Lancaster, for instructing the poor in reading, writing, and arithmetic, prove the extreme ignorance which previously existed in the *manner* of training the young; for it is in the manner alone of giving instruction that these new systems are an improvement on the modes of instruction which were formerly practised.

The arrangement of the room and many of the details in Mr Lancaster's plan, are, in some respects, better calculated to give instruction in the elements enumerated, than those recommended by Dr Bell, although some of the details introduced by the latter are very superior, and highly deserving of adoption.

The essence, however, of national training and education is to impress on the young, ideas and habits which shall contribute to the future happiness of the individuals and of the state; and this can be accomplished only by instructing them to become rational beings.

It must be evident to common observers, that children may be taught, by either Dr Bell's or Mr Lancaster's system, to read, write, account, and sew, and yet acquire the worst habits, and have their minds rendered irrational for life.

Reading and writing are merely instruments by which knowledge either true or false, may be imparted; and, when given to children, are of little comparative value, unless they are also taught how to make a proper use of them.

When a child receives a full and fair explanation of the objects and characters around him, and when he is also taught to reason correctly, so that he may learn to discover general truths from falsehood, he will be much better instructed,

[a] Samuel Whitbread (1758–1815): poor law reformer, anti-slavery advocate, Whig MP.

although without the knowledge of one letter or figure, than those are who have been compelled to *believe*, and whose reasoning faculties have been confounded or destroyed by what is most erroneously termed learning.

It is readily acknowledged that the manner of instructing children is of importance and deserves all the attention it has lately received; that those who discover or introduce improvements which facilitate the acquirement of knowledge are important benefactors of their fellow creatures. Yet the *manner* of giving instruction is one thing, the *instruction itself* another; and no two objects can be more distinct. The *worst* manner may be applied to give the *best* instruction, and the *best* manner to give the *worst* instruction. Were the real importance of both to be estimated by numbers, the manner of instruction may be compared to one, and the matter of instruction to millions: the first is the means only; the last, the end to be accomplished by those means.

If, therefore, in a national system of education for the poor, it be desirable to adopt the best *manner*, it is surely so much the more desirable to adopt also the best *matter*, of instruction.

Either give the poor a rational and useful training, or mock not their ignorance, their poverty, and their misery, by merely instructing them to become conscious of the extent of the degradation under which they exist. And, therefore, in pity to suffering humanity, either keep the poor, if you now can, in the state of the most abject ignorance, as near as possible to animal life, or at once determine to form them into rational beings, into useful and effective members of the state.

Were it possible, without national prejudice, to examine into the matter of instruction which is now given in some of our boasted new systems for the instruction of the poor, it would be found to be almost as wretched as any which can be devised. In proof of this statement, enter any one of the schools denominated national,[a] and request the master to show the acquirements of the children. These are called out, and he asks them theological questions to which men of the most profound erudition cannot make a rational reply; the children, however, readily answer as they had been previously instructed; for memory, in this mockery of learning, is all that is required.

Thus the child whose natural faculty of comparing ideas, or whose rational powers, shall be the soonest destroyed, if, at the same time, he possess a memory to retain incongruities without connection, will become what is termed the first scholar in the class; and three-fourths of the time which ought to be devoted to the acquirement of useful instruction, will be really occupied in destroying the mental powers of the children.

To those accustomed attentively to notice the human countenance from infancy to age, in the various classes and religious denominations of the British

---

See the *First Annual Report of the National Society for Promoting the Education of the Poor in the Principles of the Established Church* (1812). The Society was founded in 1811.

population, it is truly an instructive although melancholy employment, to observe in the countenances of the poor children in these schools the evident expression of mental injury derived from the well-intentioned, but most mistaken, plan of their instruction.

It is an important lesson, because it affords another recent and striking example to the millions which previously existed, of the ease with which children may be taught to receive any sectarian notions, and thence acquire any habits, however contrary to their real happiness.[a]

To those trained to become truly conscientious in any of the present sectarian errors which distract the world, this free exposure of the weakness of the peculiar tenets in which such individuals have been instructed, will, at first, excite feelings of high displeasure and horror, and these feelings will be acute and poignant in proportion to the obvious and irresistible evidence on which the disclosure of their errors is founded.

Let them, however, begin to think calmly on these subjects, to examine their own minds and the minds of all around them, and they will become conscious of the absurdities and inconsistencies in which their forefathers have trained them; they will then abhor the errors by which they have been so long abused; and, with an earnestness not to be resisted, they will exert their utmost faculties to remove the cause of so much misery to man.

Enough surely has now been said of the manner and matter of instruction in these new systems, to exhibit them in a just and true light.

The improvements in the manner of teaching children whatever may be deemed proper for them to learn – improvements which, we may easily predict, will soon receive great additions and amendments – have proceeded from the Rev. Dr Bell and Mr Lancaster; while the errors which their respective systems assist to engrave on the ductile mind of infancy and childhood, are derived from times when ignorance gave countenance to every kind of absurdity.

Mr Whitbread's scheme for the education of the poor was evidently the production of an ardent mind possessing considerable abilities; his mind, however, had been irregularly formed by the errors of his early education; and this was most conspicuous in the speech which introduced the plan he had devised to the House of Commons, and in the plan itself.

The first was a clear exposition of all the reasons for the education of the poor which could be expected from a human being trained from infancy under the systems in which Mr Whitbread had been instructed.

The plan itself evinced the fallacy of the principles which he had imbibed, and showed that he had not acquired a practical knowledge of the feelings and

[a] The 1st edn adds:

In the Lancastrian system the children are instructed in fewer of these errors, and they are consequently left somewhat more at liberty to be trained in the pure, rational, and genuine principles of religion; and it therefore possesses a fair claim to preference.

habits of the poor, or of the only effectual means by which they could be trained to be useful to themselves and to the community.

Had Mr Whitbread not been trained, as almost all the Members of both Houses of Parliament have been, in delusive theories, devoid of rational foundation, which prevent them from acquiring any extensive practical knowledge of human nature, he would not have committed a plan for the national education of the poor to the sole management and direction of the ministers, churchwardens, and overseers of parishes, whose present interests must have appeared to be opposed to the measure.[a]

He would surely, first, have devised a plan to make it the evident interest of the ministers, churchwardens, and overseers, to co-operate in giving efficacy to the system which he wished to introduce to their superintendence; and also to render them, by previous training, competent to that superintendence for which now they are in general unprepared. For, trained as these individuals have hitherto been, they must be deficient in the practical knowledge necessary to enable them successfully to direct the instruction of others; and had an attempt been made to carry Mr Whitbread's plan into execution, it would have created a scene of confusion over the whole kingdom.[b]

Attention to the subject will make it evident that it never was, and that it never can be, the interest of any sect claiming exclusive privileges on account of professing high and mysterious doctrines, about which the best and most conscientious men may differ in opinion, that the mass of the people should be otherwise instructed than in those doctrines which were and are in unison with its peculiar tenets; and that at this hour a national system of education for the lower orders, on sound political principles, is really dreaded, even by some of the most learned and intelligent members of the Church of England. Such feelings in the members of the national church are those only which ought to be expected; for most men so trained and circumstanced must of necessity acquire these feelings. Why, therefore, should any class of men endeavour to rouse the indignation of the public against them? Their conduct and their motives are equally correct, and therefore, equally good, with those who raise the cry against and oppose the errors of the church. And let it ever be remembered, that an establishment which possesses the power of propagating principles, may be rendered truly valuable when directed to inculcate a system of self-evident truth, unobstructed by inconsistencies and counteractions.

The dignitaries of the church, and their adherents, foresaw that a national system for the education of the poor, unless it were placed under the immediate

[a] See Samuel Whitbread, *Substance of a Speech on the Poor Laws* (1807).

[b] The 1st edn adds:

Mr. Whitbread, now that he has had time to reconsider the subject, may, it is probable, acquiesce in the truth of these remarks, and in that case his cordial and ardent co-operation in the proceedings to be recommended is confidently anticipated.

influence and management of individuals belonging to the church, would effectually and rapidly undermine the errors, not only of their own, but of every other ecclesiastical establishment. In this foresight they evinced the superiority of their penetration over the sectaries by whom the unexclusive system is supported. The heads of the church have wisely discovered that reason and inconsistency cannot long exist together; that the one must inevitably destroy the other, and reign paramount. They have witnessed the regular, and latterly the rapid progress which reason has made; they know that its accumulating strength cannot be much longer resisted; and, as they now see the contest is hopeless, the unsuccessful attempt to destroy the Lancastrian system of education is the last effort they will ever make to counteract the dissemination of knowledge which is now widely extending itself in every direction.

The establishment of the Rev. Dr Bell's system of initiating the children of the poor in all the tenets of the Church of England, is an attempt to ward off a little longer the yet dreaded period of a change from ignorance to reason, from misery to happiness.

Let us, however, not attempt impossibilities; the task is vain and hopeless; the Church, while it adheres to the defective and injurious parts of its system, cannot be induced to act cordially in opposition to its apparent interests.

The principles here advocated will not admit the application of any deception to any class of men; they countenance no proceedings in practice, but of unlimited sincerity and candour. They give rise to no one sentiment which is not in unison with the happiness of the human race; and they impart knowledge, which renders it evident that such happiness can never be acquired until every particle of falsehood and deception shall be eradicated from the instructions which the old force upon the young.

Let us then in this spirit openly declare to the Church, that a national unexclusive plan of education for the poor will, without the shadow of doubt, destroy all the errors which are attached to the various systems; and that, when this plan shall be fully established, not one of the tenets which is in opposition to facts can long be upheld.

This unexclusive system for the education of the poor has gone forth, and, having found a resting place in the minds of its supporters, it will never more return even to the control of its projectors; but it will be speedily so improved, that by rapidly increasing strides it will firmly establish the reign of reason and happiness.

Seeing and knowing this, let us also make it equally evident to the Church – warn it of its actual state – cordially and sincerely assist its members quietly to withdraw those inconsistencies from the system, which now create its weakness and its danger; that it may retain those rational principles alone which can be successfully defended against attack, or which rather will prevent any attack from being attempted, or even meditated.

The wise and prudent, then, of all parties, instead of wishing to destroy national establishments, will use their utmost exertions to render them so consistent and reasonable in all their parts, that every well-disposed mind may be induced to give them their hearty and willing support.

For the first grand step towards effecting any substantial improvement in these realms, without injury to any part of the community, is to make it the clear and decided interest of the Church to co-operate cordially in all the projected ameliorations. Once found a national church on the true, unlimited, and genuine principles of mental charity, and all the members of the state will soon improve in every truly valuable quality. If the temperate and discerning of all parties will not now lend their aid to effect this change by peaceable means (which may with the greatest ease and with unerring certainty be done), it is evident to every calm observer, that the struggle by those who now exist in unnecessary misery, to attain that degree of happiness which they may attain in practice, cannot long be deferred. It will therefore prove true political wisdom to anticipate and guide these feelings.

To those who can reflect and will attend to the passing scenes before them, the times are indeed awfully interesting; some change of high import, scarcely yet perhaps to be scanned by the present ill-taught race of men, is evidently in progress: in consequence, well-founded, prompt, and decisive measures are now required in the British councils, to direct this change, and to relieve the nation from the errors of its present systems.

It must surely then be the desire of every rational man, of every true friend to humanity, that a cordial co-operation and unity of action should be affected between the British Executive, the Parliament, the Church, and the People, to lay a broad and firm foundation for the future happiness of themselves and the world.

Say not, my countrymen, that such an event is impracticable; for, by adopting the evident means to form a rational character in man, there is a plain and direct road opened, which, if pursued, will render its accomplishment not only possible but certain. That road, too, will be found the most safe and pleasant that human beings have ever yet travelled. It leads direct to intelligence and true knowledge, and will show the boasted acquirements of Greece, of Rome, and of all antiquity, to be the mere weakness of mental infancy. Those who travel this road will find it so straight and well defined, that no one will be in danger of wandering from the right course. Nor is it yet a narrow or exclusive path; it admits of no exclusion: every colour of body and diversity of mind are freely and alike admitted. It is open to the human race, and it is broad and spacious enough to receive the whole, were they increased a thousandfold.

We well know that a declaration like the one now made must sound chimerical in the ears of those who have hitherto wandered in the dark mazes of ignorance, error, and exclusion, and who have been taught folly and inconsistencies only from their cradle.

But if every known fact connected with the subject proves that, from the day in which man first saw light to that in which the sun now shines, the old collectively have taught the young collectively the sentiments and habits which the young have acquired; and that the present generation and every following generation must in like manner instruct their successors; then do we say, with a confidence founded on certainty itself, that even much more shall come to pass than has yet been foretold or promised.[a] When these principles, derived from the unchangeable laws of nature, and equally revealed to all men, shall, as soon as they will, be publicly established in the world, no conceivable obstacle can remain to prevent a sincere and cordial union and co-operation for every wise and good purpose, not only among all the members of the same state, but also among the rulers of those kingdoms and empires whose enmity and rancour against each other have been carried to the utmost stretch of melancholy folly, and even occasionally to a high degree of madness.

Such, my fellow men, are some, and yet but a few, of the mighty consequences which must result from the public acknowledgement of these plain, simple, and irresistible truths. They will not prove a delusive promise of mockery, but will in reality speedily and effectively establish peace, goodwill, and an ever-active benevolence throughout the whole human race.

The public avowal of these principles, and their general introduction into practice, will constitute the invaluable secret, for which the human mind, from its birth, has been in perpetual search; its future beneficial consequences no man can yet foresee.

We will now show how these principles may be immediately and most advantageously introduced into general practice.

It has been said that 'the state which shall possess the best national system of education, will be the best governed'; and if the principle on which the reasoning of these Essays is founded be true, then is that sentiment also true. Yet (will future ages credit the fact?) to this day the British Government is without any national system of training and education even for its millions of poor and uninstructed!! The formation of the mind and habits of its subjects is permitted to go on at random, often in the hands of those who are the most incompetent in the empire; and the result is, the gross ignorance and disunion which now everywhere abound!!

(Even the recent attempts which have been made are conducted on the narrow principle of debasing man to a mere irrational military machine which is to be rapidly moved by animal force.)

Instead of continuing such unwise proceedings, a national system for the training and education of the labouring classes ought to be immediately

[a] See Mark 13:23.

arranged; and, if judiciously devised, it may be rendered the most valuable improvement ever yet introduced into practice.

For this purpose an act should be passed for the instruction of all the poor and labouring classes in the three kingdoms.

In this act, provision should be made:

First – For the appointment of proper persons to direct this new department of government, which will be found ultimately to prove the most important of all its departments; consequently, those individuals who possess the highest integrity, abilities, and influence in the state, should be appointed to its direction.

Second – For the establishment of seminaries in which those individuals who shall be destined to form the minds and bodies of the future subjects of these realms should be well initiated in the art and matter of instruction.

This is, and ought to be considered, an office of the greatest practical trust and confidence in the empire; for let this duty be well performed, and the government must proceed with ease to the people and with high gratification to those who govern.

At present there are not any individuals in the kingdom who have been trained to instruct the rising generation as it is for the interest and happiness of all that it should be instructed. The training of those who are to form the future man, becomes a consideration of the utmost magnitude; for, on due reflection, it will appear, that instruction to the young must be, of necessity, the only foundation upon which the superstructure of society can be raised. Let this instruction continue to be left, as heretofore, to chance, and often to the most inefficient members of the community, and society must still experience the endless miseries which still arise from such weak and puerile conduct. On the contrary, let the instruction to the young be well devised and well executed, and no subsequent proceedings in the state can be materially injurious. For it may truly be said to be a wonder-working power; one that merits the deepest attention of the legislature; with ease it may be used to train man into a demon of mischief to himself and to all around him, or into an agent of unlimited benevolence.

Third – For the establishment of seminaries over the United Kingdoms; to be conveniently placed, and of sufficient extent to receive all those who require instruction.

Fourth – For supplying the requisite expenditure for the building and support of those seminaries.

Fifth – For the arrangement of the plan which, for the manner of instruction, upon a due comparison of the various modes now in practice, or which may be devised, shall appear to be the best.

[a] The 1st edn adds: 'to the whole human race'.

Sixth – For the appointment of proper masters to each of the schools. And,

Last – The matter of instruction, both for body and mind, in these seminaries, should be substantially beneficial to the individuals and to the state. For this is, or ought to be, the sole motive for the establishment of national seminaries.

These are the outlines of the provisions necessary to prepare the most powerful instrument of good that has ever yet been placed in the hands of man.

The last national improvement which remains to be proposed in the present state of the public mind, is, that another legislative act should be passed, for the purpose of obtaining regular and accurate information relative to the value of and demand for labour over the United Kingdoms. This information is necessary, preparatory to the adoption of measures which will be proposed, to provide labour for those who may be occasionally unable to procure other employment.

In this act provision should be made, to obtain accurate quarterly returns of the state of labour in each country or smaller district; the returns to be made either by the clergy, justices of the peace, or other more competent persons. These returns should contain,

First – The average price of manual labour within the district for the period included in the return.

Second – The number of those in each district who depend on their daily labour or on the parish for their support; and who may be at the period of these returns unemployed, and yet able to labour.

Third – The number of those who, at the period of each return, are but partially employed; and the extent of that partial employment.

Provisions should also be made to obtain a statement of the general occupations in which the individuals had been formerly employed, with the best conjectures as to the kind and quantity of work which each may be supposed still capable of performing.

The want of due attention to this highly necessary branch of government, occasions thousands of our fellow subjects to be made wretched; while, from the same cause, the revenues of the empire are annually deteriorated to an enormous amount.

We have stated, because it is easy of proof, that the revenues of all countries are derived directly or indirectly, from the labour of man; and yet the British Government, which, with all its errors, is among the best devised and most enlightened that has hitherto been established, makes extravagant and unnecessary waste of that labour. It makes this waste, too, in the midst of its greatest pecuniary difficulties, and when the utmost efforts of every individual in the state are requisite!

This waste of human labour, as it is highly unjust to all, is not only impolitic in a national view, but is most cruel to the individuals who, in consequence of this waste, are the immediate sufferers.

It would be an Herculean task to trace through all their ramifications the various injurious effects which result from the fundamental errors by which man has been, and is governed; nor is the world yet fully prepared for such development. We shall, therefore, now merely sketch some of the most direct and palpable of these effects, relative of the oversight of governments in regard to the non-application or misapplication of the labour of the poor and unoccupied.

It has been shown that the governing powers of any country may easily and economically give the subjects just sentiments and the best habits; and so long as this shall remain unattempted, governments will continue to neglect their most important duties as well as interests. Such neglect now exists in Britain, where, in lieu of the governing powers making any effort to attain these inestimable benefits for the individuals belonging to the empire, they must content themselves with the existence of laws which must create sentiments and habits highly injurious to the welfare of the individuals and of the state.

Many of these laws, by their never-failing effects, speak in a language which no one can misunderstand, and say to the unprotected and untaught, '*Remain in ignorance, and let your labour be directed by that ignorance; for while you can procure what is sufficient to support life by such labour, although that life should be an existence in abject poverty, disease, and misery, we will not trouble ourselves with you, or any of your proceedings; when, however, you can no longer procure work, or obtain the means to support nature, then apply for relief to the parish, and you shall be maintained in idleness.*'

And in ignorance and idleness, even in this country, where manual labour is or always might be made valuable, hundreds of thousands of men, women, and children are daily supported. No one acquainted with human nature will suppose that men, women, and children, can be long maintained in ignorance and idleness, without becoming habituated to crime.

(It would, perhaps, prove an interesting calculation, and useful to government, to estimate how much its finances would be improved by giving proper employment to a million of its subjects, rather than by supporting that million in ignorance, idleness, and crime.

Will it exceed the bounds of moderation to say, that a million of the population so employed, under the direction of an intelligent government, might earn to the state ten pounds each annually, or ten millions sterling per annum? Ten millions per year would be obtained, by each individual earning less than four shillings per week; and any part of the population of these kingdoms, including within the average the too young and the too old for labour, may be made to earn, under proper arrangements, more than four shillings per week to the state, besides creating an innumerable train of other more beneficial consequences.)

Why, then, are there any idle poor in these kingdoms? Solely because so large a part of the population have been permitted to grow up to manhood in gross ignorance; and because, when they are, or easily may be trained to be willing to labour, useful and productive employment has not been provided for them.

All men may, by judicious and proper laws and training, readily acquire knowledge and habits which will enable them, if they be permitted, to produce far more than they need for their support and enjoyment: and thus any population, in the fertile parts of the earth, may be taught to live in plenty and in happiness, without the checks of vice and misery.

Mr Malthus[a] is, however, correct, when he says that the population of the world is ever adapting itself to the quantity of food raised for its support; but he has not told us how much more food an intelligent and industrious people will create from the same soil, than will be produced by one ignorant and ill-governed. It is, however, as one to infinity.

For man knows not the limit to his power of creating food. How much has this power been latterly increased in these islands! And in them such knowledge is in its infancy. Yet compare even this power of raising food with the efforts of the Bosgemens[b] or other savages, and it will be found, perhaps, as one to a thousand.

Food for man may also be considered as a compound of the original elements, of the qualities, combinations, and control of which, chemistry is daily adding to our knowledge; nor is it yet for man to say to what this knowledge may lead, or where it may end.

The sea, it may be remarked also, affords an inexhaustible source of food. It may then be safely asserted that the population of the world may be allowed naturally to increase for many thousand years; and yet, under a system of government founded on the principles for the truth of which we contend, the whole may continue to live in abundance and happiness, without one check of vice or misery; and under the guidance of these principles, human labour, properly directed, may be made far more than sufficient to enable the population of the world to live in the highest state of human enjoyment.

Shall we then continue to allow misery to predominate, and the labour of man to be most absurdly applied or wasted, when it might be easily directed to remove that misery?

The labour of every man, woman, and child, possessing sufficient bodily strength, may be advantageously employed for the public; and there is not, perhaps, a stronger evidence of the extreme ignorance and fallacy of the systems which have hitherto governed the world, than that the rich, the

[a] Thomas Robert Malthus (1766–1834): opponent of Condorcet, Godwin and later Owen, author of the immensely influential *Essay on Population* (1798), which argued that population always grew to the means of subsistence, and could be restrained only by want or the prudent marriage of the poor.

[b] 'Hottentot' tribe native to the Cape of Good Hope.

active, and the powerful, should, by tacit consent, support the ignorant in idleness and crime, without making the attempt to train them into industrious, intelligent, and valuable members of the community; although the means by which the change could be easily effected have been always at their command!

It is not, however, intended to propose that the British Government should now give direct employment to all its working population. On the contrary, it is confidently expected that a national system for the training and education of the poor and lower orders will be so effectual, that ere long they will all find employment sufficient to support themselves, except in cases of great sudden depression in the demand for, and consequent depreciation in the value of, labour.

To prevent the crime and misery which ever follow these unfavourable fluctuations in the demand for and value of labour, it ought to be a primary duty of every government that sincerely interests itself in the well-being of its subjects, to provide perpetual employment of real national utility, in which all who apply may be immediately occupied.

In order that those only who could not obtain employment from private individuals should be induced to avail themselves of these national works, the rate of the public labour might be in general fixed at some proportion less than the average rate of private labour in the district in which such public labour should be performed. These rates might be readily ascertained and fixed, by reference to the county or district quarterly returns of the average rate of labour.

This measure, judiciously managed, would have a similar effect on the price of labour, that the sinking fund produces on the Stock Exchange; and, as the price of public labour should never fall below the means of temperate existence, the plan proposed would perpetually tend to prevent an excess of nationally injurious pressure on the most unprotected part of society.

The most obvious, and, in the first place, the best source, perhaps, of employment, would be the making and repairing of roads. Such employment would be perpetual over the whole kingdom; and it will be found true national economy to keep the public roads at all times in a much higher state of repair than, perhaps, any of them are at present. If requisite, canals, harbours, docks, shipbuilding, and materials for the navy, may be afterwards resorted to; it is not, however, supposed that many of the latter resources would be necessary.

A persevering attention, without which, indeed, not anything beneficial in practice can ever be attained, will soon overcome all the difficulties which may at first appear to obstruct this plan for introducing occasional national employment into the polity of the kingdom.

In times of very limited demand for labour, it is truly lamentable to witness the distress which arises among the industrious for want of regular employment and their customary wages. In these periods, innumerable applications are made to the superintendents of extensive manual operations, to obtain any kind of employment by which a subsistence may be procured. Such applications are often made by persons who, in search of work, have travelled from one extremity of the island to the other!

During these attempts to be useful and honest, in the common acceptation of the terms, the families of such wandering individuals accompany them, or remain at home; in either case they generally experience sufferings and privations which the gay and splendid will hesitate to believe it possible that human nature could endure.

Yet, after this extended and anxious endeavour to procure employment, the applicant often returns unsuccessful; he cannot, by his most strenuous exertions, procure an honest and independent existence; therefore, with intentions perhaps as good, and a mind as capable of great and benevolent actions as the remainder of his fellow men, he has no other resources left but to starve, apply to his parish for relief, and thus suffer the greatest degradation, or rely on his own native exertions, and, to supply himself and family with bread, resort to what are termed dishonest means.

Some minds thus circumstanced are so delicately formed, that they will not accept the one or adopt the other of the two latter modes to sustain life, and in consequence they actually starve. These, however, it is to be hoped, are not very numerous. But the number is undoubtedly great, of those whose health is ruined by bad and insufficient food, clothing, and shelter; who contract lingering diseases, and suffer premature death, the effect of partial starvation.

The most ignorant and least enterprising of them apply to the parish for support; soon lose the desire of exertion; become permanently dependent; conscious of their degradation in society; and henceforward, with their offspring, remain a burden and grievous evil to the state; while those among this class who yet possess strength and energy of body and mind, with some undestroyed powers of reasoning, perceive, in part, the glaring errors and injustice of society towards themselves and their fellow sufferers.

Can it then create surprise that feelings like those described should force human nature to endeavour to retaliate?

Multitudes of our fellow men are so goaded by these reflections and circumstances, as to be urged, even while incessantly and closely pursued by legal death almost without a chance of escape, to resist those laws under which they suffer; and thus the private depredator on society is formed, fostered, and matured.

Shall we then longer withhold national instruction from our fellow men, who, it has been shown, might easily be trained to be industrious, intelligent, virtuous, and valuable members of the state?

True, indeed, it is, that all the measures now proposed are only a compromise with the errors of the present systems; but as these errors now almost universally exist, and must be overcome solely by the force of reason; and as reason, to effect the most beneficial purposes, makes her advance by slow degrees, and progressively substantiates one truth of high import after another, it will be evident, to minds of comprehensive and accurate thought, that by these and similar compromises alone can success be rationally expected in practice. For such compromises bring truth and error before the public; and whenever they are fairly exhibited together, truth must ultimately prevail.

As many of the inconsistencies of the present systems are evident to the most intelligent and well-disposed minds, the way for the public admission of the important truths which have now been in part unfolded seems to be rendered easy; and it is confidently expected that the period is at hand, when man, through ignorance, shall not much longer inflict unnecessary misery on man; because the mass of mankind will become enlightened, and will clearly discern that by so acting they will inevitably create misery to themselves.

(As soon as the public mind shall be sufficiently prepared to receive it, the practical detail of this system shall be fully developed.)

For the extensive knowledge of the facts which present themselves on the globe, makes it evident to those whose reasoning faculties have not been entirely paralysed, that all mankind firmly believe, that everybody except themselves has been grievously deceived in his fundamental principles; and feel the utmost astonishment that the nations of the world could embrace such gross inconsistencies for divine or political truths. Most persons are now also prepared to understand, that these weaknesses are firmly and conscientiously fixed in the minds of millions, who, when born, possessed equal faculties with themselves. And although they plainly discern in others what they deem inconceivable aberrations of the mental powers, yet, in despite of such facts, they are taught to believe that they themselves could not have been so deceived; and this impression is made upon the infant mind with the greatest ease, whether it be to create followers of the most ignorant, or of the most enlightened systems.

The inhabitants of the world are, therefore, abundantly conscious of the inconsistencies contained in those systems in which all have been trained out of the pale of their own peculiar, and, as they are taught to believe, highly favoured sect: and yet the number of the largest sect in the world is small, when compared with the remaining sects which have been instructed to think the notions of that larger division an error of the grossest kind, proceeding alone from the ignorance or deception of their predecessors.

All that is now requisite, previous to withdrawing the last mental bandage by which hitherto the human race has been kept in darkness and misery, is, by calm and patient reasoning to tranquillize the public mind, and thus prevent the evil effects which otherwise might arise from the too sudden prospect of freely enjoying rational liberty of mind.

To withdraw that bandage without danger, reason must be judiciously applied to lead men of every sect (for all have been in part abused), to reflect that if untold myriads of beings, formed like themselves, have been so grossly deceived as they believe them to have been, what power in nature was there to prevent *them* from being equally deceived?

Such reflections, steadily pursued by those who are anxious to follow the plain and simple path of reason, will soon make it obvious that the inconsistencies which they behold in all other sects *out of their own pale*, are precisely similar to those which all other sects can readily discover *within that pale*.

It is not, however, to be imagined, that this free and open exposure of the gross errors in which the existing generation has been instructed, should be forthwith palatable to the world; it would be contrary to reason to form any such expectations.

Yet, as evil exists, and as man cannot be rational, nor of course happy, until the cause of it shall be removed; the writer, like a physician who feels the deepest interest in the welfare of his patient, has hitherto administered of this unpalatable restorative the smallest quantity which he deemed sufficient for the purpose. He now waits to see the effects which that may produce.

Should the application not prove of sufficient strength to remove the mental disorder, he promises that it shall be increased, until sound health to the public mind be firmly and permanently established.

OBSERVATIONS ON THE COTTON TRADE, WITH A VIEW TO THE INTENDED APPLICATION TO PARLIAMENT FOR A REPEAL OF THE DUTY ON THE IMPORTATION OF COTTON WOOL
1815

To the Editor of the Glasgow Chronicle

SIR,

Having attended the meeting of Cotton Spinners, Cotton Manufacturers, and others interested in the trade and manufacture of cotton wool, held in the city of Glasgow on Wednesday last, by special requisition to the Lord Provost,[a] and having taken a different view of the subject which was submitted to the meeting from any of the gentlemen present, I request you to insert the following Statement, which explains the ideas impressed on my mind by an attentive consideration of this important business. It is the same I took the liberty of stating to the meeting.

I am Sir,

Your obedient servant,

ROBERT OWEN

New Lanark, 27th January, 1815

MY LORD,

The subject which is to engage the attention of the meeting is one of deep interest, not only to those who are immediately engaged in the cotton trade, but to every member of the community; it is one of great national importance, and it is in this view I now intend to consider it.

Little more than half a century has elapsed since, it may be said, the cotton trade commenced in this country; it is now the most considerable in the kingdom, and its ramifications extend through every part of the British Empire.

---

[a] Henry Monteith (c. 1764–1848), who was elected in October 1814, re-elected in October 1815, and later became MP for Carstairs.

It is worthy of remark that this astonishing increase has taken place not only without the aid of Government, but even against national oppression; for can a duty on the importation of a raw material which may be obtained by every nation in the world, be called anything less than a national oppression?

During this period the linen trade, although aided by bounties, has gradually diminished. The wollen trade, although unaided by bounties, has not been oppressed by duties, yet it has remained nearly stationary.

The varied qualities of cotton enable the manufacturer of it to form fabrics of every texture for clothing and furniture, from the most cool, light, and airy, to that which is almost impervious to cold. It can be produced cheaper than wool, flax, or hemp, and manufactured more easily than either. From these circumstances it may be inferred that cotton is destined to become the common clothing of mankind.

We may hence infer, that in whatever country the cotton manufacture shall finally prevail, there also may be found the greatest political power.

Hitherto, in consequence of the conflict of contenting nations for their political existence, we have had no competitors in this manufacture that could materially retard its progress. But this conflict is now terminated; peace pervades the Continent of Europe; and I trust, ere long we shall receive intelligence of the ratification of peace between the British Empire and America. We must, however, now prepare for a new rivalry – a rivalry in arts and manufactures; and as the political importance of the cotton trade is already duly appreciated in every state in Europe, from seeing and feeling the effects of the wealth and power which it has created in this country, we may rest assured that all means will be used by those States to participate in its advantages, and that each Government will willingly render its subjects every assistance to procure some share of its benefits. Favoured by our exclusion so long from the Continent, this trade has already made a progress in France, Switzerland, and Germany, that will scarcely be credited by those unacquainted with the business.

Is it then wise in our Legislators to aid the views and wishes of our rivals, to do all they can to withdraw this source of our wealth, power, and greatness, and give it to other nations? This, however, is truly the tendency of their present conduct; and if they persevere in continuing the duty on the importation of cotton, we shall most certainly be deprived of the cotton trade, and of a part of many others which depend upon it for support.

Let us now examine what this trade is, which our legislators thus put to the hazard.

On the average of the last ten years, we have imported about seventy-three millions of pounds of cotton annually, for which we have paid about five millions sterling.

This cotton has been spun into yarn, and exported or made into goods, from the coarsest fabric for household purposes and garments, to the finest muslins and lace; and, averaging these, I think it may be stated that the subjects of this country increase its value six or seven times, making a return for the cotton trade alone of from thirty to thirty-five millions sterling annually, which sum is paid to the inhabitants of this country chiefly for labour, and which they again expend within the year for food and other necessaries of life, making an annual sum paid and expended for labour of from sixty to seventy millions sterling. However extraordinary this sum may appear, I believe it will be found, on accurate investigation, to be under the real amount.

Now seventy millions sterling will support about three millions of the working classes, as they at present live in this country.

I believe this number, or more, derive their employment and support directly or indirectly from the cotton trade, for it is not those alone who are occupied in the manufacture of cotton that should be included in this number; but a considerable part of those who are engaged in almost all the other manufactures in the kingdom. It gives activity to the lead, tin, and copper, mines; to the Baltic and Canada trade in timber, tallow, etc, etc; to the manufacturers of glass, cards, leather, vegetable oil; to the whale fisheries; and to a variety of other branches of commerce too tedious here to enumerate, besides the direct consumption of food and of all the other necessaries of life required by the individuals so occupied. Such, my Lord and gentlemen, is the importance of the cotton trade.

The next question for our examination is, whether we possess the means of retaining this valuable branch of commerce? – and it is an inquiry deserving our most serious attention.

This question can be answered only by reference to the local advantages possessed by this country, and a comparison of them with those enjoyed by other countries likely to become our opponents.

Here we have the manufacture established, and a large part of the population trained to the business; there is a steady industry and application in the people, which cannot easily be outdone; our capital is perhaps superior to any rival; and, above all, our constitution gives more liberty and security to the subject than any constitution hitherto obtained by our neighbours. These are our local advantages.

We are opposed on the Continent of Europe by a strong inclination to obtain the trade, by low wages, aided by protecting import duties on the yarn and goods exported from this country, and by a comparatively low taxation.

These are indeed formidable advantages in favour of our European rivals; but against these, if we shall have a free import of the raw material, I trust we may successfully contend.

But, my Lord and Gentlemen, what are we to say to the local advantages possessed by our far more formidable rivals on the other side of the Atlantic? – Men speaking our own language, who can mix with us in all our proceedings, commcercial as well as political; who can easily induce our instructed workmen to facilitate their operations; who cannot be prevented from obtaining accurate drawings of every machine we employ; who have the raw material at their doors; who have scarcely any taxation, and a constitution equally free with our own.

These are local advantages, my Lord, to which, even with every aid your Government can lend, I am sure, sooner or later, we must yield; but should our Government persevere in its present impolitic oppression of this trade, by still exacting duties on the importation of the raw material, I am equally sure that the period when we must yield to our more fortunate rivals is near at hand.

It has however been stated from high authority, that one of the leading members of the administration has said, 'We have too much cotton trade in this country.' I know it is also a prevailing sentiment among the most respectable part of the community, not personally interested in trade and commerce, that the cotton trade is highly injurious to the population of the country, and, in consequence, they lament its introduction, and are not desirous of its increase.

I am not, my Lord, surprised at these sentiments. On the contrary, I should be surprised if they did not exist: and did I not firmly believe that events like these, which are beyond the control of individuals, have ultimate beneficial consequences, I should be inclined to draw the same conclusions, and to concur in the same wishes, because I know, from personal experience, that the labouring classes were much more happy in their agricultural pursuits, than they can be while engaged, as they now are, in most branches of the cotton manufacture. These lamentable results, however, can be known only by experience; and now the experience is acquired, it is too late to retrace our steps. Were we inclined, we cannot now return to our former state; for without the cotton trade, our increased population cannot be supported, the interest of the national debt paid, nor the expenses of our fleets and armies defrayed. Our existence as an independent power now, I regret to say, depends on the continuance of this trade, because no other can be substituted in its place. True indeed it is, that the main pillar and prop of the political greatness and prosperity of our country is a manufacture which, as it is now carried on, is destructive of the health, morals, and social comforts of the mass of the people engaged in it.

Such, my Lord, is the real state of the case; and I am anxious we should look it full in the face, that, if possible, timely measures may be devised to remove the evil and prevent the lamentable consequences which must ensure to the state itself, if a remedy cannot be found and applied.

Such, my Lord, is the present situation of our country. It possesses a manufacture which gives bread, directly or indirectly, to more than three millions of its inhabitants, and supplies the Government with a large proportion of its necessary expenses. This manufacture, however, is one which essentially injures the health, morals, and happiness of the majority of those engaged in it; yet, in consequence of the peculiar qualities of the raw material of this manufacture, no substitute is likely to be found to supersede it.

But cannot the evils be remedied, the trade sustained, and the country supported? I trust and hope they may; and to this point every friend to his country, every friend to humanity, will now direct his attention.

I know there are those who have not thought on the subject, and others who, if they are well off themselves, care little about the sufferings of those around them. To these, if there are any such present, I do not now address myself: I wish rather to fix the attention of these who can look beyond the passing hour, who can accurately trace future consequences from existing causes; those who feel an extended interest in the welfare of their species; who have discovered that wealth is not happiness, and that an apparent greatness founded on the miseries of the people, is not permanent and substantial power.

To relieve us from the dangerous and critical situation in which we are now placed, we must devise effectual measures to ameliorate the condition of the millions employed in this manufacture, which has already changed almost all the good habits of our ancestors.

It is only since the introduction of the cotton trade that children at an age before they had acquired strength of body or mental instruction have been forced into cotton-mills – those receptacles, in too many instances, for living human skeletons, almost disrobed of intellect, where, as the business is often now conducted, they linger out a few years of miserable existence, acquiring every bad habit, which they disseminate throughout society. It is only since the introduction of this trade, that children, and even grown people, were required to labour more than twelve hours in the day, including the time allotted for meals. It is only since the introduction of this trade, that the sole recreation of the labourer is to be found in the pot-house or gin-shop. It is only since the introduction of this baneful trade, that poverty, crime, and misery, have made rapid and fearful strides throughout the community.

Shall we then go unblushingly and ask the Legislators of our country to pass legislative acts to sanction and increase this trade, to sign the death-warrant of the strength, morals, and happiness, of thousands of our fellow-creatures, and not attempt to propose correctives for the evils which it creates?

If such shall be your determination, I, for one, will not join in the application; nay, I will, with all the faculties I possess, oppose every attempt to extend a trade, that, except in name, is more injurious to those employed in it, than is the slavery in the West Indies to the poor African negroes. For, deeply as I am interested in the cotton manufacture, highly as I value the extended political power of my country, yet, knowing as I do, from long experience both here and in England, the miseries which this trade, as it is now conducted, inflicts on those to whom it gives employment, I do not hesitate to say, – perish the cotton trade, perish even the political superiority of our country, (if it depends on the cotton trade,) rather than they shall be upheld by the sacrifice of everything valuable in life by those who are the means of supporting them.

The measure which appears to me alone calculated to remove the evils which I have stated, is to endeavour to procure an Act of Parliament –

First. – To prevent children from being employed in cotton or other mills of machinery, until they are twelve years old. (At present they are put in at seven years old, and upwards, – sometimes even at six.)

Secondly. – That the hours of work in mills of machinery, including one hour and a-half for meals and recreation, shall not exceed twelve per day. (In most mills, the time of working, for children, as well as adults, is fourteen hours per day; and in many cases they are dismissed during that period only for one hour, usually from twelve till one o'clock.)

And lastly, That, after a period to be fixed, no child shall be received in a mill of machinery until he shall have been taught to read, to write a legible hand, and to understand the first four rules of arithmetic; and girls also taught to sew their common garments of clothing. (At admission they are now often, most frequently indeed, destitute of all useful instruction.)

This instruction, I propose, shall be given to the children of the working classes by the country which gives them birth and to which they are afterwards to lend their aid and support.

By those who have not reflected on these subjects, or who have given them a mere passing thought, or by the recluse in his closet, I may be told that what I propose is impracticable, or, if practicable, that it would not be productive of benefits equal to other evils or inconveniences which these measures may create.

Against these I am prepared to being both argument and experience.

I do not, however, wish to take the meeting by surprise, nor will I now ask it to agree to any resolution on subjects so deeply affecting the interest of the cotton trade and of the country.

I now hold in my hand the rough outlines of a Bill[a] for the general amelioration of the poor and lower orders, which, I believe, on inspection, will be found deserving the approbation and support of those who have the most attentively considered the subject.

To give the gentlemen present, and those who are interested, time for considering what I have now advanced, I mean to propose that this meeting shall adjourn to this day week, or any other time more convenient to the Gentlemen present; before which period, if such proposition shall be approved, I will procure some hundred copies of this paper, and deposit them in the Coffee Room and elsewhere, for distribution to those who may interest themselves on the subject; and at such meeting, if the adjournment shall be acceded

[a] See Owen *Life*, vol. 1A (1858), pp. 23–6.

to, I pledge myself to prove that the measures which I have now proposed will be advantageous to all the individuals engaged in the cotton trade, to the best interests of our country, and to the cause of humanity.

I therefore now move that this meeting do adjourn, and that it shall meet again in the same place, this day-week, at twelve o'clock.

[*Copy of Title.*]

OBSERVATIONS

ON THE EFFECT OF

The Manufacturing System:

WITH HINTS FOR THE IMPROVEMENT OF THOSE PARTS OF IT WHICH ARE MOST INJURIOUS TO HEALTH AND MORALS.

DEDICATED MOST RESPECTFULLY TO

THE BRITISH LEGISLATURE.

BY ROBERT OWEN,

OF NEW LANARK.

London:

PRINTED BY RICHARD AND ARTHUR TAYLOR, SHOE LANE;

SOLD BY MESSRS. HATCHARD, PICCADILLY; RIVINGTON, ST. PAULS CHURCHYARD; CADELL AND DAVIES, STRAND; AND ARCH, CORNHILL.

1815.

Price One Shilling.

OBSERVATIONS

On the Effect of the Manufacturing System etc.[a]
(1815)

Those who were engaged in the trade, manufactures, and commerce of this country thirty or forty years ago, formed but a very insignificant portion of the knowledge, wealth, influence, or population of the Empire.

Prior to that period, Britain was essentially agricultural. But, from that time to the present, the home and foreign trade have increased in a manner so rapid and extraordinary as to have raised commerce to an importance, which it never previously attained in any country possessing so much political power and influence.

(By the returns to the Population Act in 1811, it appears that in England, Scotland and Wales, there are 895,998 families chiefly employed in agriculture – 1,129,049 families chiefly employed in trade and manufactures – 640,500 individuals in the army and navy – and 519,168 families not engaged in any of these employments. It follows that nearly half as many more persons are engaged in trade as in agriculture – and that of the whole population the agriculturists are about 1 to 3.)

This change has been owing chiefly to the mechanical inventions which introduced the cotton trade into this country, and to the cultivation of the cotton tree in America. The wants which this trade created for the various materials requisite to forward its multiplied operations, caused an extraordinary demand for almost all the manufactures previously established, and, of course, for human labour. The numerous fanciful and useful fabrics manufactured from cotton soon became objects of desire in Europe and America: and the consequent extension of the British foreign trade was such as to astonish and confound the most enlightened statesmen both at home and abroad.

The immediate effects of this manufacturing phenomenon were a rapid

[a] 2nd edn 1817; 3rd edn 1818; 4th edn 1819; another edn 1841; reprinted in Owen, *The New Existence of Man Upon the Earth* (1854), pt 1, pp. i–iv, and Owen, *Life*, vol. 1A (1858), pp. 35–45. Later reprints include 1927, 1977, 1991. In subsequent edns, 'of New Lanark' was omitted from the title. The 3rd edn added three letters, two on the employment of children in manufactories, addressed to the Earl of Liverpool (see *infra*, pp. 237–44), and to British Master Manufacturers (see *infra*, pp. 271–7); and the third on the union of churches and schools, addressed to the Archbishop of Canterbury (for the latter, see *infra*, pp. 245–9).

increase of the wealth, industry, population, and political influence of the British Empire; and by the aid of which it has been enabled to contend for five-and-twenty years against the most formidable military and *immoral* power that the world perhaps ever contained.

These important results, however, great as they really are, have not been obtained without accompanying evils of such a magnitude as to raise a doubt whether the latter do not preponderate over the former.

Hitherto, legislators have appeared to regard manufactures only in one point of view, as a source of national wealth.

The other mighty consequences which proceed from extended manufactures *when left to their natural progress*, have never yet engaged the attention of any legislature. Yet the political and moral effects to which we allude, well deserve to occupy the best faculties of the greatest and the wisest statesmen.

The general diffusion of manufactures throughout a country generates a new character in its inhabitants; and as this character is formed upon a principle quite unfavourable to individual or general happiness, it will produce the most lamentable and permanent evils, unless its tendency be counteracted by legislative interference and direction.

The manufacturing system has already so far extended its influence over the British Empire, as to effect an essential change in the general character of the mass of the people. This alteration is still in rapid progress; and ere long, the comparatively happy simplicity of the agricultural peasant will be wholly lost amongst us. It is even now scarcely anywhere to be found without a mixture of those habits which are the offspring of trade, manufactures, and commerce.

The acquisition of wealth, and the desire which it naturally creates for a continued increase, have introduced a fondness for essentially injurious luxuries among a numerous class of individuals who formerly never thought of them, and they have also generated a disposition which strongly impels its possessors to sacrifice the best feelings of human nature to this love of accumulation. To succeed in this career, the industry of the lower orders, from whose labour this wealth is now drawn, has been carried by new competitors striving against those of longer standing, to a point of real oppression, reducing them by successive changes, as the spirit of competition increased and the ease of acquiring wealth diminished, to a state more wretched than can be imagined by those who have not attentively observed the changes as they have gradually occurred. In consequence, they are at present in a situation infinitely more degraded and miserable than they were before the introduction of these manufactories, upon the success of which their bare subsistence now depends.

To support the additional population which this increased demand for labour has produced, it now becomes necessary to maintain the present extent of our foreign trade, or, under the existing circumstances of our population, it will become a serious and alarming evil.

It is highly probable, however, that the export trade of this country has attained its utmost height, and that by the competition of other states, possessing equal or greater local advantages, it will now gradually diminish.

The direct effect of the Corn-bill lately passed[a] will be to hasten this decline and prematurely to destroy that trade. In this view it is deeply to be regretted that the bill passed into a law; and I am persuaded its promoters will ere long discover the absolute necessity for its repeal, to prevent the misery which must ensue to the great mass of the people.

The inhabitants of every country are trained and formed by its great leading existing circumstances, and the character of the lower orders in Britain, is now formed chiefly by circumstances arising from trade, manufactures, and commerce; and the governing principle of trade, manufactures, and commerce, is immediate pecuniary gain, to which on the great scale every other is made to give way. All are sedulously trained to buy cheap and to sell dear; and to succeed in this art, the parties must be taught to acquire strong powers of deception; and thus a spirit is generated through every class of traders, destructive of that open, honest sincerity, without which man cannot make others happy, nor enjoy happiness himself.

Strictly speaking, however, this defect of character ought not to be attributed to the individuals possessing it, but to the overwhelming effect of the system under which they have been trained.

But the effects of this principle of gain, unrestrained, are still more lamentable on the working classes, those who are employed in the operative parts of the manufactures; for most of these branches are more or less unfavourable to the health and morals of adults. Yet parents do not hesitate to sacrifice the well-being of their children by putting them to occupations by which the constitution of their minds and bodies is rendered greatly inferior to what it might and ought to be under a system of common foresight and humanity.

Not more than thirty years since, the poorest parents thought the age of fourteen sufficiently early for their children to commence regular labour: and they judged well; for by that period of their lives they had acquired by play and exercise in the open air, the foundation of a sound robust constitution; and if they were not all initiated in book learning, they had been taught the far more useful knowledge of domestic life, which could not but be familiar to them at the age of fourteen, and which, as they grew up and became heads of families, was of more value to them (as it taught them economy in the expenditure of their earnings) than one half of their wages under the present circumstances.

It should be remembered also that twelve hours per day including the time for regular rest and meals, were then thought sufficient to extract all the working strength of the most robust adult; when it may be remarked local

[a] 55 Geo. III. c. 26 (1815), prohibiting all imports of wheat when the domestic price fell below 80/– per quarter.

holidays were much more frequent than at present in most parts of the kingdom.

At this period, too, they were generally trained by the example of some landed proprietor, and in such habits as created a mutual interest between the parties, by which means even the lowest peasant was generally considered as belonging to, and forming somewhat of a member of, a respectable family. Under these circumstances the lower orders experienced not only a considerable degree of comfort, but they had also frequent opportunities of enjoying healthy rational sports and amusements; and in consequence they became strongly attached to those on whom they depended; their services were willingly performed; and mutual good offices bound the parties by the strongest ties of human nature to consider each other as friends in somewhat different situations; the servant indeed often enjoying more solid comfort and ease than his master.

Contrast this state of matters with that of the lower orders of the present day; – with human nature trained as it now is, under the new manufacturing system.

In the manufacturing districts it is common for parents to send their children of both sexes at seven or eight years of age, in winter as well as summer, at six o'clock in the morning, sometimes of course in the dark, and occasionally amidst frost and snow, to enter the manufactories, which are often heated to a high temperature, and contain an atmosphere far from being the most favourable to human life, and in which all those employed in them very frequently continue until twelve o'clock at noon, when an hour is allowed for dinner, after which they return to remain, in a majority of cases, till eight o'clock at night.

The children now find they must labour incessantly for their bare subsistence: they have not been used to innocent, healthy, and rational amusements; they are not permitted the requisite time, if they had been previously accustomed to enjoy them. They know not what relaxation means, except by the actual cessation from labour. They are surrounded by others similarly circumstanced with themselves; and thus passing on from childhood to youth, they become gradually initiated, the young men in particular, but often the young females also, in the seductive pleasures of the pot-house and inebriation: for which their daily hard labour, want of better habits, and the general vacuity of their minds, tend to prepare them.

Such a system of training cannot be expected to produce any other than a population weak in bodily and mental faculties, and with habits generally destructive of their own comforts, of the well-being of those around them, and strongly calculated to subdue all the social affections. Man so circumstanced sees all around him hurrying forward, at a mail-coach speed, to acquire individual wealth, regardless of him, his comforts, his wants, or even his sufferings, except by way of a *degrading parish charity*, fitted only to steel the heart of man against his fellows, or to form the tyrant and the slave. To-day he labours for one master, tomorrow for a second, then for a third, and a fourth, until all ties between employers and employed are frittered down to the consideration of what immediate gain each can derive from the other.

The employer regards the employed as mere instruments of gain, while these acquire a gross ferocity of character, which, if legislative measures shall not be judiciously devised to prevent its increase, and ameliorate the condition of this class, will sooner or later plunge the country into a formidable and perhaps inextricable state of danger.

The direct object of these observations is to effect the amelioration and avert the danger. The only mode by which these objects can be accomplished is to obtain an Act of Parliament,

1st. To limit the regular hours of labour in mills of machinery to twelve per day, including one hour and a half for meals.

2nd. To prevent children from being employed in mills of machinery until they shall be ten years old, or that they shall not be employed more than six hours per day until they shall be twelve years old.

3rd. That children of either sex shall not be admitted into any manufactory, – after a time to be named, – until they can read and write in an useful manner, understand the first four rules of arithmetic, and the girls be likewise competent to sew their common garments of clothing.

These measures, when influenced by no party feelings or narrow mistaken notions of immediate self-interest, but considered solely in a national view, will be found to be beneficial to the child, to the parent, to the employer, and to the country. Yet, as we are now trained, many individuals cannot detach general subjects from party considerations, while others can see them only through the medium of present pecuniary gain. It may thence be concluded, that individuals of various descriptions will disapprove of some or all of these measures. I will therefore endeavour to anticipate their objections, and reply to them.

The child cannot be supposed to make any objection to the plans proposed: he may easily be taught to consider them, as they will prove to be by experience, essentially beneficial to him in childhood, youth, manhood, and old age.

Parents who have grown up in ignorance and bad habits, and who consequently are in poverty, may say 'We cannot afford to maintain our children until they shall be twelve years of age, without putting them to employment by which they may earn wages, and we therefore object to that part of the plan which precludes us from sending them to manufactories until they shall be of that age.'

If the poorest and most miserable of the people formerly supported their children without regular employment until they were fourteen, why may they not now support them until they shall be twelve years old? If parents who decline this duty had not been ignorant and trained in bad habits which render their mental faculties inferior to the instinct of many animals, they would understand that by forcing their children to labour in such situations at a premature age, they place their offspring in circumstances calculated to retard their growth, and make them peculiarly liable to bodily disease and mental injury, while they debar them the chance of acquiring that sound robust constitution which otherwise they would possess, and without which they cannot much happiness, but must become a burthen to themselves, their friends, and their country. Parents by so acting also deprive their children of the opportunity of acquiring the habits of domestic life, without a knowledge of which high nominal wages can procure them but few comforts, and without which among the working classes very little domestic happiness can be enjoyed.

Children thus prematurely employed are prevented from acquiring any of the common rudiments of book learning; but in lieu of this useful and valuable knowledge, they are likely to acquire the most injurious habits by continually associating with those as ignorant and as ill instructed as themselves. And thus it may be truly said, that for every penny gained by parents from the premature labour of their offspring, they sacrifice not only future pounds, but also the future health, comfort, and good conduct of their children; and unless this pernicious system shall be arrested by the introduction of a better, the evil is likely to extend, and to become worse through every succeeding generation.

I do not anticipate any objection from employers to the age named for the admittance of children into their manufactories; or to children being previously trained in good habits and the rudiments of common learning; for, upon an experience abundantly sufficient to ascertain the fact, I have uniformly found it to be more profitable to admit children to constant daily employment at ten years old, than at any earlier period; and that those children, or adults, who had been the best taught, made the best servants, and were by far the most easily directed to do every thing that was right and proper for them to perform. The proprietors of expensive establishments may object to the reduction of the *now* customary hours of labour. The utmost extent however of their argument is, that the rent or interest of the capital expended in forming the establishment is chargeable on the quantity of its produce; – and if, instead of being permitted to employ their work-people within their manufactories so long as human nature can be tempted to continue its exertions, say for fourteen or fifteen hours per day, they shall be restricted to twelve hours of labour per day from their work-people, then the prime cost of the article which they manufacture will be increased by the greater proportion of rent or interest which attaches to the smaller quantity produced. If, however, this law shall be, as it is proposed, general over England, Scotland, and Ireland, whatever difference may ultimately arise in the prime cost of the articles produced in these manufactories, will be borne by the consumers, and not by the proprietors of such establishments. And, in a national view, the labour which is exerted twelve hours per day will be obtained more economically than if stretched to a longer period.

I doubt, however, whether any manufactory, so arranged as to occupy the hands employed in it twelve hours per day, will not produce its fabric, even to the immediate proprietor, nearly if not altogether as cheap as those in which the exertions of the employed are continued to fourteen or fifteen hours per day.

Should this, however, not prove to be the case to the extent mentioned, the improved health, the comforts, useful acquirements of the population, and the diminution of poors-rates, naturally consequent on this change in the manners and habits of the people, will amply compensate to the country for a mere fractional addition to the prime cost of any commodity.

And is it to be imagined that the British Government will ever put the chance of a trivial pecuniary gain of a few, in competition with the solid welfare of so many millions of human beings?

The employer cannot be injured by being obliged so to act towards his labourers as, for the interest of the country, he should act. Since the general introduction of expensive machinery, human nature has been forced far beyond its average strength; and much, very much private misery and public injury are the consequences.

It is indeed a measure more to be deplored in a national view than almost any other that has occurred for many centuries past. It has deranged the domestic habits of the great mass of the people. It has deprived them of the time in which they might acquire instruction, or enjoy rational amusements. It has robbed them of their substantial advantages, and, by leading them into habits of the pot-house and inebriation, it has poisoned all their social comforts.

Shall we then make laws to imprison, transport, or condemn to death, those who purloin a few shillings of our property, injure any of our domestic animals, or even a growing twig; and shall we *not* make laws to restrain those who otherwise will not be restrained in their desire for gain, from robbing, in the pursuit of it, millions of our fellow creatures of their health, – their time for acquiring knowledge and future improvement, – of their social comforts, – and of every rational enjoyment? This system of proceeding cannot continue long; – it will work its own cure by the practical evils which it creates, and that in a most dangerous way to the public welfare, if the Government shall not give it a proper direction.

The public, however, are perhaps most interested in that part of the plan which recommends the training and educating of the lower orders under the direction and at the expense of the country. And it is much to be wished that the extended substantial advantages to be derived from this measure were more generally considered and understood, in order that the mistaken ideas which now exist regarding it, in the most opposite quarters, may be entirely removed.

A slight general knowledge of the past occurrences of the world, with some experience of human nature as it appears in the little sects and parties around us, is sufficient to make it evident to those, not very much misinstructed from infancy, that children may be taught any habits and any sentiments; and that these, with the bodiy and mental propensities and faculties existing at birth in each individual, combined with the general circumstances in which he is placed, constitute the whole character of man.

It is thence evident that human nature can be improved and formed into the character which it is for the interest and happiness of all it should possess, solely by directing the attention of mankind to the adoption of legislative measures judiciously calculated to give the best habits and most just and useful sentiments to the rising generation; and in an especial manner to those who are placed in situations which, without such measures, render them liable to be taught the worst habits and the most useless and injurious sentiments.

I ask those who have studied the science of government upon those enlightened principles which alone ought to influence the statesman – What is the difference, in a national view, between an individual trained in habits which give him health, temperance, industry, correct principles of judging, foresight, and general good conduct; and one trained in ignorance, idleness, intemperance, defective powers of judging, and in general vicious habits? Is not one of the former of more real worth and political strength to the state than many of the latter?

Are there not many millions in the British dominions in whom this difference can be made? And if a change which so essentially effects the well-being of those individuals, and, through them, of every member of the empire, *may* be made, is it not the first duty of the government and the country to put into immediate practice the means which *can* effect the change?

Shall then such important measures be waived, and the best interests of this country compromised, because one party wishes its own peculiar principles to be forced on the young mind; or because another is afraid that the advantages to be derived from this improved system of legislation will be so great as to give too much popularity and influence to the Ministers who shall introduce it?

The termination of such errors in practice is, I trust, near at hand, and then Government will be no longer compelled to sacrifice the well-doing and the well-being of the great mass of the people and of the empire, to the prejudices of comparatively a few individuals, trained to mistake even their own security and interests.

Surely a measure most obviously calculated to render a greater benefit to millions of our fellow-creatures than any other ever yet adopted, cannot be much longer suspended because one party in the state may erroneously suppose it would weaken their influence over the public mind unless that party shall alone direct that plan; but which direction, it is most obvious, the intelligence of the age will not commit to any party exclusively. Or because others, trained in very opposite principles, may imagine that a national system of education for the poor and lower orders, under the sanction of Government, but superintended and directed in its details by the country, would place a dangerous power in the hands of ministers of the Crown.

Such sentiments as these cannot exist in minds divested of party considerations, who sincerely desire to benefit their fellow-men, who have no private views to accomplish, and who wish to support and strengthen the Government, that the Government may be the better enabled to adopt decisive and effectual measures for the general amelioration of the people.

I now therefore, in the name of the millions of the neglected poor and ignorant, whose habits and sentiments have been hitherto formed to render them wretched, call upon the British Government and the British Nation to unite their efforts to arrange a system to train and instruct those who, for any good or useful purpose, are now untrained and uninstructed; and to arrest by a clear, easy, and practical system of prevention, the ignorance and consequent poverty, vice, and misery, which are rapidly increasing throughout the empire; for, 'Train up a child in the way he should go, and when he is old he will not depart from it.'

ADDRESS DELIVERED TO THE INHABITANTS OF NEW LANARK[a] 1816

On Opening the Institution for the Formation of Character, on the 1st of January, 1816

Dedicated to those who have no private ends to accomplish, who are honestly in search of truth, for the purpose of ameliorating the condition of society, and who have the firmness to follow the truth wherever it may lead, without being turned aside from the pusuit by the prepossessions or prejudices of any part of mankind.

We have met today for the purpose of opening this Institution; and it is my intention to explain to you the objects for which it has been founded.

These objects are most important.

The first relates to the immediate comfort and benefit of all the inhabitants of this village.

The second, to the welfare and advantage of the neighbourhood.

The third, to extensive ameliorations throughout the British dominions.

The last, to the gradual improvement of every nation in the world.

I will briefly explain how this Institution is to contribute towards producing these effects.

Long before I came to reside among you, it had been my chief study to discover the extent, causes, and remedy of the inconveniences and miseries which were perpetually recurring to every class in society.

The history of man informed me that innumerable attempts had been made, through every age, to lessen these evils; and experience convinced me that the present generation, stimulated by an accession of knowledge derived from past times, was eagerly engaged in the same pursuit. My mind at a very early period took a similar direction; and I became ardently desirous of investigating to its source a subject which involved the happiness of every human being.

---

[a] 2nd edn 1816; 3rd edn 1817; 4th edn 1819; another edn 1841, entitled *Address on Opening the Institution for the Formation of Character, at New Lanark*. Also reprinted in *New Moral World*, vol. 1, no. 64 (16 January 1836), pp. 89–92, no. 65 (23 January 1836), pp. 97–102; *The New Existence of Man Upon the Earth* (1854), pt 2, pp. iii–xxiv, Owen, *Life*, vol. 1 (1857), pp. 333–60. Later reprints include 1927, 1977, 1991.

It soon appeared to me, that the only path to knowledge on this subject had been neglected; that one leading in an opposite direction had alone been followed; that while causes existed to compel mankind to pursue such direction, it was idle to expect any successful result: and experience proves how vain their pursuit has been.

In this enquiry, men have hitherto been directed by their inventive faculties, and have almost entirely disregarded the only guide that can lead to true knowledge on any subject – experience. They have been governed, in the most important concerns of life, by mere illusions of the imagination, in direct opposition to existing facts.

Having satisfied myself beyond doubt with regard to this fundamental error; having traced the ignorance and misery which it has inflicted on man, by a calm and patient investigation of the causes which have continued this evil, without any intermission from one generation to another; and having also maturely reflected on the obstacles to be overcome, before a new direction can be given to the human mind; I was induced to form the resolution of devoting my life to relieve mankind from this mental disease and all its miseries.

It was evident to me that the evil was universal; that, in practice, none was in the right path – no, not one; and that, in order to remedy the evil, a different one must be pursued. That the whole man must be re-formed on fundamental principles the very reverse of those in which he had been trained; in short, that the minds of all men must be born again, and their knowledge and practice commence on a new foundation.

Satisfied of the futility of the existing modes of instruction, and of the errors of the existing modes of government, I was well convinced that none of them could ever effect the ends intended; but that, on the contrary, they were only calculated to defeat all the objects which human instructors and governors had proposed to attain.

I found, on such a patient consideration of the subject as its importance demanded, that to reiterate precept upon precept, however excellent in theory, while no decisive measures were adopted to place mankind under circumstances in which it might be possible to put those precepts in practice, was but a waste of time. I therefore determined to form arrangements preparatory to the introduction of truths, the knowledge of which should dissipate the errors and evils of all the existing political and religious systems.

Be not alarmed at the magnitude of the attempt which this declaration opens to your view. Each change, as it occurs, will establish a substantial and permanent good, unattended by any counteracting evil; nor can the mind of man, formed on the old system, longer interpose obstacles capable of retarding the progress of those truths which I am now about to unfold to you. The futile attempts which ignorance may for a short time oppose to them, will be found to accelerate their introduction. As soon as they shall be comprehended in all their bearings, everyone will be compelled to acknowledge them, to see their benefits in practice to himself and to each of his fellow creatures; for, by this system, none, no not one, will be injured. It is a delightful thought, an animating reflection, a stimulus to the steady prosecution of my purpose, beyond – nay, far beyond – all that riches, and honour, and praise can bestow, to be conscious of the possibility of being instrumental in introducing a practical system into society, the complete establishment of which *shall give happiness to every human being through all succeeding generations*. And such I declare was the sole motive that gave rise to this Institution, and to all my proceedings.

To effect any permanently beneficial change in society, I found it was far more necessary to *act* than to *speak*. I tried the effect of the new principles on a limited scale in the southern part of the Island. The result exceeded my most sanguine anticipations; and I became anxious for a more enlarged field of action. I saw New Lanark: it possessed many of the local circumstances proper for my purpose; and this establishment became at my disposal. This event, as many of you may recollect, occurred upwards of sixteen years ago. Sixteen years of action is not a short period: extensive changes are the result. You have been witnesses of my proceedings here, from the time I undertook the direction of the establishment to the present hour. I now ask, and I will thank you to make either a public or a private reply – have any of you discovered even *one* of my measures that was not clearly and decisively intended to benefit the whole population? But I am satisfied that you are all now convinced of this truth. You also know some of the obstacles which were opposed to my progress; but you know not a tithe of them. Yet, after all, these obstacles have been few, compared with those which I expected and was prepared to meet; and which I trust I should have overcome.

When I examined the circumstances under which I found you, they appeared to me to be very similar to those of other manufacturing districts; except with regard to the boarding-house, which contained the young children who were procured from the public charities of the country. That part of the establishment was under an admirable arrangement, and was a strong indication of the genuine and extensive benevolence of the revered and truly good man (the late David Dale of Glasgow), who founded these works and this village. His wishes and intentions towards you all were those of a father towards his children. You knew him and his worth; and his memory must be deeply engraven upon your hearts. Little indeed could he be conscious, when he laid the first stone of this establishment, that he was commencing a work, from whence not only the amelioration of his suffering countrymen should proceed, but the means of happiness be developed to every nation in the world.

I have stated that I found the population of this place similar to that of other manufacturing districts. It was, with some exceptions, existing in poverty, crime, and misery; and strongly prejudiced, as most people are at first, against any change that might be proposed. The usual mode of proceeding on the principles which have hitherto governed the conduct of men, would have been to punish those who committed the crimes, and to be highly displeased with everyone who opposed the alterations that were intended for his benefit. The principles, however, upon which the new system is founded, lead to a very different conduct. They make it evident, that when men are in poverty – when they commit crimes or actions injurious to themselves and others – and when they are in a state of wretchedness – there must be substantial cause for these lamentable effects; and that, instead of punishing or being angry with our fellow men because they have been subjected to such a miserable existence, we ought to pity and commiserate them, and patiently to trace the causes whence the evils proceed, and endeavour to discover whether they may not be removed.

This was the course which I adopted. I sought not the punishment of any delinquent, nor felt anger at your conduct in opposition to your own good; and when apparently stern and decisive, I was not actuated by a single feeling of irritation against any individual. I dispassionately investigated the source of the evils with which I saw you afflicted. The immediate causes of them were soon obvious; nor were the remote ones, or the causes of those causes, long hid from me.

I found that those which principally produced your misery, were practices you had been permitted to acquire – of falsehood, of theft, of drunkenness, of injustice in your transactions, want of charity for the opinions of others, and mistaken notions, in which you had been instructed, as to the superiority of your religious opinions, and that these were calculated to produce more happiness than any of the opinions impressed on the minds of an infinitely more numerous part of mankind. I found, also, that these causes were but the effects of others; and that those others might all be traced to the ignorance in which our forefathers existed, and in which we ourselves have continued to this day.

But from this day a change must take place, a new era must commence; the human intellect, through the whole extent of the earth, hitherto enveloped by the grossest ignorance and superstition, must begin to be released from its state of darkness; nor shall nourishment henceforth be given to the seeds of disunion and division among men. For the time is come, when the means may be prepared to train all the nations of the world – men of every colour and climate, of the most diversified habits – in that knowledge which shall impel them not only to love but to be actively kind to each other in the whole of their conduct, without a single exception. I speak not an unmeaning jargon of words, but that which I know – that which has been derived from a cool and dispassionate examination and comparison, during a quarter of a century, of the facts which exist around us. And, however averse men may be to resign their early taught prejudices, I pledge myself to prove, to the entire satisfaction of the world, the truth of all that I have stated and all that I mean to state. Nay, such is my confidence in the truth of the principles on which the system I am about to introduce is founded, that I hesitate not to assert their power heartily to incline all men to say, 'This system is assuredly true, and therefore eminently calculated to realize those invaluable precepts of the Gospel – universal charity, goodwill, and peace among men. Hitherto we must have been trained in error; and we hail it as the harbinger of that period when our swords shall be turned into ploughshares, and our spears into pruning-hooks;[a] when universal love and benevolence shall prevail; when there shall be but one language and one nation; and when fear of want or of any evil among men shall be known no more.'

Acting, although unknown to you, uniformly and steadily upon this system, my attention was ever directed to remove, as I could prepare means for their removal, such of the immediate causes as were perpetually creating misery amongst you, and which, if permitted to remain, would to this day have continued to create misery. I therefore withdrew the most prominent incitements to falsehood, theft, drunkenness, and other pernicious habits, with which many of you were then familiar: and in their stead I introduced other causes, which were intended to produce better external habits; and better external habits have been introduced. I say better *external* habits; for to these alone have my proceedings hitherto been intended to apply. What has yet been done I consider as merely preparatory.

This institution, when all its parts shall be completed, is intended to produce permanently beneficial effects; and, instead of longer applying temporary expedients for correcting some of your most prominent external habits, to effect a complete and thorough improvement in the *internal* as well as *external* character of the whole village. For this purpose the Institution has been devised to afford the means of receiving your children at an early age, as soon almost as they can walk. By this means many of you, mothers and families, will be enabled to earn a better maintenance or support for your children; you will have less care and anxiety about them; while the children will be prevented from acquiring any bad habits, and gradually prepared to learn the best.

The middle room of the storey below will be appropriated to their accommodation; and in this their chief occupation will be to play and amuse themselves in severe weather: at other times they will be permitted to occupy the enclosed area before the building; for, to give children a vigorous constitution, they ought to be kept as much as possible in the open air. As they advance in years, they will be taken into the rooms on the right and left, where they will be regularly instructed in the rudiments of common learning; which, before they shall be six years old, they may be taught in a superior manner.

[a] See Isaiah 2:4.

These stages may be called the first and second preparatory schools: and when your children shall have passed through them, they will be admitted into this place (intended also to be used as a chapel), which, with the adjoining apartment, is to be the general schoolroom for reading, writing, arithmetic, sewing, and knitting; all which, on the plan to be pursued, will be accomplished to a considerable extent by the time the children are ten years old; before which age, none of them will be permitted to enter the works.

For the benefit of the health and spirits of the children both boys and girls will be taught to dance, and the boys will be instructed in military exercises; those of each sex who may have good voices will be taught to sing, and those among the boys who have a taste for music will be taught to play upon some instrument; for it is intended to give them as much diversified innocent amusement as the local circumstances of the establishment will admit.

The rooms to the east and west on the storey below, will also be appropriated in bad weather for relaxation and exercise during some part of the day, to the children who, in the regular hours of teaching, are to be instructed in these apartments.

In this manner is the Institution to be occupied during the day in winter. In summer, it is intended that they shall derive knowledge from a personal examination of the works of nature and of art, by going out frequently with some of their masters into the neighbourhood and country around.

After the instruction of the children who are too young to attend the works shall have been finished for the day, the apartments shall be cleaned, ventilated, and in winter lighted and heated, and in all respects made comfortable, for the reception of other classes of the population. The apartments on this floor are then to be appropriated for the use of the children and youth of both sexes who have been employed at work during the day, and who may wish still further to improve themselves in reading, writing, arithmetic, sewing, or knitting; or to learn any of the useful arts: to instruct them in which, proper masters and mistresses, who are appointed, will attend for two hours every evening.

The three lower rooms, which in winter will also be well lighted and properly heated, will be thrown open for the use of the adult part of the population, who are to be provided with every accommodation requisite to enable them to read, write, account, sew, or play, converse, or walk about. But strict order and attention to the happiness of every one of the party will be enforced, until such habits shall be acquired as will render any formal restriction unnecessary; and the measures thus adopted will soon remove such necessity.

Two evenings in the week will be appropriated to dancing and music: but on these occasions every accommodation will be prepared for those who prefer to study or to follow any of the occupations pursued on the other evenings.

One of the apartments will also be occasionally appropriated for the purpose of giving useful instruction to the older classes of the inhabitants. For, believe me, my friends, you are yet very deficient with regard to the best modes of training your children, or of arranging your domestic concerns; as well as in that wisdom which is requisite to direct your conduct towards each other, so as to enable you to become greatly more happy than you have ever yet been. There will be no difficulty in teaching you what is right and proper; your own interest will afford ample stimulus for that purpose; but the real and only difficulty will be to unlearn those pernicious habits and sentiments which an infinite variety of causes, existing through all past ages, have combined to impress upon your minds and bodies, so as to make you imagine that they are inseparable from your nature. It shall, however, ere long be proved to you, that in this respect as well as in many others, you and all mankind are mistaken. Yet think not, from what I have said, that I mean to infringe, even in the most slight degree, on the liberty of private judgement or religious opinions. No! they have hitherto been unrestrained; and the most effectual measures have been adopted by all the parties interested in the concern, to secure to you these most invaluable privileges. And here I now publicly declare (and while I make the declaration I wish my voice could extend to the ear, and make its due impression on the mind, of every one of our fellow creatures), 'that the individual who first placed restraint on private judgement and religious opinions, was the author of hypocrisy, and the origin of innumerable evils which mankind through every past age have experienced'. The right, however, of private judgement, and of real religious liberty, is nowhere yet enjoyed. It is not possessed by any nation in the world; and thence the unnecessary ignorance, as well as endless misery, of all. Nor can this right be enjoyed until the principle whence opinions originate shall be universally known and acknowledged.

The chief object of my existence will be to make this knowledge universal, and thence to bring the right of private judgement into general practice; to show the infinitely beneficial consequences that will result to mankind from its adoption. To effect this important purpose is a part, and an essential part, of that system which is about to be introduced.

I proceed to show how the Institution is to contribute to the welfare and advantage of this neighbourhood.

It will be readily admitted, that a population trained in regular habits of temperance, industry, and sobriety; of genuine charity for the opinions of all mankind, founded on the only knowledge that can implant true charity in the breast of any human being; trained also in a sincere desire to do good to the utmost of their power, and without any exception, to every one of their fellow creatures, cannot, even by their example alone, do otherwise than materially increase the welfare and advantages of the neighbourhood in which such a population may be situated. To feel the due weight of this consideration, only imagine to yourselves 2,000 or 3,000 human beings trained in habits of licentiousness, and allowed to remain in gross ignorance. How much, in such a case, would not the peace, quiet, comfort, and happiness of the neighbourhood be destroyed! But there is not anything I have done, or purpose to do, which is not intended to benefit my fellow creatures to the greatest extent that my operations can embrace. I wish to benefit all equally; but circumstances limit my present measures for the public good within a narrow circle. I must begin to act at some point; and a combination of singular events has fixed that point at this establishment. The first and greatest advantages will therefore centre here. But, in unison with the principle thus stated, it has ever been my intention that as this institution, when completed, will accommodate more than the children of parents resident at the village, any persons living at Lanark, or in the neighbourhood anywhere around, who cannot well afford to educate their children, shall be at liberty, on mentioning their wishes, to send them to this place, where they will experience the same care and attention as those who belong to the establishment. Nor will there be any distinction made between the children of those parents who are deemed the worst, and of those who may be esteemed the best, members of society: rather, indeed, would I prefer to receive the offspring of the worst, if they shall be sent at an early age; because they really require more of our care and pity; and by well-training these, society will be more essentially benefited, than if the like attention were paid to those whose parents are educating them in comparatively good habits. The system now preparing, and which will ultimately be brought into full practice, is to effect a complete change in all our sentiments and conduct towards those poor miserable creatures whom the errors of past times have denominated the bad, the worthless, and the wicked. A more enlarged and better knowledge of human nature will make it evident that, in strict justice, those who apply these terms to their fellow men are not only the most ignorant, but are themselves the immediate cause of more misery in the world than those whom they call the outcasts of society. *They* are, therefore, correctly speaking, the most wicked and worthless; and were they not grossly deceived, and rendered blind from infancy, they would become conscious of the lamentably extensive evils, which, by their well-intended but most mistaken conduct, they have, during so long a period, inflicted on their fellow men. But the veil of darkness must be removed from their eyes; their erroneous proceedings must be made so palpable that they shall thenceforth reject them with horror. Yes! they will reject with horror even those notions which hitherto they have from infancy been taught to value beyond price.

To that which follows I wish to direct the attention of all your faculties. I am about to declare to you the cause and the cure of that which is called wickedness in your fellow men. As we proceed, instead of your feelings being roused to hate and to pursue them to punishment, you will be compelled to pity them; to commiserate their condition; nay, to love them, and to be convinced that to this day they have been treated unkindly, unjustly, and with the greatest cruelty. It is indeed high time, my friends, that our conduct – that the conduct of all mankind, in this respect, should be the very reverse of what it has been; and of this truth, new as it may and must appear to many of you, you shall, as I proceed, be satisfied to the most complete conviction.

That, then, which has been hitherto called wickedness in our fellow men, has proceeded from one of two distinct causes, or from some combination of those causes. They are what is termed bad or wicked,

1st. Because they are born with faculties and propensities which render them more liable, under the circumstances, than other men, to commit such actions as are usually denominated wicked. Or

2nd. Because they have been placed, by birth or by other events, in particular countries; have been influenced from infancy by parents, playmates, and others; and have been surrounded by those circumstances which gradually and necessarily trained them in the habits and sentiments called wicked. Or

3rd. They have become wicked in consequence of some particular combination of these causes.

Let us now examine them separately, and endeavour to discover whether any, and which of them, have originated with the individuals; and, of course, for which of them they ought to be treated by their fellow men in the manner those denominated wicked have to this day been treated.

You have not, I trust, been rendered so completely insane, by the ignorance of our forefathers, as to imagine that the poor helpless infant, devoid of understanding, made itself, or any of its bodily or mental faculties or qualities: but, whatever you may have been taught, it is a fact, that every infant has received all its faculties and qualities, bodily and mental, from a power and cause, over which the infant had not the shadow of control.

Shall it, then, be unkindly treated? And, when it shall be grown up, shall it be punished with loss of liberty or life, because a power over which it had no control whatever, formed it in the womb with faculties and qualities different from those of its fellows? – Has the infant any means of deciding who, or of what description, shall be its parents, its playmates, or those from whom it shall derive its habits and its sentiments? – Has it the power to determine for itself whether it shall first see light within the circle of Christendom; or whether it shall be so placed as inevitably to become a disciple of Moses, of Confucius, of Mahomed; a worshipper of the great idol Juggernaut,[a] or a savage and a cannibal?

If then, my friends, not even one of these great leading and overwhelming circumstances can be, in the smallest degree, under the control of the infant, is there a being in existence, possessing any claim even to the smallest degree of rationality, who will maintain that any individual, formed and placed under

[a] Large cart associated with Vishnu cult, dragged annually by thousands of followers.

such circumstances, ought to be punished, or in any respect unkindly treated? When men shall be in some degree relieved from the mental malady with which they have been so long afflicted, and sound judgement shall take the place of wild and senseless imagination, then the united voice of mankind shall say, 'No!' And they will be astonished that a contrary supposition should ever have prevailed.

If it should be asked – Whence, then, have wickedness and misery proceeded? I reply, *Solely from the ignorance of our forefathers!* It is this ignorance, my friends, that has been, and continues to be, the only cause of all the miseries which men have experienced. This is the evil spirit which has had dominion over the world – which has sown the seeds of hatred and disunion among all nations – which has grossly deceived mankind, by introducing notions the most absurd and unaccountable respecting faith and belief; notions by which it has effectually placed a seal on all the rational faculties of man – by which numberless evil passions are engendered – by which all men, in the most senseless manner, are not only made enemies to each other, but enemies to their own happiness! While this ignorance of our forefathers continues to abuse the world, under any name whatever, it is neither more nor less than a species of madness – rank insanity – to imagine that we can ever become in practice good, wise, or happy.

Were it not indeed, for the positive evils which proceed from these senseless notions, they are too absurd to admit of a serious refutation; nor would any refutation be necessary, if they did not from infancy destroy the reasoning faculties of men, whether Pagans, Jews, Christians, or Mahomedans; and render them utterly incompetent to draw a just conclusion from the numberless facts which perpetually present themselves to notice. Do we not learn from history, that infants through all past ages have been taught the language, habits, and sentiments of those by whom they have been surrounded? That they had no means whatever of giving to themselves the power to acquire any others? That every generation has thought and acted like preceding generations, *with such changes only as the events around it, from which experience is derived, may have forced upon it?* And, above all, are we not conscious that the experience of every individual now existing is abundantly sufficient, on reflection, to prove to himself that he has no more power or command over his faith and belief than he possesses over the winds of heaven? nay, that his constitution is so formed, that in every instance whatsoever, the faith or belief which he possesses has been given to him by causes over which he had no control?

Experience, my friends, now makes these conclusions clear as the sun at noonday. Why, then, shall we not instantly act upon them? Having discovered our error, why shall we longer afflict our fellow men with the evils which these wild notions have generated? Have they ever been productive of one benefit to mankind? Have they not produced, through all past ages – are they not at this moment engendering, every conceivable evil to which man, in every nation of the world, is subjected? Yes; these alone prevent the introduction of charity and universal goodwill among men. These alone prevent men from discovering the true and only road which can lead to happiness. Once overcome these obstacles, and the apple of discord will be withdrawn from among us; the whole human race may then, with the greatest ease, be trained in one mind; all their efforts may then be trained to act for the good of the whole. In short, when these great errors shall be removed, all our evil passions will disappear; no ground of anger or displeasure from one human being towards another will remain; the period of the supposed Millennium will commence, and universal love prevail.

Will it not, then, tend to the welfare and advantage of this neighbourhood, to introduce into it such a practical system as shall gradually withdraw the cause of anger, hatred, discord, and every evil passion, and substitute true and genuine principles of universal charity and of never-varying kindness, of love without dissimulation, and of an ever-active desire to benefit to the full extent of our faculties all our fellow creatures, whatever may be their sentiments and their habits – wholly regardless whether they be Pagans, Jews, Christians, or Mahomedans? For anything short of this can proceed only from the evil spirit of ignorance, which is truly the roaring lion going about seeking whom he may devour.[a]

We now come to the third division of the subject, which was to show that one of the objects of this Institution was to effect extensive ameliorations throughout the British dominions. This will be accomplished in two ways:

1st. By showing to the master manufacturers an example in practice, on a scale sufficiently extensive, of the mode by which the characters and situation of the working manufacturers whom they employ may be very materially improved, not only without injury to the masters, but so as to create to them also great and substantial advantages.

2nd. By inducing, through this example, the British legislature to enact such laws as will secure similar benefits to every part of our population.

The extent of the benefits which may be produced by proper legislative measures, few are yet prepared to form any adequate idea of. By legislative measures I do not mean any party proceeding whatever. Those to which I allude are – laws to diminish and ultimately prevent the most prominent evils to which the working classes are now subjected – laws to prevent a large part of our fellow subjects, under the manufacturing system, from being oppressed by a much smaller part – to prevent more than one half of our population from being trained in gross ignorance and their valuable labour from being most injuriously directed – laws to prevent the same valuable part of our population from being perpetually surrounded by temptations, which they have not been

[a] See Psalms 22:13.

trained to resist, and which compel them to commit actions most hurtful to themselves and to society. The principles on which these measures are to be founded being once fairly and honestly understood, they will be easy of adoption; and the benefits to be derived from them in practice to every member of the community, will exceed any calculation that can be made by those not well versed in political economy.

These are some of the ameliorations which I trust this Institution will be the means of obtaining for our suffering fellow subjects.

But, my friends, if what has been done, what is doing, and what has yet to be done here, should procure the benefits which I have imperfectly enumerated, to this village, to our neighbourhood, and to our country, only, I should be greatly disappointed; for I feel an ardent desire to benefit all my fellow men equally. I know not any distinction whatever. Political or religious parties or sects are everywhere the fruitful sources of disunion and irritation. My aim is therefore to withdraw the germ of all party from society. As little do I admit of the divisions and distinctions created by any imaginary lines which separate nation from nation. Will any being, entitled to the epithet intelligent, say that a mountain, a river, an ocean, or any shade of colour, or difference of climate, habits, and sentiments, affords a reason sufficient to satisfy the inquiries of even a well-trained child, why one portion of mankind should be taught to despise, hate, and destroy another? Are these absurd effects of the grossest ignorance never to be brought to a termination? Are we still to preserve and encourage the continuance of those errors which must inevitably make man an enemy to man? Are these the measures calculated to bring about that promised period when the lion shall lie down with the lamb,[a] and when uninterrupted peace shall universally prevail? – peace, founded on a sincere goodwill, instilled from infancy into the very constitution of every man, which is the only basis on which universal happiness can ever be established? I look, however, with the utmost confidence to the arrival of such a period; and, if proper measures shall be adopted, its date is not far distant.

What ideas individuals may attach to the term Millennium, I know not; but I know that society may be formed so as to exist without crime, without poverty, with health greatly improved, with little, if any, misery, and with intelligence and happiness increased a hundredfold; and no obstacle whatsoever intervenes at this moment, except ignorance, to prevent such a state of society from becoming universal.

I am aware, to the fullest extent, what various impressions these declarations will make on the different religious, political, learned, commercial, and other circles which compose the population of our empire. I know the particular shade of prejudice through which they will be presented to the minds of each

[a] See Isaiah 11:6.

of these. And to none will they appear through a denser medium than to the learned, who have been taught to suppose that the book of knowledge has been exclusively opened to them; while in fact, they have only wasted their strength in wandering through endless mazes of error. They are totally ignorant of human nature. They are full of theories, and have not the most distant conception of what may or may not be accomplished in practice. It is true their minds have been well stored with language, which they can readily use to puzzle and confound the unlettered and inexperienced. But to those who have had an opportunity of examining the utmost extent of their acquirements, and of observing how far they have been taught, and where their knowledge terminates, the deception vanishes, and the fallacy of the foundation upon which the superstructure of all their acquirements has been raised, at once becomes most obvious. In short, with a few exceptions, their profound investigations have been about words only. For, as the principle which they have been taught, and on which all their subsequent instruction proceeds, is erroneous, so it becomes impossible that they can arrive at just conclusions. The learned have ever looked for the cause of human sentiments and actions in the individual through whom those sentiments and actions become visible – and hitherto the learned have governed the opinions of the world. The individual has been praised, blamed, or punished, according to the whims and fancies of this class of men, and, in consequence, the earth has been full charged with their ever-varying absurdities, and with the miseries which these absurdities hourly create. Had it not been a law of our nature, that any impression, however ridiculous and absurd, and however contrary to fact, may be given in infancy, so as to be tenaciously retained through life, men could not have passed through the previous ages of the world without discovering the gross errors in which they had been trained. They could not have persevered in making each other miserable, and filling the world with horrors of every description. No! they would long since have discovered the natural, easy, and simple means of giving happiness to themselves and to every human being. But that law of nature which renders it difficult to eradicate our early instruction, although it will ultimately prove highly beneficial to the human race, serves now but to give permanence to error, and to blind our judgements. For the present situation of all the inhabitants of the earth may be compared to that of one whose eyes have been closely bandaged from infancy; who has afterwards been taught to imagine that he clearly sees the form or colour of every object around him; and who has been continually flattered with this notion, so as to compel his implicit belief in the supposition, and render him impenetrable to every attempt that could be made to undeceive him. If such be the present situation of man, how shall the illusion under which he exists be withdrawn from his mind? To beings thus circumstanced, what powers of persuasion can be applied, to make them comprehend their misfortune, and manifest to them the extent of the darkness in which they exist? In what language and in what manner shall the attempt be made? Will not every such attempt irritate and increase the malady, until means shall be devised to unloose the bandage, and thus effectually remove the cause of this mental blindness? Your minds have been so completely enveloped by this dense covering, which has intercepted the approach of every ray of light, that were an angel from heaven to descend and declare your state, you would not, because so circumstanced you could not, believe him.

Causes, over which I could have no control, removed in my early days the bandage which covered my mental sight. If I have been enabled to discover this blindness with which my fellow men are afflicted, to trace their wanderings from the path which they were most anxious to find, and at the same time to perceive that relief could not be administered to them by any premature disclosure of their unhappy state, it is not from any merit of mine; nor can I claim any personal consideration whatever for having been myself relieved from this unhappy situation. But, beholding such truly pitiable objects around me, and witnessing the misery which they hourly experienced from falling into the dangers and evils by which, in these paths, they were on every side surrounded – could I remain an idle spectator? Could I tranquilly see my fellow men walking like idiots in every imaginable direction, except that alone in which the happiness they were in search of could be found?

No! The causes which fashioned me in the womb – the circumstances by which I was surrounded from my birth, and over which I had no influence whatever, formed me with far other faculties, habits, and sentiments. These gave me a mind that could not rest satisfied without trying every possible expedient to relieve my fellow men from their wretched situation, and formed it of such a texture that obstacles of the most formidable nature served but to increase my ardour, and to fix within me a settled determination, either to overcome them, or to die in the attempt.

But the attempt has been made. In my progress the most multiplied difficulties, which to me at a distance seemed almost appalling, and which to others seemed absolutely insurmountable, have on their nearer approach diminished, until, at length, I have lived to see them disappear, like the fleeting clouds of morning, which prove but the harbingers of an animating and cheering day.

Hitherto I have not been disappointed in any of the expectations which I had formed. The events which have yet occurred far exceed my most sanguine anticipations, and my future course now appears evident and straightforward. It is no longer necessary that I should silently and alone exert myself for your benefit and the happiness of mankind. The period is arrived when I may call numbers to my aid, and the call will not be in vain. I well knew the danger which would arise from a premature and abrupt attempt to tear off the many-folded bandages of ignorance, which kept society in darkness. I have therefore been many years engaged, in a manner imperceptible to the public, in gently and gradually removing one fold after another of these fatal bands, from the mental eyes of those who have the chief influence in society. The principles on which the practical system I contemplate is to be founded, are now familiar to some of the leading men of all sects and parties in this country, and to many of the governing powers in Europe and America. They have been submitted to the examination of the most celebrated universities in Europe. They have been subjected to the minute scrutiny of the most learned and acute minds formed on the old system, and I am fully satisfied of their inability to disprove them. These principles I will shortly state.

Every society which exists at present, as well as every society which history records, has been formed and governed on a belief in the following notions, assumed as *first principles*:

1st. That it is in the power of every individual to form his own character.

Hence the various systems called by the name of religion, codes of law, and punishments. Hence also the angry passions entertained by individuals and nations towards each other.

2nd. That the affections are at the command of the individual.

Hence insincerity and degradation of character. Hence the miseries of domestic life, and more than one half of all the crimes of mankind.

3rd. That it is necessary that a large portion of mankind should exist in ignorance and poverty, in order to secure to the remaining part such a degree of happiness as they now enjoy.

Hence a system of counteraction in the pursuits of men, a general opposition among individuals to the interests of each other, and the necessary effects of such a system – ignorance, poverty, and vice.

Facts prove, however,

1st. That character is universally formed *for* and not *by*, the individual.

2nd. That *any* habits and sentiments may be given to mankind.

3rd. That the affections are *not* under the control of the individual.

4th. That every individual may be trained to produce far more than he can consume, while there is a sufficiency of soil left for him to cultivate.

5th. That nature has provided means by which population may be at all times maintained in the proper state to give the greatest happiness to every individual, without one check of vice or misery.

6th. That any community may be arranged, on a due combination of the foregoing principles, in such a manner, as not only to withdraw vice, poverty, and, in a great degree, misery, from the world, but also to place *every* individual under circumstances in which he shall enjoy more permanent happiness than can be given to *any* individual under the principles which have hitherto regulated society.

7th. That all the assumed fundamental principles on which society has hitherto been founded are erroneous, and may be demonstrated to be contrary to fact. And

8th. That the change which would follow the abandonment of those erroneous maxims which bring misery into the world, and the adoption of principles of truth, unfolding a system which shall remove and for ever exclude that misery, may be effected without the slightest injury to any human being.

Here is the groundwork – these are the data, on which society shall ere long be rearranged; and for this simple reason, that it will be rendered evident that it will be for the immediate and future interest of everyone to lend his most active assistance gradually to reform society on this basis. I say *gradually*, for in that word the most important considerations are involved. Any sudden and coercive attempt which may be made to remove even misery from men, will prove injurious rather than beneficial. Their minds must be gradually prepared by an essential alteration of the circumstances which surround them, for any great and important change and amelioration in their condition. They must be first convinced of their blindness, this cannot be effected, even among the least unreasonable, or those termed the best part of mankind, in their present state, without creating some degree of irritation. This irritation must then be tranquillized before another step ought to be attempted; and a general conviction must be established of the truth of the principles on which the projected change is to be founded. Their introduction into practice will then become easy – difficulties will vanish as we approach them – and, afterwards, the desire to see the whole system carried immediately into effect will exceed the means of putting it into execution.

The principles on which this practical system is founded are not new; separately, or partially united, they have been often recommended by the sages of antiquity, and by modern writers. But it is not known to me that they have ever been thus combined. Yet it can be demonstrated that it is only by their being *all brought into practice together*, that they are to be rendered beneficial to mankind; and sure I am that this is the earliest period in the history of man when they could be successfully introduced into practice.

I do not intend to hide from you that the change will be great. 'Old things shall pass away, and all shall become new.'[a]

But this change will bear no resemblance to any of the revolutions which have hitherto occurred. These have been alone calculated to generate and call forth all the evil passions of hatred and revenge: but that system which is now contemplated will effectually eradicate every feeling of irritation and ill will which exists among mankind. The whole proceedings of those who govern and instruct the world will be reversed. Instead of spending ages in telling mankind what they ought to think and how they ought to act, the instructors and governors of the world will acquire a knowledge that will enable them, in one generation, to apply the means which shall cheerfully induce each of those whom they control and influence, not only to think, but to act in such a

[a] See 2 Corinthians 5:17.

manner as shall be best for himself and best for every human being. And yet this extraordinary result will take place without punishment or apparent force.

Under this system, before commands are issued it shall be known whether they can or cannot be obeyed. Men shall not be called upon to assent to doctrines and to dogmas which do not carry conviction to their minds. They shall not be taught that merit can exist in doing, or that demerit can arise from not doing, that over which they have no control. They shall not be told, as at present, that they must love that which, by the constitution of their nature, they are compelled to dislike. They shall not be trained in wild imaginary notions, that inevitably make them despise and hate all mankind out of the little narrow circle in which they exist, and then be told that they must heartily and sincerely love all their fellow men. No, my friends, that system which shall make its way into the heart of every man, is founded upon principles which have not the slightest resemblance to any of those I have alluded to. On the contrary, it is directly opposed to them; and the effects it will produce in practice will differ as much from the practice which history records, and from that which we see around us, as hypocrisy, hatred, envy, revenge, wars, poverty, injustice, oppression, and all their consequent misery, differ from that genuine charity and sincere kindness of which we perpetually hear, but which we have never seen, and which, under the existing systems, we never can see.

That charity and that kindness admit of no exception. They extend to every child of man, however he may have been taught, however he may have been trained. They consider not what country gave him birth, what may be his complexion, what his habits or his sentiments. Genuine charity and true kindness instruct, that whatever these may be, should they prove the very reverse of what we have been taught to think right and best, our conduct towards him, our sentiments with respect to him, should undergo no change; for, when we shall see things as they really are, we shall know that this our fellow man has undergone the same kind of process and training from infancy which we have experienced; that he has been as effectually taught to deem his sentiments and actions right, as we have been to imagine ours right and his wrong; when perhaps the only difference is, that we were born in one country, and he in another. If this be not true, then indeed are all our prospects hopeless; then fierce contentions, poverty, and vice, must continue for ever. Fortunately, however, there is now a superabundance of facts to remove all doubt from every mind; and the principles may now be fully developed, which will easily explain the source of all the opinions which now perplex and divide the world; and their source being discovered, mankind may withdraw all those which are false and injurious, and prevent any evil from arising in consequence of the varieties of sentiments, or rather of feelings, which may afterwards remain.

In short, my friends, the New System is founded on principles which will enable mankind to *prevent*, in the rising generation, almost all, if not all the evils and miseries which we and our forefathers have experienced. A correct knowledge of human nature will be acquired; ignorance will be removed; the angry passions will be prevented from gaining any strength; charity and kindness will universally prevail; poverty will not be known; the interest of each individual will be in strict unison with the interest of every individual in the world. There will not be any counteraction of wishes and desires among men. Temperance and simplicity of manners will be the characteristics of every part of society. The natural defects of the few will be amply compensated by the increased attention and kindness towards them of the many. None will have cause to complain; for each will possess, without injury to another, all that can tend to his comfort, his well-being, and his happiness. Such will be the certain consequences of the introduction into practice of that system for which I have been silently preparing the way for upwards of five-and-twenty years.

Still, however, much more preparation is necessary, and must take place, before the whole can be introduced. It is not intended to put it into practice here. The establishment was too far advanced on the old system before I came amongst you, to admit of its introduction, except to a limited extent. All I now purpose doing in this place is, to introduce as many of the advantages of the new system as can be put into practice in connection with the old: but these advantages will be neither few nor of little amount. I hope, ere long, even under the existing disadvantages, to give you and your children far more solid advantages for your labour, than any persons similarly circumstanced have yet enjoyed at any time or in any part of the world.

Nor is this all. When you and your children shall be in the full possession of all that I am preparing for you, you will acquire superior habits; your minds will gradually expand; you will be enabled to judge accurately of the cause and consequences of my proceedings, and to estimate them at their value. You will then become desirous of living in a more perfect state of society – a society which will possess within itself the certain means of preventing the existence of any injurious passions, poverty, crime, or misery; in which every individual shall be instructed, and his powers of body and mind directed, by the wisdom derived from the best previous experience, so that neither bad habits nor erroneous sentiments shall be known; in which age shall receive attention and respect, and in which every injurious distinction shall be avoided – even variety of opinions shall not create disorder or any unpleasant feeling; a society in which individuals shall acquire increased health, strength, and intelligence – in which their labour shall be always advantageously directed – and in which they will possess every rational enjoyment.

In due time communities shall be formed possessing such characters, and be thrown open to those among you, and to individuals of every class and denomination, whose wretched habits and whose sentiments of folly have not been too deeply impressed to be obliterated or removed, and whose minds can be sufficiently relieved from the pernicious effects of the old system, to permit them to partake of the happiness of the new.

(The communities alluded to shall be more particularly described in a future publication.)

Having delivered this strange discourse, for to many of you it must appear strange indeed, I conceive only one of two conclusions can be drawn by those who have heard it. These are – that the world to this day has been grossly wrong, and is at this moment in the depth of ignorance – or, that I am completely in error. The chances then, you will say, are greatly against me. True: but the chances have been equally against every individual who has been enabled to make any discovery whatsoever.

To effect the purposes which I have long silently meditated, my proceedings for years have been so far removed from, or rather so much in opposition to, the common practices of mankind, that not a few have concluded I was insane. Such conjectures were favourable to my purposes, and I did not wish to contradict them. But the question of insanity between the world and myself will now be decided; either they have been rendered greatly insane – or I am so. You have witnessed my conduct and measures here for sixteen years; and the objects I have had in progress are so far advanced that you can now comprehend many of them. You, therefore shall be judges in this case. Insanity is inconsistency. Let us now try the parties by this rule.

From the beginning I firmly proposed to ameliorate your condition, the condition of all those engaged in similar occupations, and, ultimately, the condition of mankind, whose situation appeared to me most deplorable. Say, now, as far as you know, did I not adopt judicious measures to accomplish these purposes?

Have I not calmly, steadily, and patiently proceeded to fill up the outline of the plan which I originally formed to overcome your worst habits and greatest inconveniences, as well as your prejudices? Have not the several parts of this plan, as they were finished, fulfilled most completely the purposes for which they were projected? Are you not at this moment deriving the most substantial benefits from them? Have I in the slightest degree injured any one of you? During the progress of these measures have I not been opposed in the most determined and formidable manner by those whose interests, if they had understood them, would have made them active co-operators? Without any apparent means to resist these attempts, were they not frustrated and overcome, and even the resistance itself rendered available to hasten the execution of all my wishes? In short, have I not been enabled, with one hand to direct with success the common mercantile concerns of this extensive establishment, and with the other hand to direct measures which now seem more like national than private ones, in order to introduce another system, the effects and success of which shall astonish the profound theologian no less than the most experienced and fortunate politician? – a system which shall train its children of twelve years old to surpass, in true wisdom and knowledge, the boasted acquirements of modern learning, of the sages of antiquity, of the founders of all those systems which hitherto have only confused and distracted the world, and which have been the immediate cause of almost all the miseries we now deplore?

Being witnesses of my measures, you alone are competent to judge of their consistency. Under the circumstances it would be mere hypocrisy in me to say that I do not know what must be your conclusions.

During the long period in which I have been thus silently acting for your benefit and for the benefit of each of my fellow men – what has been the conduct of the world?

Having maturely contemplated the past actions of men, as they have been made known to us by history, it became necessary for my purpose that I should become practically acquainted with men as they now are, and acquire from inspection a knowledge of the precise effects produced in the habits and sentiments of each class, by the peculiar circumstances with which the individuals were surrounded. The causes which had previously prepared my mind and disposition for the work – which had removed so many formidable difficulties in the early part of my progress – now smoothed the way to the easy attainment of wishes. By the knowledge of human nature which I had already acquired, I was enabled to dive into the secret recesses of a sufficient number of minds of the various denominations forming British society, to discover the immediate causes of the sentiments of each, and to trace the consequences of the actions that necessarily proceeded from those sentiments. The whole, as though they had been delineated on a map, were laid open to me. Shall I now at this eventful crisis make the world known to itself? Or shall this valuable knowledge descend with me to the grave, and you, our fellow men, and our children's children, through many generations, yet suffer the miseries which the inhabitants of the earth have to this day experienced? These questions, however, need not be asked. My resolutions were taken in early life; and subsequent years have added to their strength and confirmed them. I therefore proceed regardless of individual consequences. I will hold up the mirror to man – show him, without the intervention of any false medium, what he *is*, and then he will be better prepared to learn what he *may be*. Man is so constituted, that, by the adoption of proper measures in his infancy, and by steadily pursuing them through all the early periods of his life to manhood, he may be taught to think and to act in any manner that is not beyond the acquirement of his faculties: whatever he may have been thus taught to think and do, he may be effectually made to believe is right and best for all mankind. He may also be taught (however few may think and act as he does), that all those who differ from him are wrong, and even ought to be punished with death if they will not think and act like him. In short, he may be rendered insane upon every subject which is not founded on, and which does not remain in never-varying consistency with, the facts that surround mankind. It is owing to this peculiarity in the constitution of man, that when he is born he may be taught any of the various dogmas which are known, and be rendered wholly unfit to associate with any of his fellow men who have been trained in any of the other dogmas. It is owing to this principle that a poor human being duly initiated in the mysteries of Juggernaut, is thereby rendered insane on everything regarding that monster. Or, when instructed in the dogmas of Mahomedanism, he is thus rendered insane on every subject which has reference to Mahomed. I might proceed and state the same of those poor creatures who have been trained in the tenets of Brahma, or Confucius, or in any other of those systems which serve only to destroy the human intellect.

I have no doubt, my friends, you are at present convinced, as thoroughly as conviction can be formed in your minds, that none of you have been subjected to any such process – that you have been instructed in that which is true – that it is evident, Pagans, Jews, Turks, every one of them, millions upon millions almost without end, are wrong, fundamentally wrong. Nay, you will allow, also, that they are truly as insane as I have stated them to be. But you will add – 'We are right – we are the favoured of Heaven – we are enlightened, and cannot be deceived.' This is the feeling of every one of you at this moment. I need not be told your thoughts. Shall I now pay regard to you or to myself? Shall I be content and rest satisfied with the sufficiency which has fallen to my lot, while you remain in your ignorance and misery? Or shall I sacrifice every private consideration for the benefit of you and our fellow men? Shall I tell you, and the whole of the civilized world, that, in many respects, none of those have been rendered more insane than yourselves – than every one of you is at this moment; and that while these maladies remain uncured, you and your posterity cannot but exist in the midst of folly and misery?

What think you now, my friends, is the reason why you believe and act as you do? I will tell you. It is solely and merely because you were born, and have lived, in this period of the world – in Europe – in the island of Great Britain – and more epecially in this northern part of it. Without the shadow of a doubt, had every one of you been born in other times or other places, you might have been the very reverse of that which the present time and place have made you: and, without the possibility of the slightest degree of assent or dissent on your own parts, you might have been at this moment sacrificing yourselves under the wheels of the great idol Juggernaut, or preparing a victim for a cannibal feast. This, upon reflection, will be found to be a truth as certain as that you now hear my voice.

Will you not, then, have charity for the habits and opinions of all men, of even the very worst human beings that your imaginations can conceive? Will you not, then, be sincerely kind to them, and actively endeavour to do them good? Will you not patiently bear with, and commiserate, their defects and infirmities, and consider them as your relatives and friends?

If you will not – if you cannot do this, and persevere to the end of your days in doing it – you have not charity; you cannot have religion; you possess not even common justice; you are ignorant of yourselves, and are destitute of every particle of useful and valuable knowledge respecting human nature.

Until you act after this manner, it is impossible that you can ever enjoy full happiness yourselves, or make others happy.

Herein consists the essence of philosophy – of sound morality – of true and genuine Christianity, freed from the errors that have been attached to it – of pure and undefiled religion.

Without the introduction of this knowledge into full and complete practice, there can be no substantial and permanent ameliorations effected in society; and I declare to you, that until all your thoughts and actions are founded on and governed by these principles, your philosophy will be vain – your morality baseless – your Christianity only calculated to mislead and deceive the weak and the ignorant – and your professions of religion but as sounding brass or a tinkling cymbal.[a]

Those, therefore, who with singleness of heart and mind are ardently desirous to benefit their fellow men, will put forth their utmost exertions to bring this just and humane system of conduct forthwith into practice, and to extend the knowledge of its endless advantages to the uttermost parts of the earth – *for no other principles of action can ever become universal among men*!

Your time now makes it necessary that I should draw to a conclusion, and explain what ought to be the immediate result of what I have stated.

Direct your serious attention to the cause why men think and act as they do. You will then be neither surprised nor displeased on account of their sentiments or their habits. You will then clearly discover why others are displeased with you – and pity them. As you proceed in these inquiries, you will find that mankind cannot be improved or rendered reasonable by force and contention; that it is absolutely necessary to support the old systems and institutions under which we now live, until another system and another arrangement of society shall be proved by practice to be essentially superior. You will, therefore, still regard it as your duty to pay respect and submission to what is established. For it would be no mark of wisdom to desert an old house, whatever may be its imperfections, until a new one shall be ready to receive you, however superior to the old that new one may be when finished.

Continue to obey the laws under which you live; and although many of them are founded on principles of the grossest ignorance and folly, yet obey them – until the government of the country (which I have reason to believe is

[a] See 1 Corinthians 13:1.

in the hands of men well disposed to adopt a system of general improvement),[a] shall find it practicable to withdraw those laws which are productive of evil, and introduce others of an opposite tendency.

With regard to myself, I have not anything to ask of you, which I have not long experienced. I wish you merely to think that I am ardently engaged in endeavouring to benefit you and your children, and, through you and them, to render to mankind at large great and permanent advantages. I ask not for your gratitude, your love, your respect; for on you these do not depend. Neither do I seek or wish for praise or distinction of any kind; for to these, upon the clearest conviction, I am not entitled, and to me, therefore, they could be of no value. My desire is only to be considered as one of yourselves – as a cotton spinner going about his daily and necessary avocations.

But for you I have other wishes. On this day a new era opens to our view. Let it then commence by a full and sincere dismissal from your minds of every unpleasant feeling which you may entertain towards each other, or towards any of your fellow men. When you feel these injurious dispositions beginning to arise – for, as you have been trained and are now circumstanced, they will arise again and again – instantly call to your recollection how the minds of such individuals have been formed – whence have originated all their habits and sentiments: your anger will then be appeased; you will calmly investigate the cause of your differences, and you will learn to love them and to do them good. A little perseverance in this simple and easily acquired practice will rapidly prepare the way for you, and everyone around you, to be truly happy.

[a] Owen thought the Tory administration of Lord Liverpool favoured his proposals, and later claimed that only ecclesiastical intervention prevented their being adopted. See *Manifesto of Robert Owen* (5th edn, 1840), p. 12.

REPORT

To the Committee of the Association for the Relief of the Manufacturing and Labouring Poor, referred to the Committee of the House of Commons on the Poor Laws. March, 1817.[a]

TO THE CHAIRMAN OF THE COMMITTEE ON THE POOR LAWS

SIR,
In obedience to the recommendation of the Committee of the Association for the Relief of the Manufacturing and Labouring Poor, I present the accompanying Report to the Committee on the Poor Law.

I have the honour to be, Sir,
Your most obedient Servant.
ROBERT OWEN

49, Bedford Square, 12th March, 1817

MY LORDS AND GENTLEMEN,
Having been requested by you to draw up a detailed Report of a Plan for the general Relief of the Manufacturing and Labouring Poor, I have the honour to submit the following.

In order to do justice to this interesting subject, it is necessary to trace the operation of those leading causes to which the distress now existing to an unprecedented extent in this country, and in other countries in no very slight degree, is to be ascribed. The evil will be found to flow from a state of things to which society has given birth: a development of this will, therefore, suggest the means of counteracting it.

The immediate cause of the present distress is the depreciation of human labour. This has been occasioned by the general introduction of mechanism into the manufactures of Europe and America, but principally into those of Britain, where the change was greatly accelerated by the inventions of Arkwright and Watt.

[a] Reprinted in *New State of Society*, no. 2 (1817), *New View of Society. Tracts Relative to This Subject* (1818), *The New Existence of Man Upon the Earth* (1854), pt 1, pp. vi–xiv, Owen, *Life*, vol. 1A (1858), pp. 53–64. Later reprints include 1927, 1977.

The introduction of mechanism into the manufacture of objects of desire in society reduced their price; the reduction of price increased the demand for them, and generally to so great an extent as to occasion more human labour to be employed after the introduction of machinery than had been employed before.

The first effects of these new mechanical combinations were to increase individual wealth, and to give a new stimulus to further inventions.

Thus one mechanical improvement gave rise to another in rapid succession; and in a few years they were not only generally introduced into the manufactures of these kingdoms, but were eagerly adopted by other nations of Europe, and by America.

Individual wealth soon advanced to national prosperity, as that term is generally understood; and the country, during a war of twenty-five years, demanding exertion and an amount of expenditure unknown at any former period, attained to a height of political power which confounded its foes and astonished its friends. Both were alike unable to assign the real cause. So steadily, yet rapidly, did our country advance to this envied state, that there appeared to be no limit to its acquirement of riches, and the kind of power which wealth creates. The war itself, when it had extended its ravages over Europe, to Asia, and to America, seemed but a new stimulus to draw forth our exhaustless resources; and in its effects the war did so operate. The destruction of human life in its prime, which it caused throughout the world, and the waste of all the materials necessary for war on so large a scale – perhaps unparalleled in ancient or modern times – created a demand for various productions, which the overstrained industry of British manufacturers, aided by all the mechanism they could invent and bring into action, was hardly competent to supply.

But peace at length followed, and found Great Britain in possession of a new power in constant action, which, it may be safely stated, exceeded the labour of *one hundred millions* of the most industrious human beings, in the full strength of manhood.

(To give an instance of this power, there is machinery at work in one establishment in this country, aided by a population not exceeding 2,500 souls, which produces as much as the existing population of Scotland could manufacture after the mode in common practice fifty years ago! And Great Britain contains several such establishments!)

Thus our country possessed, at the conclusion of the war, a productive power, which operated to the same effect as if her population had been actually increased fifteen or twenty fold; and this had been chiefly created within the preceding twenty-five years. The rapid progress made by Great Britain, during the war, in wealth and political influence, can therefore no longer astonish; the cause was quite adequate to the effect.

Now, however, new circumstances have arisen. The war demand for the productions of labour having ceased, markets could no longer be found for them; and the revenues of the world were inadequate to purchase that which a power so enormous in its effects did produce: a diminished demand consequently followed. When, therefore, it became necessary to contract the sources of supply, it soon proved that mechanical power was much cheaper than human labour; the former, in consequence, was continued at work, while the latter was superseded; and human labour may now be obtained at a price far less than is absolutely necessary for the subsistence of the individual in ordinary comfort.

(Human labour, hitherto the great source of wealth in nations, being thus diminished in value at the rate of not less than from two to three millions sterling per week in Great Britain alone, that sum, or whatever more or less it may be, has consequently been withdrawn from the circulation of the country, and this has necessarily been the means by which the farmer, tradesman, manufacturer, and merchant, have been so greatly impoverished.) A little reflection will show that the working classes have now no adequate means of contending with mechanical power; one of three results must therefore ensue:

1. The use of mechanism must be greatly diminished; or,

2. Millions of human beings must be starved, to permit its existence to the present extent; or,

3. Advantageous occupation must be found for the poor and unemployed working classes, to whose labour mechanism must be rendered subservient, instead of being applied, as at present, to supersede it.

But under the existing commercial system, mechanical power could not in one country be discontinued, and in others remain in action, without ruin to that country in which it should be discontinued. No one nation, therefore, will discontinue it; and although such an act were possible, it would be a sure sign of barbarism in those who should make the attempt. It would, however, be a far more evident sign of barbarism, and an act of gross tyranny, were any government to permit mechanical power to starve millions of human beings. The thought will not admit of one moment's contemplation; it would inevitably create unheard-of misery to all ranks. The last result therefore alone deserves to be considered, which is, 'that advantageous occupation must be found for the unemployed working classes, to whose labour mechanism must be rendered subservient, instead of being applied, as at present, to supersede it.'

To conduct a change so important and of such vital necessity to our well-being, demands a comprehensive view and an accurate knowledge of the real state of society.

The measure should be well considered with respect to its present bearings and connections, and its consequences traced by minds uninfluenced by prejudices of party or of class.

The circumstances of the times render a change in our internal policy respecting the poor and working classes absolutely necessary; and the first question to be decided by every man of all ranks is, Shall the alteration be made under the guidance of moderation and wisdom, foreseeing, and gradually preparing each step, one regularly after another, thereby preventing a single premature advance – or shall the change be effected by ignorance and prejudice, under the baneful influence of the angry and violent passions? Should these prevail, then will the truly disinterested, those whose ardent wish is to ameliorate the condition of mankind, withdraw from the contest, and society be involved in confusion. But, surely, the experience of past ages, and particularly of the last twenty-five years, will have taught men wisdom, and prepared the minds of all for a calm and dispassionate inquiry – how the evils which at present afflict society can best be remedied.

I proceed, therefore, with the subject, and shall endeavour to show in what manner advantageous employment can be found for all the poor and working classes, under an arrangement which will permit mechanical improvements to be carried to any extent.

Under the existing laws, the unemployed working classes are maintained by, and consume part of, the property and produce of the wealthy and industrious, while their powers of the body and mind remain unproductive. They frequently acquire the bad habits which ignorance and idleness never fail to produce; they amalgamate with the regular poor, and become a nuisance to society.

Most of the poor have received bad and vicious habits from their parents; and so long as their present treatment continues, those bad and vicious habits will be transmitted to their children, and, through them, to succeeding generations.

Any plan, then, to ameliorate their condition, must prevent bad and vicious habits from being taught to their children, and provide the means by which only good and useful ones may be given to them.

The labour of some individuals is far more valuable than that of others; and this arises principally from the training and instruction they receive.

Means should therefore be devised to give the most useful training and instruction to the children of the poor.

The same quantity and quality of labour, under one direction, will produce a much more valuable result than under another.

It is necessary, then, that the labour of the poor should be exerted under the best.

One mode of management as to their expenditure will create many more advantages and comforts than another.

Such arrangements should, therefore, be made in this department, as would produce the largest benefits at the smallest expense.

Most of the vices and misery of the poor arise from their being placed under circumstances in which their apparent interest and their apparent duty are opposed to each other, and in consequence of their being surrounded by unnecessary temptations which they had not been trained to overcome.

It would, therefore, be a material improvement in the management of the poor, to place them under such circumstances as would obviously unite their real interest and duty, and remove them from unnecessary temptation.

Under this view of the subject, any plan for the amelioration of the poor should combine means to prevent their children from acquiring bad habits, and to give them good ones – to provide useful training and instruction for them – to provide proper labour for the adults – to direct their labour and expenditure so as to produce the greatest benefit to themselves and to society; and to place them under such circumstances as shall remove them from unnecessary temptations, and closely unite their interest and duty.

These advantages cannot be given either to individuals or to families separately, or to large congregated numbers.

They can be effectually introduced into practice only under arrangements that would unite in one establishment a population of from 500 to 1,500 persons, averaging about 1,000.

I now submit to the Committee the following plan, founded on the foregoing principles, which, it is presumed, will combine all the advantages that have been enumerated, and, in progress of time, lead to many others of equal importance.

As the seeming novelty of the plan might possibly induce a hasty or premature decision respecting it on the part of those who have not had much practical experience among the poor, or who may be under the influence of some favourite theory of political economy, to which it might appear to be opposed, I beg to submit it as the result of daily experience among the poor and working classes, on an extensive scale, for twenty-five years; and during which the most unceasing attention has been directed to discover the primary causes of their poverty and misery, and the best means of providing a remedy for both.

A casual or superficial consideration of the plan now proposed cannot be expected to impart a sufficient knowledge of the various beneficial results of such a combination, or to form the ground of a reasonable opinion as to its practicability.

I now beg leave to solicit the attention of the Committee to the drawings and explanations which accompany this Report.

The drawing exhibits, in the foreground, an establishment, with its appendages and appropriate quantity of land; and at due distances, other villages of a similar description.

Squares of buildings are here represented sufficient to accommodate about 1,200 persons each; and surrounded by a quantity of land, from 1000 to 1500 acres.

Within the squares are public buildings, which divide them into parallelograms.

The central building contains a public kitchen, mess-rooms, and all the accommodation necessary to economical and comfortable cooking and eating.

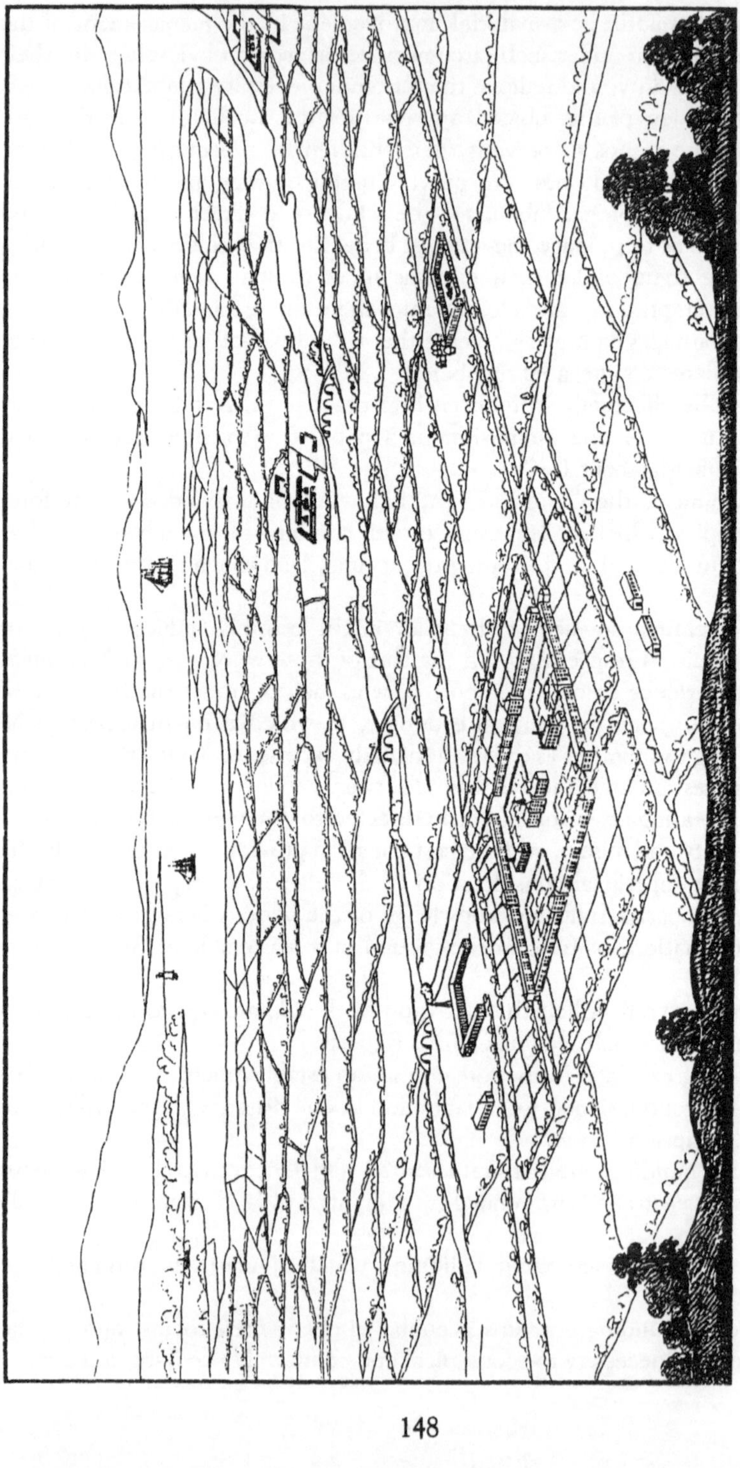

A View and Plan of the Agricultural and Manufacturing Villages of *Unity* and *Mutual* Co-operation.

To the right of this is a building, of which the ground-floor will form the infant school, and the other a lecture-room and a place of worship.

The building to the left contains a school for the elder children, and a committee-room on the ground floor; above, a library and a room for adults.

In the vacant space within the squares, are enclosed grounds for exercise and recreation: these enclosures are supposed to have trees planted in them.

It is intended that three sides of each square shall be lodging houses, chiefly for the married, consisting of four rooms in each; each room to be sufficiently large to accommodate a man, his wife, and two children.

The fourth side is designed for dormitories for all the children exceeding two in a family, or above three years of age.

In the centre of this side of the square are apartments for those who superintend the dormitories: at one extremity of it the infirmary; and at the other a building for the accommodation of strangers who may come from a distance to see their friends and relatives.

In the centres of two sides of the squares are apartments for general superintendents, clergyman, schoolmasters, surgeon &c.; and in the third are store-rooms for all the articles required for the use of the establishment.

On the outside, and at the back of the houses around the squares, are gardens, bounded by roads.

Immediately beyond these, on one side, are buildings for mechanical and manufacturing purposes. The slaughter-house, stabling, &c., to be separated from the establishment by plantations.

At the other side are offices for washing, bleaching, &c.; and at a still greater distance from the squares, are some of the farming establishments, with conveniences for malting, brewing, and corn-mills, &c.: around these are cultivated enclosures, pasture-land, &c., the hedge-rows of which are planted with fruit-trees.

The plan represented is on a scale considered to be sufficient to accommodate about 1,200 persons.

And these are to be supposed men, women, and children, of all ages, capacities, and dispositions; most of them very ignorant; many with bad and vicious habits, possessing only the ordinary bodily and mental faculties of human beings, and who require to be supported out of the funds appropriated to the maintenance of the poor – individuals who are at present not only useless and a direct burthen on the public, but whose moral influence is highly pernicious, since they are the medium by which ignorance and certain classes of vicious habits and crimes are fostered and perpetuated in society.

It is evident that while the poor are suffered to remain under the circumstances in which they have hitherto existed, they and their children, with very few exceptions, will continue unaltered in succeeding generations.

In order to effect any radically beneficial change in their character, they must be removed from the influence of such circumstances, and placed under those which, being congenial to the natural constitution of man and the well-being of society, cannot fail to produce that amelioration in their condition which all classes have so great an interest in promoting.

Such circumstances, after incessant application to the subject, I have endeavoured to combine in the arrangement of the establishment represented in the drawings, so far as the present state of society will permit. These I will now attempt to explain more particularly.

Each lodging-room within the squares is to accommodate a man, his wife, and two children under three years of age; and to be such as will permit them to have much more comforts than the dwellings of the poor usually afford.

It is intended that the children above three years of age should attend the school, eat in the mess room, and sleep in the dormitories; the parents being of course permitted to see and converse with them at meals and all other proper times; – that before they leave school they shall be well instructed in all necessary and useful knowledge; – that every possible means shall be adopted to prevent the acquirement of bad habits from their parents or otherwise; – that no pains shall be spared to impress upon them such habits and dispositions as may be most conducive to their happiness through life, as well as render them useful and valuable members of the community to which they belong.

It is proposed that the women should be employed, –

1st. – In the care of their infants, and in keeping their dwellings in the best order.

2ndly. – In cultivating the gardens to raise vegetables for the supply of the public kitchen.

3rdly. – In attending to such of the branches of the various manufactures as women can well undertake; but not to be employed in them more than four or five hours in the day.

4thly. – In making up clothing for the inmates of the establishment.

5thly. – In attending occasionally, and in rotation, in the public kitchen, mess-rooms, and dormitories; and, when properly instructed, in superintending some parts of the education of the children in the schools.

It is proposed that the elder children should be trained to assist in gardening and manufacturing for a portion of the day, according to their strength; and that the men should be employed, all of them, in agriculture, and also in manufactures, or in some other occupation for the benefit of the establishment.

The ignorance of the poor, their ill-training, and their want of a rational education, make it necessary that those of the present generation should be actively and regularly occupied through the day in some essentially useful work; yet in such a manner as that their employment should be healthy and productive. The plan which has been described will most amply admit of this.

In order to offer some practical idea of the expenses that would be incurred such an establishment of 1200 souls, that following items are submitted.

SCHEDULE *of* EXPENSES *for forming an Establishment for* 1,200 MEN, WOMEN, AND CHILDREN.

If the land be purchased,

1,200 acres of land, at 30*l.* per acre	£36,000
Lodging apartments for 1,200 persons	17,000
Three public buildings within the square	11,000
Manufactory, slaughter-house, and washing-house	8,000
Furnishing 300 lodging-rooms, at 8*l.* each	2,400
Furnishing kitchen, schools, and dormitories	3,000
Two farming establishments, with corn-mill, and malting and brewing appendages	5,000
Making the interior of the square and roads	3,000
Stock for the farm under spade cultivation	4,000
Contingencies and extras	6,060
	£96,000[a]

This sum, being divided by 1,200, gives a capital to be advanced of 80*l.* per head; or, at 5 per cent. per annum, 4*l.* each per year.

Thus, at so small an expense as a rental of 4*l.* per head, may the unemployed poor be put in a condition to maintain themselves; and, as may be easily conceived, quickly to repay the capital advanced, if thought necessary.

But, if the land be rented, only 60,000*l.* capital would be required.

There are several modes by which this plan may be effected.

It may be accomplished by individuals, – by parishes, – by counties, – by districts, &c. comprising more counties than one, – and by the nation at large, through its Government. Some may prefer one mode, some another; and it would be advantageous certainly to have the experience of the greatest variety of particular modes, in order that the plan which such diversified practice should prove to be the best might afterwards be generally adopted. It may therefore be put into execution by any parties according to their own localities and views.

The first thing necessary is, to raise a sum of money adequate to purchase the land (or it may be rented) – to build the square, manufactories, farm-houses, and their appendages – to stock the farm – and to provide everything to put the whole in motion.

Proper persons must be procured to superintend the various departments, until others should be trained in the establishment to supply their places.

The labour of the persons admitted may then be applied to procure a

[a] The total is £95,460, which Owen has rounded upwards.

comfortable support for themselves and their children, and to repay, as might be required, the capital expended on their establishment.

When their labour shall be thus properly and temperately directed, under an intelligent system, easy of practice, it will soon be found to be more than sufficient to supply every reasonable want of man. How vain and useless to acknowledge the truth of the principle that men may be trained to produce more than they will consume, unless the means shall be devised by which the principle may be carried into practice! The period is arrived when it may be most advantageously put into practice. And the period is also arrived when the state of society imperiously requires the adoption of some measures to relieve the wealthy and industrious from the increasing burdens of the poor's rate, and the poor from their increasing misery and degradation.

It is impossible to find language sufficiently strong to express the inconsistency, as well as the injustice, of our present proceedings towards the poor and working classes. They are left in gross ignorance; they are permitted to be trained up in habits of vice, and in the commission of crimes; and, as if purposely to keep them in ignorance and vice, and goad them on to commit criminal acts, they are perpetually surrounded with temptations which cannot fail to produce all those effects.

The system, or rather want of system, which exists with regard to the management of the poor, has been emphatically condemned by a long and painful experience.

The immense sums annually raised for their relief are lavished in utter disregard of every principle of public justice or economy. They offer greater rewards for idleness and vice than for industry and virtue; and thus directly operate to increase the degradation and misery of the classes whom they are designed to serve. No sum, however enormous, administered after this manner, could be productive of any other result; rather will pauperism and wretchedness increase along with the increase of an expenditure thus applied.

The poor and unemployed working classes, however, cannot, must not, be abandoned to their fate, lest the consequences entail misfortune on us all. Instead of being left, as they now are, to the dominion of ignorance, and to the influence of circumstances which are fatal to their industry and morals – a situation in which it is easy to perceive the inefficacy, or rather the injuriousness, of granting them a provision in a mere pecuniary shape – they should, on the contrary, be afforded the means of procuring a certain and comfortable subsistence by their labour, under a system which will not only direct that labour and its earnings to the best advantage, but, at the same time, place them under circumstances the most favourable to the growth of morals and of happiness. In short, instead of allowing their habits to proceed under the worst influence possible, or rather, as it were, to be left to chance, thus producing unintentionally crimes that render necessary the severities of our penal code, let a system for the prevention of pauperism and of crimes be adopted, and the operation of our penal code will soon be restricted to very narrow limits.

The outlines of such a plan, it is presumed, have been, however imperfectly, suggested and sketched in this Report.

It may be hoped, that the Government of this country is now sufficiently alive to the necessity of abandoning the principle on which all our legislative measures on this subject have hitherto proceeded; for nothing short of this can place the Empire in permanent safety. Until the preventive principle shall become the basis of legislative proceedings, it will be vain to look for any measures beyond partial temporary expedients, which will leave society unimproved, or involve it in a much worse state.

If such should be the conviction of Government, the change proposed in the management of the poor and unemployed working classes will be much better directed nationally than privately.

In fact, many of the benefits to be derived to society at large will not be realised until the plan becomes national.

Should the practical outline which is now submitted be approved, and engage the attention of Parliament, the next consideration would be, in what manner it may be carried into effect with the least loss of time, and without immediate or future injury to the resources of the country.

The money necessary for founding establishments on the principle of the plan now proposed, may be obtained by consolidating the funds of some of the public charities; by equalising the poor rates and borrowing on their security. The poor, including those belonging to public charities, should be made national.

(Or the funds may be raised by borrowing of individuals who have now a surplus capital unemployed; by borrowing from the Sinking Fund; or by any other financial arrangement that may be deemed preferable. The establishments rapidly increasing in value by the labour of the individuals on the land, will soon become a sufficient security for a large proportion of the money that may be expended in this purchase.)

Hence will arise a superabundance of funds and labour.

The country should be surveyed, and the best situations for these agricultural and manufacturing establishments be ascertained.

Such as can be the most easily procured, in various parts of the kingdom, should be fairly valued, and purchased by the nation, on perpetual lease or otherwise, and be properly laid out by competent persons for the purposes required. The labour of the poor and unemployed may be most advantageously applied to the execution of every part of this work, under the direction of proper persons appointed to superintend the various departments.

Nothing new would be required; all that could be wanted is in daily practice all over the kingdom.

The land and houses would not only possess their original worth, but, as the plan advanced, both would materially increase in value; and all the districts in the neighbourhood of these communities would partake of the general amelioration which they could not fail to introduce in a very extensive degree.

When these arrangements shall be adopted and carried into execution, (and sooner or later they must be, in order to permanently relieve the national distress,) new and extraordinary consequences will follow. The real value of the land and labour will rise, while all the productions of land and labour will fall; mechanism will be of more extensive worth and benefit to society; every encouragement may be given to its extension; and its extension will go on *ad infinitum*, but only in aid of, and not in competition with, human labour.

A summary of the advantages to be derived from the execution of such a plan may be presented under the following heads:-

1. Expensive as such a system for the unemployed poor may appear to a superficial observer, it will be found, on mature investigation by those who understand all the consequences of such a combination, to be by far the most economical that has yet been devised.

2. Many of the unemployed poor are now in a state of gross ignorance, and have been trained in bad habits; evils which, under the present system, are likely to continue for endless generations. The arrangements proposed offer the most certain means, in a manner gratifying to all the parties interested, and to every liberal mind, of overcoming both their ignorance and their bad habits in one generation.

3. The greatest evils in society arise from mankind being trained in principles of disunion. The proposed measures offer to unite men in the pursuit of common objects for their mutual benefit, by presenting an easy practicable plan for gradually withdrawing the causes of difference among individuals, and making their interest and duty very generally the same.

4. This system will also afford the most simple and effectual means of giving the best habits and sentiments to all the children of the unemployed poor, accordingly as society shall be able to determine what habits and sentiments, or what character, ought to be given to them.

5. It will likewise offer the most powerful means of improving the habits and conduct of the present unemployed adult poor, who have been grossly neglected by society from their infancy.

6. Owing to the peculiar arrangement of the plan, it will give to the poor, in return for their labour, more valuable, substantial, and permanent comfort, than they have ever yet been able to obtain.

7. In one generation it will supersede the necessity for poor-rates or any pecuniary gifts of charity, by preventing any one from being poor or subject to such unnecessary degradation.

8. It will offer the means of gradually increasing the population in unpopulous districts of Europe and America in which such increase may be deemed necessary, and of enabling a much greater population to subsist in comfort on

a given spot, if requisite, than existed before; in short, of increasing the strength and political power of the country in which it shall be adopted, more than tenfold.

9. It is so easy, that it may be put into practice with less ability and exertion than are necessary to establish a new manufacture in a new situation. Many individuals of ordinary talent have formed establishments which possess combinations much more complex. In fact, there would not be anything required which is not daily performed in common society, and which, under the proposed arrangement, might not be much more easily accomplished.

10. It will effectually relieve the manufacturing and labouring poor from their present deep distress, without violently or prematurely interfering with the existing institutions of society.

11. It will permit mechanical inventions and improvements to be carried to any extent; for by the proposed arrangement every improvement in mechanism would be rendered subservient to and in aid of human labour.

12. And lastly, every part of society would be essentially benefited by this change in the condition of the poor.

Some plan founded on such principles as have been developed herein, appears absolutely necessary, to secure the well-being of society, as well as to prevent the afflicting spectacle of thousands pining in want amidst a superabundance of means to well-train, educate, employ, and support in comfort, a population of at least four times our present numbers.

ROBERT OWEN

LETTER

Published in the London Newspapers of July 30th, 1817[a]

LONDON, JULY 25, 1817

MR EDITOR,

SIR, – As a meeting is intended shortly to be held, to take into consideration a plan which I have proposed to relieve and remoralise the poor and the unemployed of the working classes, I feel it incumbent on me, previously, to put the public in possession of a greater development of the principles on which it is founded, in order that the details may be afterwards more fully comprehended. An early insertion, therefore, of the following, will promote the object of,

Sir, your obliged,

R. OWEN

49, Charlotte Street, Portland Place.

A Further Development of the Plan contained in the Report to the Committee of the Association for the Relief of the Manufacturing and Labouring Poor; with answers to objections. And an account of the Effects produced on the Female Prisoners in Newgate by the Application in Practice of these Principles, carried into Execution by Mrs Fry[b] *and other benevolent Individuals of the Society of Friends. And a Personal Sketch.*

It is generally known and acknowledged that from obvious causes greater distress exists among the poor and working classes than they have experienced

[a] See for example *The Times*, no. 10211 (30 July 1817), pp. 3–4. The full title was: A Further Development of the Plan Contained in the Report to the Committee of the Association for the Relief of the Manufacturing Poor; with Answers to Objections. And an Account of the Effects Produced on Female Prisoners in Newgate by the Application in Practice of These Principles, Carried into Execution by Mrs. Fry and other Benevolent Individuals of the Society of Friends. And a Personal Sketch. Also printed in *New View of Society. Extracted from the Daily Papers of 30th July, and 9th and 10th of August, 1817* (1817). Reprinted in *New View of Society. Tracts Relative to This Subject* (1818), *A Report of the British and Foreign Philanthropic Society* (Dublin, 1823), *The New Existence of Man Upon the Earth* (1854), pt 1, pp. xv–xxxi, and in Owen, *Life*, vol. 1A (1858), pp. 65–83. Later reprints include 1991.

[b] Elizabeth Fry (1780–1845): Quaker prison reformer active from c. 1813; formed association for the improvement of female prisoners at Newgate in 1817.

at any former time. The country, however, possesses the most ample means to relieve their distress; and a plan has been proposed by me to enable either the Government, parishes, or individuals, to put those means into practice. The plan has been also generally circulated, and many objections, as it was anticipated, have been made to it by those who are theorists only, or who are wholly unacquainted with the kind of practice requisite to give them any useful knowledge on the subject. Many misconceptions also exist respecting the details, which some of lively, and others of gloomy imagination, have fancied belong of necessity to the plan. To meet the objections of the first in the most direct manner, and to obviate the misconceptions of the last, I have arranged the subject in the form of questions and answers.

The principles and plan are now more fully before the public. If the former contain error, or the latter be impracticable, it becomes the duty of many to expose either. If, however, the plan shall prove, on investigation, to be correct in principle, to be easy of practice, and that it can relieve the poor and unemployed of the working classes from the grievous distresses and degradation under which they suffer, it becomes equally the duty of all who profess to desire the amelioration of the lower orders, to exert themselves without further delay to carry it into execution, in order that another year of extensive and unnecessary suffering and demoralisation, from the want of a sufficiency of wholesome food and proper training and instruction, may not uselessly pass away.

Question. Are you the principal proprietor of the works and village of New Lanark, and have you the sole direction and superintendence of them?

Answer. Yes.

Q. *How long have you had the management of that establishment?*

A. Eighteen years in August next.

Q. *Of what description is the population of New Lanark?*

A. Of manufacturers of cotton thread chiefly; but also of iron and brass founders, iron and tin smiths, millwrights, turners in wood and metals, sawyers, carpenters, masons, tilers, painters, glaziers, tailors, shoemakers, butchers, bakers, shopkeepers, farmers, labourers, surgeons, ministers of religion, instructors of youth, male and female superintendents of various departments, clerks, and policemen; forming a mixed society of trades and workpeople.

Q. *Had you any experience among the working classes before you undertook the management of the works at New Lanark?*

A. Yes; I superintended large manufacturing establishments in Manchester and its neighbourhood for about eight years preceding, in which great numbers of men, women, and children were employed.

Q. *What has been the chief object of your attention during the number of years that you have had so many persons under your care and superintendence?*

A. To discover the means by which the condition of the poor and working classes could be ameliorated, and with benefit to their employers.

Q. *To what conclusions have you now come upon this subject?*

A. That the situation of these classes may be easily greatly improved; and that their natural powers may be far more beneficially directed, for themselves, and for society at large, without creating injury of any kind, to any class, or to any individual.

Q. *Have you generally succeeded in improving the condition and moral habits of those who have been under your care?*

A. Yes, and with even fewer exceptions than I anticipated, considering the obstacles I had to encounter, with the nature of the influence that I possessed to enable me to overcome them.

Q. *What are those obstacles?*

A. The ignorance and ill-training of the people, which had given them the habits of drunkenness, theft, falsehood, and want of cleanliness; with opposition to each other's interests; sectarian feelings; strong national prejudices, both political and religious, against all attempts on the part of a stranger to improve their condition; to which may be added the unhealthy nature of their employment.

Q. *On what leading principles did you act, so as to remove those obstacles?*

A. On the principle of prevention solely. Instead of wasting time and talent in considering an endless variety of individual effects, I patiently studied the causes producing those effects, exerting myself to remove them; and by thus acting, it appeared that the same time and talent, when employed under the system of prevention, could produce results very much greater than under the system of coercion and punishment. For instance, in the case of habitual drunkenness, it appeared to me useless to apply to the individuals who had been taught to acquire the practices of intoxication, to desist from it, while they remained surrounded by the circumstances that perpetually tempted them to continue the habit. The first step adopted in that case was to convince the parties when sober, of the advantages they would derive from having the temptation removed; which, when attempted in a mild and proper spirit, was never difficult to accomplish. The next step was to remove the temptation; and then the evil itself, with all its endless injurious consequences, ceased altogether. The whole process, when completely understood, is simplicity itself, and may be easily carried into practice to the fullest extent by those who possess the usual ordinary talents; and society would rapidly improve without any retrogression. But while the notions which have influenced the conduct of mankind up to the present period shall prevail and be acted upon, society cannot substantially and permanently improve. Those notions confine the attention to effects, and, from want of useful inquiry, lead to the conclusion that the causes from which they really proceed, however injurious, cannot be altered or controlled by man. Under such notions the world is now governed.

Facts, however, prove that the reverse of these notions is true: let men, therefore, attend to facts, and to facts only, and it will be obvious that they can, with ease, remove the real causes which create bad habits, errors, and crimes; and, without difficulty, replace them with other causes, the certain effects of which would be to establish generally throughout society, good habits, correct sentiments, and a kind, charitable, and virtuous conduct, free from the prejudices that would create unkind feelings and thence render them unjust to those who had been taught to differ from them in opinion. It must, therefore, absolutely follow, that to attempt to improve mankind on any other principle whatever, than by a close, accurate, and undeviating attention to facts, is as absurd and as unavailing as to expect that the most barren soil and sterile climate shall spontaneously produce abundance; as to expect that a full and steady light shall issue from the darkest abyss; or that man, immersed in ignorance, surrounded by every vicious temptation, shall be better, wiser, and happier, than when trained to be intelligent and active, amidst circumstances only which would perpetually unite his interests, his duty, and his feelings. While, then, we permit the causes to remain that must leave mankind in ignorance, that must create in them intemperance, idleness, uncharitableness, vice, crime, and every evil passion, and, at the same time, expect or wish them to become the reverse, – there is precisely as much wisdom in such expectation, as to imagine, contrary to all the experience of the world, that effects shall no longer continue to follow their natural causes. To inflict, therefore, upon men, pains and penalties for having vicious qualities (more unfortunate for themselves than others) which are produced in them by the existing circumstances, is to act upon notions devoid of every pretension to sound judgment and rationality.

Q. Has all your practice been founded upon these principles?

A. Yes; and the results have not once disappointed my expectations; on the contrary, in every instance they have exceeded my most sanguine hopes. It is not, as it appears to me, to any natural superiority of mind, or early-acquired advantages, (for I possess none,) that my success in these endeavours can be attributed; but solely to the accidental circumstances of being enabled, early in life, to see, in part, the important benefits that would result to society from the adoption of the system of prevention; and acting uniformly upon the well-known fact 'that human character is always formed *for*, and not *by*, the individual.'

Q. How many complaints have been brought before you by the inhabitants of New Lanark, in your capacity of a magistrate for the county?

A. Not one, for many years past.

Q. Having turned your attention to the subject, to what causes do you attribute the distress existing among the poor and working classes?

A. To a misapplication of the existing powers of production in the country, both natural and artificial, when compared to the wants and demands for those productions. Much of our natural power, consisting of the physical and intellectual faculties of human beings, is now not only altogether unproductive, but a heavy burden to the country; under a system, too, which is rapidly demoralising it; while a very large part of our artificial or mechanical agency is employed to produce that which is of little real value to society, and which, in its act of production, entails innumerable evils of the most afflicting kind, at the present time, upon the producers, as well as upon a very large part of society; and, through them, upon the whole of our population.

Q. Does your experience enable you to suggest a more advantageous application of these productive powers?

A. It induces me to say, that they may be applied more advantageously, for society, and for the individuals; that they may, with ease, be so directed as to remove speedily the present distress of the labouring poor, and gradually to carry the prosperity of the country to a point much higher than it has ever yet attained.

Q. How can this be done?

A. By forming well-digested arrangements to occupy the apparent surplus of the labouring poor, who are competent to work, in productive employment, in order that they may maintain themselves first, and afterwards contribute to bear their proportion of the expenses of the State.

Q. Do the means exist by which employment could be given to the unoccupied of the working classes?

A. It appears to me that the country possesses the most ample means to attain this object, if they were called into action. Those means consist of land unemployed; land imperfectly cultivated; money employed unprofitably; manual powers of labour idle, demoralising, and consequently generating every kind of evil in society; artificial or mechanical agency almost unlimited, and which might be made available for the most important purposes. These are the means, which, if properly combined and put into action, would soon relieve the country from poverty and its attendant evils.

Q. How can they be put into action?

A. By bringing them all into useful and profitable combinations, so as to create limited communities of individuals, on the principle of united labour and expenditure, having their basis in agriculture, and in which all should have mutual and common interests.

Q. What are your reasons for recommending such a combination of human powers?

A. The knowledge that I possess of the very superior advantages which each person could derive by this means, beyond any application of his own exertions for his own exclusive purposes.

Q. What are those superior advantages?

A. Communities of 500 to 1,500 persons, founded on the principle of united labour and expenditure, and having their basis in agriculture, might be arranged so as to give the following advantages to the labouring poor, and through them to all the other classes – for every real benefit to the latter must come from the former. All the labour of the individuals under this system would be naturally and advantageously directed; first to procure for themselves abundance of all that was necessary for their comfortable subsistence; next, they would obtain the means to enable them to unlearn many, almost all indeed, of the bad habits which the present defective arrangements of society have forced upon them: then, to give only the best habits and dispositions to the rising generation, and thus withdraw those circumstances from society which separate man from man, and introduce others, whose entire tendency shall be to unite them in one general interest that shall be clearly understood by each. They will afterwards be enabled to cultivate the far more valuable, the intellectual part of their nature; that part which, when properly directed, will discover how much may yet be put into practice to promote human happiness.[a]

They will then proceed to create that surplus which will be necessary to repay the interest of the capital expended in the purchase of the establishment, including all its appendages; or, in other words, the rent of it. And lastly, to contribute their full share to the exigencies of the State, in proportion to the value of their property. By these arrangements they will add a new strength to the political power of the country, that few are yet able to estimate.

Q. Should the arrangements you describe be practicable, many objections have been urged against the plan?

A. Inexperienced as the world is in regard to the combinations here contemplated, I am aware that many difficulties and doubts will arise in most minds; but if the objections be separately stated, they may be removed; and an experience of nearly thirty years, added to an unceasing, honest, and I hope unbiased attention to the subject, assures me beforehand that they may.

Q. For instance – can the poor and working classes be associated together to act cordially in any general measures, considering what is everywhere evinced in the state of the workhouses and houses of industry?

A. Trained as the poor have been, and arranged as even the best of those establishments now are, such unfavourable results must follow. The poor exist previously in a state of extreme ignorance; and when they are brought together under one roof, they are perpetually in contact with each other, but without a single principle of union which they can understand. Owing to the bad habits they have acquired, and a want of proper instruction, they cannot discover the mutual interest they have in each other's happiness; and as these houses are now constituted, no effective arrangements can be made to overcome the one, or to impart the other. Workhouses and houses of industry have originated with those who had but a limited knowledge of human nature, and who were

[a] Some debt to William Godwin may be evident here. See for example Godwin, *The Enquirer* (1797), p. 173.

also unacquainted with the true principles of political economy. But very different results may be made to ensue from the establishment of these agricultural and manufacturing villages; most of the causes of opposition among the individuals thus associated will be removed, and others tending to unite them in good offices and in one interest will be introduced.

Q. *But will men in a community of mutual and combined interests be as industrious as when employed for their individual gain?*

A. The supposition that they will not, I apprehend to be a common prejudice, and not at all founded on fact. Wherever the experiment has been tried, the labour of each has been exerted cheerfully. It is found that when men work together for a common interest, each performs his part more advantageously for himself and for society, than when employed for others at daily wages, or than when working by the piece. When employed by the day, they feel no interest in their occupation, beyond the receipt of their wages; when they work by the piece, they feel too much interest, and frequently overwork themselves, and occasion disease, premature old age, and death. When employed with others in a community of interests, both these extremes are avoided; the labour becomes temperate, but effective, and may be easily regulated and superintended. Besides, the principles and practices are now quite obvious, by which any inclinations, from the most indolent to the most industrious, may be given to the rising generation.

Q. *But will not the parties dispute perpetually about the division and possession of the property?*

A. Certainly not. The labour and expenditure of individuals are now applied so ignorantly, wastefully, and under so many disadvantages, that the mass of mankind cannot procure sufficient to support themselves in ordinary comfort without great exertion and anxiety; they therefore acquire, under the influence of a strong necessity, a tenacious love of that property which costs them so much to procure; thus making the feeling itself appear, to a superficial observer, as one implanted by nature in the constitution. No conclusion can, however, be more erroneous; for if men were placed in a situation, where, by moderate occupation, without care or agitation of mind, they could procure the necessaries and comforts of life in abundance, they might be trained to dispute as little about the division of them as they now do about the commonly attainable products of nature – such as water; neither would they have a desire to accumulate an unnecessary quantity of the one, any more than they now wish an excess of the other. I might add, that under this plan, each individual would soon discover that he possessed more for his own enjoyment without any anxiety, than he could have acquired under the existing system amongst the poor, with all the cares and troubles they now experience.

Q. *But can these establishments be well managed, unless by men of great talents and benevolence, such men not being very numerous?*

A. Here also I may be permitted to say, that a mistake exists, in consequence of the principles upon which this plan is founded and ought to be conducted not being as yet sufficiently understood. In the management of workhouses, &c., there is no unity of action; each part is so placed as to feel an interest at variance with the others; they are, in fact, a compound of the same errors that pervade common society, where all are so circumstanced as to counteract each other's intentions, and thus render even extraordinary energies and talents of no avail, which, under another combination, would produce the most extensive and beneficial effects. From my own experience, however, I can aver that such means and regulations may be adopted for the management of these villages, as would enable any one possessing fair talents, so to manage them as to give entire satisfaction to all the parties under his direction and care, with the greatest pleasure to himself, and with unspeakable advantage to the country. Numbers may be found who would soon be competent to such management and who would be satisfied with the living and comforts these villages would offer, without desiring compensation of any kind; and the annual expense of such living would not amount to £20 in value.

Q. Is it not to be feared that such arrangements as you contemplate would produce a dull uniformity of character, repress genius, and leave the world without hope of future improvements?

A. It appears to me that quite the reverse of all this will follow; that the means provided in these establishments will give every stimulus to bring forth and to perfect the best parts only of every character, by furnishing the inhabitants with such valuable instruction as they could not acquire by any other means, and by affording sufficient leisure and freedom from anxiety to promote the natural direction of their powers. When thus prepared by early-imbibed temperate habits, by an accurate knowledge of facts, and by a full conviction that their efforts are directed for the benefit of mankind, it is not easy to imagine, with our present ideas, what may be accomplished by human beings so trained and so circumstanced. As for the probability of a dull uniformity of character being produced, let us for a moment imagine individuals placed as the inhabitants of these villages will be, and contemplate the characters that must be formed solely by the circumstances that will surround them. From the hour they are born, treated with uniform kindness, directed by reason, and not mere caprice, weakness, and imbecility; not one habit acquired to be again unlearned; the physical powers trained and cultivated to attain their natural strength and health; the mental faculties furnished with accurate data, by all the useful facts that the ingenuity and experience of the world have acquired and demonstrated, aided by the power of minds trained to draw only just and consistent conclusions, and each left to declare freely those conclusions, to compare them with others, and thus in the most easy and rapid manner to correct any errors that might otherwise arise; – children so trained, men so circumstanced, would soon become, not a dull uniform race, but beings full of health, activity, and energy; endowed by means of instruction with the most kind and amiable dispositions, and who, being trained free from the motives, could not form one *exclusive* wish for themselves. It is only when the obscurities by which society is now enveloped are in some degree removed, that the benefit of these new villages can be even in part appreciated. So far from genius being depressed, it will receive every aid to enable it to exert itself with unrestrained delight, and with the highest benefit to mankind. In short, experience will prove that no objection against the 'New View of Society' will be found more futile than that which supposes it not competent, nor calculated, to train men to attain the utmost improvement, in arts, sciences, and every kind of knowledge.

Q. *Will not these establishments be expensive, and require a large expenditure in the outset; and can such a capital be easily obtained?*

A. The expenditure will prove the greatest possible economy, and the capital may be had, without difficulty, as rapidly as it would be required. A large and anticipated revenue, occasioned by the war expenditure in this and other countries, having ceased, distress of the most grievous nature has ensued: the only remedy that can be found will be a greatly increased expenditure applied to labour that will be reproductive, equal, at least, to the interest of the capital invested, and to the remuneration of the labour employed, both physical and mental. These establishments offer means for the investment of capital on security that ought to be considered of the highest value to the country. Every shilling thus expended would be national gain, create national improvement, find ample support for and remoralise the population employed, and return five per cent. interest for the capital expended, leaving the property annually and rapidly increasing in intrinsic value. Did the situation of the country admit of such a slow progress, I should be satisfied to see a few of these villages set on foot by way of national experiment; well knowing that their manifold advantages, and superiority over every other plan for the employing of the labouring classes, would be obvious to every capacity; but I know that the peculiar circumstances of this country, and of Europe, will not admit of this slow proceeding. Value must be restored to manual labour, and this cannot be done except by employment on land. When the mode of effecting this shall be fairly and fully before the public, they will readily discover that there are no means within our present knowledge competent to give to individuals and to the country the innumerable advantages that this will accomplish for both. With this conviction before them, the public will feel the strong necessity for, and naturally require, a liberal expenditure, in order that a rapid progress may be made in forming these asylums for the health, comfort, improvement, and happiness, of the working classes and the rising population.

Q. *But should many of these villages be founded, will they not increase the products of agricultural and manufacturing labour, which are already too abundant, until no market can be found for them, and thus injure the present agriculture, manufactures, and commerce of the country?*

A. This is a part of the subject that requires to be understood better than, at present, it appears to be by any party. Is it possible that there can be too many productions desirable and useful to society? and is it not to the interest of all, that they should be produced with the least expense and labour, and with the smallest degree of misery and moral degradation to the working classes; and, of course, in the greatest abundance to the higher classes, in return for their wealth? It is surely to the interest of all, that everything should be produced with the least expense of labour, and so as to realise the largest portion of comfort to the producing classes: and there are no means of effecting these desirable ends that will bear any comparison with the combined agricultural and manufacturing villages, colleges of industry, county or district establishments for the poor and industrious, or by whatsoever name they may be called. It is true that as they increase in number they may come into competition with the existing agricultural and manufacturing systems, if society shall permit them so to do; otherwise, they can restrain them to the amount of their own immediate wants; and constituted as they will be, they can have no motives to produce an unnecessary surplus. When society shall, however, discover its true interests, it will permit these new establishments gradually to supersede the others; inasmuch as the latter are wretchedly degrading, and directly opposed to the improvement and well-being of those employed either in agriculture or manufactures, and consequently are equally hostile to the welfare and happiness of all the higher classes. We know full well the misery and vice in which the manufacturing population is involved; we know also the ignorance and degradation to which the agricultural labourer is reduced; and it is only by such a re-arrangement of this part of society that these enormous evils can ever be removed.

Q. But will not these establishments tend to increase population, beyond the means of subsistence, too rapidly for the well-being of society?

A. I have no apprehension whatever on this ground. Every agriculturist knows that each labourer now employed in agriculture can produce five or six times more food than he can eat; and therefore, even if no other facilities were given to him than those he now possesses, there is no necessity in nature for 'the population to press against subsistence,'[a] until the earth is fully cultivated. There can be no doubt that it is the artificial law of supply and demand, arising from the principles of individual gain in opposition to the general well-being of society, which has hitherto compelled population to press upon subsistence. The certain effect of acting on the principle of individual gain is, ever to limit the supply of food, in an average season, to a sufficiency, according to the customs of the times, for the existing inhabitants of the earth; consequently, in a favourable season, and in proportion as the season may be favourable, there

[a] See T. R. Malthus, *Essay on Population* (5th edn, 1817), pp. 1–35.

will be abundance of food, and it will be cheap; and, in an unfavourable season, in proportion as the season may be unfavourable, food will be scarce and dear, and famines will ensue. And yet, no one who understands anything practically on the subject can for a moment doubt that, at the period immediately preceding the most grievous famine ever known, the means existed, in ample profusion, to have enabled the population, under proper arrangements, had they possessed the knowledge to form them, to produce a stock of food amounting even to an excessive superabundance. Whatever may have been imagined by intelligent individuals, who have written and thought upon the subject, the annual increase of population is really one by one; we know its utmost limit – it is only, it can be only, an arithmetical increase; whereas, each individual brings into the world with him the means, aided by the existing knowledge of science, and under proper direction, sufficient to enable him to produce food equal to more than ten times his consumption. The fear, then, of any evil to arise from an excess of population, until such time as the whole earth shall become a highly-cultivated garden, will, on due and accurate investigation, prove a mere phantom of the imagination, calculated solely to keep the world in unnecessary ignorance, vice, and crime, and to prevent society from becoming what it ought to be, well-trained and instructed, and, under an intelligent system of mutual good-will and kindness, active, virtuous, and happy; a system which might easily be created so as to pervade the whole of society, and extend through all its ramifications.

Q. By thus altering the general habits and existing arrangements of the lower orders, would it not give an increased value to manual labour?

A. My intention was to combine the means of accomplishing objects which appear to me to be inevitably required by the existing state of the country; and to prevent the violent derangement of society, arising from the distress and extreme demoralisation which is hourly advancing and must go on till effectual and counteracting measures shall be adopted. I saw the poor and working classes surrounded by circumstances that necessarily entailed misery on them and their posterity; that if they were allowed to continue and proceed much longer, they would further demoralise and violently subvert the whole social system. To prevent this catastrophe, it becomes absolutely indispensable that their habits be changed; and this cannot be done without altering the existing arrangements with regard to them and to the rising generation. If the plan proposed shall be found to be much, nay, infinitely, more complete, in all its parts, and in its entire combination, than any hitherto suggested, and if it can be immediately and gradually introduced without causing the least shock to society, or prematurely disturbing existing institutions, then is the proper time arrived – then are the circumstances duly prepared, for its reception; and I feel a perfect confidence in saying, that however, through mistaken private interests, it may be attempted to retard it, it will be inevitably introduced, and firmly established, even against all opposition. It is, indeed, of that nature, that opposition will but hasten its adoption, and fix the principles more generally and deeply in and through society. The circumstances that have been silently, for nearly twenty years past, preparing for this end, are so far completed, as to answer all the purposes intended; and the future welfare of mankind, in this and also in other countries, may be considered secure, beyond the power of accident. Combined labour and expenditure, for a common object, among the working classes, with proper training and instruction for their offspring, and surrounded by the circumstances devised for the whole, will create and secure the present safety of society, the present and future comfort and happiness of the individuals, and the ultimate well-being of all. I may, therefore, confidently believe, that no combination of human powers can now be formed to prevent its permanent adoption. After having made this statement, it is necessary for me to add, that the knowledge I have acquired on this subject has been forced upon me by a long and extensive experience; which, under similar circumstances, would have been acquired by the generality of mankind. None, I believe not one, of the principles, have the least claim to originality; they have been repeatedly advocated and recommended by superior minds, from the earliest period of history. I have no claim even to priority in regard to the combinations of these principles in theory; this belongs, as far as I know, to John Bellers,[a] who published them, and most ably recommended them to be adopted in practice, in the year 1696. Without any aid from actual experience, he has most distinctly shown how they might be applied to the improvement of society, according to the facts then known to exist; thus evincing that his mind had the power to contemplate a point extended 120 years beyond his contemporaries. His work appeared to be so curious and valuable, that on discovering it, I have had it reprinted, verbatim, in order to bind up with the papers I have written on the same subject.[b] Whatever merit can be due to an individual for the original discovery of a plan that, in its consequences, is calculated to effect more substantial and permanent benefit to mankind than any ever yet perhaps contemplated by the human mind, it all belongs exclusively to John Bellers.

Q. *Is it then your decided opinion, that land, labour, and capital, may be employed under a new combination so as to produce more valuable results to all parties than they do at present?*

A. If I have derived any distinct knowledge by my long experience and extensive practice, I am enabled to say, with a confidence that fears no refutation, that any given quantity of land, labour, and capital, may be so combined as to support at least four times the present number of human beings,

[a] John Bellers (1654–1725): Quaker philanthropist; author of the *Proposals for Raising a College of Industry* (1695), a communitarian and co-operative scheme reprinted by Owen in 1818 (see *Life*, vol. 1A (1858), pp. 155–81).

[b] See Owen, *Life*, vol. 1A (1858), pp. 155–81.

and in tenfold comfort than the same is maintained at present, under the existing practices in this country; and, of course, that the intrinsic value of land, labour and capital, may be increased in the same proportion: that, consequently, we possess the most ample means to carry now, without loss of time, the prosperity of the country to a point it has not before attained – to a height that no country has ever yet experienced. If any parties suppose these to be mere assertions without sound foundation, or to be a visionary scheme derived from the regions of fancy, they will be mistaken; for they are the result of a patient and unwearied attention to discover accurate and practical data, and to try an endless variety of experiments, to enable me to draw correct conclusions, and thus bring the theories of learned men in their closets to the only test of truth. By thus proceeding I have been more and more satisfied of the errors of mere theories, and of the little real value they have hitherto been to mankind. I have no wish, however, that any more confidence should be placed in what I say, than to induce the public to give a fair trial to the plan. If I am in error, the loss and inconvenience, compared with the object, will be small; but if I am right, the public and the world will be gainers indeed! I ask nothing for myself; and, except good-will and the interchange of kind and friendly offices, I will not accept any thing from any party. I merely ask to be permitted to relieve the poor and working classes from their present distress, and to render an essential service to the wealthy and to all the higher classes. I am, therefore, desirous that competent persons of business should be named to investigate all the details which I have to propose; knowing, as I do from experience, that this is the only practical measure that can be adopted to enable the public to comprehend a subject so extensive and important as this will ultimately prove to be.

Q. On the supposition that the plan may be unexceptionable in all its parts, how can it be carried into execution, as far as relates to the poor who receive parochial aid?

A. First, by passing an Act of Parliament to nationalize the poor. Secondly, by borrowing, from time to time, on the national security, sufficient sums to build these villages, and to prepare the land for cultivation; the Government holding security upon these establishments until both interest and capital shall be paid; by which means the whole process would be straightforward, equitable, and just to all the parties; and the country would enable the Government to carry it into execution, without opposition from any interested party.

July 26.

After closing the above on Thursday morning, the 24th inst., I little expected that before it was ready for publication, two events were to arise, sufficiently important to render a narrative of the one useful, and an explanation to the other necessary. Such events, however, have occurred. That which is useful is so valuable and interesting, that I lose not a moment in making it known.

Fortunately, it admits not of a difference of opinion; it comprises simple matter of fact, that may be seen and investigated by every one who will devote time to visit the principal prisons in the metropolis.

Having heard from various quarters what highly beneficial effects had been produced by Mrs Fry, of St Mildred's Court, Poultry, among the female prisoners in Newgate, I yesterday, by previous appointment, accompanied that Lady, and was conducted by her through all the apartments of the prison occupied by the unfortunate females of every description. I shall not easily, if ever, forget the impressions I experienced; they were of a mixed and very opposite nature. In passing from room to room we were met in every instance (there was not one exception,) with kind looks and the most evident feelings of affection in every prisoner towards Mrs Fry. Not a feature in the countenance of any, however hardened they might have been on entering the prison, that did not evince, in stronger expression than language can define, their love and admiration for what she had done for them. With an alacrity and pleasure that would be commended in the best-trained children in attending to parental requests, they were ready and willing to comply with her advice. It was evidently a heartfelt consolation to these poor creatures to know her wishes, that they might show their gratitude by an immediate compliance with them. She spoke in manner and voice the language of confidence, kindness, and commiseration, to each; and she was replied to in such accordant feelings as are, and ever will be, produced in human beings, whenever they shall be spoken to and treated thus rationally. On quitting the prison the eyes of all were directed towards her until she was no longer in their sight. The apartments and the persons of the prisoners were clean and neat; order, regularity, decency, and almost cheerful content, pervaded the whole of these heretofore miserable and degraded wretches! With the constant habit, for years, of reading the mind in the countenance among the lower classes, I could not discover, throughout the numerous apartments we visited, one line of feature that denoted any inclination to resist, in the slightest degree, Mrs Fry's wishes; but, on the contrary, the looks and manner of each female prisoner strongly indicated a full acquiescence in this new government of well-directed kindness. The only regret I heard expressed was by those who were unemployed, 'that they had no work.' All who had something to do were far more cheerful than I had previously supposed human beings could be in the situation, with the accommodation and under the circumstances here described. We next proceeded to the female school; and, on our entering, every eye was fixed on their benefactress. The little girls, children of the prisoners and convicts, looked on her as human creatures might be imagined to look upon beings of a superior, intelligent, and beneficent nature. They were all clean and neat; and some of their countenances very interesting. The school was in excellent order, and appeared to be under good management. I could not avoid contrasting the present with the former situation of all these poor unfortunates. What a change must they have experienced! from filth, bad habits, vice, crime – from the depth of degradation and wretchedness – to cleanliness, good habits, and comparative comfort and cheerfulness! Had not experience long made known to me the simplicity and certain effects of the principles which had here been carried into practice, I might have been led to inquire what profound statesman had been here? what large sums had been expended? how many years of active and steady perseverance had been necessary to accomplish this extraordinary improvement, which has foiled even the British Government and Legislature to effect during the centuries they have existed. And what would have been my astonishment at the simple narrative which was told me? That this change, from the depth of misery to the state described, was effected by Mrs Fry and a few benevolent individuals of the Society of Friends, in three months, without any increased expense, and with feelings of high gratification to herself! We left the female side of the prison, and passed on to the rooms, courts, &c., occupied by the males. We went first to the boys' court, and found the school, which was formed at Mrs Fry's request, had been just dismissed. The person acting as master asked if he should muster the boys; to which she consented, and it was instantly done. What a melancholy sight did they offer! A collection of boys and youths with scarcely the appearance of human beings in their countenances; the most evident sign that the Government to which they belong had not performed any part of its duty towards them. For instance; there was one boy, only sixteen years of age, double-ironed! Here a great crime has been committed, and a severe punishment has been inflicted, which under a system of proper training and prevention would not have taken place.

My Lord Sidmouth[7] will forgive me, for he knows I intend no personal offence. His dispositions are known to be mild and amiable; but the Chief Civil Magistrate of the country, in such case, is far more guilty than the boy; and, in strict justice, if a system of coercion and punishment be rational and necessary, he ought rather to have been double-ironed, and in the place of the boy. The Secretary of State for the Home Department has long had the power, and ought to have used it, to give that boy, and every other boy in the empire, better habits, and to place them under circumstances that would train them to become moral.

We left these boys, and visited the men who were yet to be tried, those who had been tried, and others under sentence of death. Everything on this side of the prison was most revolting to common sense and human feelings; but it serves to exhibit the contrast between the practice that results, and ever will result, from acting upon rational and irrational principles. I wish the Members of Government would now investigate these extraordinary facts. If they were to inspect them, with this benevolent female, I am sure they would learn the

[a] Henry Addington, 1st Viscount Sidmouth (1757–1844): Whig MP; Home Secretary 1811–21.

principles which have guided her practice, and adopt them in all their future measures. They would then enjoy only the highest satisfaction.

It was admitted by the attendants of the prison, that a few months ago the women were more depraved than the men are now; they were both pronounced to be irreclaimable: but the state of the females has been entirely changed, and that in the short space of three months! Notwithstanding this fact, the men are still pronounced to be irreclaimable! Blame, however, is by no means to be attached to any of the attendants of the prison, who appear inclined to do their duty as far as they have received instructions.

Let Ministers attend here, and they will discover that the most powerful instruments of government have hitherto been dormant in their hands and in those of their predecessors. If they will study the subject as it deserves to be studied, and afterwards make a proper use of their power, in legislating on the principle of prevention, under the influence of a persevering well-directed kindness, the distress of the country will be found to vanish – the ignorance, poverty, and misery of the lower classes to disappear, as though it were by a miracle; and they would then look in vain for disaffection, discontent, or opposition to any of their measures. The present period is, of all others, the best adapted to introduce the change, and every circumstance now imperiously calls for its commencement.

I would here rivet the attention of the world! It has been said that there are numerous difficulties in training children to good habits and right conduct, even previous to their having received any contrary bias; but here is a proof that the most deep-rooted and long continued habits of depravity may be easily and speedily overcome by a system of kindness, which, when properly directed and persevered in, no human beings have ever yet been found long inclined to resist.

This principle, when it shall be well understood and rightly acted upon, will effect more for the substantial happiness of mankind, than all the moral and religious systems that have ever yet, at any period, or in any country, been forced upon the human mind.

Hitherto the world has been tormented by useless *talking* – by much speaking; all of which has proved to be of no avail. Henceforward, *acting* will render precepts unnecessary; and, in future, systems for the government of mankind will be estimated and valued *by their effects in practice only*.

I must now refer to that which is *necessary*. Immediately before and after the late meeting at the George and Vulture, I discovered that some secret emissaries were at work to counteract my progress by insinuations of various kinds, which evidently produced the effect intended on the minds of some who had previously expressed themselves favourable to my plan.[a] All this was very

[a] See also *infra*, vol. 4, p. 215.

natural. No ordinary individual could attack the errors and prejudices of mankind, as I have done, without encountering, at each step, opposition of every description.

When the weapons used in this warfare, however unfair and illegitimate they may have been, were directed against the individual only, they were disregarded. I cared, and I do still care, as little for the individual as any of his opponents did or can. I make him, as they shall now be made, an instrument to forward measures for our mutual and the general benefit. He has been hitherto so employed, without regard to his vanity or self-consequence of any kind; and until the object shall be effectually secured, he shall continue to be so employed.

But as the absurd and ridiculous insinuations now set afloat are intended to retard the work I have undertaken, they must be met; and they have determined the next step that I shall adopt, and about which I was deliberating.

It is, that a Public Meeting shall be held at the City of London Tavern, on Thursday, the 14th day of August, to take into consideration a plan to be proposed to relieve the country from its present distress, to remoralize the poor, reduce the poor's-rate, and abolish pauperism and all its injurious consequences. At that meeting I invite those parties, and any others whom they can enlist in their cause, to come forward and make every thing they have to say against me publicly known. I wish to gratify them to the utmost of their desires; and as they may not possess all the requisites for the purpose, I will give them the clue by which they may pursue and discover all the errors of my past life.

I was born in Newtown, Montgomeryshire; left it, and came to London, when about ten years of age; soon after went to Mr James M'Guffog,[a] of Stamford in Lincolnshire; where I remained upwards of three years; returned to town, and was a short time with Messrs Flint and Palmer, London Bridge.[b] I went afterwards to Manchester, and was some time with Mr John Satterfield,[c] whom I left, while yet a boy, to commence business on a limited scale in making machinery and spinning cotton, part of the time in partnership with Mr Jones,[d] and part on my own account. Afterwards I undertook to manage the spinning establishments of the late Mr Drinkwater[e] of Manchester, at the latter place and at Northwich in Cheshire, in which occupation I remained

[a] James McGuffog (1747–1829), linen and woollen draper.

[b] William Flint and Benjamin Palmer, haberdashers, London Bridge, Southwark.

[c] John Satterfield, who founded Satterfield and Co., a firm of silk mercers and linen drapers, in 1775. This was located at 5 St Ann's Square in 1794.

[d] Probably John Jones, a machine-maker.

[e] Peter Drinkwater (1742–1801), whose mill opened in 1790, applied the first Bolton and Watt steam engine to cotton-spinning in Manchester. Owen errs by a year here, as his interview with Drinkwater was in April 1792, not 1791. See W. H. Chaloner, 'Robert Owen, Peter Drinkwater and the Early Factory System in Manchester, 1788–1800', *Bulletin of the John Rylands Library*, 37 (1954), 92.

three or four years. I then formed a partnership to carry on a cotton-spinning business with Messrs Moulson and Scarth[a] of Manchester; built the Chorlton Mills, and commenced a new firm, under the designation of the Chorlton Twist Company, along with Messrs Borrodale and Atkinson,[b] of London, and Messrs H. and J. Barton and Co.,[c] of Manchester. Some time afterwards we purchased the mills and establishments at New Lanark, where I have been before the public for eighteen years past; and I am now forty-six years old. Here is a clue to my whole life for any parties who may wish to make use of it; not because the conduct of the individual, whether it has been the best or the worst, can alter one tittle of the truth or falsehood of the principles and practices for which I contend; these stand solely on their own foundation, and will ultimately resist the shock of ages; nor because he has acted better, or with more wisdom, than the average of persons at the same time of life, and under the same circumstances; for he has never, in a single instance, set any value on himself, or on any of his actions; – but because I wish that every thing which can be said against *the individual* may be urged by those who are desirous so to do, in order to have done with these trifling and insignificant personalities, and that I may proceed onward to the accomplishment of that which is of real practical utility. Let them, therefore, at such public meeting, bring forward every saying and action of mine that has displeased them: I only ask that the attack shall be fair, open, and direct; it shall then be met, and it shall be overcome. In the meantime, I ask no favour; let them be industrious, and be prepared to secure all the success at which they aim. I shall not ask for, or accept, any quarter. My purposes have been long fixed; and my determination is, not to give any quarter to the errors and evils of the existing systems, civil, political, and religious, and until they shall become so obvious, that their removal shall be desired by all parties, even by those who now feel the strongest interest in, and inclination to support them. The Rubicon is passed, and the public will soon experience the beneficial consequences.

ROBERT OWEN

P.S. A more complete view of the Plan, accompanied by perspective drawings and a full detail of all its practical advantages, will be shortly submitted to the public.

---

[a] Moulson & Scarth, the firm of Richard Percival Moulson and Jonathan Scarth (1772–c. 1850).

[b] William Borradaile (1751–1831) was a merchant and hat-manufacturer at Salford whose London headquarters was at 34 Fenchurch Street (in 1790). John Atkinson, also of Salford, was his partner.

[c] Henry and James Barton, merchants and cotton-manufacturers, of 6 Phoenix Street, Manchester (in 1794).

LETTER

Published in the London Newspapers of August 9th, 1817[a]

August 7th, 1817

Mr Editor,

Sir – Strict justice to the public renders it necessary that my sentiments and views should be fully and fairly before it, prior to the Meeting to be held at the City of London Tavern, at Twelve o'Clock, on Thursday next, the 14th instant. Your early insertion, therefore, of the following, will confer a favour on,

Sir, your obliged,

49, Charlotte Street, Portland Place. R. Owen

A Sketch of some of the Errors and Evils arising from the Past and Present State of Society, with an Explanation of some of the peculiar advantages to be derived from the Arrangement of the Unemployed Working Classes into 'Agricultural and Manufacturing Villages of Unity and Mutual Co-operation,' limited to a Population of from 500 to 1,500 Persons.

To enable the public more easily to comprehend the subject, it is necessary to begin with first principles.

The object of all human exertions is to be happy.

Happiness cannot be attained, enjoyed, and secured, unless all men possess health, real knowledge, and wealth.

Hitherto health and real knowledge have been neglected for the attainment of wealth and other exclusive individual objects; but which, when acquired,

[a] See *The Times*, no. 10220 (9 August 1817), p. 4. The full title was: 'A Sketch of Some of the Errors and Evils Arising from the Past and Present State of Society, with an Explanation of Some of the Peculiar Advantages to be Derived from the Arrangement of the Unemployed Working Classes into "Agricultural and Manufacturing Villages of Unity and Mutual Co-operation", Limited to a Population of from 500 to 1,500 persons'. Reprinted in *New State of Society. Extracted From the Daily Papers of 30th July, and 9th and 10th of August, 1817* (1817), *New View of Society. Tracts Relative to This Subject* (1818), *A Report of the British and Foreign Philanthropic Society* (Dublin, 1823), *The New Existence of Man Upon the Earth* (1854), pt 1, pp. xxxi–xxxviii, and in Owen, *Life*, vol. 1A (1858), pp. 83–92. Later reprints include 1991.

even in the greatest profusion, have been, and ever will be, found to destroy happiness.

The world is now saturated with wealth – with inexhaustible means of still increasing it – and yet misery abounds! Such at this moment is the actual state of human society. No arrangement, proceeding from a defined intention to attain an object of desire, could be worse devised than that which is now in practice throughout all the nations of the earth. Immense, invaluable energies, competent with ease to procure everything beneficial to humanity, lie waste, or are so misdirected as to defeat the object of all their wishes.

The world, however, is now amply supplied with the means to stop the current of human folly, to call those dormant powers into action, and to give a right straightforward direction to all the energies of man.

The means are wanted to give health, real knowledge, and wealth, to all men.

The means surround us, are at our instant disposal, and exist in a superfluity of abundance; yet the great mass of the world is in the depth of ignorance, without the comforts of life; a large proportion of them are in want of a sufficiency of food, subject to every privation, and are to be found at this hour in the midst of almost inconceivable distress and wretchedness.

Is the change then from the one state to the other difficult? Are there any insurmountable obstacles in the way, to prevent the accomplishment of that which is so desirable?

On the contrary, extraordinary as it may seem, the change will be most easy. No difficulty or obstacle of magnitude will be found in the whole progress. THE WORLD *knows* AND *feels* THE EXISTING EVIL: IT WILL LOOK AT THE NEW ORDER OF THINGS PROPOSED – APPROVE – WILL THE CHANGE – AND IT IS DONE.

Who, or what, shall now prevent man from being well-trained, instructed, and productively employed? Who, or what, shall now prevent him from being so trained, instructed, and employed, amidst every comfort and enjoyment, when it shall be proved, even to demonstration, that all, *without a single exception*, shall be essentially benefited by the change?

To proceed systematically in the subject, it is necessary here to state that man is by nature. what he has been made by the previous circumstances which have surrounded him; and afterwards to show what he may be made by surrounding him with new circumstances, all of which are now at the control of society.

Man, then, is born with combined propensities and qualities, differing in degree of power and in combination, sufficient to create through life individuality and distinctness of person and character.

But however much the power and combination of these propensities and qualities may differ in individuals at birth, they may be all so directed by subsequent circumstances, as to be made to form general characters; and these characters to be of any, of the most opposite nature – even to be made entirely *irrational* or *rational*.

The progress shall now be slightly traced, as well as the means, by which the first has been completely effected: and a hasty sketch shall also be given, by which the last may with equal certainty be accomplished.

In every known region of the earth, up to the present hour, man has been compelled from infancy to acquire the peculiar notions of some sect, some class, some party, and of some country. In consequence, each individual has been surrounded by four dense atmospheres of error and prejudice, and through which he must look at every object around him. These mental atmospheres vary materially in different countries; but in all they are so dense, that (as every object must be observed through them) each object becomes distorted or indistinct; none of them, in any country, or by a single individual, can yet be seen in their just proportions; and, in consequence, nature has hitherto been hidden from man.

Throughout all past ages a limited number of individuals on various spots of the earth have been surrounded with atmospheres, the shades of which have been more or less differently combined; and each of these combinations has presented to the individual within its influence a particular distortion of all the objects of nature peculiar to itself. When individuals thus differently surrounded happen to meet and converse together, they soon discover that they do not see objects alike; and, wholly unconscious of the real cause of difference between them, an opposition of *feeling*, as well as of seeing, is created; extending from a slight degree of dislike, to anger, hatred, revenge, death, and destruction in every form and shape. Hence, from differences of opinion on notions of *sect*, arise the evils and miseries of human life, which, more than all the other atmospheres, of class, party, and of country, has in every age separated man from man, and made him a wretched and degraded being.

The several atmospheres of *class* have also created various feelings of strong separation among men, and have essentially tended to increase their irrationality and their misery.

The atmospheres of *party* and of *country* have been equally injurious: they have, even until now, compelled man to remain a stranger to his fellows.

A combination of every conceivable degree of ignorance, weakness, and inconsistency, has been the natural consequence of men's actions during such a state of existence.

All the past and present institutions of the world are a proof of the ever-changing insanity with which the human mind has been enveloped.

The result of each change, under these circumstances, has disappointed the fondest hopes and the most sanguine expectations; and while the circumstances are permitted to remain, folly alone will expect any other result, from any change whatever, except their entire removal.

Happiness is not one jot nearer the grasp of a single individual *now*, than it was at the period when we have the first records of man. Born in ignorance, he imagined first, and he has ever since been systematically taught, that he himself created the motives for his own actions: his mind has been formed on this base; it has been, and is now, the very foundation of his thoughts; it has been combined into all the associations of his ideas; and only doubt, disorder, and confusion of intellect could follow!

It was truly said, that before man could be wise and happy, his mind 'must be born again' – that is, it must be discharged of all the inconsistent associations which have been formed within it; the foundation must be laid anew, and a superstructure raised of just and useful proportions, consistent in each and in all its parts, and such as shall please, gratify, and delight the eye of all beholders; that shall bear the test of the most scientific investigations; and through all future ages shall satisfy each mind as it advances, well trained and formed, to maturity, that it is the abode of happiness proceeding from correct conduct, under the guidance of the best intelligence and the soundest wisdom!

Man is born in ignorance, and from his birth he is surrounded with the errors of some sect, some class, frequently of some party, and always of some country.

He is consequently rendered ignorant of himself, of his fellow creatures, and of nature.

The seeds of disunion and separation are deeply and extensively sown during infancy and childhood.

He is individualised, and made openly or covertly, to oppose every other human being.

His natural wishes are to press onward towards happiness; but he is strongly and successfully opposed by the multitudes around him, and by the ignorantly devised institutions of society.

As he advances to youth and manhood, the soil into which the seeds of disunion and separation have been put, is cultivated with the greatest care, and every conceivable means are adopted to cherish the plants, ensure their growth, and secure a plentiful crop.

Such care and culture cannot fail of success; opposition to his natural feelings, and to all his exertions to attain happiness, brings forth in due time an abundant harvest of discontent, dislikes, and displeasure, envy, hatred, revenge, and all the evil passions; and at length he becomes intimately involved in all the irrationality which must inevitably arise from such a mode of training and culture!

He is compelled to be insincere; and this circumstance alone will destroy human happiness! Were any individual to speak the truth within either of these deranging atmospheres of the human intellect, he would at once be termed a fool and a madman!

His finest feelings, his highest intellectual powers, and his best energies, must lie waste, or be so misdirected as to produce evil continually.

Such is a just and accurate outline of man as he has been made – as he is made – under all the past and present systems.

Were I now to descend to particulars; to give a faithful representation in detail of the errors, inconsistencies, and of the miseries which arise from the existing arrangements of society throughout all its parts, the public mind would be too suddenly enlightened for its own good: ignorant and untrained as it yet is, it would not retain the requisite patience to allow the change to be *gradually* effected; to proceed only as speedily as practical measures will admit; it would too eagerly press forward to seize the good which in due time shall be certainly placed within its grasp; and by such over haste it would injure and destroy many in its course. In effecting this change – and where is the existing mind that can yet comprehend its magnitude? – it is my most ardent wish, my anxious desire, that the least possible irritation should be created; that it should be accomplished without any real injury to a human being! Those who possess comprehension of mind and some practical knowledge of the existing state of society will understand the purport of this language, and will of course act accordingly.

Yes, my friends, full of folly, inconsistency, and wretchedness, as all the existing systems are, *they must not be touched by ill-informed and rude hands*. A single premature or ill-advised step, were it now to be taken, might retard our best founded hopes, and deprive some generations yet to come of that happiness which otherwise we and our children shall surely enjoy in no inconsiderable degree.

Allay, therefore, your present irritations – do not urge forward any ill-digested, or rather undigested, plans of premature reform; yet attend, with all your powers of earnestness, to the proceedings which are about to commence; and in the shortest possible time for your own good and for the benefit of posterity, you shall be relieved from the existing miseries – you shall be put in possession of all the comfort and enjoyment that can be advantageous to human beings.

To accomplish, however, this great end, without injury to any one, it is absolutely necessary that all the existing institutions should be supported, for a time, as they are; to enable them to protect, and beneficially to direct and controul, the mighty change which is coming rapidly upon us and upon all nations; from which it is utterly impossible for us to escape; and from which, when it shall be properly understood, not one of us shall desire to escape; on the contrary, one and all of us will hail it as the harbinger of whatever is good for individual man, and advantageous for him in his social capacity.

When right principles are acted upon, it is, and ever will be, unnecessary to deceive the public: the truth may be told for or against any national impressions with advantage to every just cause; and this course shall be now adopted.

The present governing Powers of Europe and America, with a few unimportant exceptions, are not in reality opposed to the practical improvement of society; they wish its advance; and, when they shall fully understand how this can be effected, they will not withhold their active assistance.

The Ministers of this country – and I know them well – do not possess sufficient energies and practical knowledge to lead the public mind as it now ought to be led; and their political opponents possess still less useful, practical, knowledge. *Statesmen in all countries have yet to learn the principles of the science that will enable them to govern States so as to make themselves and the people happy.*

But our Ministers possess kind and amiable dispositions, and a real desire to ameliorate the condition of all ranks. I have for five years put their patience, their tempers, and their inclinations, to a test which cannot deceive me; and although it is correctly true that they do not possess the requisites to lead the national mind into new and untried, but absolutely necessary, improvement – for this they leave to others – yet it is my belief that many of them are sincerely willing and desirous to go with and accompany the public in that course, whenever the public shall be duly prepared and provided for the journey. They are now as conscious as any other class in society, that the way in which they find themselves fast advancing *is the high road to confusion and misery*.

And here, as I am anxious that not one of my motives should be misunderstood, it is necessary to say, that when in a preceding publication[a] I stated that it would be more just for the Secretary of State for the Home Department to be double-ironed and in Newgate, rather than the poor boy, sixteen years of age, who from his birth had been neglected by society; although this statement was then, as it is now, the genuine expression of my feelings and judgment, yet it was not in any degree intended to wound the feelings of my Lord Sidmouth. Some part of the public, it seems, has supposed otherwise, although his Lordship could not mistake my meaning. I have received numberless marks of kindness and attention from him; I have at this moment a lively impression of the urbanity of his manners: and it is but justice to him to say, that he readily gave his assistance to Mrs Fry, to enable her to proceed with her good work among the female prisoners in Newgate. Still, however, the Secretary of State for the Home Department is pursuing, and for some time to come I fear must pursue, a course which creates, in its consequences, more cruelty and injustice than may be obvious to him and many others; and therefore, notwithstanding I feel a real regard for the individual, I must oppose, with all my powers, the errors of the system under which he acts; and I hope the time is not far distant when he also will lend his utmost ministerial aid to introduce a better.

Of the existing systems I trust it is unnecessary for me now to say more, than that I consider them wretched indeed! but, bad as they are, they must be protected until a better shall be actually in practice.

We will now view man under the new circumstances in which he is about to be placed.

In the new, as under the old, he will be born in ignorance.

---

[a] See *infra*, p. 170.

He will be trained from earliest infancy to acquire only kind and benevolent dispositions.

He will be taught facts only. These will enable him very early in life to understand clearly how his own character and the character of his fellow-creatures have been formed and are forming. He will thus be secured from being enveloped by any of the evil and demoralising atmospheres with which every man yet born has been surrounded.

No circumstances will exist to compel him to acquire feelings of disunion and separation from any other human being. On the contrary, his heart will be open to receive, and his hand ready to assist, each of his fellow creatures, whatever may be his sect, his class, his party, his country, or his colour. Anger, hatred, and revenge will have no place on which to rest: the pabulum on which all the evil passions fed, will no longer exist: unity and mutual co-operation, to any extent, will become easy of execution, and the common practice of all.

Men will soon read their past history, only to retain a remembrance of the errors and inconsistencies from whence they emerged; and to compare the happiness around them with the misery of former times.

Look now at the drawing exhibited, and compare the scenes which it but faintly represents, with the situation of the existing poor and working classes in the manufacturing towns; and yet the expense and trouble of the latter are tenfold those of the one represented.

We will very hastily and slightly sketch the contrast.

In the Manufacturing Towns, – the poor and working classes now usually live in garrets or cellars, within narrow lanes or confined courts.

In the Proposed Villages, – the poor and working classes will live in dwellings formed into a large square, rendered in every way convenient, and usefully ornamented.

In the Manufacturing Towns, – they are surrounded with dirt, enveloped in smoke, and have seldom a pleasant object on which to fix their eye.

In the Proposed Villages, – they will be surrounded by gardens, have abundance of space in all directions to keep the air healthy and pleasant: they will have walks and plantations before them, within the square, and well cultivated grounds, kept in good order around, as far as the eye can reach.

In the Manufacturing Towns, – parents are oppressed with anxiety to secure the means of subsistence for themselves and children.

In the Proposed Villages, – in consequence of the principle of mutual co-operation being understood and practiced to its full extent, the necessaries and comforts of life are enjoyed by all in abundance.

In the Manufacturing Towns, – each family has the care and trouble of going to market to supply their individual wants, and under every disadvantage.

In the Proposed Villages, – the same trouble will provide for 1000 as is now required for one family; and all articles will be procured on the best terms.

In the Manufacturing Towns, – each family must have domestic arrangements for cooking, &c., and one person must be wholly occupied in preparing provisions, &c., for a family of ordinary numbers.

In the Proposed Villages, – the best provisions will be cooked in the best manner, under arrangements that will enable five or six individuals to prepare provisions for 1000.

In the Manufacturing Towns, – the parents must toil from ten to sixteen hours in the day to procure the wretched subsistence which they obtain for themselves and children, and very often under circumstances the most unfavourable to health and natural enjoyments.

In the Proposed Villages, – the parents will be healthfully and pleasantly occupied not more than eight hours in the day.

In the Manufacturing Towns, – in bad times, and which frequently occur, the parties experience a distress not easily to be described.

In the Proposed Villages, – no bad time can occur from a change of markets, or from any commercial uncertainties, as the parties will always have a plentiful stock of all things necessary.

In the Manufacturing Towns, – in cases of sickness, every evil takes place among these individualised beings.

In the Proposed Villages, – in the event of sickness, the utmost attention and care will be experienced; every one, both from principle and interest, will be active and have pleasure in rendering the situation of the invalid as comfortable as possible.

In the Manufacturing Towns, – the early death of parents leaves the children orphans, and subject to every evil.

In the Proposed Villages, – the early death of parents leaves the children in all respects well provided for and protected.

In the Manufacturing Towns, – the children are usually sickly, and, as well as their parents, ill-clothed.

In the Proposed Villages, – the children will be ruddy and healthy, and, as well as their parents, neat, clean, and properly clothed.

In the Manufacturing Towns, – the young children are much neglected, and hourly acquire bad habits.

In the Proposed Villages, – the children will be well looked after, prevented from acquiring bad, and taught good, habits.

In the Manufacturing Towns, – the education of the children is neglected.

In the Proposed Villages, – the children all well trained and well informed.

In the Manufacturing Towns, – the children sent early in life to some one trade of manufacture, usually of a very unhealthy nature, and at which they must attend from ten to sixteen hours per day.

In the Proposed Villages, – the children gradually instructed in gardening, agriculture, and some trade or manufacture, and only employed according to age and strength.

In the Manufacturing Towns, – the children trained under ignorant persons, possessing many bad habits.

In the Proposed Villages, – the children will be trained by intelligent persons, possessing only good habits.

In the Manufacturing Towns, – scolding, coercion, and punishments, are the usual instruments of training.

In the Proposed Villages, – kindness and good sense will be the only instruments of training.

To proceed with the contrast would be endless; the mind of the reader will easily supply the remainder: suffice it therefore to say –

That the Manufacturing Towns are the abode of poverty, vice, crime, and misery.

While the Proposed Villages will ever be the abode of abundance, active intelligence, correct conduct, and happiness.

[The *Times* of the 9th of August, 1817, had the following remarks in a leading article:

'Mr Owen's communication occupies so large a space in our columns this day, that we can do no more than claim for it that attention to which his enlightened zeal in the cause of humanity must at all times entitle the author.'

The *Morning Post* of the same date noticed Mr Owen's proceedings in a leading article as follows:

'We have this day with much pleasure again devoted a considerable portion of our columns to the further elucidation of the admirable plans of that distinguished philanthropist Mr Owen of Lanark, for the improvement of the condition, the morals, and the consequent comfort and happiness of the lower orders of society. Like all Mr Owen's other productions on this perhaps most interesting of all subjects to the community, his present Essay abounds in reasoning at once creditable to the head and the heart of its author. His appeal, founded as it is upon genuine reason, virtue, and humanity, cannot possibly fail of success; and while he is earnestly entitled to the thanks and gratitude of his country, future ages will have cause to revere his memory, as the virtuous author of universal public good, and as one of the most distinguished and worthy benefactors of the human race.']

ADDRESS

Delivered at the City of London Tavern, on Thursday, August 14th, and published in the London Newspapers of August 15th, 1817[a]

In consequence of the following Advertisement; namely,

'A Public Meeting will be held at the City of London Tavern, on Thursday, 14th of August next, when those interested in the subject will consider a Plan to relieve the Country from its present Distress, to remoralise the Lower Orders, reduce the Poor's-rate, and gradually abolish Pauperism, with all its degrading and injurious consequences.'

A Meeting was accordingly held, at which Mr Owen delivered the following Address.

It is not to gratify a weak and useless vanity that I am here to-day. I appear before you to perform a solemn and most important duty. Popularity and future fame I value not; neither of them appear to me of any estimation whatever. The only personal motive that influences my conduct is a desire, which disease and death alone can overcome, to see you and my fellow creatures everywhere in the actual enjoyment of the happiness which, in the utmost profusion, Nature has prepared for our acceptance.

Had wisdom been given to the world, it would have perceived long ago, during all the ages which have passed, at this ever-sought-for boon, this gift beyond the means and power of wealth to purchase, has ever been at the world's disposal, even for the least regarded of all the human beings who have lived. But, in whatever profusion the means of happiness have been shed around us, ignorance has veiled them from our sight; enveloped them securely within an atmosphere of the grossest errors, so dense and well guarded from

[a] The full title was: Address, August 14, 1817, at a Public Meeting Expressly Convened to Consider a Plan to Relieve the Country from its Present Distress; to Re-Moralize the Lower Orders, to Reduce the Poor's Rate; and to Gradually Abolish Pauperism, With All Its Degrading and Injurious Consequences; Which Adjourned to Thursday, August 21, 1817. See *The Times*, no. 10225 (15 August 1817), p. 3. Also published separately as a pamphlet. Reprinted in *New View of Society*, no. 2 (1817), *New View of Society. Tracts Relative to This Subject* (1818), *The New Existence of Man Upon the Earth* (1854), pt 1, pp. xlix–lii, Owen, *Life*, vol. 1A (1858), pp. 92–104. Later reprints include 1927, 1977, 1991.

every bold adventurer, that even the experience of time itself could not heretofore penetrate through all its shades.

This dominion of thick darkness, however, protected as it was by myriads of hydras of every appalling shape and aspect, has at length been passed.

Experience laid her plans deep in former ages, persevered in her righteous course, without fatigue, misgiving, or one moment's relaxation; proceeded while her opponents slept, and silently crept on when they were inattentive to her movements. Difficult, intricate, and dangerous as was each step in advance, she at length, to the astonishment and confusion of her foes, attained the outward barriers. All the powers of darkness were instantly in portentous movement, and preparing to inflict vengeance on this audacious intruder.

Experience, however, the parent of true wisdom and real knowledge, therefore wise and determined in all her measures, having till now hidden her might and majesty from their sight, suddenly displayed her all-efficient mirror of truth, burnished to such divine brilliancy, that when beheld by the whole host of darkness, they shrunk astounded from its piercing light, which instantly struck them to the heart; they fled, overwhelmed with despair; and are even now rapidly hastening, in every direction to quit our abodes for ever, and leave us in the full enjoyment of perfect unity, real virtue, permanent peace, and substantial happiness. It is, my friends, under the banners of this successful leader, Experience, that I this day wish to enlist you. Be not alarmed at this proposal. I shall even now proceed one step further, having been previously tutored by this unerring instructress; and I now say to you, that on this day, which will be stamped indelibly on the memory of future time, you shall be *compelled* to join the standard of Experience; and hereafter you will be unable to swerve from your allegiance to it. The rule and sway of this leader will prove to you so just and equitable, that no oppression shall be known; no cries of hunger and distress shall be heard in her streets; the prisons raised by ignorance and superstition shall have their doors always open; and their instruments of punishment shall be reserved as her legitimate trophies of victory. Under the unerring laws of Experience you shall make such physical and intellectual advances, you shall all be so well trained, instructed, and employed, usefully, pleasantly, and advantageously, for yourselves and others, that no motive will be left within you to desert your righteous cause; nay, each of you will, ere long, rather suffer any death whatever, than be forced for a moment from her all-attractive and ever-delightful service. And, by thus acting, the world will speedily be relieved from the overwhelming mental slavery in which it has heretofore been held fast bound.

We will now quit the language of metaphor, and attend closely and accurately to what facts may say; and they will speak a language so interesting to each, and so important to all, that they will merit your most fixed and earnest attention. Listen to what they say of our distress and misery, and of the practicable means by which only that distress and misery may be removed.

They say – and whenever doubts exist they are always ready to advance proof: –

That the Empire of Great Britain and Ireland is now in greater misery, distress, and wretchedness, than, in reality, it has been known to be for centuries past.

That, whatever specious appearance of improvement may at this moment exist, the real distress and demoralisation of the country is going on, and will rapidly proceed until the causes which create both shall be removed, and until they shall be replaced by other causes of a quite opposite nature.

That the United Empire of Great Britain and Ireland never in any former period possessed such an excess of superabundant means to relieve the whole of the population from this misery, degradation, and danger.

That from the Governing Powers of the country no rational means have ever yet been proposed to give a permanent and substantial relief to the thousands who are now pining in want, and whose dwellings are the unnecessary abode of every species of afflicting wretchedness.

That without other aid they do not possess sufficient power and practical knowledge of the subject to enable them to make a proper use of the means with which the country superabounds to relieve its inhabitants from their ignorance and vice, whence all the existing evils have arisen.

That this aid of power and practical knowledge can alone be given by the public voice, expressed distinctly and clearly, by the reflecting, most intelligent, and best cultivated part *of the community in their several local districts.*

And facts also prove, that the public voice should declare to the following effect:

1. – That a country can never be beneficially wealthy while it supports a large portion of the working classes in idle poverty or in useless occupation.

2. – That partial information and poverty, without any training but the worst that can be imagined, must demoralise the inhabitants of any country.

3. – That such population, when surrounded by gin-shops, low pot-houses, and every temptation to public gambling, must necessarily become either imbecile and useless, or vicious, criminal, and dangerous.

4. – That strong coercion, and severe, cruel, and unjust punishment, must necessarily follow.

5. – That discontent, disaffection, and every kind of opposition to the governing powers, must consequently ensue.

6. – That while these incentives to everything vile, criminal, and wicked, shall be permitted and encouraged by the Government, it is downright mockery of common sense to talk about religion, and of improving the conditions and morals of the poor and working classes.

7. – That to talk and act thus is a weak and silly attempt to deceive the public – that the public is not now deceived by it – and that hereafter such inconsistent and unmeaning jargon will not deceive any one.

(But, my friends, be not angry with these proceedings; rather endeavour with me to remove the existence of those circumstances which could produce such perverted intellects. Pity the individuals who have been thus injured: aid them, and do them good.)

8. That, to expect any national improvement while these and similar circumstances are permitted to remain, exhibits as much wisdom and fore-knowledge as to wait for the drying of the ocean while all the rivers of the earth are continually pouring their streams into its waters.

9. – That to remove these evils, and to introduce good habits, valuable intellect, and permanent happiness, – the large accumulated masses of poverty, vice, crime, misery, and pernicious habits, must be gradually separated, divided into manageable portions, and distributed over the country.

10. – That to succeed in ameliorating the condition of the lower orders, and of society generally, it is absolutely requisite that means should be devised to well-train, instruct, and advantageously employ, every child that shall be born among the working classes, and to give them all the necessaries and beneficial comforts of life.

11. – That such arrangements should be formed as would enable the working classes to attain all these blessings by their own labour, temperately exerted under the government of mild and equitable laws, that would admit an increase of freedom in proportion to the improved moral conduct and intellectual acquirements of the great body of the people.

12. – That the experience and means now exist to form those arrangements, without creating one particle of injury to a single individual; but, on the contrary, each one, from the most oppressed and degraded of the human race, to the highest ruler of States, shall be essentially and permanently benefited by the change.

And *facts* farther declare that the learned inexperienced men of the present times are wrong when they imagine that pauperism will be created, increased, and perpetuated by the plans now to be submitted to the public for the abolition of poverty, vice, and crime.

I feel myself, however, greatly indebted to these gentlemen, for bringing before the public every objection that acute and intelligent minds can suggest. My wish is that the whole subject should be so investigated and scrutinised that not one of its immediate effects, or most remote consequences, should be hidden from the world. *It shall withstand the full blaze of the most intense and steady light,*[a] *or I shall not be found its defender.*

I say it, however, with a confidence fearless of any opposition, having a distinct and accurate knowledge of all parts of this extensively combined subject before me, that it will bear the test of this trial: that after each proof to

[a] See Isaiah 9:2.

which it can be put, even by its most powerful opposers, it will be more and more purified from the misconceptions of ignorance; and will present itself, as future ages will find it, consistent and complete for all the purposes for which it was devised.

I would here beg leave to ask these gentlemen, –

If to train a child carefully and well, from earliest infancy, be a likely means to create, increase, and perpetuate pauperism?

If to instruct a child in an accurate and correct knowledge of facts, be a likely means to create, increase, and perpetuate pauperism?

If to give a child health, kind and benevolent dispositions, other good habits, and an active cheerful industry, be a likely means to create, increase, and perpetuate pauperism?

If, among the working classes, to instruct each male in the practice and knowledge of gardening, of agriculture, and in at least some one other trade, manufacture, or occupation – if to instruct each female in the best method of treating infants and training children, in all the usual domestic arrangements to make themselves and others comfortable, – in the practice and knowledge of gardening, and in some one useful, light, and healthy manufacture; – I ask, if all or any of these parts of the plan be a likely means to create, increase, and perpetuate pauperism?

If to remove the causes of ignorance, anger, revenge, and every evil passion, be a likely means to create, increase, and perpetuate pauperism?

If to train the whole population of a country to be temperate, industrious, and moral, be a likely means to create, increase, and perpetuate pauperism?

If to unite in cordial union and mutual co-operation, without one feeling of distrust on the part of any, be a likely means to create, increase, and perpetuate pauperism?

If to increase the wealth of the world four-fold – perhaps ten-fold, not improbably a hundred-fold – be a likely means to create, increase, and perpetuate pauperism?

But I might proceed to ask these gentlemen many other questions, and to which, perhaps, they would not make so ready a reply as to those now put: one, however, shall suffice.

How do they propose to relieve the people from the ignorance, distress, and immorality, with which the country abounds; and which, if not speedily checked, must soon overwhelm all ranks in one general scene of confusion, disorder, and ruin?

I know they have no reply to make, founded on any sound practical knowledge of the subject. I should have been delighted beyond anything which I can now find language to express, to discover that the Government, the Legislature, or any Parties in the country, had possessed the requisite knowledge and practical experience to remove the physical and mental evils under which we and other nations are now suffering. I, patiently and calmly, for years, sought for this knowledge among the most intelligent, enlightened, and experienced of all classes, sects, and parties, in the State. I neglected no source whatever, from whence it appeared to me possible to derive the information required. While thousands of my fellow-creatures were most unnecessarily pining in want, and their offspring hourly wasting away before their eyes, I anxiously attended to the proceedings of both Committees of Parliament, to learn if help was near. Soon, however, to my mortification, I discovered that the knowledge and experience necessary to enable them to comprehend this subject, in its various parts, and in its entire connexion, did not in any degree exist among them. They speedily involved themselves in a heterogeneous mass of particulars, admirably calculated to confound their intellects, and to disappoint every hope of the country. My duty now compels me to say, that were they to proceed thus for a century, they would continue in the dark, and remain incompetent to pass one rational legislative act on this vital subject to the well-being of the Empire. With such knowledge before me, and as distinctly before my mental vision as you are now to my sight, could I remain a quiet, inactive observer? Ought I to have held my tongue, and been mute, in deference to unmeaning forms and customs? Nay, with the knowledge permitted me to acquire, should I not have been the most criminal of all human beings, if regarding any personal considerations whatever, I had not attempted to make the still small voice of truth heard among my fellow-men. It has gone forth, like the dove from the ark,[a] never more to return.

This truth will not rest in its progress until it has visited and pervaded all parts of the earth; and its influence will dispel and destroy every pestilential vapour, and whatever is noxious and evil; and, my friends, it will thus render our country, and all countries, a fit abode for rational beings. But, my friends, before this period can arrive (and I now speak to you as a plain practical man, long and intimately acquainted with the transactions of men,) you have *much to unlearn – much to learn*. This change in your proceedings is not to be, cannot be, created by magic. It can be effected only gradually, by individual steps – by correct principles being carried into actual practice – by imperfect attempts at first, until Experience shall point out that which is better and more beneficial.

I have been long aware – I have so stated it some years ago – that when you should have the new order of things distinctly placed before your minds, so as to enable you to compare it with things which have passed and which exist, you would become too impatient for the change; that you would be inclined to destroy your old habitation before the new one could be erected and made ready for your reception. To feel thus is natural; but so to act would be most unwise. From this day forward I shall have no occasion to urge you to adopt in practice the plans proposed. Your wishes and inclinations to be in the actual

[a] See Genesis 8:8.

possession of the happiness which they cannot fail to give you and your children, to endless generations, will greatly exceed the present power of human beings to prepare the means to put the plans into execution. These considerations, however, should not prevent us from making all the practical preparation possible to relieve us from the existing evils and distress, and to replace them with the least loss of time by those new circumstances which, without a shadow of doubt, must produce a happiness that the world has not yet experienced, and of which none of you can now form a clear and distinct estimate.

There are various modes by which the measures now proposed can be carried into practice: and should this Meeting approve of the outlines of the plans which I have submitted so generally to public notice, it is next to consider which, if any, of the following modes deserve the most commendation; or whether any other that may be proposed from some other quarter, should be recommended, if equally good. The adoption of the latter would please me infinitely more than to see any of my own preferred. You know not, my friends, how I shall rejoice when we shall sink the individual and unite him cordially with his fellows.

The practical modes that have hitherto suggested themselves to me, or have been mentioned to me by others, are the following; –

The first plan I shall mention, and it is an admirable one, has been sent to me by a Mr James Johnson, of Chelsea.[a] I have not the pleasure of knowing this gentleman; but whoever he is, and whatever he may be, the letter he has sent to me, and which, with your permission, I will now read, evinces a clear understanding, a sound judgment, and much practical knowledge. It is as follows:

'MR OWEN,

Sir, – I have taken the liberty of addressing you in consequence of reading your very able and judicious Plan for the amelioration and Employment of the Poor, which has appeared in the Public Papers, and which does appear to be the best calculated for the general happiness and prosperity of the nation which can be possibly adopted. No doubt, like all great undertakings, many improvements may suggest themselves from time to time in the course of its progress, but none but what may be easily introduced without the slightest impediment to the original design. It wants nothing but the support and protection of Government to enable it to be the most efficient national establishment in the kingdom; and it would be the means of drawing forth the prayers and gratitude of the poor, and would also meet the general approbation

[a] Possibly James Johnson (1777–1845), physician, medical editor and author of *The Influence of Tropical Climates on European Constitutions* (1812), who however was normally resident at Portsmouth until 1818. No other James Johnson seems to have been resident in Chelsea in 1817.

of every good individual in the country. It would soon change the feelings of many thousands of the present unhappy and discontented class of the community, into gratitude and respect towards their superiors, and obedience to the laws of the country. It is distress that first produces indifference, and that leads imperceptibly, from time to time, to depravity and desperation; and then general misery gets established throughout the country.

Open once a prospect to future comfort, there will not be found any want of patience to wait for the enjoyment of it. – My motive for addressing this is, merely to suggest a simple plan for raising the means for the accomplishment. I will suppose, by way of foundation, £100,000 will be sufficient, either for one establishment, or to be divided into smaller ones, as may be deemed expedient; the common interest upon this will be £5,000. There will be but little difficulty, I should imagine, to find one hundred Gentlemen who would most willingly give every encouragement to promote any undertaking that will add comfort to the Poor. We have proof, and proof sufficient, in every benevolent establishment throughout the kingdom, to evince there never has been any want of liberal feeling, when it has been required.

If one hundred persons of sufficient property will undertake the promotion of the plan, it can easily be accomplished in this way: If Government will advance, in the first instance, the £100,000, and each of the one hundred persons will consider himself as a kind of Trustee to the Establishment, subject to the payment of an annual sum of £50 to Government – this will discharge the interest. The Trustees, in proportion as they can, to employ on the Establishment the present unemployed Poor, which will give considerable relief to the Poor Rates. The Trustees then shall have a power to receive a reduced rate from the parishes accordingly as the unemployed Poor get off the parish books. This will lessen the claim upon the private property of the Trustees upon the interest which they have to pay to Government. If I understand correctly, the Establishment, ultimately, is to produce profit. If so, the present Trustees, or their Assigns, shall have a power to discharge the original advance of the £100,000 by Government; but not to have power to make alterations in what has once been established, but as the wisdom of Government sees proper; otherwise, for the sake of profit, it might become a kind of speculative concern, and occasion its own destruction. It does appear strongly to my view, that Government giving protection to it will give it strength and security not to be obtained by any other means. The Trustees, and not Government, shall possess the power of executing the arrangements, but not the power to alter the Plan once laid down, without the consent of Government. I hope this rough outline will not be considered impertinent; and I most sincerely wish every success may attend your truly benevolent effort.

I am, Sir, with the highest respect,

Your very obedient servant,

Chelsea, Aug. 4th, 1817 JAMES JOHNSON.'

This plan appears to me very unexceptionable. But other modes may be asked for, and others offer themselves. Individuals possessing £100 each, and the means of support for one year, may unite on this plan, and carry it most successfully into execution. Extensive parishes, in which the poor are numerous and the annual expenditure large, may put the plan into immediate execution; or several parishes, according to their number of poor and annual expenditure, may unite under the Gilbert Act,[a] and carry the plan into practice, most advantageously for themselves and the poor.

Or, one or more wealthy individuals, who may be desirous of ameliorating the conditions of the ignorant, the ill-taught, the vicious, and the miserable of their own dependants, or others, may form such establishments as the proposed, and effect thereby the greatest possible good to their fellow-creatures – most certainly increase their revenue, and add a new zest and pleasure to every hour of their lives. But before either or any of these plans can be put into execution, I have still other duties to perform. I must direct a complete model to be made of the whole arrangements proposed; and draw up rules and regulations by which the population within these villages can be *alone* governed, to enable them to attain all these promised benefits, and never to recede or be stationary in their progress of improvement.

These I will yet do; and at all times while my health, strength, and other circumstances will admit, I will render all the personal aid in my power to put any establishments, on the plan now advocated, into execution: or, if I can be of any real service in aiding any superior plan, devised by, and proceeding from any party whatever, I shall have equal, nay, and I speak from my genuine feelings, I shall have more real pleasure in giving such aid, than I could derive from giving support to any plans of my own.

But now, permit me to say that, opposed by the ignorance and folly of the world, I have devoted nearly thirty years to deep research and active experiment in order that the plans before us might be well matured. In thus acting, and in bringing the principles on which they are founded prominently before the public, I have expended sums that would have stayed an ordinary or short-sighted prudence in its course. I have not, – up to this hour, I do not, regret one moment of this time or one shilling of the money which has been so spent and expended. I ask for no return – none is due to me: I have simply performed my duty. The great leading object of my life, from my youth upwards, is this day accomplished; the principles and plan are even now so fixed and permanent, that hereafter the combined power of the world will be found utterly incompetent to extract them from the public mind. It will from this hour go on with an increasing celerity. 'Silence will not retard its course, and opposition

[a] Gilbert's Act (22 Geo. III, c. 68): 1782 Act which separated the able-bodied from the infirm poor, only the latter being sent to the workhouse. Work was to be provided for the able-bodied poor with wages supplemented from the poor rate if necessary.

will give increased celerity to its movements.' It may now be said, my great task is done; I resign it with unspeakable pleasure into the hands and unto the guidance of others. When death approaches, he will not, he cannot now be to me an unwelcome visitor. I shall receive him, come when he may, and as he will, with a satisfaction of which none of you, perhaps, can now form any just conception.

I should rejoice, however, to see these delightful associations of unity and mutual co-operation flourishing in this country, and in others; and should my life be longer spared, the utmost bounds of my ambition is to become an undistinguished member of one of these happy villages; and in which my personal expenses would not exceed £20 a year.

I ought to apologise for having spoken so much of myself; but it appeared to me somewhat *necessary*, in order that no part of the subject might be misunderstood.

It now becomes an important question to consider what resolutions ought to be proposed to this meeting. Many offer themselves, and probably a material advance might now be made towards carrying the plan proposed into immediate execution, and in several places. But I am most anxious that not one premature step should be taken in this business.

By the observations of several public writers and public men I perceive the subject is *not understood*. They have hitherto caught a few only of the parts, as I contemplate them; and have mixed them in an incongruous manner with various notions of their own, which have no connexion whatever with the plan I recommend. Many sensible and intelligent individuals, whose minds had not been previously directed to such subjects, are so confounded and astonished at this new and extraordinary combination of human powers, that they very naturally conclude the proposer must be either mad, a visionary, or an enthusiast; not in the least suspecting the truth, that I have ever been a plodding, practical, persevering, matter-of-fact man, who has been engaged for thirty-five years, in all the common and in extensive transactions of business. Under all these considerations, and as I do not wish to take any party by surprise, it appeared to me to be due to the subject, due to the country, and due to the individuals who are desirous of promoting the plan if it should be found to possess the advantages I have stated, that it should undergo the most severe scrutiny, in its details separately, and as a whole combined, proper for a great national and universal system, to relieve mankind from the ignorance, vice, poverty, crime, and misery, with which the whole earth is now degraded and oppressed, to the deep hurt and injury of all ranks and descriptions of men, none of whom can be happy under the fundamentally erroneous notions on which society has been hitherto constituted.

And that this high and important duty – a task worthy the present age and period – shall be committed to the calm and mature investigation and deliberation of a sufficient number of the most respectable characters in this kingdom, for rank, intellect, practical experience, and active benevolence; and without distinction of parties, sect, or class; that they should form a National Committee, in order that strict justice may be done to the plan proposed, to the country, and to the world. By this procedure every part of this interesting and important subject would be well and effectually sifted to its lowest foundation and through all its extensive and multiplied ramifications, and thus prove, by a full and fair examination, all its defects and advantages; and whether it will be proved, as I have stated, to possess that high claim to public notice and universal adoption.

It is for the Meeting to decide what encouragement shall be now given to an immediate experiment of the Plan, in one, or in more instances.

In conformity with these views I beg leave first to read the following Resolutions, as they stand in connection; and afterwards to propose them separately for your opinion and decision.

1. – That many of the poor and working classes in Great Britain and Ireland cannot now procure employment to enable them to earn a proper subsistence.

2. – That in Great Britain and Ireland the poor, the unemployed, and the inefficiently employed, are now supported at a ruinous expense to many parishes, and by extensive and injurious private charities.

3. – That under these circumstances the poor and working classes generally experience privations and distress to a greater extent, probably, than they have suffered at any former period in the history of this country.

4. – That this arises from manual labour being of less value now, compared with the price of provisions and the habits of the people generally, than it has been at any former known period.

5. – That it is not probable manual labour can regain its proper and necessary value under circumstances beneficial to the country, unless other arrangements shall be formed by society, purposely devised to give productive employment to all who are competent and willing to labour.

6. – That it is the highest practical point in political economy, as it most essentially involves the well-being and happiness of all ranks, to attain the means by which the labour of any country can be the most advantageously employed.

7. – To reduce the Poor's Rate, and to gradually abolish Pauperism, with all its degrading and injurious consequences.

8. – That, – as a solemn and grave judgment ought not to be given hastily on a subject in which the vital interests of this Empire and other countries are involved, – the plan now proposed shall be submitted to the scrutiny and investigation of a Committee composed of many of the leading, most intelligent, and best disposed, from among all ranks, who, by their previous acquirements, may be competent to give a useful opinion upon the subject. For something must be done.

9. – That the Committee of General Investigation be composed of the

following Noblemen and Gentlemen, or such of them as may be inclined to perform this high and important duty, for themselves, their country, and for posterity. The Committee to have power to add from time to time to their number, and to be a quorum.

10. – That this Committee shall report the result of their investigations and labours to a General Meeting to be called for that purpose, early in May next year, or sooner if they shall so determine.

11. – That the Proposer of the Plan shall give from time to time to the Committee, all the information in his power, that they may ask or require.

It was not my intention to have proceeded further at present; but a most benevolent and public-spirited Gentleman, whose name I am not at liberty yet to mention, called upon me last night, and, in the most liberal manner made me an unlimited offer of about 1,500 acres of land, proper in all respects to try one experiment upon, and of at least £50,000 in value, which I might use for such purpose at any time after October next.[a] I cannot, therefore, refrain from proposing the following additional Resolutions:-

12. – That it is now most desirable that one or more experiments should be tried with the least possible loss of time.

13. – That for this purpose a subscription be now opened, and that whenever £100,000 in money or land shall be subscribed, one experiment shall be commenced forthwith, and a second when £200,000 shall be subscribed; and so on, as each following £100,000 shall be subscribed.

14. – That the following Gentlemen, or such of them as may be inclined to act, shall be a Select Acting Committee, to direct and superintend such experiments, assisted by the proposer of the plan.

15. – That the most warm and cordial thanks of this meeting be given to the Gentleman who has so nobly stept forward to offer his Land to the Country, for the use of an experiment, at the moment it was wanted.

[a] Possibly A. J. Hamilton, on whose lands the later Orbiston community was built.

LETTER

Published in the London Newspapers of August 19th, 1817[a]

LONDON, AUGUST 16

MR EDITOR,

As the adjourned Public Meeting to consider 'A Plan to relieve the country from its present distress,' &c., is to be held on Thursday next at the City of London Tavern, it is important that the public should be put in possession of the following with the least possible delay. Your early insertion of it, therefore, will confer another favour on,

Sir, your obliged,

49, Charlotte Street, Portland Place. R. OWEN

The First Public Meeting,[b] to consider A *Plan of amelioration and reformation without revolution*, has passed, under circumstances peculiarly interesting. An unaided individual, directly opposed to all the existing errors and prejudices of every sect, party, and class in the State – I called that meeting. I was anxious to discover the real tendency of the public mind, when left unfettered by the influence of name or authority. I therefore purposely went unattended by any one, except Mr Rowcroft and Mr Carter.[c] The former had more experience in public meetings within the City of London than perhaps any other individual: the latter was the Secretary to the Committee of the Association for the Relief of the Manufacturing and Labouring Poor, (in which Committee my public proceedings on this subject originated,) and therefore, as he already possessed greater knowledge in these matters than any other gentleman, his services were

[a] See *The Times*, no. 10228 (19 August 1817), p. 3. Reprinted in *New View of Society*, no. 2 (1817), *New View of Society. Tracts Relative to This Subject* (1818), *The New Existence of Man Upon the Earth* (1854), pp. liii–lxii, Owen, *Life*, vol. 1A (1858), pp. 104–8. Later reprints include 1991.

[b] The meeting of 14 August 1817.

[c] Thomas Rowcroft (d. 1824), Tory candidate for Parliament in the 1818 elections, a Lombard Street provision merchant, was involved in a variety of London philanthropic enterprises, such as the Fish Association, established in 1813 to promote the consumption of fish among the poor. 'Carter', the solicitor William George Carter (1787–1861), of Temple Chambers, Fleet Street, was also active in this organisation. Both were later members of the British and Foreign Philanthropic Society. Rowcroft was only drawn into this particular meeting at the last minute, somewhat unwillingly. See *The Globe*, no. 4840 (13 June 1818), p. 2.

truly desirable in aid of the measures about to commence. With these two gentlemen I entered the room, having previously determined to leave the choice of the Chairman really to the Meeting, for to *me* it was truly indifferent who was named. Mr Rowcroft requested the company present (which then appeared to be as numerous as the room could contain,) to appoint their own Chairman. His name was immediately called out by many voices, and no other was put into competition with it. He declined, and gave the best reasons for so doing – 'that the state of his health made it imprudent for him to fill the situation.' It therefore had not been in his contemplation for a moment to accept that office; although, if an honest devotion to the cause of the poor, long experience, and very strong rational powers of mind, though greatly tried by severe exertions, rendered any individual (partially acquainted with the subject to come before the meeting,) proper to fill that place, Mr R. was certainly entitled to it. After an ineffectual resistence he acquiesced in the wishes of the meeting; and, without knowing one sentence that I was going to utter, or one resolution that I was going to propose, at length took the chair, read the advertisement, and stated what I had prepared for the meeting. I may here mention that in consequence of the incessant and numerous applications, by letter and personally, made to me for some days previous to the meeting, I could not finish my preparations for it in time even to read over a fair copy of them, as it was not ready when I left home at eleven o'clock in the morning. Under these circumstances the business of the day commenced. I knew then, however, as I did before, and as I know now, that the subject would carry me through; and it will continue to do so, whatever obstacles, trivial or important, may intervene.

Those who opposed the principles and plan that I advocated were some of the younger disciples of the much-dreaded notions respecting the evils of a too rapid population; the advocates of reform, not founded on previous training, instruction, and productive employment of the people; and some of the opposers of all the measures of Government.

A knowledge of the extent of land in this empire and the world, advantageous for cultivation, but now waste and useless, with the known practice of every farmer in the kingdom, whose servants raise ten times the food they could eat, would suggest sufficient to enable every thinking mind to discover that no position can be more fallacious than the one which states that 'population has a tendency to increase geometrically, while food can be increased, only arithmetically.'

A reform of any of our great national institutions, without preparing and putting into practice means to well-train, instruct, and advantageously employ, the great mass of the people, would inevitably create immediate revolution, and give new and extensive stimulus to every bad passion: violence would follow; every party, whether more or less virtuous, ignorant, or intelligent, would equally suffer in their turn; and in a short period this empire, and all

Europe and the Americas, would be plunged in one general scene of anarchy and dreadful confusion, of which the late French Revolution will give but a faint anticipation.

Such must be the consequences of any premature national reform. Unless the people are first made temperate and intelligent, and unless productive employment and useful occupation be provided, sudden and ill-prepared reform is greatly to be dreaded, and cannot be too much guarded against. All, every one, the poor and the rich, reformers and opposers, would be severe suffers by the change. All such ill-digested and short-sighted proceedings, in any party whatever, ought to be firmly opposed by every reflecting individual.

The remaining opposition was on the part of those who have long been in the habit of systematically opposing the measures of the existing Administration; supposing, as I have no doubt they do sincerely, that they could direct matters, under the existing circumstances, better than they are now managed: but hitherto, nothing really beneficial, that is practical, has been advanced by them. I have for years very coolly and dispassionately observed both these parties, and put their professions and practices to the test. There are some exceptions on both sides to the following conclusions; but, as parties, and acting as a body, I cannot, after so many years' intimate experience of the conduct of both, be now mistaken. These conclusions are: That the present Ministers are thoroughly satisfied that the principles on which, from previously existing circumstances, they have been hitherto compelled to act, are erroneous, and that the system they support is full of error, and productive of many serious and grievous evils: that they heartily and sincerely wish to remove the latter, if they know how; but they do not, as a Ministry, possess sufficient practical knowledge to enable them to carry their wishes and inclinations into execution. They are in search of it; and ultimately they will find it among individuals who combine science and practice, and who are sufficiently intelligent and independent not to be influenced by any party or interested motives;-and thus may the country and its inhabitants be safely and rapidly improved.

The Opposition[a] have involved themselves in a maze of false intelligence; somewhat gratifying to discourse about, because it possesses the appearance of much learning; but when examined accurately it possesses no substance, it cannot be rendered of any practical use whatever; and were they to be placed in power tomorrow, they would be found, with the exception of Lord Granville[b] and a few others, to be mere theorists, and quite inadequate to the task of removing the distress of the country.

There is, however, a far greater portion of genuine good intention and disposition among all parties, even among the premature Reformists, than is in

[a] Under the Liverpool administration (1812–27), the Whigs were in opposition.

[b] Leveson-Gower, Lord Granville (1773–1846), Staffordshire MP, friend of Canning, and staunch Whig.

any degree conjectured by their opponents. I know many of them well; and, as men and friends, I respect and love many among all the parties. I only wish I could now dispel the atmosphere of separation and distortion that has been formed around the mind of each, that they might be permitted to see each other without prejudice; and I trust the time is not far distant when this will be accomplished.

The particular objections brought forward at the meeting by the several speakers who advocated them, were so little to the purpose, so futile and contrary to daily experience, and evinced so much real ignorance of the subject before them, that the Chairman restrained me, on account of the exhausted state of the meeting, from making more than a general reply; and to which I the more readily acceeded, inasmuch as a complete answer to their objections, and to many others, was contained in the printed papers distributed at the meeting, and which I recommend to the calm and deliberate consideration of every individual who has sincerely at heart the safety of his country, the improvement of the condition of the poor and working classes, and the well-being of all, without any exception whatever.

At the next meeting, now that the more preliminary but necessary part of the subject has appeared, I will give the minute details of the plan; with which I learn many present were wholly unacquainted, as they had not seen the Report and papers previously published. I mean also to ask for a general, that is, a numerous and highly-intelligent Committee of severe scrutiny and investigation, to report on the plan, both as a limited and as a general National measure. My impression, nay, my cool dispassionate conviction, is, that it will be found highly beneficial for both, and perfectly safe and advantageous for all countries, and for each individual.

At the last meeting I was satisfied to discover that while the business proceeded regularly, the impression was most unequivocally and decidedly in favour of the measures I had recommended; and to the last the majority was against the amendments that were opposed to my Resolutions. For a considerable time I noticed with interest the proceedings of those who wished to defeat the objects of the meeting. The parties were all new to me. I wished to discover the depth of their minds, and the peculiar atmosphere by which each was enveloped: this was very soon done. Afterwards, when the adverse parties (if adverse they ought to be called, who have done the cause great and important service,) proceeded to excite tumult, I looked upon the scene before me with precisely the same feelings with which I should have noticed so many individuals in a very ill-managed lunatic asylum. Yet they must not be left thus, – they really merit our sympathy; and we must, at least, endeavour to do them service, even in opposition to their present prejudices and their consequent feelings.

ROBERT OWEN

NEW STATE OF SOCIETY.

MR. OWEN's SECOND ADDRESS,

DELIVERED AT

THE CITY OF LONDON TAVERN,

On Thursday, August 21, 1817,

At the Adjourned Public Meeting,

TO CONSIDER

A PLAN

To relieve the Country from its present Distress;
To re-moralize the lower Orders;
To reduce the Poor's Rate; and
To gradually abolish Pauperism, with all its degrading and injurious consequences.

TO WHICH IS ADDED,

A FARTHER DEVELOPEMENT OF THE PLAN.

As published in the LONDON Daily Newspapers of Sept. 10, 1817;

TOGETHER WITH

AN ADDRESS TO THE PUBLIC,

ON THE

IMMEDIATE RELIEF OF THE POOR.

NEW STATE OF SOCIETY[a]
1817

ADDRESS

The last Meeting terminated under circumstances of some disorder:[b] but I trust and look forward with hope that these assemblages will be in future conducted with more order and decorum. I was not prepared to find, as I then discovered, so very little practical knowledge among some of the prominent speakers of the day; they have yet to acquire all the elements of the system of political economy. I had indeed abundant proof at the last Meeting that they have not made one step in advance in the right course to enable them to arrive at one useful practical result. I hope, therefore, all the supporters of premature reform who are here will listen to what I am going to say, as they would attend to any one in whom they have full confidence that their welfare alone was the object of the discourse. You say that you wish to improve the condition of the poor and working classes by giving them more freedom, and by reducing the taxes and expenses of Government. We will suppose both these apparently important objects gained; that the most ignorant and licentious had full liberty to act as they pleased, and that the expenses of Government and the taxes were diminished ten millions a year, – would you, do you think, be better off than you are now? You would not; – but the reverse would be soon experienced. The ten millions now raised by the government, and which they expend again in some particular channel for labour, would be withdrawn, and all those labourers would be thrown upon the parishes, and would thereby create new sources of misery and degradation. It is true the ten millions raised and expended by Government, if not so raised, would be expended by individuals in another channel; but not one labourer more would, or could, be employed in the latter

[a] See for example *The Times*, no. 10231 (22 August 1817), p. 3. Reprinted in *New State of Society*, no. 3 (1817), *New View of Society. Tracts Relative to This Subject* (1818), *The New Existence of Man Upon the Earth* (1854), pt 1, pp. liii–lxii, Owen, *Life*, vol. 1A (1858), pp. 108–18, with the title 'Address Delivered at the City of London Tavern on Thursday, August 21st, and Published in the London Newspapers of August 22nd, 1817'. Later reprints include 1927, 1977, 1991.

[b] See *infra*, vol. 4, p. 211.

case than at present, although much distress would inevitably arise from the change of employment from one set of labourers to another. Should greater liberty be now given than the British Constitution can with safety afford to all its subjects, the lives and properties of the well-disposed, and the safety of the State, would be put to imminent hazard; and until better training, more useful knowledge, and productive constant employment shall be given to the poor and working classes, no really intelligent person could venture to give more freedom to such a population as ours has gradually become, than the British Constitution in its ordinary state now admits. It is a mistake to suppose the existing Government possesses power independent of the genuine voice of the public. It has been for several years past solely governed by that voice, and my present proceedings are the most unequivocal proof of the truth of this statement. If you wish really to improve the Government, the only beneficial *practical* step you can take is, to increase the knowledge and improve the conduct of the public, and then both your objects would be safely and effectually obtained. The Government of this country cannot now resist the influence of the public voice, whether it be right or wrong: it becomes therefore of the highest importance, both to the Government and to the people, that the public should not be superficially trained or instructed, but that it should be substantially well-informed, and that effective means should be devised to train it as human beings intended to be rational ought to be trained. Believe me, my friends, that after you have in vain searched in every possible direction to attain your object by any of the childish, impracticable, and futile schemes, which have been hitherto proposed for your relief and improvement, you will at last discover that the only road in which it can be found is through productive employment for all the working classes, connected with good instruction. Now let me request you to consider all I have said calmly, at your leisure, when at home, after every feeling of anger has subsided; – for while these exist in any degree, you cannot be in a situation to use your judgment to any rational purpose. Act in this manner, and I am sure the time is not far distant when you will agree with me in all that I have stated.

I must now proceed to other matters, important for you and all present to understand thoroughly and well. It has been stated by me, that a gradual alteration in the arrangement of the working classes is absolutely necessary, owing to the new circumstances in which the country has been placed. It may be useful for me to make my ideas on this part of the subject better understood by the public.

At the commencement of the late war, all the products of Great Britain and Ireland were produced by about *five millions and a-half* of the working classes, aided by a comparatively limited proportion of mechanical agency. The war created a large demand for men in the prime of life for all the purposes of war, and it also created a demand for all the materials of war in such a manner as to give a most extraordinary stimulus to the rapid extension of mechanism. The result of these combined proceedings was to leave this country at the commencement of peace with a working population of about *six millions*, and an increased mechanical agency, which is now daily at work, that effects as much as could be accomplished by the united labour of *one hundred and fifty millions more;* and without consuming either food or raiment, and requiring but a few of other articles of manufacture. The certain results of this unnoticed change in the manner of supplying the wants of this and other countries, was to add in a most extraordinary manner to the amount of annual products, without increasing the power of consumption in the same proportion. The one, therefore, greatly outran the other, and a very material diminution of products became necessary. Individual interest immediately made the calculation, and found mechanism to be a cheaper agency than manual labour; human beings were therefore dismissed from employment, their labour in consequence rapidly fell in value, and with it fell almost every other article of commerce, and misery at once and most extensively followed. This is the grand cause that is constantly operating every hour to grind you to misery; and while it continues, without other arrangements being made to give a right direction to this magic power hitherto unknown to the world, you must be subjected not only to the misery that now exists, but to much greater. Were every shilling of your national debt and taxes removed to-morrow, and were the Government wholly unpaid for all its services, – in a very few years either this or some other country must suffer more than you now experience. Mechanism, which may be made the greatest of blessings to humanity, is, under the existing arrangements, its greatest curse. Those who direct the affairs of men ought to make themselves masters of this subject, and thoroughly to understand all its mighty influence and consequences. They are overwhelmed with the labour of picking useless straws, while they ought to be engaged in gathering the most precious and valuable of all products; and which they might collect in unlimited quantities with only the labour they now bestow in collecting the veriest trash. Investigate this subject now, or ere long dire necessity will compel you to give due attention to it. We, and all countries, are already so placed by it, that a very large portion of human beings are thrown idle greatly against their will, and they must be supported or starve, or be so placed as to be enabled to create their own subsistence. *Something, therefore, must be done* for them, and done soon, or society will speedily be in a confusion of which the human mind can previously form but inadequate conceptions. *That something must be employment on land. There is no alternative.*

The question then is, – How are men to be most advantageously employed on land to create their own subsistence and well supply their own wants? Is there a single individual in existence who has been placed in a situation to enable him to understand this subject even partially? If one exists, let him now be named, and brought forward to instruct us in the practice of what ought to be, what can be, done. For five years I have in vain sought for one, and if I had found such, I would have given to him all the knowledge and experience which, though nearly forty years of active inquiry and practice, I have collected, with the sole view of benefiting my fellow men of every rank and description, of every country and colour; and I would have remained secluded and unknown to the public to the latest day of my existence; – and when such individual shall appear, and will advocate this most interesting subject so as to make it practical to the world and give its endless benefits to man, I will again retire to the shade and rejoice; for, whether you believe me or not, it is a *fact*, that with the sentiments and feelings I possess, the full blaze of popularity would give me far more pain than pleasure. – A rational being will not, never can, derive gratification from the ignorance and imbecility of his fellows; and there is no other source whatever from whence popularity or fame can proceed. In the absence of such individual as I have asked for, I will now give you the result of the practical knowledge that experience has given me. It is solely for your use and benefit, and I give it you at the hazard of all that is usually valued by man. The question is: How can men be most advantageously employed to create their own subsistence and supply their own wants? I answer,

First, – *Not* by any of the existing arrangements in society: *they have now been fully proved to be quite inadequate to the purpose.*

Secondly, – *Not* by any arrangements that it is possible to make by individualising man in his proceedings, either in a cottage or in a palace; for while his character shall be so formed, and while the circumstances around him shall be, as they then must be, in unison with that character, he cannot but be an enemy to all men, and all men must be in enmity and opposed to him; nay, more, while this arrangement of society shall continue, the best parts, the only valuable parts, of Christianity, can never be brought into action. You may as well attempt to unite oil and water; individualised man, and all that is truly valuable in Christianity, are so separated as to be utterly incapable of union through all eternity. Let those who are interested for the universal adoption of Christianity, endeavour to understand this, and discover that which for nearly two thousand years has rendered it impossible to unite their theory with the practice of the world.

Thirdly, – I admit that to purchase a cottage, and let it to a labourer, with land sufficient to support an industrious family, would do much to relieve and improve society; but when all the details of such arrangements shall be known, it will found very difficult of execution, very expensive, and very defective in all the results which are now required to remoralise and improve the working classes. As we advance in this interesting inquiry, it will be discovered that a limited knowledge only of our physical and intellectual powers could induce any parties to recommend this mode in preference to united labour, expenditure, and instruction, in conformity to a practical plan suggested 120 years ago by John Bellers, in complete unison with the soundest principles of political economy. Let us now contrast this plan, only somewhat enlarged, with the separate individualised cottage system, which is beyond all comparison the best that the existing arrangements of society now offer.

In the first place, – Under the Cottage system there must be a separate dwelling and all the usual appendages for each family, which will be at first greatly more expensive and far more incomplete than the arrangement proposed in the plans lately submitted to the public; and all the domestic labour to produce usual comfort would be double at least.

In the second place, – One half more land would be required to feed the parties on the Cottage system, than on the new plan; and of course one half more labour would be necessary in cultivation.

In the third place, – The Cottage system would not admit, without greater expense and inconvenience, of an effective system to well-train and instruct the children of such parents as we now find profoundly ignorant under that system.

While under the new, the best possible arrangements are made, not only to prevent the acquirement of bad habits, but to give good ones, and the soundest and best instruction; and all this will be given more under the eye of their parents than in any way in which this important object can now be attained, except under constant family tuition, and this in many respects will be found greatly inferior to it.

In the fourth place, – The Cottage system offers no obvious advantageous mode to employ the children, so as to render them afterwards so valuable to themselves, to their neighbours, or to their country, as the plan proposed.

Under the Cottage system, they become stupid, ignorant, and brutally selfish.

In the plan now advocated, they will be made lively, intelligent, and rationally selfish – that is, truly disinterested and benevolent.

Under the Cottage system, the parents are subjected to all the restraints to which ignorance and brutal selfishness must ever be liable.

Under the other now proposed, such injurious restraints may be gradually withdrawn, and in the second generation, punishment of every kind will not only be unnecessary, but the reason why punishment is pernicious will be evident to all. Under this system kindness, properly directed, will easily and shortly accomplish that which punishment, if permitted to try its power, could not effect through all the ages of time. For punishment is the instrument of ignorance and barbarism only.

While the working classes shall remain individualised, the world will be liable to famine from unfavourable seasons. It never can be the interest of the growers of food, on this system, to raise more than sufficient for the consumption of the year in an average season; and the Cottage system will be subject also to this evil.

The new arrangements will easily admit of granaries, and to have always on hand at least twelve months' stock for each village, in readiness to prevent the melancholy effects of a season of scarcity. The new villages would combine within them all the advantages of the largest town, without one of its innumerable evils and inconveniences; and with all the benefits of the country, without any of the numerous disadvantages that secluded residences now present.

In fact, the entire labour of the country, by the proposed arrangements, would be directed under all the advantages that science and experience could give; while now it is wasted in the most useless efforts, and generally exerted under the grossest ignorance. This difference in the application of human powers will soon produce an advantageous result in favour of the new system, far exceeding the annual amount in value of all the taxes and Government expenditure. *But who is yet prepared to understand this kind of political arithmetic?*

The Cottage system renders each individual of every family subject to those evils which all have witnessed and experienced, or are hourly liable to experience: the husband suddenly deprived of his wife, the wife of her husband – parents bereft of their children, children deprived of their parents. The ties of endearment are separated in a moment, and, under your system, what remains to the survivors? A wreck and desolation of all that before made life desirable; often anguish not to be described or imagined, for the irreparable loss of the only loved object in existence; no friend remaining that feels, or can feel, one particle of interest in all those nameless associations which had been formed by and with the departed object; and at the same time liable to insult, poverty, and every kind of oppression, and no one inclined to help or relieve. All are individualised, cold, and forbidding; each being compelled to take an hundredfold more care of himself than would be otherwise necessary; because the ignorance of society has placed him in direct opposition to the thousands around him.

Under the proposed system, what a reverse will take place in practice when any of these dispensations of life occur! In these happy villages of unity, when disease or death assail their victim, every aid is near; all the assistance that skill, kindness, and sincere affection can invent, aided by every convenience and comfort, are at hand. The intelligent resigned sufferer waits the result with cheerful patience, and thus most effectually parries every assault of disease, when unaccompanied by his fell companion, death; and, when death attacks him, he submits to a conqueror who he knew from childhood was irresistible, and whom for a moment he never feared! He is gone! The survivors lose an intelligent, a sincere and truly-valued friend; a beloved child; they feel their loss, and human nature ever must regret it; – but the survivors were not unprepared, or unprovided, for this natural event. They have, it is true, lost one endeared and beloved object; and endeared and beloved in proportion as it was intelligent and excellent; but they have consolation in the certain knowledge that within their own immediate circle they have many, many others remaining; and around them on all sides, as far as the eye can reach, or imagination extend, thousands on thousands, in strict, intimate, and close union, are ready and willing to offer them aid and consolation. No orphan left without protectors; no insult or oppression can take place, nor any evil result whatever, beyond the loss of one dear friend or object from among thousands who remain, dear to us as ourselves. Here may it be truly said, 'O death, where is thy sting? O grave, where is thy victory?'[a]

It may now be asked, 'If the new arrangements proposed really possess all the advantages that have been stated, why have they not been adopted in universal practice during all the ages which have passed?' –

'Why should so many countless millions of our fellow-creatures, through each successive generation, have been the victims of ignorance of superstition, of mental degradation, and of wretchedness?'

My friends, a more important question has never yet been put to the sons of men! Who *can* answer it? who *dare* answer it, – but with his life in his hand; a ready and willing victim to truth, and to the emancipation of the world from its long bondage of disunion, error, crime, and misery?

Behold that victim! On this day – in this hour – even now – shall those bonds be burst asunder, never more to reunite while the world shall last. What the consequences of this daring deed shall be to myself, I am as indifferent about as whether it shall rain or be fair to-morrow. Whatever may be the consequences, I will now perform my duty to you, and to the world; and should it be the last act of my life, I shall be well content, and know that I have lived for an important purpose.

Then, my friends, I tell you, that hitherto you have been prevented from even knowing what happiness really is, solely in consequences of the errors – gross errors – that have been combined with the fundamental notions of every religion that has hitherto been taught to men. And, in consequence, they have made man the most inconsistent, and the most miserable being in existence. By the errors of these systems he has been made a weak, imbecile animal; a furious bigot and fanatic; or a miserable hypocrite; and should these qualities be carried, not only into the projected villages, but *into Paradise itself, a Paradise would be no longer found!*

In all the religions which have been hitherto forced on the minds of men, deep, dangerous, and lamentable principles of disunion, division, and separation, have been fast entwined with all their fundamental notions; and the certain consequences have been all the dire effects which religious animosities have, through all the past periods of the world, inflicted with such unrelenting stern severity, or mad and furious zeal!

If, therefore, my friends, you should carry with you into these proposed villages of intended unity and unlimited mutual co-operation, one single particle of *religious intolerance*, or sectarian feelings of *division* and *separation*, –

[a] See 1 Corinthians 15:54–5.

maniacs only would go there to look for harmony and happiness; or *elsewhere*, as long as such insane errors shall be found to exist!

I am not going to ask impossibilities from you – I know what you *can* do; and I know also what you *cannot* do. Consider again on what grounds each man in existence has a full right to the enjoyment of the most unlimited liberty of conscience. I am not of your religion, nor of any religion yet taught in the world! – to me they all appear united with much – yes, with very much – error!

Am *I* to blame for thinking thus? Those who possess any real knowledge of human nature know that I cannot think otherwise – that it is not in my power, of myself, to change the thoughts and ideas which appear to me to be true. Ignorance, bigotry, and superstition, may again, as they have so often done before, attempt to force belief against conviction – and thus carry the correct-minded conscientious victim to the stake; or *make a human being wretchedly insincere!*

Therefore, unless the world is now prepared to dismiss all its erroneous religious notions, and to feel the justice and necessity of publicly acknowledging the most unlimited religious freedom, it will be futile to erect villages of union and mutual co-operation; for it will be vain to look on this earth for inhabitants to occupy them, *who can understand how to live in the bond of peace and unity*; or who can love their neighbour as themselves, whether he be Jew or Gentile, Mahomedan or Pagan, Infidel or Christian. Any religion that creates one particle of feeling short of this, is *false*; and must prove a curse to the whole human race!

And now, my friends, – for such I will consider you to the last moment of my existence, although each of you were now armed for my immediate destruction – such, my friends, and no other, is the change that must take place in your hearts and minds, and in all your conduct, before you can enter into these abodes of peace and harmony. You must be attired in proper garments before you can partake of all the comforts and blessings with which they will abound.

Such are my thoughts and conclusions; and I know that you will hereafter ponder them well in your minds, and TRUTH WILL PREVAIL!

When you shall be thus prepared, if life be spared to me, I will be ready to accompany you, and to assist with all my power in every particular step that may be necessary to secure your immediate happiness and future well-being.

Now, my friends, I am content that you call me an infidel; that you esteem me the most worthless and wicked of all the human beings who have yet been born: still, however, even this will not make what I say one jot less true.

No name can make falsehood truth. How can any name whatever make truth more true? Of what use then can names be, except to give a false validity to gross error? [See note at the end of the fourth letter.][a]

---

[a] See *infra*, vol. 1, p. 224.

No one here is implicated in the slightest degree in these sentiments. I do not wish to pledge any one beyond the most severe scrutiny and investigation, only to approve of what may appear practically beneficial, and to reject all that may be proved wrong in principle, or any way injurious in practice.

The interest of those who govern has ever appeared to be, and under the present systems ever will appear to be, opposed to the interest of those whom they govern. Law and taxation, as these are now necessarily administered, are evils of the greatest magnitude. They are a curse to every part of society. *But while man remains individualised they must continue*, and both must unavoidably still increase in magnitude of evil.

Under the system proposed both these scourges of society will gradually diminish; and the diminution will be in exact proportion as men are made rational, moral, and intelligent.

Each village will ultimately be governed by a committee of all its own members, from forty to fifty years of age; or, should this number be too numerous, it may be composed of all from forty-five to fifty years of age; which would form a permanent, experienced, local government, never opposed to, but always in closest union with each individual governed.

This Committee, through its oldest member, might communicate direct with the Government; and the utmost harmony be thus established between the executive, the legislature, and the people.

No change whatever in our national institutions need take place for many years, except among the working classes: nor at any period, until the benefits of the arrangements proposed shall become fully evident to all parties.

Every great national change hitherto proposed has rendered it necessary to sacrifice the interests of some parties, by which only, the proposers imagined, the welfare of the others could be attained. But, my friends, the improvement I now advocate will remove many evils from all, and not introduce one to any. The change contemplated has no tendency, even in the slightest degree, to remove those who enjoy any supposed advantages in eminent stations to which they have attained. No one will envy them their privileges, whatever they may be; and every hair of their heads will be securely guarded by the rapidly improving condition of the great mass of the people.

This gradual and well-prepared change now advocated has no tendency whatever to drag down from their stations those whom a course of events, far, far beyond their control, has placed there. It has solely for its object to raise from abject poverty, misery, and degradation, those whom the same course of events has now sunk to the very depths of wretchedness. If the principles for which I contend be true, then there can be no permanent and beneficial change in human society that does not enable every one of the working classes to produce his own subsistence, to improve his bodily and mental powers, and to secure to himself the natural comforts of life; and which by his own labour, properly directed, will be very easily attainable.

I hastily notice these particulars, in order that you may understand *that a mere change of sufferers, whether it be from one part of a class to another – from one entire class to another – or from one nation to the other – is no remedy for the great and increasing evils which the world now suffers.* But this is the dilemma to which the systems that have hitherto regulated the conduct of men has reduced them; and while their principles shall be acted upon, a choice of severe evils only lies before them.

Every intelligent mind will comprehend, that to give the British population now, in its present state, greater freedom than the constitution has heretofore admitted, would put to hazard the safety of the state. The contending and selfish passions of mankind, irritated, goaded, and aggravated, by the hitherto unperceived operation of the new and irresistible power of mechanism, if let loose before ameliorating circumstances could be introduced, would expose all that is valuable in the country to certain destruction. But not a moment should be lost in applying the proper remedies to relieve the country at the present alarming crisis.

The plan proposed will effectually accomplish this object, in a manner most advantageous to each, and not injurious to any. The objections made against it proceed from a gross misconception of each of its parts separately, and a total want of knowledge of its effects when combined. The poor will not be required to go into these villages appropriated for them, when they can do better; or remain in them one hour longer than they wish.

But I have no idea that these villages will be occupied by the present poor only; for they will be found to afford the most desirable arrangements for all the present surplus working population, who cannot procure a comfortable support in their present situations.

I will, as I promised at the last meeting, give directions for a model to be made, and draw up the regulations necessary for the government and arrangement of these villages, on the principles that have been stated, and on which alone they can be successfully conducted.

In the meantime, however, it is highly necessary for the well-being of society, that the whole of this important subject should be immediately submitted to a Committee, composed of the most intelligent, scientific, and practically experienced individuals the country affords. A few of the most prominent names from among all ranks and parties are selected – not that many others, equally entitled to this high trust might not be still named; but as it is proposed that power be given to the Committee to increase the number, these may be afterwards added.

I will not now offer to the consideration and adoption of this meeting the Resolutions which were read to the last, but which were not proceeded on to a vote upon them. The discussions in a Committee will best prepare them for further consideration on a future day.

Peace on Earth—Good Will towards Men!

DEVELOPEMENT OF THE PLAN

FOR THE

RELIEF OF THE POOR,

AND THE

EMANCIPATION OF MANKIND.

By ROBERT OWEN, Esq.

London:
Printed and Sold by G. Smeeton, 17, St. Martin's Lane, Charing Cross.
[PRICE THREE PENCE.]

DEVELOPMENT OF THE PLAN FOR THE RELIEF OF THE POOR[a] 1817

THE adjourned or second public meeting, to consider the plan I have proposed, has passed;[b] and from its commencement to the end, it far more than satisfied all my wishes. Each prominent figure moved correctly to the wire that was touched for the purpose. The opposition to the measures recommended to these meetings for their concurrence has well accomplished the part assigned to it,[c] and has thereby forwarded all my views, and brought the adoption of the plan in its whole extent some years nearer than otherwise could have been possible. My chief apprehension previous to the meeting was that there would not be a sufficiently decisive stand made by its opponents, to elicit all the arguments which could be urged against it; for I was anxious the public should discover all their fatuity and weakness.

I therefore put forth in the newspapers that were published and very extensively distributed during the two or three weeks preceding, as much stimulus to all the parties, as, without creating personal animosity, would call into action all the opposition they could offer: and my object was attained. I thus distinctly discovered its quality and amount; and was astonished to find both so inefficient. It was, indeed, far beyond my most sanguine expectations to find the plan opposed only by the remnant of a party, who cannot discern that the first step of their own success would inevitably secure their own destruction. I have long known that the utmost resistance which could be made, in its greatest

[a] See for example *The Times*, no. 10247 10 September 1817, p. 2. Also published separately as a pamphlet in 1817. Reprinted in *New State of Society*, no. 3 (1817), *New View of Society. Tracts Relative to This Subject* (1818), *The Crisis*, vol. 3, no. 26 (22 February 1834), pp. 210–14, *The New Existence of Man Upon the Earth* (1854), pp. lxii–lxxvi, and reprinted in Owen, *Life* vol. 1A (1858), pp. 119–38, with the title, 'Letter Published in the London Newspapers of September 10th, 1817. A Further Development of the Plan for the Relief of the Poor, and the Emancipation of Mankind'. Later reprints include 1927, 1977, 1991.

[b] Of 21 August 1817. See *infra*, pp. 201–10.

[c] Owen was strongly opposed mainly by plebeian radicals, especially Robert Wedderburn, Henry Hunt, William Hone, and Thomas Wooler, who suggested that he sought to reintroduce feudalism; as well as by the political economist Robert Torrens. See *The Times*, no. 10231 (22 August 1817), p. 2. In print, he was also attacked by William Cobbett (*Cobbett's Weekly Political Register*, vol. 32, no. 18, 2 August 1817, pp. 569–70); and in private, by, among others, Francis Place (see British Library Add. MSS. 35,152 ff. 218–21; 37,949 f. 45).

aggregate amount, would not ultimately be more than a feather opposed to a whirlwind; but to experience so little opposition at the outset of my progress, is a sure proof that society is abundantly ripe for all the important improvements about to take place.

The gentlemen who opposed the plan at the public meetings, (for whom, however, I do not entertain one unsocial feeling,) did not surely imagine I wished to have the opinions of the ill-trained and uninformed on any of the measures intended for their relief and amelioration. No! On such subjects, until they shall be instructed in better habits, and made rationally intelligent, their advice can be of no value.

I called the meetings to discover the best practical means to effect those objects for them, in the shortest possible time. The first was convened simply to ascertain whether it would be prudent to proceed in my long determined measures with a greater rapidity towards their execution than I had intended when I left home early in the year; for on my arrival in town I found public inquiry and anxiety for the practical part of the plan beginning to out-strip my most sanguine hopes, as well as my preparations to carry it into immediate execution.

This first experiment upon public opinion satisfied me that the most intelligent and uninfluenced part of the meeting was much further advanced than I had calculated upon; and this knowledge, combined with my previous personal communications among all ranks and classes, convinces me thát seven out of ten of the reflecting part of society are *in heart* already prepared to go with me; and that while the supporters of the old errors and evils are considering how to defend that which is indefensible, two of the remaining three will come over to the *New View*, and the third will be paralysed.

The second meeting now became absolutely necessary to enable me to advance; for I could not proceed another step until I had ascertained whether the hour was come when FREEDOM OF OPINION, *the natural right of all human beings*, could be obtained for the world. Two modes presented themselves by which this object might be accomplished: – one was, to go to a Committee of the best disposed, best informed, and most intelligent, from among all parties, and to claim from their united wisdom, *perfect freedom of opinion*, as the first necessary step to ameliorate the condition of mankind. The other mode was to put public feeling at once to the test; and to ascertain, at every personal risk, what was the real state of the public mind on this most interesting subject. I determined to attempt both modes, that if one failed, the other might be resorted to. The appeal to public feeling, therefore, formed part of my address; and when it was delivered, the instantaneous burst of genuine heartfelt approbation that followed, told me in language I could not misunderstand, that the world was delivered from mental slavery – that the shackles of ignorance, superstition, and hypocrisy, were burst asunder for ever – that the road was fairly opened for the introduction of those principles which would, in practice, withdraw all uncharitableness, and remove every other cause of disunion and separation from among human beings. [See note, at end of this letter.]

Happiness never can be attained or secured while men shall be trained to hate and to be wholly ignorant of each other.

Having by this means ascertained, the real progress of intellect, I gained all the purposes I wished by the meeting. Those who remained at seven o'clock could only be of service to my object by carrying some amendment that would prevent the appointment of a committee. For had the committee been appointed, the discordant principles of which it would have been composed (highly useful on that account for the purpose originally intended,) could not have failed to retard all my subsequent movements by its necessary forms and consequently slow procedure. Such is the peculiar nature of my operations, that I cannot yet derive useful aid from Class, Sect, or Party.

The popular leaders among the Livery,[a] and others, and their well-trained followers, fortunately came to their assistance, and an amendment being at length carried, I was relieved from the only difficulty that presented itself to my mind, and was again set at liberty to put in train the most vigorous and decisive measures for carrying the plan into extensive execution.

No time shall now be unnecessarily lost; but the public must be guarded against precipitancy of expectation. It is folly to draw conclusions without data; and it is equally unwise to suppose that practice can proceed with the rapidity of thought. The greatest change which the world has ever yet experienced cannot be effected in a few days. It is now but one month, from the time I am now writing, since that change was publicly announced; and already, in the minds of all, the existing order of things has no secure spot on which to rest; beneath it, all is slippery and unsound. Where are its defenders? *Has one come forward who possesses any real knowledge of human society, or of mankind?* Not one – nor will any such appear to defend that which *they* know to be indefensible. Silence in them is true wisdom. Soon they will acquire courage to support that which THEY know to be *alone* true, and which in practice can and will give more happiness than has yet been promised. In a little time the new order of things shall penetrate the hearts and understandings of the intelligent, and be established for ever on an immoveable foundation. A little time longer only shall men have eyes, and see not; ears, and hear not; understandings and understand not.[b] Is there not room and are there not means, *now*, to make many thousand millions more of human beings happy than exist this day on earth? *Universal practical knowledge, derived from experience*, replies, Yes; and all men, except a few whom a melancholy theory benights, assent to the dictates of experience.

[a] Notably Alderman Robert Waithman (1764–1833), a political reformer who was a member of the Society of Framework Knitters.

[b] See Jeremiah 5:21.

Vociferators for freedom while subjected to the lowest mental slavery, – chained to the earth by the most violent and injurious passions, – bound hand and foot by the worst habits and most degrading ignorance, – and existing amidst intellectual and physical wretchedness, cry out to their deliverers not to touch their bonds, and beseech them to leave them in possession of *all* the liberty they enjoy! Mistaken helpless beings! They must not, they shall not, be left thus! Their deliverance is near at hand, and they shall enjoy *true liberty, both of body and mind!*

Were I *now* to proceed to ALL the details of the plan which shall be in due time completed; to throw full light and exhibit to them in native brilliancy that which ere long they shall possess; their present existence would become loathsome; they would not longer abide these dens of poverty, of crime, and of torment; and their sight would be destroyed by the intensity of the day that is beginning to dawn upon them. Suffice it to say, to those who are in some degree prepared to understand the change, that the following arrangements have been made to enable society to pass from the OLD to the NEW State without inconvenience, and in order that not one of the prejudices with which men have been afflicted shall be prematurely or ignorantly attacked, or opposed in any way so as unnecessarily to hurt the feelings of a single individual. Under a proper treatment those prejudices will all gradually and imperceptibly die away, until the knowledge of their existence shall be obliterated from memory.

The first Villages of Unity and Mutual co-operation may each be occupied by those only who have been trained in the same class, sectarian notions, and party feelings; by which means many of the most unpleasant counteractions experienced in ordinary society will be at once avoided, and many important advantages will be gained.

The *cause* of disunion of feelings on account of *Class*, of differences respecting *Religious Notions* or *Political Parties*, will be removed; and should any individual, after the trial of a residence in the village he first selected, have his mind changed on the subject of *Class*, *Sect*, or *Party*, he may at any period remove into another in which the occupiers of it will agree with him in all these respects; or he may retire with his property into common society.

A large part of mankind will be immediately and ESSENTIALLY benefited by quitting the OLD state of society and forming themselves under the NEW.

THE FIRST CLASS will be from the PARISH PAUPERS, etc, and may be arranged in the following order:

1. *The Parish Poor*, properly so-called, that is, *the infirm and aged who cannot now help themselves in any way, and for whom everything must be done.*

In future (under the new order of things,) such helplessness will not be created. The first business of Society is to provide for these sufferers, and if, as will be the case, *much more comfort* under the new order of things can be given to these miserable beings with less trouble and expense than they require at present, a substantial practical good will be at once obtained.

2. *The children of the Poor whom the parishes are now compelled to support, and which in general they accomplish at a great expense, and with little or no benefit either to the children or to society.*

No one can doubt that under the new arrangements *these children may be better trained, instructed, employed, and associated,* than they are at present; and *at much less expense.*

3. *Those who can labour, are willing to work, but who cannot procure employment; and whom, therefore, the parishes must support.*

Under the new order of things these may be made to create all their own subsistence, and to repay the interest of all the capital invested in the outfit of the establishment formed to give activity to their industry.

These three descriptions of poor, who must of course be under parish direction, may be advantageously combined, in certain proportions, into each 'Parish Employment Settlement.' And the payers of the poor's rate will soon discover it to be their interest to establish these settlements with the least possible delay, and those who permit next year to pass without creating the change, will suffer materially in many respects for their neglect.

But it will not be necessary to FORCE *any one to go into these parish establishments, or to retain them there for an hour against their inclination..* These establishments should be known as the *only* mode by which parish relief will be administered; and as it will be a very improved mode, compared with the present system, no applicant for such relief ought to receive it from any other parochial source. Over the pauper establishment properly instructed superintendants and assistants must be placed, to direct them under regulations duly prepared for their easy and regular government, *which will be formed throughout on consistent principles for the Prevention of Evil.*

THE SECOND, OR WORKING CLASS, will be composed of these who are WITHOUT PROPERTY, and must be employed in and for the voluntary and independent associations of the 4th class.

THE THIRD, OR WORKING CLASS, will be composed of the present LABOURERS, ARTISANS, AND TRADESMEN, WITH PROPERTY from £100 to £2,000 each. THESE *will form twelve voluntary associations*, or divisions.

The 1st division of this class will consist of members who possess £100 each, whether men, women, or children, who can for one year, or until the village residences be prepared, continue to maintain themselves, provided the adults are likely, from their age and strength, to perform a reasonable day's work for five years to come. The class can from the first have much better accommodations than those described in my report to the Committees of the Association for the relief of the Manufacturing and Labouring Poor, and of the House of Commons on the Poor Law.[a]

---

[a] See *infra*, pp. 143–55.

The divisions of this class, from the 2nd to the 12th inclusive, will be composed of individuals and families, who, besides maintaining themselves until the new residences shall be ready, can advance from £200 to £2,000 each person; and who, on joining their respective divisions, are willing to enter upon the regular employment of the establishment; it being understood that all their occupations will be as healthy, pleasant, and productive, as it is possible to make them, under arrangements in which MECHANISM AND SCIENCE *will be extensively introduced to execute all the work that is over-laborious, disagreeable, or in any way injurious to human nature.* And their accommodations of all kinds will be in proportion to the capital they can at first advance or may hereafter acquire; and ultimately they cannot fail *all* to attain the highest division of the voluntary associations, and to render MECHANISM AND SCIENCE *the only slaves or servants of men.*

The members of these associations will be all upon an equality, and governed by a general committee, chosen at first by themselves; which will select sub-committees of – 1. Health. 2. Instruction. 3. Agriculture. 4. Manufactures. 5. Merchandise. 6. Domestic Economy. 7. External Communication, including the Government of the Empire. Each of these sub-committees to choose a head, who will be the executive of each department, and the remainder will form his council or assistant associates, and the several departments mentioned will be directed by their respective committees. In a few years, when all shall be properly trained and instructed, the general committee will be formed of all from forty to fifty years of age, with power in the majority to add particular talents of any age to their number.

THE FOURTH CLASS, or VOLUNTARY INDEPENDENT ASSOCIATIONS, will be composed of persons unwilling or unable to be productively occupied, possessing from £1,000 to £20,000 each, and who by their capital will employ the 2nd class; and they may be divided into associations in proportion to the amount of their property.

The associations of this class will each be governed by a general committee and seven sub-committees (same as 3rd class). The persons of the 2nd class employed therein will not be eligible to be elected or to elect to the general committee for the government of the establishment; but this 2nd, or working class, employed in each of these voluntary independent associations, shall elect seven out of their own number, who, with one appointed out of each of the sub-committees, shall form another sub-committee, which shall choose a head among themselves by ballot, and which committee, so chosen, shall superintend all the arrangements and transactions between the employer and the employed. It being understood that the employed shall be well provided with all the necessaries of life, and have a reasonable proportion of recreation, during seven years; at the termination of which, each adult who has attained the age of twenty-five years, shall have the option to receive £100 from the community to become a member of the 1st division of the 3rd, or working class, with property; or to remain five years longer, and then to receive £200, to enable him to become a member of the 2nd division of the 3rd class; or, at his option, to go into the old society and provide for himself, or to serve the very wealthy or higher ranks, while they continue to prefer their present mode of life.

I conclude, however, that every class in society, below the very wealthy and the highest ranks, will give a decided preference to physical and intellectual liberty, over bodily and mental slavery; to temperance, health, and rational enjoyment, over intemperance, disease, and suffering; and to have thousands and tens of thousands of well disposed, well-informed, and sincere friends around them, on all sides, all acting for each other in one bond of love and interest, rather than exist among the folly, insincerity, and counteraction of society as it is now constituted; and more especially *when the same property and care will produce them* MORE THAN TEN-FOLD *advantages beyond what any of the existing arrangements can afford*. In short, when the time shall arrive when it will be prudent to develop the whole plan in its more minute detail and general combination, it will be obvious to the meanest capacity that the OLD state of society will not bear one moment's comparison with the NEW; and *that the only real practical difficulty will be to restrain men from rushing too precipitately from one to the other*.

By the adoption of the plan proposed for the PAROCHIAL POOR, the parishes of England and Wales will soon materially diminish their poor's rate, and gradually reduce them, until they shall be extinguished. They will also essentially benefit and improve the poor, and render a service of the highest magnitude to their country and mankind. I therefore take it for granted that as soon as they understand the plan, so as to be capable of putting it into execution, they will be eager to adopt it.

To enable them to adopt it, *the first step necessary is, that several parishes combine together* in order to carry the plan into execution. *The second step will be to form arrangements to enable them to borrow a capital on the revenue of one-third, or half, of their average poor's rate for the last three years.* The interest of the sum so borrowed to be paid out of the annual rate, which, owing to the reduced number and expenditure of their poor, will gradually diminish after the first year, from the present amount down to entire extinction. By the time the parishes shall have accomplished these arrangements, the model of the establishment and its appendages, with the regulations for its government, will be ready, and then the execution of the plan may commence and proceed without loss of time.

It may be useful here to remark, that the plan developed in my Report to the Committees of the Association for the Relief of the Manufacturing and Labouring Poor, and of the House of Commons on the Poor Laws, was intended for the parish poor *only*; and of course no part of society will long continue in a worse condition than the individuals within such proposed establishments. Under these arrangements the parish poor will soon lose their ignorant and vulgar habits, and acquire such an improved character as the new circumstances will imperceptibly and speedily give then. When these results irresistibly force themselves on the minds of all, the meanest and most miserable beings now in society will thus become the envy of the rich and indolent under the existing arrangements. The change from the OLD system to the NEW must become universal. To resist the introduction of this plan, in any part of the world, will *now* be as vain and useless, as for man by his puny efforts to endeavour to preclude from the earth the vivifying rays of the sun.

Such as has been described must be the beneficial change that will be created among the existing paupers, and at a greatly reduced expenditure. But, under proper arrangements, the effective and independent members of society may in a short time be surrounded by circumstances that will afford them all they can desire, all that can be of real service or add permanently to their happiness.

The first class of the voluntary and independent Associations will possess benefits and be surrounded by advantages of which no one can yet form an adequate idea. *No part of their powers will be wasted* – all will be employed to the greatest benefit for the individual, who, though not individualised, will enjoy far more than the most successful of his class have yet experienced.

The members of this class will soon be instructed to conduct the affairs of their own village with ease, order, and success. They may come in, or sell out, whenever they choose; they may acquire all the endless advantages to be gained from such an association; and should they ever feel inclined to try a change, and wish to return to old society, they will experience every facility for the purpose. But I do not contemplate that such a wish will ever arise, or exist in any one, after they shall have experienced and shall comprehend all the advantages which the new societies will produce. Shortly they will have no inducements, no motive, to commit crime, or to be immoral; but they will have every motive to be active, cheerful, and humane. They will rapidly acquire such useful knowledge as will make them ardent in their endeavours to improve the condition of all around them. Each will acquire such irresistible energy in this cause, as no one now comprehends, but which will perpetually keep these societies in the most delightful activity, and afford full scope for all the physical and intellectual powers of our nature; and both will be directed in the right course only. But these valuable qualities will not be confined to their own villages or associations. Persons, when properly trained for the purpose, will be sent from time to time to travel, in order to collect and communicate knowledge, to benefit and harmonise the world by their superior wisdom and, conduct, and thereby to cement and extend more and more the bond of union, good will, and mutual co-operation among all mankind.

By these improved characters, prejudices of every kind will be overlooked; they will know how to draw forth the best qualities of the heads and hearts of all men, and to allow the worst and inferior ones to lie dormant; and they will *act* upon their knowledge. They will go forth to do good; and the happiness they will derive from such conduct will *alone* compensate them for their absence from their own abodes of health, intelligence, activity, and happiness. And thus the change from insanity to rationality will take place with the least possible inconvenience to society.

It is to prepare the way for this change, that the combinations are made so numerous, in order that those who have till now existed within one kind of atmosphere, may not be opposed by those who have been subjected to another.

And, to accomplish this important object, in the best way, and to the greatest practicable extent that the existing arrangements of society will admit, I have composed tables which at one view exhibit the most general combination of minds in the British Empire, as they have been formed by the present and preceding generation.

The tables show, – First, the various classes into which old society may be conveniently and naturally arranged in the new order of things. Secondly, the more general sects and parties which now prevail. Thirdly, the various combinations of sect and party, which are, or may be, united with each class.

These tables have been arranged *in compassion to the weakness, prejudice, and error which have been gradually created for the existing race of men; who have been so afflicted in consequence of a chain of causes which may be easily traced beyond their present powers of mind to comprehend.* These tables have been formed *to enable all men more readily to understand their real situation in society – to discover how the minds of others have been filled with impressions which hitherto they have not understood, and to show the gross folly of being angry or displeased with those who have been thus forced to differ from us in the association of their ideas or sentiments, and consequently also in their conscientious feeling of what appears to them right or wrong.*

TABLES

Shewing the various Combinations of CLASS, SECT, and PARTY.

CLASSES

According to the arrangements of the *Proposed Villages.*

1. *Parish Pauper Class*, consisting of the infirm and aged, children of the poor, and those who can labour and are willing to work, but who cannot procure employment.

2. *Working Class*, without Property, employed by 4th Class.

3. *Working Class, or Voluntary Association*, from the present Labourers, Artisans, and Tradesmen, with property from £100 to £2,000 each, to be productively occupied in Agriculture and Manufactures.

Divisions of 3rd Class					
1st £ 100	2nd £ 200	3rd £ 300	4th £ 400	5th £ 500	6th £ 650
7th £ 800	8th £ 1,000	9th £ 1,200	10th £ 1,300	11th £ 1,800	12th £ 2,000

4. *Voluntary and Independent Class, or Association*, with Property from £1,000 to £20,000 each person, who, by their capital, will employ 2nd, or *Working* Class.

Division of 4th Class					
1st £ 1,000	2nd £ 2,000	3rd £ 3,000	4th £ 4,000	5th £ 5,000	6th £ 6,500
7th £ 8,000	8th £ 10,000	9th £ 12,000	10th £ 15,000	11th £ 18,000	12th £ 20,000

Five hundred of either of the *Classes*, or of the *Voluntary and Independent Associations*, may form a Community to commence ONE VILLAGE.

Every individual, from the lowest to the highest, will enjoy the greatest possible advantages of Instruction, Health, Comfort, Liberty, and Recreation: and all their accommodations will be in proportion to the Capital they at first advance, or may hereafter acquire.

SECTS AND PARTIES

As they now chiefly prevail in the British Empire

RELIGIOUS SECTS				POLITICAL PARTIES
CHRISTIANS	CATHOLICS			*Violent* Ministerialists
	PROTESTANTS	*Lutherans*	Baptists – (Arminian) Episcopalians – (High Ch. & Low Ch. of Eng.) Methodists – (Wesleyans) Moravians	*Moderate* Ministerialists
			Evangelicals	
		Calvinists	Antinomians – Baptists – (Calvinist) Congregationalists – Independents Methodists – (Whitfieldites) Presbyterians, or Church of Scotland Seceders	*Violent* Whigs
			Arians – Friends – Swedenborgians – Unitarians – Universalists	*Moderate* Whigs
JEWS	PORTUGUESE GERMAN			*Violent* Reformists
BRAMINS				
CONFUCIANS				*Moderate* Reformists
MAHOMEDANS				
PAGANS				*Independent*, or of no Party.

Religious Sect and Political Party in their various Combinations.

1 Armin. Meth. & *Violent Min.*	16 Antinomians & *Viol. Min.*	31 Calv. Method. & *Mod. Whigs.*	46 Armin. Bap. & *of no party.*	61 Armin. Meth. & *Vio. Whigs.*
2 Seceders & *of no party.*	17 Low. Ch. Eng. & *Mod. Refor.*	32 Catholics & *Mod. Ref.*	47 Presbyterians & *Vio. Whigs.*	62 Friends & *Mod. Ref.*
3 Evangelicals & *Violent Min.*	18 Baptists & *of no party.*	33 Presbyterians & *Mod. Min.*	48 Independents & *Mod. Min.*	63 Antinomians & *Mod. Min.*
4 Arm. Bapt. & *Viol. Whigs.*	19 Arm. Baptists & *Mod. Min.*	34 Calv. Baptists & *Mod. Whigs.*	49 Unitarians & *of no party.*	64 Moravians & *Vio. Whigs.*
5 Jews & *Moderate Whigs.*	20 Presbyterians & *Mod. Whigs.*	35 Friends & *Vio. Min.*	50 Jews & *Mod. Ref.*	65 Seceders & *Mod. Min.*
6 Presbyterians & *of no party.*	21 Congregation. & *Viol. Ref.*	36 Antinomians & *Mod. Whigs.*	51 Moravians & *Mod. Min.*	66 Calv. Bap. & *Mod. Ref.*
7 Calv. Method. & *Mod. Min.*	22 Unitarians & *Mod. Whigs.*	37 High Ch. Eng. & *Vio. Min.*	52 High Ch. Eng. & *Mod. Min.*	67 Universalists & *Mod. Whigs.*
8 Jews & *Viol. Whigs.*	23 Calv. Method. & *Viol. Min.*	38 Arians & *Vio. Ref.*	53 Catholics & *Mod. Min.*	68 Universalists & *Mod. Ref.*
9 Friends & *Viol. Whigs.*	24 Jews & *Vio. Reformists.*	39 Independents & *Mod. Whigs.*	54 Jews & *Vio. Min.*	69 Unitarians & *Mod. Ref.*
10 Arians & *Mod. Ministerial.*	25 Evangelicals & *Mod. Ref.*	40 Armin. Meth. & *of no party.*	55 Armin. Bap. & *Mod. Ref.*	70 High Ch. Eng. & *Mod. Ref.*
11 Swedenborg. & *of no party.*	26 Moravians & *of no party.*	41 Antinomians & *Vio. Whigs.*	56 Friends & *Vio. Ref.*	71 Low Ch. Eng. & *of no party.*
12 Unitarians & *Violent Min.*	27 Seceders & *Vio. Min.*	42 Calv. Bap. & *Vio. Min.*	57 Calv. Meth. & *Vio. Ref.*	72 Antinomians & *Vio. Ref.*
13 High Ch. Eng. & *of no party.*	28 Unitarians & *Mod. Min.*	43 Evangelicals & *of no party.*	58 Congregation. & *Mod. Whigs.*	73 Independents & *of no party.*
14 Catholics & *Violent Min.*	29 Swedenborg. & *Vio. Whigs.*	44 Seceders & *Mod. Ref.*	59 Independents & *Mod. Ref.*	74 Evangelicals & *Vio. Whigs.*
15 Arians & *of no party.*	30 Independents & *Vio. Whigs.*	45 Moravians & *Vio. Min.*	60 Calv. Bap. & *Vio. Whigs.*	75 Arians & *Vio. Min.*

Religious Sect and Political Party in their various Combinations – *Continued.*				
76 Presbyterians & *Vio. Ref.*	89 Calvin. Meth. & *Mod. Ref.*	102 Moravians & *Mod. Ref.*	115 Swedenborg. & *Mod. Min.*	128 Moravians & *Vio. Ref.*
77 Evangelicals & *Mod. Whigs.*	90 Catholics & *Vio. Ref.*	103 Calv. Bap. & *Vio. Ref.*	116 Presbyterians & *Vio. Min.*	129 Antinomians & *of no party.*
78 Calv. Meth. & *Vio. Whigs.*	91 Universalists & *Mod. Whigs.*	104 Antinomians & *Mod. Ref.*	117 Universalists & *Vio. Min.*	130 Armin. Bap. & *Mod. Whigs.*
79 Low Ch. Eng. & *Mod. Whigs.*	92 Low Ch. Eng. & *Vio. Ref.*	105 Evangelicals & *Mod. Min.*	118 Arians & *Vio. Whigs.*	131 Universalists & *Vio. Ref.*
80 Friends & *Mod. Min.*	93 Friends & *of no party.*	106 Arians & *Mod. Ref.*	119 Congregation & *Mod. Ref.*	132 Low Ch. Eng. & *Vio. Min.*
81 Unitarians & *Vio. Whigs.*	94 High Ch. Eng. & *Vio. Ref.*	107 Congregation. & *Vio. Min.*	120 Unitarians & *Vio. Ref.*	133 Jews & *Mod. Min.*
82 Swedenborg. & *Mod. Ref.*	95 Armin. Bap. & *Vio. Ref.*	108 Catholics & *Mod. Whigs.*	121 Seceders & *Mod. Whigs.*	134 Seceders & *Vio. Whigs.*
83 Catholics & *Vio. Whigs.*	96 Congregation. & *Mod. Min.*	109 Independents & *Vio. Min.*	122 Congregation. & *of no party.*	135 Swedenborg. & *Vio. Ref.*
84 Armin. Meth. & *Vio. Ref.*	97 Armin. Meth. & *Mod. Whigs.*	110 Arians & *Mod. Whigs.*	123 High Ch. Eng. & *Mod. Whigs.*	136 Armin. Meth. & *Mod. Min.*
85 Friends & *Mod. Whigs.*	98 Jews & *of no party.*	111 Low Ch. Eng. & *Mod. Min.*	124 Calv. Meth. & *of no party.*	137 Swedenborg. & *of no party.*
86 Low Ch. Eng. & *Vio. Whigs.*	99 Moravians & *Mod. Whigs.*	112 Presbyterians & *Mod. Ref.*	125 Armin. Meth. & *Mod. Ref.*	138 Universalists & *Vio. Whigs.*
87 Armin. Bap. & *Vio. Min.*	100 Congregation. & *Vio. Whigs.*	113 Calv. Bap. & *Mod. Min.*	126 Evangelicals & *Vio. Ref.*	139 Swedenborg. & *Vio. Min.*
88 High Ch. Eng. & *Vio. Whigs.*	101 Seceders & *Vio. Ref.*	114 Independents & *Vio. Ref.*	127 Catholics & *of no party.*	140 Universalists & *Mod. Min.*
There are numberless other minute combinations of mind now formed in the British empire; but to descend to every varied shade of Class, Sect, and Party, would be endless, and would turn the subject, of all others the most serious to humanity, into one fit only for jest and ridicule.				

N.B. – Those who shall be solely governed by the RELIGION OF CHARITY, can, and will, unite with all, or any, of the above Sects and Parties.

Offices shall speedily be opened in London, and in other places over the kingdom, where books will be kept, *and any person wishing to join either of these new Associations may call and state his wish to become an inhabitant or member of one of the* NEW VILLAGES – *of* (suppose) CLASS No. 2, 3, or 4 – and DIVISION in *that* Class, *1, 2, 3, 4, 5, 6, 7, 8, 9, 10, 11, or* 12, *and to be associated with* SECT *and* PARTY *No.* *in the table of Sect and Party*. His name will be entered in the proper column, to designate his Class, Sect, and Party, to which he will affix his signature and address, paying a small charge to cover the expense of registry, &c.[a] *And as soon as there shall be a sufficient number, say 500, of any of these Associates, entered in the book, then the operations for one of the establishments may commence; and afterwards, as each 500 shall be entered, others may follow in rotation; or many may commence at once and together, as soon as the preparations for one shall be completed.*

To enter further into details would be to create a desire for the attainment of the object that would be injurious to its sound and beneficial progress. The change cannot be effected in a week or a month, – although much, very much, may be put into action next year; so much, indeed, as with ease to relieve the country from the most grievous evils of poverty. And it will be done. Should it be asked on what principle is this assertion made? – the reply is, on the well-known principle of self-interest, which compels all men to prefer their happiness, when easily attainable, to a continuance in wretchedness and misery.

The multitude, the uninformed part of the public, – those, in short, whose field of vision is confined within the circle of ordinary localities, could form no conjecture why I disclaimed connection with the errors of all existing systems, political and religious. They could not know that, to secure to them solid, substantial, and permanent good, my course must be such as they have seen. The declaration made at the last meeting was a step absolutely necessary then to take. To oppose myself to all the most inveterate and hitherto unconquerable prejudices with which the human intellect has been afflicted, could not have been a premature and hasty measure on my part. I long knew that to deliver from abject slavery of intellect, from the grossest ignorance, from the vilest passions, from crime, from poverty, and from every species of wretchedness, – I must for a time offend all mankind, and create in many feelings of disgust and horror at this apparent temerity of conduct, which, without a new understanding, a new heart, and a new mind, they could never comprehend; but these in due time shall now be given to them. Ere long there shall be but one action, one language, and one people. Even now the time is near at hand – almost arrived – when swords shall be turned into ploughshares, and spears into pruning hooks[b] – when every man shall sit under his own vine and his own

[a] See *infra*, pp. 201–10.
[b] See Isaiah 2:4.

fig-tree, and none shall make him afraid.[a] But, what is still more marvellous, the time is also at hand, when your respect, esteem, and love, for those who oppose all your prejudices, will be much greater than for those who now defend them; because you will discover that the instructions of the latter tend only to perpetuate endless evils throughout society.

Yes, my friends, in the day and hour when I disclaimed all connexion with the errors and prejudices of the old system – a day to be remembered with joy and gladness henceforward throughout all future ages – the Dominion of FAITH ceased; its reign of terror, of disunion, of separation, and of irrationality was broken to pieces like a potter's vessel.[b] The folly and madness of its votaries became instantly conspicuous to the world. When the benighted intellects of humanity were opened, and it was clearly perceived that *any* faith, however horrible and absurd, could be given to all of the sons of men, – it was in the same hour made known, that, therefore, Faith could be of no practical value whatever; but that its longer Dominion on earth must be productive of error and misery; and, if permitted to remain, that its continuance among the children of light would produce only evil continually.

Now from henceforth CHARITY presides over the destinies of the world. Its reign, deep rooted in principles of DEMONSTRABLE TRUTH, is permanently founded; and against it hell and destruction shall not prevail.

Yes, on this day, the most glorious the world has seen, the RELIGION OF CHARITY, UNCONNECTED WITH FAITH, is established for ever. *Mental liberty for man is secured; and hereafter he will become a reasonable, and consequently a superior being.*

What is the character of this NEW RELIGION?

It is throughout consistent with all facts, and therefore TRUE. It suffereth long and is kind;[c] envieth not; vaunteth not itself; is not puffed up; doth not behave itself unseemly; seeketh not its own; is not easily provoked; thinketh no evil;[d] rejoiceth not in iniquity, but rejoiceth in the truth. Beareth all things, believeth all things[e] (WHEN DEMONSTRATED BY FACTS, – BUT NOTHING THAT IS DISTINCTLY OPPOSED TO THE EVIDENCE OF OUR SENSES.)

What is the power of Charity?

It never faileth. But whether there be prophesies, they shall fail; whether there be tongues, they shall cease;[f] whether there be (FALSE) knowledge, it shall vanish away.

What has been foretold of Charity?

[a] See 1 Kings 4:25.
[b] See Psalms 2:9.
[c] See 1 Corinthians 13:4.
[d] See 1 Corinthians 13:5.
[e] See 1 Corinthians 13:7.
[f] See 1 Corinthians 13:8.

That it has been known only in part, and prophesied of in part;[a] but when that which is perfect is come,[b] then that which is in part shall be done away. When I was a child, I spake as a child, I understood as a child, I thought as a child; but when I became a man, I put away childish things.[c] For now we see through a glass darkly,[d] but when CHARITY REIGNETH ALONE, we shall see face to face. Now I know in part; but then shall I know even also as I am known.[e]

THE GREATEST OF ALL THINGS IS CHARITY.[f]

What are the signs of the last days of misery on earth? '*And there shall be signs in the sun, and in the moon, and in the stars; and upon earth, distress of nations, with perplexity; the sea and the waves roaring; men's hearts failing them for fear and for looking after those things which are coming on earth; for the powers of heaven shall be shaken.*' '*And then shall they see the son of man*' (or TRUTH) '*coming in a cloud with power and glory. And when these things begin to come to pass, then look up and lift up your heads, for your redemption*' (FROM CRIME AND MISERY) '*draweth nigh.*'[g] 'THIS GENERATION SHALL NOT PASS AWAY UNTIL ALL SHALL BE FULFILLED.'[h]

What immediate and permanent consequences will follow from the Religion of Charity alone, unconnected with Faith?

PEACE ON EARTH AND GOOD WILL TOWARDS MEN.[i]

What will be its conduct to those irrational persons who for a time must oppose it?

Commiseration for their mental infirmities; but an unceasing kindness will be continually exerted to benefit them; and thus evil shall be overcome of good, until its nature shall be changed, and its injurious propensities shall disappear from among the children of men. 'Then shall the wolf dwell with the lamb, and the leopard shall lie down with the kid; and the calf, and the young lion, and the fatling together, and a little child shall lead them. They shall not hurt nor destroy in all my holy mountain; for the earth shall be full of the knowledge of the Lord, as the waters cover the sea.'[j]

What overwhelming power has done this? Where is the arm that has crushed the mighty ones of the earth, and made them afraid?[k] Who has said, Let there be light, and there was light, and all men saw it?[l]

This marvellous change, which all the armies of the earth could not effect

[a] See 1 Corinthians 13:9.
[b] See 1 Corinthians 13:10.
[c] See 1 Corinthians 13:11.
[d] See 1 Corinthians 13:12.
[e] See 1 Corinthians 13:12.
[f] See 1 Corinthians 13:13.
[g] See Luke 21:25.
[h] See Matthew 24:34.
[i] See Luke 2:14.
[j] See Isaiah 11:6.
[k] See Jeremiah 46:5.
[l] See Genesis 1:3.

through all the ages that have passed, has been accomplished, (without an evil thought or desire toward a being with life or sensation,) by the invincible and irresistible power of TRUTH alone; and for the deed done, *no human being can claim a particle of merit or consideration*. That hitherto Undefined, Incomprehensible Power, which directs the atom and controls the aggregate of nature, has in this era of creation made the world to wonder at itself.

The nations of the earth will be astonished! Their heretofore esteemed sacred institutions – their far-famed complex political arrangements – and their varied domestic manners, habits, and languages – will be no longer esteemed among men. – 'Old things shall pass away, and all shall become new.'[a] (See the 58th and 59th chap. of Isaiah, for the *calamities of ignorance*, and the *requisite changes therein described*; and the 65th chap. on the OMNIPOTENCE OF TRUTH, *and the changes to take place in the fulness of time*.)

I may now be asked, – What are the characteristic differences between Old and New Society?

They are decisive and manifold.

Old society has supposed, contrary to every fact that has been observed from the earliest period of known time to this hour, that MAN FORMS HIS OWN CHARACTER!! *and all the transactions of mankind have been governed by this absurd notion!!*

New society will be instructed, by close and accurate attention to all existing and provable facts, THAT THE CHILD DOES NOT FASHION ITSELF IN THE WOMB; OR DIRECT THE LANGUAGE, MANNERS, HABITS, SENTIMENTS, AND ASSOCIATIONS, WHICH SHALL BE AFTERWARDS IMPRESSED UPON ITS NATURAL PHYSICAL AND INTELLECTUAL POWERS; *and that the whole character of man is a compound of these combined circumstances*. Old society, therefore, from the hour the child was born, began a system of conduct diametrically contrary to fact, *and nature was counteracted by all the efforts of Ignorance*. Nature, however continually opposed Ignorance, and all the force and violence of the latter could not keep the former in subjection. Ignorance then called in Superstition and Hypocrisy to its aid; and together they invented all the faiths or creeds in the world; – a horrid crew, armed with every torture both for body and mind. A dreadful conflict ensued; Nature was overcome, and compelled for a long season to receive laws from her conquerors, and to be the slave of Ignorance and Superstition.[b] Nature was then treated with indescribable severity; and would have been put to death if she had not been immortal, and possessed of powers capable of gradual reaction, equal, and superior, to any force that could be permanently exerted against her. As time advanced, the appalling terrors of Ignorance and Superstition, Faith and Hypocrisy, imperceptibly diminished.

---

[a] See 2 Corinthians 5:17.

[b] Here there are echoes of John Bunyan, *The Pilgrim's Progress* (1678), pt 1.

Experience united herself to Nature, and produced Real Knowledge and Demonstrable Truth. These grew up together; and, in close bond of union with their parents, they became strong, felt conscious of their strength, and were soon eager for attack. But Nature and Experience knowing the wiles and power of their opponents, restrained their ardour, but inured them to continual opposition and severe contest, until Knowledge and Truth became assured that their united efforts would be irresistible. War was then openly declared against Ignorance, Superstition, Faith, Hypocrisy, and all their dire associates. The latter instantly sounded the alarm, collected their forces, and began to prepare for battle. To their utter dismay, however, Charity, who till now had been compelled by force, contrary to her nature and inclinations, to be their ally, and to appear in their front ranks, escaped their toils, and declared she would henceforward unite herself solely with Nature, Experience, Real Knowledge, and Demonstrable Truth; but, to prevent all future devastation and misery, she would use her mediation and obtain the best possible terms for the weakened and now disheartened enemies of Nature and her invincible allies. This offer, seeing all resistance vain and hopeless, was readily accepted, and Truth and Charity dictated the terms, which, in consequence, were kind and benevolent, evincing that they were not influenced by anger, revenge, or any evil motive whatever. Ignorance, Superstition, Faith, and Hypocrisy, were permitted to retain all their possessions; – to remain free and unmolested in the conquered country. But they were to leave it solely to the government of Nature, aided by Experience and Real Knowledge, as counsellors. And Charity, assisted by Demonstrable Truth and Sincerity, was to preside as the active agent over the whole dominions of the New State of Society.

Their first care was to make a new code for the government of the people, *in unison with all Nature's laws.* They decreed it to be just, *that as Nature was always passive before birth – in infancy, childhood, and youth – and was made beneficially or injuriously active by the treatment she had previously experienced –* NATURE COULD DO NO WRONG, *and, therefore, could never become a proper subject for punishment: that the cause of all her errors proceeded from the powers that acted upon her passive state; and that if these were consistent and proper,* NATURE WOULD BECOME ACTIVELY GOOD, *and in consequence* UNIVERSALLY BELOVED; *but if there were irrational and improper,* NATURE WOULD BECOME DISGUSTING AND WICKED, *and in consequence* DISLIKED AND HATED BY ALL. Charity, Truth, and Sincerity, therefore, decreed, that NOT ONE CHILD OF NATURE OUGHT TO BE NEGLECTED OR IMPROPERLY TREATED; *that all should be trained, instructed, associated, and occupied, and placed amidst circumstances most congenial to the genuine feelings of Nature,* and which were to be arranged by the twin sisters SCIENCE and PRACTICE, *who were to unite their efforts in the execution of everything that was to be accomplished.* – Every minor regulation was in strict unison with these general laws; and Truth was ever watchful to mark the *least* deviation from her favourite rule, 'THAT INCONSISTENCY IS ERROR,' and therefore *inconsistency* must never be admitted into any transactions within the dominions of the New State of Society.

Such as have now been described are the fundamental differences between man in the OLD and man in the NEW state of society. In the first he *has been* a wretched, credulous, superstitious, hypocrite: – in the *last* he *must become* rational, intelligent, wise, sincere, and good. In the OLD, the earth has been the residence of poverty, luxury, vice, crime, and misery; – in the NEW, it will become the abode of health, temperance, wisdom, virtue, and happiness. The change from the one to the other, however, must not be too hasty. All I ask is, – *let it be gradual,* and conducted in the *true spirit of benevolence*; and let no one be injured in mind, body, or estate.

We have, therefore, my friends, a most important duty now to perform. The institutions of our forefathers, erroneous as they are, must not be handled with violence, or rudely touched. No: they must be still preserved with care, supported, and protected, until the new state of society shall be far advanced in quiet practice, – until it has proved its numberless important benefits to mankind, even to the conviction of the most unbelieving.

None must suffer in *person, property, or comfort*; all will be soon reconciled to the change, and lend a helping hand.

The instructors of the endless, varied, and existing creeds or faiths, which have deluged the world with blood, and rendered it a curse and desolation, will all become the unresisting *teachers of Charity. Benevolence will pervade all their language and all their conduct; and an evident and substantial success will crown every step of their future progress.* They will no longer say, 'we piped unto you, and ye have not danced,'[a] or '*we preached in vain.*'[b]

The whole frame of society may remain as it is. The British Constitution will readily admit of every improvement requisite to ensure the interest and happiness of the empire. A CHANGE of the most extensive magnitude the world ever contemplated will be accomplished without violence or confusion, or any very apparent opposition. *The feelings and the interests of mankind imperiously demand this change;* THE WORLD APPROVES – AND NONE CAN RESIST.

THUS, IN THE FULNESS OF TIME, ERE ITS COMMENCEMENT WAS WELL KNOWN, IS THE GREAT WORK ACCOMPLISHED.

THE CHANGE HAS COME UPON THE WORLD LIKE A THIEF IN THE NIGHT!

NO MAN KNOWS WHENCE IT COMETH, NOR WHITHER IT GOETH!

ROBERT OWEN.

September 6th, 1817.

[a] See Matthew 11:17.
[b] See 1 Corinthians 15:14.

NOTE: No intelligent mind will for a moment suppose from what I have said, that I am an enemy to all religion. On the contrary, my efforts have been, and will be, directed to secure the interests of true religion, and to establish it permanently throughout the world. I well know, and am now competent to prove, that the real enemies to truth, to genuine religion, and to the happiness of mankind, among all people, are those parts of every religion that are in direct and palpable contradiction to existing facts, and which have been added to pure and undefiled religion, either by weak, mistaken, or by designing men. Withdraw these from the Christian system, and then it will become a religion of universal benevolence, competent to make, and it will make, men rational and happy. Let but this change be effected, and I will become a Christian indeed.

ADDRESS

Dated September 19th, 1817; on Measures for the Immediate Relief of the Poor[a]

The urgent applications which are hourly made to me from those who suffer in almost every conceivable manner from the effects of the present wretched system, render it an imperative duty on my part to state such practical measures as are in progress to give the relief so anxiously sought for.

The evils experienced are both mental and bodily; but those which effect the body require removal with the least possible delay; and every individual who can feel for the afflictions of others is called upon to give his earnest attention to the means devised for the purpose. Whatever inexperienced or theoretic men may write to say on the subject, it will now be discovered that no other measures than those I have proposed possess, in their ultimate results, any practical value. I therefore again call upon the public to do its duty to itself – to strive to overcome its prejudice, its weakness, and its errors. These, I well know, cannot be conquered in a day or a week, and time must be allowed for them to disappear gradually and almost imperceptibly. But the measures devised and recommended need not interfere with those diseases of the mind from which separation between man and man proceeds.

The practical means of relief for your suffering and degraded population are before you. They may be easily adopted, and united to all your various creeds, and acted upon without much inconvenience until your minds shall attain sound health and enable you to discover and secure the good things which so abundantly surround you, and until you acquire the power to discern the manifold advantages of demonstrable truth, over the evils which perpetually arise from pursuing systems founded on and involving the most palpable inconsistencies.

Many of various classes, sects, and parties, enter with a hearty sincerity into all these practical measures, with a determination to do their duty to their fellow creatures, and yet retain the integrity of those religious notions in which they have been instructed – nor have I any wish or desire that they should act otherwise. It is no part of my plan to form a sect, or to induce individuals to

[a] Reprinted in *New State of Society*, no. 3 (1817), *The New Existence of Man Upon the Earth* (1854), pp. lxviii–lxxix, Owen, *Life*, vol 1A (1858), pp. 138–41. Later reprints include 1927, 1977, 1991.

change one creed for another. My practice has ever been otherwise. It has always been to encourage the utmost liberty of conscience – the only true freedom of mind, and source of truth and wisdom.

I know that all mankind, ere long, will think as I now do respecting the formation of human character and the inutility and grievous evils of faith; for with me this subject has long been known as a science which at pleasure I can force upon the world: and in due time it shall be so developed; that is, when the minds of men shall be prepared to receive it without injury to themselves or their fellow creatures. But let me not be misunderstood. I wish not that the world should change old names for a new one, or be subjected to any false influence. I came not among you to establish a name, but to relieve you from the errors and evils of all names. Ponder well on that which I shall now state, and consider all its important consequences to yourselves and to posterity.

I have not the smallest desire to leave a name to be remembered by men for an hour after my death, although I know I shall afterwards retain existence through all eternity. I would not now give one straw for the homage or even worship of all mankind. All such vain wishes and desires appear to me, and soon will appear to others, to be weakness itself, and of less value than I can find present language to express.

THE SOLE OBJECT OF ALL MY EFFORTS IS TO DO YOU GOOD – TO RELIEVE YOU FROM THE MOST WRETCHED MENTAL AND BODILY SLAVERY AND MISERY; *and the time is fast approaching when you can no longer doubt these sayings.*

To procure that good for you in the best way, and in the shortest time that practice will admit, an Office is to be immediately opened in Temple Chambers, Fleet Street, under the superintendence of a gentleman who in all respects is well qualified and most willing to give every explanation of the practical part of the system to those of all ranks and descriptions, from the highest to the lowest, who may be sincerely desirous of acquiring such information. And such knowledge cannot fail to make the means obvious by which the poor and working classes may be, advantageously to all, relieved from their present distress, and the country saved from all the evils of poor's-rates and pauperism; – by which also health, temperance, affectionate association, cheerful industry, and increasing intelligence and happiness, will take the place of disease, intemperance, severe labour, counteraction, ignorance, and misery; – by which, in short, mankind will be benefited in the most simple manner, and to the greatest extent that the present knowledge and experience of the world will admit.

I am, however, most anxious to guard against precipitancy of expectation in those who are now prevented from employing their talents to benefit themselves or others. Of the full distress of their situation I am well aware, and it is a correct knowledge of their sufferings that stimulates my exertions to obtain for them the most speedy relief.

The first Village of unity and mutual co-operation that shall be erected, will be in part a model for all others in this country and over the world. It should, therefore, possess all the advantages that modern science can give, to exhibit in practice the extraordinary difference of results, between human faculties blindly moved to action by ignorance, individualised, – and when they are governed in all their operations and transactions by the combined intelligence and experience of all past times. This will soon be proved by practice to be almost as infinity is to unity. When these results shall be rendered obvious to common minds, truly has it been said, 'that the world will wonder at itself. –[a] Yes! it will become at once conscious of the intensity of the darkness in which it heretofore existed.'

But to complete a scientific arrangement like this, which involves the comfort, well-being, and happiness of the present and all future generations, will require much calm consideration, and the co-operation of various minds, the best versed in each minute part, in order that the most weak and helpless should have common justice, and to prove that we are really actuated solely by motives of pure and undefiled religion – of charity – of genuine love to our brothers, unmixed with any motive that would give to self what they would not freely bestow on others.

Such arrangements as these cannot be completed before the beginning of next year; but I hope they may be in forwardness to enable as many parties as may be prepared to act upon them, to commence the foundation of Villages and all their appendages early in the ensuing spring.

And that the public mind may keep pace with this important work, a paper, entitled the 'MIRROR OF TRUTH,' will be published twice a month, in which every objection to the New State of Society shall be candidly answered, and all doubts of its truth and happy results removed.[b] The light shall be made to appear, so as that none shall remain in darkness.[c]

In the 'Mirror of Truth,' the supporters of the Old and the New System will be *equally* admitted; strict impartiality to the candid representations of every class, sect, and party, will mark all its proceedings; and, as *Truth alone* is the object in view, the most intelligent opposition is earnestly solicited. The Prospectus to this Paper will soon be advertised and published.

In the meantime, on the first of next month all inquiries on the subject connected with the New State of Society are to be made, in person, or by letter, *post paid*, addressed to Dr Wilkes,[d] New State of Society Enrolment Office, Temple Chambers, Fleet Street, London.

---

[a] See Revelations 13:3.

[b] Two numbers of the *Mirror of Truth* appeared in October-November 1817, edited by one Lindsay. Owen used the phrase, 'the mirror of truth', in an address the previous month. See *infra*, p. 176.

[c] See for example Luke 1:79.

[d] Presumably Dr James Wilkes, of Haymarket, Piccadilly.

Immediate and patient attention will be given to every inquiry in person or by correspondence, dictated by a spirit of benevolence; and all information that may be of practical use in this undertaking will be thankfully received.

It may be useful to add, that until the Office is opened in Temple Chambers, Books of Enrolment continue at Lindsell's, Wimpole Street; Longman and Co., Paternoster Row; Cadell and Davies, Strand; Hatchard, Piccadilly; and Archs', Cornhill.

R. OWEN

49, Charlotte Street, Portland Place.
September 19th, 1817.

ON THE EMPLOYMENT OF CHILDREN IN MANUFACTORIES[a] 1818

To The Right Honourable The Earl of Liverpool

MY LORD, – Permit me to address your Lordship[b] in your capacity of Prime Minister of the British Empire, on a subject of national concern, which, though it has excited considerable interest in certain quarters, appears not to be understood or appreciated by the public at large in any degree commensurate with its real importance.

A bill on the employment of children in manufactories has been read twice in the House of Commons, passed through the Committee, had its blanks filled up, and is to be read a third time the first Monday in April.

I noticed the debates which took place on its first and second reading, and have just received a copy of the Bill as amended by the Committee.[c]

This bill is opposed, it seems, by a number of active wealthy cotton spinners, good men of business, several of whom are members of the House of Commons, and who are capable of raising a formidable opposition to any measure which they imagine will affect their interests.

Its supporters are those who deem the practices which at present prevail in our manufactories to be in many cases injurious to the children.

The subject, however, seems to be taken up by both parties on very confined grounds.

Its extensive bearings on the general interests of the nation have been very imperfectly, or hardly at all, considered; and its strong claims on the attention of government and of the country, in consequence, very feebly insisted upon.

The manufacturers look at it simply as mercantile men, under an alarm that the regulations proposed may in some way or other diminish a fraction of their profits.

The fear of loss of pecuniary gain to men trained in the principles of trade

---

[a] Published in London newspapers c. 20 March 1818 (see for example *The Examiner*, no. 535 (20 March 1818), pp. 194–6. Reprinted in *The Crisis*, vol. 2, no. 9 (9 March 1833), pp. 66–8; no. 10 (16 March 1833), pp. 74–6, *New Moral World*, vol. 12, no. 42 (14 April 1844), p. 330, no. 43 (20 April 1844), p. 339, *Robert Owen's Journal*, no. 21 (22 March 1851), pp. 162–4, no. 22 (29 March 1851), pp. 171–4, and in Owen, *Life*, vol. 1A (1858), pp. 185–93. Later reprints include 1991.

[b] Robert Banks Jenkinson, 2nd Earl of Liverpool (1770–1828), Prime Minister 1812–27.

[c] See *Parliamentary Debates*, vol. 33 (1816), pp. 884–7.

and manufactures is very natural. Their station in society, and, in many instances, their very subsistence, depends on success in their several occupations. Their labours and anxieties, too, are very great, and, except in a few instances, which in consequence are always prominent, they are very inadequately remunerated for their toil and care. Under these circumstances it is reasonable to conclude that every object must be viewed by them through the medium of mercantile calculation; and no one can justly blame them for, or be surprised at, the jealous activity which they exhibit on all occasions where their interests, real or imaginary, are attacked.

For these and other reasons, the natural course of trade, manufactures, and commerce, should not be disturbed, except when it interferes with measures affecting the well-being of the whole community; in which case minor considerations ought of course at all times to give way.

The practices which prevail in our manufactories form, in a peculiar manner, one of these exceptions.

They interfere essentially with the best interests of society, without benefit to any particular class, or to any individual.

And very little explanation, I presume, will demonstrate to your Lordship the truth of this statement.

Generally speaking, the occupation which manufactures under the existing arrangements afford, is more or less unhealthy to those employed in them; who are called upon to sacrifice their strength and substantial comforts for the advantage of others, and not unfrequently for the benefit of their enemies.

The numbers thus employed now constitute an important part of the population – so great indeed, as necessarily to disseminate the good or evil effects of the practices which obtain among them, over every corner of the Empire.

These practices are –

1st. – The employment of children before they possess sufficient strength for their work; before they can be initiated in their necessary domestic duties; and before they can acquire any fixed moral habits or knowledge that may render them useful, or not injurious, members of the community.

2dly. – The employment of adults, both male and female, in situations unfavourable to health, for an excessive and unreasonable number of hours per day.

The Bill before the House of Commons is intended to apply to the former evil only, and to remedy which it is surely very inadequate.

It permits children to be employed at nine years of age for twelve hours and a half per day, allowing them only an hour and a half during this period for meals and for exercise in the open air.

Experience proves that men may be habituated by early practice to consider the most inhuman and barbarous customs, not only with indifference, but as amusements from which they derive exquisite enjoyment. Even the best natural dispositions may be trained with ease to delight in cannibalism. It would be clearly unjust, therefore, to blame manufacturers for practices with which they have been familiar from childhood; or to suppose that they have less humanity than any other class of men.

Those practices, however, to which they have been familiarised from early life, are nevertheless unjust in the extreme to their fellow creatures, and peculiarly injurious to the best interests of the country.

To detail all their consequences would exceed the limits of a letter; and it is presumed that a sketch of the outline of them will be sufficient at once to disclose to your Lordship the high importance of the subject, and to establish its claim to the immediate attention of government.

To govern well and justly, is to form arrangements by which the greatest benefits that circumstances admit shall be given to the inhabitants of the country governed; and by which, especially, the most helpless part of the population shall be protected from unnecessary oppression.

Allow me, my Lord, to apply these principles to the subject of this letter.

From causes which it is unnecessary here to explain, the value of mere manual labour has been so much reduced, that the working man in this and other countries is now placed under circumstances far more unfavourable to his happiness than the serf or villain was under the feudal system, or than the slave was in any of the nations of antiquity.

I have myself, within the last three years, been but too often obliged to refuse the services of men willing to exert their strength to the very uttermost, when those services were offered and urged upon me by entreaties most distressing to decline, at wages which could not afford the applicant for himself and family the most bare and common necessaries of life.

With the small pittance they asked, they could in fact only gradually starve, amidst wretchedness of which the wealthy can form no adequate conception.

Under these circumstances the working man and his family are now truly become even in this country pitiable objects.

Yet it is from this class the wealthy derive all which they hold. The rich wallow in an excess of luxuries injurious to themselves, solely by the labour of men who are debarred from acquiring for their own use a sufficiency even of the indispensable articles of life, – much less any of those numberless comforts which they see around them.

And yet, if their capabilities were permitted to be brought into action, they could multiply these in such abundance as would not only afford themselves a participation in them, but would yield to the higher classes a still larger proportion of wealth than the latter can possibly obtain under existing circumstances.

Such being the fact, my Lord, which at any time I can prove to the satisfaction of every intelligent reflecting mind, surely the working man and his family have a fair and just claim for some aid and protection from the legislature of their country.

In a majority of cases he is now, whenever required, compelled by dire necessity to labour fourteen, sixteen, or even eighteen hours per day, in employments from which often every idea of comfort must be banished, which are frequently very unhealthy, and sometimes revolting to human nature; but, my Lord, his sons and his daughters, and even his children, male and female, of a tender age, are now subjected to the same necessity; they must all thus labour, when they can procure work even of this wretched description, to support a bare existence.

To effect more than this many of them never hope, but live in perpetual fear, should sickness overtake them, that they must sooner or later be compelled to accept even this in the degrading capacity of parish paupers.

You will, I am sure, my Lord, readily grant that this state of things cannot last; and its continuance will annihilate every proper feeling between the governed and their rulers; and that confusion and misery will go on increasing.

If you ask me where is the remedy? or say, as modern politicians are apt to say, that the evil in time will cure itself, I contend there are remedies; and I deny that the evil, if unchecked, will cure itself in any other way than by perpetually increasing the necessity for the adoption of those remedies.

A truly enlightened statesman will avert by wise ameliorating measures, those increasing evils, which, if permitted to proceed unremedied, will inevitably derange the social system which it is his duty to direct and control.

Past history exhibits no combination of circumstances which bears any analogy to the present crisis; the time never existed when knowledge and misery were so closely and extensively united.

That such an union can be of long duration is impossible. One or other must prevail; and no mind competent to look into futurity can be at any loss to conjecture which must yield to the other.

The only safe course which governments can now pursue, is, not to oppose, but to lead and direct knowledge.

Those governments which will not or cannot act thus, will have increasing difficulties to encounter, which no artificial power opposed to the permanent well-being of the people whom they govern, can long withstand.

I trust, my Lord, the British government is not destined to be one of these.

I feel confident that there is too much good intention and intelligence afloat among us to permit this evil to be inflicted on a nation so willing to sacrifice its temporary interests to the security of its future liberty and happiness.

It is these considerations which induce me to bring before your Lordship those natural remedies for existing evils which can be alone effectual. Security can now be found only in that system of policy which regards the proper training, education, and advantageous employment of the working classes as the primary objects of government. Every other remedy which may be attempted will prove a mere palliative, and now a very short-lived palliative.

But, my Lord, how utterly vain must it be to attempt these objects while so large a part of the population as I have described – while not adults only of either sex, but even children of a tender age, are compelled to labour in unhealthy occupations for fourteen or fifteen hours per day?

Such a practice has arisen from the blind efforts of ignorance, that, in its eagerness to grasp at immediate wealth, destroys the only sure means of securing its permanence and its benefits.

The opposers of the ameliorations proposed would be themselves great gainers by their adoption.

Let the subject be viewed fairly even as one of mere gain or pecuniary profit only, and it would be easy to prove to the satisfaction of every one who has not been trained to become a mere manufacturer, or whose mind has not been too deeply imbued with the prejudices of trade, that all parties interested must necessarily be gainers under the regulations which ought now to be adopted – that is, that more wealth shall be created for all, at a less cost, and with more comfort to each.

But I need not occupy your Lordship's time with the details of an argument necessary only to those whose ideas have been confined within the limits of a certain class, and who are consequently incompetent to any process of reasoning in which it is necessary to view society as a whole, and not in little detached and unconnected portions.

The question is now before the legislature, and the country, where I have long wished to see it, that its principles might be fairly and fully discussed by statesmen who have no interest, either real or imaginary, in the present destruction of the health, morals, and happiness of their fellow creatures – whose only resource afterwards is parish relief.

I regret, however, to see that the ameliorating clauses which the bill before me contains in its present form are inadequate to remedy the evils which now exist, and which long ago ought to have been prevented.

Its enactments limit its intended ameliorations to Cotton Mills only: and permit children at nine years old to be employed in them, from that period to sixteen years of age, twelve hours and a half per day, allowing only one hour and a half for meals and exercise in the open air.

I have no doubt the honourable member who first introduced this bill into Parliament,[a] and who has devoted so much time to the subject, is aware that these enactments are very inadequate to meet the existing evils.

He was probably afraid to ask more, lest he should increase the opposition of those who think themselves interested in perpetuating an oppression on their fellow creatures, worse than any slavery of the same extent with which the human race has been hitherto afflicted.

We are unacquainted with any nation, ancient or modern, that has suffered

[a] Sir Robert Peel.

its hundreds of thousands of children of seven to twelve years of age to work incessantly for fifteen hours per day in an overheated unhealthy atmosphere, allowing them only forty minutes out of that time for dinner and change of air, which they breathe often in damp cellars or in garrets, in confined narrow streets or dirty lanes.

And this system of oppression will be sanctioned by the British Legislature if the Bill proposed shall be allowed to pass in its present state; for it is in evidence, taken before a Committee of the House of Commons appointed to investigate the subject, that such practices prevail in other manufactories as unhealthy as that of cotton.

It cannot for a moment be supposed that the Legislature will now compromise its character by giving its countenance to such abuses.

Far better would it be that the evil should remain in its full extent, than that the poor sufferer should be mocked by enactments which merely hold out a petty, paltry relief to those employed in one branch of our manufactures, while thousands and hundreds of thousands in other situations are left to experience all the oppression and slavery of which I now complain.

My Lord, I do hope that this important subject will be taken up and defended by the ministers of the Crown on its broad and true principles. I trust they will prove to the country at large that revolution or violent reformation is not necessary to compel them to protect the oppressed and the helpless; and that they are willing of themselves to begin the work of gradual reformation at that point from which alone any beneficial reformation can ever commence – that is, by attending well to the proper training and education of the rising generation.

Let this point be adopted as the polar star of the domestic policy of Great Britain, and it may safely be predicted that her past fleeting prosperity and success will become as shadows when contrasted with her future permanent strength and glory.

A fortunate opportunity at the proper moment now presents itself to begin this admirable work; and let us hope it will be seized with avidity by our most enlightened statesmen, who, discarding the ignorant and degrading feelings of party, will unite all their efforts in a cause in which all have a common interest, and, by the adoption of timely preventive measures, founded on principles leading to union and good-will among mankind, will overcome those evils in the social system, which now in every direction threaten forcibly to dissolve all existing governments and institutions.

But, my Lord, and I put the question to you as a practical statesman, can the habits of the rising generation be well and properly formed while they continue to be immured almost from infancy within our demoralizing and unhealthy manufactories for fourteen or fifteen hours per day? Or rather, my Lord, could the greatest enemy to human nature devise more effectual means by which to blight every hope of improvement or happiness to man? Could such a being in the plenitude of his cunning and hatred so surely settle in any other way a blasting curse on human beings, or so certainly inflict upon them every form and degree of misery to which their nature is liable?

To advance *one step* beyond a mere pretence to ameliorate the wretched condition of the working classes, – the sole instruments by which our necessaries, our comforts, and our luxuries are produced, – they must be protected from that oppression to which they are now exposed, and their children must be placed under circumstances in which they may be trained in habits useful to themselves and to society.

If the Bill now before the legislature secure not these objects, it will not effect anything that had not much better be left undone.

Instead of confining the provisions of the Act to Cotton Mills only, they should extend to all manufactures whatever not carried on in private houses.

Instead of children being admitted at nine years of age to work in Cotton Mills twelve and a half hours per day, with only an hour and a half for meals and recreation, no child should be admitted to work in any manufactory before ten years of age and not for more than six hours per day until he is twelve years old.

And no manufacturer should be permitted to employ either young or old for a longer period than twelve hours per day, allowing them out of that time one hour for breakfast and another for dinner, leaving ten hours for full and constant work, which is one more than our ancestors thought beneficial; and I doubt whether nine hours of regular and active employment, established as the measure of daily labour to be required from the working classes, would not be still more economical and profitable for the country.

I am fully aware of the clamour which these propositions will at first call forth from the blind avarice of commerce; for commerce, my Lord, trains her children to see only their immediate or apparent interest; their ideas are too contracted to carry them beyond the passing week, month, or year at the utmost.

They have been taught, my Lord, to consider it to be the essence of wisdom to expend millions of capital, and years of extraordinary scientific application, as well as to sacrifice the health, morals, and comforts of the great mass of the subject of a mighty empire, that they may uselessly improve the manufacture of, and increase the demand for, pins, needles, and threads; – that they may have the singular satisfaction, after immense care, labour, and anxiety on their own parts, to destroy the real wealth and strength of their country by gradually undermining the morals and physical vigour of its inhabitants, for the sole end of relieving other nations of their due share of this enviable process of pin, needle, and thread making.

I trust, my Lord, it is not by such men that our great national concerns are henceforward to be directed.

If their voice is to predominate in our councils, the vital interests of the country must soon be utterly sacrificed to the grossest political errors.

It is the creed of this class, that no effort or expense should be spared to improve these trifling baubles and luxuries which when perfected are of no intrinsic value whatever, which cannot add a particle of strength or comfort to the empire; (no real advantage has occurred from enabling our fashionable females to purchase fine lace and muslins at one-fourth of the former prices; but, to produce them at this price, many thousands of our population have existed amidst disease and wretchedness, and have been carried prematurely to their graves;) while any attempts to ameliorate the condition of human beings are decried as unnecessary and visionary, as travelling out of the proper business of life, which to them is solely and exclusively to accumulate wealth – wealth which is not only acquired at the expense of every thing that is truly great or valuable in the character of a nation, but which, when acquired, is useless, nay, in the highest degree injurious, to themselves and others.

It is, my Lord, to such kind of influence as I have now described that the best interests of the country have been sacrificed for years; and if the government cannot proceed without such aid, it is not difficult to see to what it will speedily lead.

Should it be urged upon you, my Lord, that these and other ameliorating measures will give such a stimulus to population that the world will soon be too small for its inhabitants, I cannot imagine that your Lordship will contemplate such an argument with any alarm.

I intend to take an early opportunity of showing that this dread of an excess of population has no better foundation than exists for the nursery terrors of ghosts and hobgoblins; that at this moment the earth is a comparative desert; that all its present inhabitants are suffering for the want of a much more extended population; and that when the subject comes to be properly understood, no real evil will ever be apprehended from this source.

Being strongly impressed with this view of the subject I have felt it a duty imperative upon me thus publicly to recommend to your Lordship, as Prime Minister of the Country, to adopt, by means of the Bill now under the consideration of the legislature, a declared principle of gradually and systematically reforming the growing evils of the country by well and properly forming the habits of the rising generation.

It is obviously a necessary preliminary to this work of reformation, that the manufacturer should relinquish the premature and oppressive employment of children.

The importance of the subject of this letter renders it unnecessary to apologize for having thus occupied so much of your Lordship's time.

Be assured that, with every proper feeling of respect for the long sacrifice which you have made of your private comforts in the discharge of public duties,

I remain, my Lord, your Lordship's most obedient humble Servant,

New Lanark, March 20, 1818. ROBERT OWEN.

ON THE UNION OF CHURCHES AND SCHOOLS[a] 1818

To His Grace The Archbishop[b] of Canterbury

My Lord, – You have now presided for several years with assiduity and regularity over the society for educating the poor in the principles of the national church; and you have witnessed the almost miraculous change which has been produced on the young mind by your influence, and by those who have acted under your directions.

You have seen ignorance and vicious conduct rapidly give place to comparative intelligence and good habits. The public look on with amazement at the effects which are daily exhibited by the children at the Central School[c] in Baldwin's Gardens. They can scarcely however yet believe, that by a similar process the most neglected and wretched part of our population, – that part which disturbs the public peace, which fills our prisons, and which is left to suffer an ignominious death, – might all have been thus trained, and thus rendered respectable, efficient, and happy members of the British Empire.

But, my Lord, this knowledge is hourly extending; and the inference must soon become most apparent to every one capable of even ordinary reflection. It is utterly impossible to hide it another year from the public eye. One and all will then ask of you and of every member of the government – 'If society possesses this overwhelming influence over the habits and conduct of the rising generation, and that influence is in your hands, why do you not exert it for the safety of the state?'

The responsibility with which you and they are invested at this crisis is of the most awful nature. The power is with you to lead the public mind to all that is truly excellent, and to secure the permanent well-being of the country on a foundation which neither domestic dissention nor foreign foe could in the slightest degree disturb; and the power is also with you to oppose the progress of true knowledge for a time, and thereby create a conflict which in the end

[a] First appended to the 3rd edn (1818) of *Observations on the Effect of the Manufacturing System* (1815). Reprinted in Owen, *Life*, vol. 1 (1857), pp. 361–7 and in *A Supplement to the Revolution in the Mind and Practice of the Human Race* (1849), pp. 42–75.

[b] Richard Reardon (1737–1824), Archbishop 1802–24.

[c] The National Society for Promoting the Education of the Poor in the Principles of the Established Church School, run by the Central Council of the Church for Religious Education.

must prove more disastrous to those who govern than any of former times; for power and knowledge never before met, since the world was created, upon terms so nearly equal.

Why do I thus express myself to your Lordship? – It is because I am anxious that the attention of government should be immediately directed to those measures which can alone relieve the country from the dangers with which it is surrounded, and to which it must continue to be exposed while they persevere in acting on notions they can no longer defend – notions, the errors of which every school-boy will soon detect.

You have obtained from Parliament the grant of a million for the erection of churches; and to the principle of the measure no one has objected. It has been thus liberally bestowed in order to improve the character of the population; and if it be at all times requisite that the public money should be expended in the most advantageous manner possible, it becomes a sacred duty under existing circumstances, (when, in the fourth year of peace, fourteen millions must be borrowed to make up the deficiency of the revenue,) that every pound should be appropriated so as to produce the greatest beneficial result.

The experience of past ages, and particularly of the present times, has proved that early training and education produce a more durable impression than can be given by instruction at a later period in life; and that, in consequence, the teaching of the school, without the learning of the church, is far more efficacious than the learning of the church can be without the previous teaching of the school.

To those, however, who have confidence in the good effects to be derived from each, it must be most desirable to have all the benefits of both, when they may be obtained with the same, or nearly the same, expense and trouble.

I well know the lively interest which your grace, and many of the highest dignitaries of the church, in common with the public, now feel in the cause of early education. The experience which has been lately acquired on this most important of all subjects must have removed whatever doubt remained as to the power which may be given to it to well-form the character of every human being.

But your Grace well knows that there is no utility to be derived from the most accurate knowledge of any principles, until those principles shall be carried into practice.

Your Grace, and every real friend to the gradual and rational improvement of society, will rejoice to hear, that buildings may be erected to serve most advantageously the double purpose of church and school; that they may be so contrived as to be complete for each, without the one interfering in any manner with the best known arrangements of the other; and that, thus combined, they would most effectually co-operate in securing to the rising generation every advantage that both are calculated to give.

I do not venture thus to address your Lordship on any mere theoretic opinion; – the fact exists under my own eye; the experiment has been tried, and is complete in all its parts; and, instead of any inconvenience having arisen from this combination of church and school, experience has proved that they ought never to be separated.

And if I greatly mistake not, the period is near at hand – almost arrived – when this combination of church and school shall become a bond of union among mankind; when the violence of opposing opinions shall be calmed by a true knowledge of the source of all disputed opinions; and rational selfishness, or true benevolence, shall take place of ignorant dissension.

All, from the highest to the lowest, are deeply interested in this change; and none, My Lord, will be so essentially benefited by it, as those on whom rests the present responsibility of governing mankind.

If they will not now actively lead on in the right course, – is it possible they can yet be so blind as not to see, what is obvious to many, that the force of circumstances will drive them into measures most hazardous for them and for society?

To avert this crisis – to produce the change gradually and by universal consent, I would willingly forego every private consideration, and deem life itself no sacrifice in such a cause.

I will now state some of the advantages which the country may derive from having the new churches so erected as to serve the double purpose of church and school.

1st. In those situations in which churches are now deficient for the population, schools will be deficient also; and Your Grace will admit that, as a foundation for the improvement of society, schools are quite as necessary as churches.

2nd. That fundamentally and substantially to improve the population, schools should be established prior to churches, or, at the latest, at the same period.

3rd. That these new churches and schools, if the measure here recommended be adopted, may be made the instruments of uniting the jarring feelings of mankind on disputed points, which from their nature do not admit of proof, and which therefore ought never to be forced on the young mind; but should be placed before it when the judgment is ripe and capable of forming a rational conclusion for itself.

Any thing short of this has no pretension to be called liberty of conscience; and until it can be obtained for the rising generation, man must continue, as he has been, little more than an ignorant animal, incompetent to discern the means which surround him to secure the happiness of his species.

4th. These churches, although when used as churches they disseminate only the peculiar doctrines of the established religion, may on the week days be safely made to give school instruction to the children of every persuasion. All contribute to their expense; all should therefore derive some benefit from them – nothing exclusive ought here to be admitted.

It is to be hoped that the church of England will set the first example of a church establishment opening its doors to instruct the children of a mixed population, not in its own peculiar religious tenets, but in good habits and substantial knowledge, so as to enable them to become useful men and respectable members of society, either in the persuasion of their parents, or of any other sect to which their maturer judgment may lead them.

This measure would be sound policy in the church. By such wise and just conduct she would disarm her enemies, withdraw the hostility of those who dissent from her, and obtain time gradually to reform herself as society advanced in knowledge.

These considerations are abundantly sufficient to prove the utility and wisdom of the plan of combining the object of a school with every church to be hereafter erected; and the time approaches when the school will become the best protection and safeguard of the church.

All who can anticipate the evils of a violent revolution will adopt every prudent measure to prevent it; and surely none will be more efficacious in this respect than to form a union between the church and the school.

There is however another view of the subject, which must remove all doubt from every mind as to the necessity of the measure recommended. The legislator is about to emancipate the manufacturing labourer from the oppression to which he and his children have been subjected. To secure health and time for instruction to the mass of the people, is a measure of the soundest policy; it is the first step to improve the condition of society. Without it, indeed, the population of these Islands would soon become little better than miserable brutes, having scarcely the form of men.

Yet to give the population time for instruction, and not provide that instruction, would be to mock the reasonable expectations of every reflecting mind; nay, My Lord, it could not fail to prove the certain means of hastening the period when, without the application of effectual remedies society will find itself involved, through ignorance, in violence and confusion.

But, happily for all parties – for the improvement of the poor – for the safety of the rich – at the moment when required, an opportunity presents itself when the ignorance and bad habits of the rising generation may be removed by the influence of the new schools, of the new churches; and those poor children who have latterly been made the victims of a miscalculating cupidity in the manufacturing districts, will come from those schools competent and prepared to return fourfold advantages to the public for the expense and labour which shall be thus bestowed upon them.

You, My Lord, from the experience which the national schools have afforded you, may have some faint idea of what may be obtained by proper attention to the young mind.

But, My Lord, (and I say it as a practical man from my youth up to the present period,) without some such similar experience you can form no adequate conception of the power which the government and the public possess to add to the comfort and well-being of all ranks, by forming and directing the physical and mental capabilities of the working classes in the best manner for themselves and for society.

When these principles shall be thoroughly understood; when the legislature of this and other countries shall steadily act upon them, and legislate solely in conformity with them; and when the astonishing effects shall be witnessed which they are sure to produce in practice; – then will one and all express their astonishment that that which is so obviously true, so plain, and simple, and so perfectly in unison with every known fact – and moreover so easy of application to all the purposes of life, – should have been disregarded for so many ages of the world, and left to be brought into action at this late period of human existence.

I trust, my Lord, that you are destined to lend a helping hand to forward this great work; and that you will take very prudent step, not only to combine schools with the churches, but to hasten as far as possible their completion, in order that our manufacturing population may not be compelled to acquire bad and vicious habits, because no efficient means have been prepared to make them virtuous and useful members of society.

I have the honour to be, My Lord, Most respectfully, Your Grace's Obt. hum. Ser.

ROBERT OWEN

New Lanark, 2nd May, 1818.

[*Copy of Title as published in* 8*vo.*]

TWO MEMORIALS

ON BEHALF OF THE WORKING CLASSES;

THE FIRST PRESENTED TO

THE GOVERNMENTS

OF

EUROPE AND AMERICA,

THE SECOND TO

THE ALLIED POWERS

ASSEMBLED IN CONGRESS

AT

Aix-la-Chapelle.

BY ROBERT OWEN.

London:

PRINTED FOR LONGMAN, HURST, REES, ORME, AND BROWN, PATERNOSTER ROW; CADELL AND DAVIES, STRAND; J. HATCHARD, PICCADILLY; MURRAY, ALBEMARLE STREET; CONSTABLE AND CO., AND OLIPHANT AND CO., EDINBURGH; SMITH AND SONS, AND BRASH AND REID, GLASGOW; AND SOLD BY ALL BOOKSELLERS.

1818.

MEMORIAL

To the Governments of Europe and America, on behalf of the Working Classes. September 20, 1818[a]

The Memorialist has devoted the last thirty years of his life to the study and practice of political economy; and, by permitting practice in all cases to correct theory, he has attained the most important results for the well-being of society.

In consequence of the numberless benefits which the knowledge thus acquired is calculated to give to the inhabitants of every country, the Memorialist is desirous of making it known, in the shortest time, to those who govern the civilised world, and to the public.

He therefore presents memorials on the subject to the Governments of Europe and America.

The Memorialist is not influenced to this proceeding by partiality or prejudice for or against any class, sect, party, or country. He views the whole human race as men created originally with the same general faculties and qualities, though varied in degree, and trained by circumstances, over which society has now a complete control, to despise, hate, and oppose each other, even to death, although the path is now clear by which, with more ease, society may train them to esteem, to love, and to aid each other.

Nor yet has the Memorialist been actuated to the conduct which he adopts by a desire for wealth, for popularity, for honours, or for future fame; to him these already appear the playthings of infants.

But he is induced to act thus because he can shew the causes which perpetually generate misery in human society; and also develop the means by which, without injury to any, those causes may be gradually, and, at no very distant period, effectually, removed. To witness this change in part, or, if that shall not be permitted, to know that it must soon commence and rapidly proceed, is his reward; and it is already secured to him.

---

[a] Partly reprinted in *The New Harmony Gazette*, vol. 1, no. 43 (19 July 1826), pp. 337–8, *The Crisis*, vol. 1, no. 1 (28 July 1832), pp. 81–2, *A Supplement to the Revolution in Mind and Practice of the Human Race* (1849), pp. 42–75, *The New Existence of Man Upon the Earth* (1854), pt 2, pp. xxiv–xxxvi. Later British editions were appended to the *Manifesto of Robert Owen* (1840) (e.g., 6th edn, 1840). Reprinted in Owen, *Life*, vol. 1A (1858), pp. 207–22, where Owen noted that French and German translations were published. See *Mémoire de M. Robert Owen . . . addressé aux souverains alliés assemblés à Aix-la-Chapelle* (1818); *Denkschrift zugunsten der arbeitenden Klassen an den Kongress der verbündeten Mächte* (Aachen, 1818). Later reprints include 1991.

Under these circumstances the Memorialist claims not that kind of attention which is usually given to ordinary questions of policy; but he asks for the devotion of the minds of the parties whom he addresses, that they may comprehend subjects not yet open to common capacities, and which involve all the valuable interests of society.

For a period has arrived in which a greater change in human affairs will be forced on the world than the world has yet witnessed; but in all its extent the change will be highly beneficial to every individual and to all states.

It is a period when the errors which have hitherto perplexed mankind are about to be unravelled; and, in consequence, the obstacles which stood in the way of human improvement and enjoyment will be removed.

The immediate causes which make this change certain and necessary are the overwhelming effects of new scientific power, and the rapid increase of knowledge among all classes of men. The former will soon render human labour of little avail in the creation of wealth; while the latter will make evident to the people the absolute necessity which has thus arisen for them to give a different direction to their powers, and will inform them, also, how the change is to be effected.

To this day the means of consumption, or of obtaining the necessaries of life, by the working classes, have been acquired solely through the medium of their labour, the value of which the new power has already much diminished. And the certain consequences of the undirected progress of this power will be to reduce the unchangeable value of manual labour, until it falls below the means of procuring a wretched subsistence for any large proportion of the working classes; while the remainder of them must be starved out of existence.

Such is the nature of the contest which has already continued for some time, and which now exists in full activity, between scientific Power and manual Labour, between Knowledge and Ignorance; but no one who comprehends anything of the subject can, for one moment, doubt the result.

It is presumed that the powers thus addressed cannot desire an increase to the misery of the people, while, in consequence, new dangers to every state must continually arise on every side.

On these grounds solely the Memorialist requests attention and co-operation.

He is now ready to communicate the full details of these important subjects to any or to all of the Powers whom he addresses, that, if those details shall appear, on examination, to be derived from facts and experience, as he presumes they will be found, the requisite measures to stop the progress of the existing distress among the working classes may be adopted by the respective Governments, before the period shall have passed when the combined extended sufferings and knowledge of the people will permit the requisite time for calm deliberation.

The Memorialist adds an appendix, which contains some of the general results which he has derived from long study, multiplied experiments on a large scale, and personal communication with acute, intelligent, and enlightened men, of all classes, sects, and parties, more varied and confidential than has ever, perhaps, fallen to the lot of one individual.

And thus circumstanced, he awaits the deliberation and reply of the Powers whom he has now addressed.

APPENDIX

To first Memorial, containing some of the General Results, derived from the Memorialist's long study and experience

FIRST GENERAL RESULT

That the period is arrived when the means are become obvious, by which, without force or fraud, or disorder of any kind, riches may be created in such abundance, and so advantageously for all, that the wants and desires of every human being may be over-satisfied.

In consequence, the dominion of wealth and the evils arising from the desire to acquire and accumulate riches are on the point of terminating.

SECOND GENERAL RESULT

That the period is arrived when the principles of the science are become obvious, by which, without force or punishment of any kind, the rising generation may be, with ease and advantage to all, surrounded by circumstances which shall form them into any character that society may predetermine; and if any defect shall afterwards appear in those characters, except what nature has made uncontrollable by human means, the cause will not be in the individuals, but will be solely owing to the inexperience of the parties who attempt to put those invaluable principles into practice.

In consequence, the dominion of Ignorance, of Fraud, and of Violence, is also on the point of terminating.

THIRD GENERAL RESULT

That is it is the interest, and that it will soon *appear* to be the interest, of each individual, in every rank, in all countries, that judicious measures should be adopted, with the least delay, to secure these beneficial results in practice. It is, however, greatly to be desired that they should be carried into effect by general consent, gradually and temperately, in order that no party or individual may be injured by the changes which must necessarily arise.

In consequences, any attempt to stop or retard the introduction of these measures will be unavailing. Already the principles and consequent practice are placed effectually beyond the power of human assault. It will be found that silence cannot now retard their progress, and that opposition will give increased celerity to their movements.

Frankfort, 20th September, 1818.

MEMORIAL

To the Allied Powers assembled in Congress at Aix-La Chapelle,[a] *on behalf of the Working Classes. October 22, 1818*

SHEWETH,

That your Memorialist has addressed a Memorial to the Governments of Europe and America, on subjects deeply interesting to the working classes and to all ranks in these countries.

That he has presented the said Memorial to many of the European Governments; and will take the earliest opportunity to lay it before the remaining Governments of Europe, and before the States of America.

That the said Memorial was a preliminary one, being intended to call the attention of the civilised world –

First, To the new and extraordinary effects produced by the introduction of improved scientific power into the manufactures of Europe and America; and which has already materially affected the value of labour in these countries, and the health, comfort, and happiness of the working classes employed in manufactures. And,

Second, To the overwhelming influence which experience has now given to the adult part of society, over the rising generation, to educate them, by the arrangement of new circumstances around them from infancy, to become the best characters for their own happiness and the permanent good of the community to which they may belong.

That your Memorialist stated his willingness to develop the details of his experience on these important subjects, to all or to any of the Governments whom he addressed.

That, as the unaided deliberations of Governments are necessarily slow, and the people are daily injured by the effects of the new scientific power, and the want of a well-digested system of training and instruction, from infancy, applicable to every child of the poor, he deems it his duty, with a view to facilitate and accelerate the execution of an object which the Allied Powers must have so much at heart, and in which their immediate interest is so deeply

[a] At the Congress of Aix-la-Chapelle in 1818, the European great powers met to settle French affairs after Napoleon's defeat.

involved, to submit to Congress, as he now does, preliminary explanations of *the three general results contained in the Appendix to the former Memorial*, and which the subjects naturally divide into three parts.

FIRST PART

The First General Result stated in the Appendix to the Memorial addressed to the Governments of Europe and America was as follows:-

'That the period is arrived when the means are become obvious, by which, without force or fraud, or disorder of any kind, riches may be created in such abundance, and so advantageously for all, that the wants and desires of every human being may be more than satisfied.'

In consequence, the dominion of wealth, and the evils arising from the desire to acquire and accumulate riches are on the point of terminating.

Preliminary explanation of the foregoing result.

The general proof of the truth of this statement shall be drawn from the changes which have occurred within the last quarter of a century, or since the introduction of Messrs Watt[a] and Arkwright's improved mechanism, first into the manufactures of Britain, and subsequently into those of other countries.

At the commencement of the period mentioned, a much larger proportion of the population of Great Britain was occupied in agriculture than in manufactures; and it is probable that the inhabitants of the British isles then experienced a greater degree of substantial prosperity than they had attained before, or than they have enjoyed since.

The reasons are obvious:

The new manufacturing system had then attained that point which gave the highest value to manual labour, compared with the price of the necessaries and comforts of life which it was calculated to afford; and it had not yet introduced the demoralizing effects which soon afterwards began to emanate from this system.

At the period mentioned, then, the manual and scientific productive powers of Great Britain were sufficient to create a degree of prosperity which placed all her population in a state of comfort, at least equal, if not superior, to that of the inhabitants of any other part of the world. The value of her national funds was higher in 1792 than at any other period; and pauperism among the working class was but little known.

The productive powers which created this high degree of prosperity consisted of temperate manual labour, and mechanical and other scientific power, which had been gradually and very slowly accumulating through the previous periods of her history.

[a] James Watt (1736–1819), inventor of the steam engine.

The manual labour was chiefly performed by men, unaided by the premature exertions of children; and its whole amount in 1792 may be estimated at about that of one-fourth of the population, which was then about *fifteen millions*.

The scientific power at the same period was probably about three times the amount of its labour; in which case,

The manual labour would be	3,750,000
And the scientific	11,250,000
And the aggregate productive power	15,000,000
The population was also	15,000,000

Thus the aggregate productive power and the population in 1792 appear to have been equal, or as one to one.

The introduction, however, of the improved steam-engine and spinning machinery, with the endless variety of mechanical and other scientific inventions to which they gave rise, and which have been applied to almost all the useful purposes and ornamental arts of life, have created a change in the productive powers of Great Britain, of the most extraordinary amount.

Manual labour has been increased, by calling into action the unceasing long daily labour of women and children in manufactures; and, consequence, its whole amount may be now estimated at about that of one third of the population, which, in 1817, was calculated to be *eighteen millions* – or in twenty-five years to have increased *three millions*; and this estimate will give *six millions* for the present manual power.

But, since the introduction of Arkwright and Watt's improved mechanism there has been a real addition made in Great Britain to the power of creating wealth, equal to that of much more than *two hundred millions* of stout, active, well-trained labourers; or to more than *ten times* the present population of the British Isles, or than *thirty times* the manual labour which they now supply for the production of wealth.

The following changes have, then, occurred from 1792 to 1817:-

The *population*, increased from fifteen millions to	18,000,000
The *manual labour*, from one-fourth to fifteen millions to one-third of eighteen millions, or to	6,000,000
The *new-created productive power*, from 1792 to 1817, will be under-stated at two hundred millions, say	200,000,000
While the *old scientific power*, if but three times the manual power in 1792, will be, as stated	11,250,000
Which together makes the *aggregate productive power*, in 1817	217,250,000

Or, in proportion to the population in 1817, as *twelve and a fraction* to *one*.

It follows that Great Britain has thus acquired a new aid from science in twenty-five years, which enables her to increase her riches, annually, twelve times in quantity beyond what she possessed the power of creating prior to that period; and which excess she may either waste in war, dissipate in unprofitable foreign commerce, or apply directly to improve and ameliorate her own population.

This enormous accession to the productive powers of Great Britain is, however, trifling, compared with that which she may now acquire. She has still capital and industry unemployed or misapplied, sufficient to create, annually, an addition to her present productive powers, for exceeding the amount of her actual manual labour.

Already, with a population under *twenty millions*, and a manual power not exceeding *six millions*, with the aid of the new power, undirected, except by a blind private interest, she supplies her own demand, and overstocks with her manufactures all the markets in the world into which her commerce is admitted. She is now using every exertion to open new markets, even in the most distant regions; and she could soon, by the help of science, supply the wants of another world equally populous with the earth.

Instead, however, of thus contending with other nations to supply their wants, and thereby, under the present arrangements of society, diminish the value of their manual labour, and depress their working classes, she might, most advantageously for herself and them, extend the knowledge which she has herself acquired of creating wealth or new productive power, to the rest of Europe, to Asia, Africa, and America.

It is the grand interest of society to adopt practical measures by which the largest amount of useful and valuable productions may be obtained at the least expense of manual labour and with the most comfort to the producers.

By applying this principle to practice now, when scientific power offers such unlimited aid to the world, wealth may be created in all parts of the earth more than sufficient for every useful purpose.

It is then strictly true,

'That the period has arrived when the means are become obvious, by which, without violence or fraud, or disorder of any kind, riches may be created in such abundance and so advantageously for all, that the wants and desires of every human being may be oversatisfied.'

Thus have two men, Watt and Arkwright, by introducing improved scientific power of a peculiar description, given to the world the means of creating wealth far more rapidly than it can be used. No intelligent practical man, who has devoted his mind to the subject, will, it is presumed, longer contend against this conclusion.

The grand question now to be solved, is, not how a sufficiency of wealth for all may be produced; but how the excess of riches which may be most easily created, may be generally distributed throughout society advantageously for all, and without *prematurely* disturbing the existing institutions or arrangements in any country.

[N.B. – Now, in 1857, the scientific, mechanical, and chemical productive powers of Great Britain may be estimated as equal to at least *one thousand millions* of men; or, in proportion to the present population, as *thirty-three to one*; and *this is continually increasing, and is capable of illimitable augmentation.* R. O.]

PART SECOND

The Second General Result stated in the Appendix to the Memorial addressed to the Governments of Europe and America was as follows:-

'*That the period is arrived when the principles of the science of political economy are become obvious, by which, without disorder, force, or punishment of any kind, the rising generation may be, with ease and advantage to all, surrounded by new circumstances, which shall form them into any character that society may predetermine; and if any defect shall afterwards appear in those characters, except what nature has made uncontrollable by human means, the cause will not be in the individuals, but will be solely owing to the inexperience of the parties who attempt to put those invaluable principles to practice.*'

'In consequence, the continuance of ignorance, of fraud, and violence, is also on the point of termination.'

Preliminary Explanations of the foregoing Result

It is a fact obvious to our senses, that children are born with certain faculties and qualities, or with the germs or seeds of them; and that these combined constitute what is called human nature.

In conformity with what appears to be a universal law in creation, these faculties and qualities differ in each individual in strength and in combination, and to so great an extent as to render it highly improbable that any two infants have been, or ever will be, born alike.

It is also a fact, obvious to our reason, that whatever these powers may be in each child, he could not create the smallest part of them; they are formed *for* him, by Providence, by Nature, by that Power (whatever name men may give it,) which creates him; and, whether those faculties and qualities are inferior or superior, it is contrary to reason to say that the infant can be entitled to merit or deserve blame for them.

He has received his natural constitution as the lamb and the tiger have received theirs; and there is precisely as much reason in finding fault with the one as with the others.

The child is also born in some country, of parents belonging to some class, and who possess characters peculiar to themselves.

Over these circumstances, also, the child can have no influence whatever; each of them has arisen from causes over which the child could have no power of any kind.

These circumstances, however unheeded they may be by ordinary minds, have hitherto fixed,

First: – Whether the child shall be a Jew, – a disciple of Confucius, – a Mahomedan, – a Christian, – a worshipper of Juggernaut, – or a savage – even a cannibal.

Second: – To what country he shall belong, and, in consequence, what national prejudices shall be forced upon him.

Third: – What sectarian notions, if any, shall be impressed on his mind.

Fourth: – What language he shall be taught; and language influences character more than is usually supposed.

Fifth: – In what class he shall be trained.

Sixth: – What peculiar habits and notions he shall imbibe from his parents and those immediately around him in childhood.

So completely, indeed, has he been hitherto enveloped within these various mediums, that it is unlikely that a single individual has yet been able to resist their influence, except in a comparatively slight degree, even aided by the infinite variety of natural faculties and qualities which have been given to children in every part of the world.

Now, however, with the experience acquired, society may form new circumstances around children, in every part of the world, which shall enable each of them to pass this sixfold barrier of error and prejudice.

It is true the power of society over the individual is not without limit. It cannot recreate and altogether change the natural faculties and qualities which are given to children at birth; nor can it make those faculties and qualities superior, which nature has originally made inferior. But the power over human nature which it has already gained by experience, may be so applied as to effect every purpose that can be rationally desired.

Such, indeed, is the overwhelming influence which experience has now given to society over the rising generation, that it may surround children from their birth with new circumstances, which shall form each of them, bodily and mentally, in such a manner that his habits, disposition, and general character, shall be greatly superior to the habits, dispositions, and general character which the circumstances of birth have yet formed for man in any part of the world.

He may also, by the same means, be so trained, placed, and employed, in proper unity with others, and aided by mechanical, chemical, and other scientific power, that he shall create a surplus of new wealth, or property, far beyond what he will or can desire for his own use.

Under these circumstances, until the whole earth shall be well cultivated, and the seas refuse to furnish additional food, each child born in the working class will become a blessing to parents, and a new acquisition of productive riches to society.

And these beneficial changes may now be created with much less expense and trouble than are required to continue the present defective and most injurious systems.

It is to be particularly remarked, that the statements are founded on and supported by actual and incontrovertible facts. The Memorialist has acted upon these principles for many years; and all the practical results have exceeded his most sanguine expectations. He has proved, by the most decisive experience, the vast, the incalculable, superiority of legislating for the arranging of circumstances, over the past and present feeble system of legislating for the individuals and allowing the circumstances to remain unchanged. The latter mode is truly laying hold of the wrong end of the lever. It is violating the progressive principle of society, founded on a universal law of nature.

Some uninformed, inexperienced, and prejudiced persons, have lightly and hastily concluded that your Memorialist is a visionary, and therefore he occupies himself with public affairs. Whenever the subject shall be thoroughly investigated to its foundation, it will be found the fact is not so. He has long witnessed the happy effects of the principles which he recommends, even very imperfectly executed in practice; and, in consequence, he cannot but feel anxious to see them generally introduced and acted upon in all countries in which there are any who are poor, ignorant, and unprovided with proper employment.

At New Lanark, in Scotland, the Memorialist, while opposed by all the prejudices of birth existing in that part of the world, patiently, for many years silently, occupied himself in withdrawing some of the *old circumstances* which he found injurious to the well-being of this little colony, and in arranging new circumstances, within which 500 or 600 children and young persons are now daily educated, without punishment or individual reward of any kind; and their habits, dispositions, and general character are allowed by strangers who visit them to be superior to the general habits, dispositions and character of the same class to be found elsewhere.

And about 1600 persons of this colony are daily employed, who, with the aid of scientific power, complete as much work (and in a better manner), than could have been executed in Scotland, of the same kind, forty years ago, by 160,000 persons; or, in other words, one now, with this new aid, performs the work of one hundred.

Extraordinary as these facts may appear to many who are unacquainted with such kind of facts, society may now create new arrangements to train, educate, and employ the ignorant and unprovided of the working classes under circumstances far more advantageous for them and for the public than it was in the power of the Memorialist to accomplish.

He commenced his task without education, without friends who could render him assistance, and without fortune; and he has been opposed in his whole progress by the mistaken notions of the world.

If, then, an individual of ordinary capacity, thus circumstanced, could create the arrangements which have been stated, solely because he was influenced by principles which are true and in strict unison with nature, how much more could have been effected in the same time for the improvement of society by an individual so influenced, if he had possessed superior natural talents, a good education, friends in power, and a fortune sufficient to enable him to put his knowledge into practice under all the proper circumstances, and taking agriculture instead of manufactures for the foundation of his new arrangements?

Yet how much more could have been attained in the same period for the permanent improvement of all classes, if, instead of an individual, the whole of society had been influenced by these rational principles, and had acted upon them?

With this explanation, it is surely then not too much to say,

'That the period is arrived, when the principles of the science of political, economy are become obvious, by which, without disorder, force, or punishment of any kind, the rising generation may be, with ease and advantage to all, surrounded by new circumstances, which shall form them into any character that society may predetermine; and if any defect shall afterwards appear in those characters, except what nature has made uncontrollable by human means, the cause will not be in the individuals, but will be solely owing to the inexperience of the parties who attempt to put those invaluable principles into practice.'

PART THIRD

The Third General Result stated in the Appendix to the Memorial addressed to the Governments of Europe and America was as follows:

'*That it* IS *the interest, and that it will soon* APPEAR *to be the interest, of each individual, in every rank, in all countries, that judicious measures should be adopted, with the least delay, to secure these beneficial results in practice. It is, however, greatly to be desired that they should be carried into effect by general consent, gradually and temperately, in order that no party or individual may be injured by the changes which must necessarily follow.*'

'In consequence, any attempt to stop or retard the introduction of these measures will be unavailing. Already the principles and consequent practice are placed effectually beyond the power of human assault. It will be found that silence cannot now retard their progress, and that opposition will give increased celerity to their movements.'

Preliminary Explanations of the foregoing Result

'Your Memorialist submits that in the explanations of the *first* general result it has been shown that the means have been discovered and brought into action by which a great accumulation of wealth has been made, and that, by the extension of new scientific power, riches may be increased beyond any assignable limit.'

That in the *second* general result it has been shown that the principles of the science of political economy are become obvious, by which, without disorder, violence, or punishment of any kind, the rising generation may be, with ease and advantage to all, surrounded by new circumstances, which shall form them into any character that society may predetermine.

Under the existing arrangements in all countries the mass of the people derive their subsistence through a nominal value of their labour, which rises and falls on the common commercial principle of supply and demand.

This arrangement served the purpose in a tolerable degree while wealth was produced chiefly by manual labour. But it has been shown that latterly a power of production unlimited in extent and which scarcely consumes at all has been introduced; that it has already created a most unfavourable disproportion between the demand for and supply of manual labour; and in its daily undirected progress this disproportion will go on increasing.

As long, however, as manual labour shall continue thus depressed, the mass of the people, who derive their subsistence solely from that source, must be subjected to poverty and misery; while a few (not nearly one in a thousand of the population of the world,) will be in possession of accumulated wealth, which, under those circumstances, must destroy their happiness. They must be perpetually involved in the opposition of evil passions and struggles which must arise in such a lamentable state of society. It is not indeed possible, with the knowledge now in the world and which is daily advancing, that such a state of society can long exist. The overwhelming strength of knowledge and interest on one side will render all contest vain, and the folly of contest must be severely felt.

No one, therefore, can for a moment doubt that 'it *is* the interest of each individual, in every rank, in all countries, that judicious measures should be adopted with the least delay, to insure these beneficial results in practice.'

Nor can it be doubted that, with the hourly increase of knowledge in many parts of Europe and America, the period cannot be distant, when it will *appear* to be the interest of all, that these ameliorations should be speedily effected.

Conclusion

Thus has your Memorialist given preliminary explanations of the Three General Results stated in the Appendix to the Memorial on these subjects addressed to the governments of Europe and America.

He submits these preliminary explanations to satisfy Congress that he has had much experience on these subjects, and that he understands them thoroughly to their foundation. And upon that knowledge he now re-states.

I. *That all countries possess the means, and many the most ample, to give riches, good habits and dispositions, and useful learning and intelligence, to all their inhabitants.*

II. That the practical measures to effect these important results are unknown to the Governments and People; otherwise, as the benefits to each would be beyond estimate, they would without loss of time be carried into execution.

III. That your Memorialist is desirous of developing these measures in the most minute detail to Congress and to the Governments of Europe and America, that they may take the lead in directing, under the established order of things, those changes which can *alone* relieve the world from the practical evils of the present system, which is experienced to be now so productive of error and misery that everyone exclaims, '*Something must be done;*' though no one has yet attempted to state *what should be done.*

IV. That your Memorialist is most desirous of cordially uniting the governments and people in those measures which he is ready to prove *ought now to be put in practice* for the interests of both.

V. That he has hitherto, except in part, withheld this knowledge from the people; because he has been afraid they would act upon it, in their present neglected and unprepared state, with too much precipitancy to benefit themselves and others. He still withholds it from them until he shall discover that they will use it calmly and temperately for their advantage, without having the desire to apply it to the injury of any class, sect, party, or individual. This period, however, for many reasons, he considers to be rapidly drawing near; and he will patiently await its arrival.

In the common acceptation of the term, your Memorialist has no private object whatever in pursuing the measures with which he has so long occupied himself for the public benefit, and in which he has expended large sums, in experiments, and in various other ways.

He asks nothing – he wants nothing – and he fears nothing, individually, either from the governments or the people.

Before he moved one step in this course, 'he put his life in his hand;'[a] and all personal objects he considered 'as a feather in the balance,'[b] compared with the immensity of good which he knew, under such circumstances, might be accomplished for his fellow-creatures. And to attain this amelioration for them is the sole object which now influences his conduct.

To understand this motive, however, in all its bearings and extent, the mind must be enabled to overcome and pass through the six-fold barrier of error and prejudice with which the circumstances of birth have hitherto encompassed every one. In fact, 'the mind must be born again,' by a new training from infancy, on the principle that the character of man ever has been, and ever must be, formed *for* him.

Then will this motive be distinctly comprehended by all; and it will influence every action of their lives.

---

[a] See 1 Samuel 19:5.

[b] See Isaiah 40:15.

Under these circumstances, which your Memorialist is aware are not of an ordinary nature, he proposes that the Allied Powers assembled in Congress should appoint a commission to examine, personally, the effects produced at New Lanark by a very partial and defective application to practice of the principles which he recommends. Also to investigate minutely the whole of the new arrangements, which, under modifications, he has to propose for adoption in all countries; and to report their opinion thereon to Congress, when it next assembles;- the frequent meeting of which may be substantially useful to Europe and the world.

Yes! the finest opportunity that has ever occurred in history now presents itself to Congress, to establish a permanent system of peace, conservation, and charity, in its true sense, and effectually to supersede the system of war, destruction, and of almost every evil, arising from uncharitable notions among men, produced solely by the circumstances of birth.

Aix-la-Chapelle, 22nd October, 1818.

AN

ADDRESS

TO THE

MASTER MANUFACTURERS

OF

Great Britain,

On the Present existing Evils

IN THE

MANUFACTURING SYSTEM

BY MR. OWEN, OF NEW LANARK

BOLTON:

PRINTED BY H. & A. SWINDELLS, DEANSGATE.

1819.

ADDRESS TO THE MASTER-MANUFACTURERS OF GREAT BRITAIN[a]
1819

I Beg to address you, Gentlemen, on behalf of a cause in which, as men and fellow-subjects, we are all deeply interested – the amelioration of the circumstances of those whom we employ as operatives in our various manufactures. Many of you, who have received a liberal education, will, I am sure, acknowledge that it is a subject of great national importance, and will consider it with more just and enlarged views, than the narrow principles of *immediate gain* might suggest. To such it would be presumption in me to offer any explanation of that which must already be obvious to them: but there are others who have not been so fortunate – who have never had the leisure to study or think about matters of this nature: and for these only are the following observations intended.

Practices prevail in our manufacturing system, which have been produced by circumstances not under the controul of any individual, and for which, therefore, no individual can be justly blamed. They are, however, notoriously the source of most grievous evils, and stand in the way of improvements in the condition of our working classes, which are essential to the well-being of the State, and without which indeed its security must rest on a very precarious foundation. I refer to the premature employment of children; and to the unreasonable term of daily labour, now exacted from persons of all ages who are employed within our manufactories. It is to these practices that we may attribute the worst effects of the manufacturing system; and, if we permit them to continue, through mere indifference to the subject, or from the egregious and fatal delusion that they are connected with the prosperity of our manufactures, we must be content to suffer all the evils arising from the increasing misery and demoralization of the working classes. But it is my most earnest wish to excite the public attention to this important question, and to do away with any delusion that may exist in your quarter respecting it – to convince you

[a] Originally printed as both a pamphlet and broadsheet. Reprinted in Owen, *Life*, vol. 1A (1858), pp. 195–204, with the title 'Letter Dated March 30th, 1818, Addressed to British Master Manufacturers, "On the Employment of Children in Manufactories"'. Later reprints include 1927.

that the continuance of these practices is directly opposed to every individual interest in the country; and that these fruitful sources of evil may be effectually closed without even diminishing the *immediate gains* of the master manufacturer.

Let us direct our attention, in the first place, in the unnatural circumstances in which the younger part of our operatives are now placed. Children are permitted to be employed, almost from infancy in our manufactures, all of which are more or less unhealthy. They are condemned to a routine of long protracted and unvarying toil within doors, at an age when their time should be exclusively divided between healthful exercises in the open air, and their school education. The utmost violence is thus offered to nature at their very outset in life. Their intellectual, as well as their physical powers, are cramped and paralysed, instead of being allowed their proper and natural developement; while every thing about them conspires to render their moral character depraved and dangerous. Without a vigorous constitution and good habits, children can never become really useful subjects of the State, nor can their lives be rendered comfortable to themselves or uninjurious to others. While so many obstacles are unnecessarily opposed to that mode of training for the rising generation which humanity and expediency so strongly recommend, society is alone to blame for the imbecility and suffering that may arise within it: the offspring of our poor must continue to be squalid and wretched, to be untaught for any good or really useful purpose, but admirably trained to effect their own misery, – destined to disturb the peace of society in their younger days, and at an early period to become a burthen on the community for the remainder of life, eating that bread in idleness, which, if the State did justice to them or to itself, would never be claimed by any not naturally infirm, except as the reward of useful industry. I conceive it to be a fact which consists equally with the experience of every one of you as it does with mine, that the labour of a child, strong and healthy, possessed of intelligence and of good habits and dispositions, is infinitely more valuable than that of one who is weak and unhealthy, imbecile in mind, and of depraved habits and dispositions. But though this fact is abundantly clear, it may not occur to you to trace the cause of this difference between the two individuals, and to perceive that in almost every case this great disparity is to be referred altogether to the different circumstances under which they have been trained and educated. A very little examination and reflection, however, will convince you that this is the true state of the case; and I will not allow myself to suppose, that in the face of so striking a fact, you will any longer have any desire to employ the inferior instrument, when, by means of regulations as practicable as they are humane, you may with certainty procure the best.

No child should be employed within doors in any manufacture, until he is twelve years of age. In those manufactures in which dexterity of operation is much more easily required by children at an early, than at a more advanced period of life, they might perhaps be employed, in order, to attain such facility, for five or six hours a day when between ten and twelve years of age; but I am of opinion that any advantage thus procured can be obtained only by tenfold sacrifices on the part of the children, their parents, and their country. I think an intelligent slave-master would not, on the sole principle of pecuniary gain, employ his young slaves even ten hours of the day at so early an age. And we know that judicious farmers will not prematurely put their young beasts of burthen to work; and that when they do put them to work, it is with great moderation at first, and, we must remember too in a healthy atmosphere. But children from seven to eight years of age are employed with young persons and men and women of all ages, for 14 or fifteen hours per day in many of our manufactories, carried on in buildings in which the atmosphere is by no means the most favourable to human life.

If the well being of our fellow creatures be a more important object than a fractional diminution of the prime cost of a few articles of commerce – often very useless ones – and if that object be a primary consideration in any change in the practices and habits of society, then surely the present generation has gone far astray from the right course, when it has expended the hours of healthy and really productive labour, for 14 hours of unhealthy, and often of useless or pernicious employment. To mark the contrast of the two systems, look at the healthy, comparatively well-trained Scottish peasant boy, who attends the parochial school until he is 14 or 15 years old, – and then turn your eyes to the feeble, pale, and wretched flax of cotton spinning children, who, at an early age, are doomed all the year round to one unvarying occupation for 14 or 15 hours a day, going to their work in winter before it is light in the morning, and returning long after dark. And here I may well ask – how should *we* like our children, girls as well as boys, to be thus employed? Would any of us permit our slaves, if we were obliged to maintain them, to be so treated? Surely it is but necessary to call your attention to these facts, and you must instantly be aware of the injustice and useless cruelty, which we thus inflict upon the most helpless beings in society. At this moment I feel almost ashamed to address any human being on such a subject.

You may perhaps admit that the Legislature has a right to regulate the labour of these helpless children, and that you would not suffer much inconvenience from being obliged to employ persons of more advanced age in their place: but the free labourer, you may say, should be permitted to work as long as he is willing, for hire. If the operatives in our manufactories were really free, and had the option to work nine or 15 hours a day, it might be less necessary to legislate on this subject. But what is their actual situation in this respect? Are they, in any thing but appearance, free labourers? Would they not, in fact, be compelled to work the customary hours though they were 20? What alternative have they, or what freedom is there in this case, but the liberty of starvation? An excess of labour and confinement prematurely weakens and destroys all the functions of the animal frame; and few constitutions can be preserved in health and vigour under a regular occupation in our manufactories for more than ten hours per day, exclusive of the time requisite for meals. It may, however, perhaps appear to you that you have no particular interest in attending to the health and comforts of the working classes, provided you can get your work well and cheaply performed by them. Every master manufacturer is most anxious to have his work cheaply performed, and as he is perpetually exerting all his faculties to attain this object, he considers low wages to be essential to his success. By one master or other, every means are used to reduce wages to the lowest possible point, and if but one succeeds the others must follow in their own defence. Yet, when the subject is properly considered, no evil ought to be more dreaded by master manufacturers than low wages of labour, or the want of the means to procure reasonable comfort among the working classes. These, in consequence of their numbers, are the greatest consumers of articles; and it will always be found that when wages are high the country prospers; when they are low, all classes suffer from the highest to the lowest, but more particularly the manufacturing interest; for food must be first purchased, and the remainder only of the labourer's wages can be expended in manufactures. It is therefore essentially the interest of the master manufacturer that the wages of the labourer should be high, and that he should be allowed the necessary time and instruction to enable him to expend them judiciously – which is not possible under the existence of our present practices. And this brings me to the main point of this letter: – Is it or is it not the interest of the master manufacturers that their operatives should be employed longer than ten hours per day?

The most substantial support to the trade, commerce, and manufacturers of this and of every country, are the labouring classes of its population; and the real prosperity of any nation may be at all times accurately ascertained by the amount of wages or the extent of the comforts, which the productive classes can obtain in return for their labour. – It is evident that food must be procured by the working man and his family before he can purchase any other article. If therefore this class of our population is so degraded and oppressed, that they can only procure the bare necessaries of life, they are lost as customers to the manufacturer; and it is to be recollected that at least two-thirds of the population of all countries derive their immediate support from the wages of labour, and in this country chiefly from trade and manufactures. The working classes may be injuriously degraded and oppressed in three ways. 1st. When they are neglected in infancy; 2dly. Where they are over worked by their employer, and are thus rendered incompetent from ignorance to make a good use of high wages when they can procure them; and, 3dly. When they are paid low wages for their labour. But when ignorance, overwork, and low wages are combined, not only is the labourer in a wretched situation, but all the higher classes are essentially injured, although none will suffer in consequence more severely than the master manufacturer, for the reason which has been before stated. Let your minds dwell a little longer on this subject, and you will soon discover that it is most obviously your interest that your operatives should be well taught in infancy, and during their future lives rendered healthy, and put in possession of the means of being good customers to you. But they cannot be well-taught, healthy, or competent to spend moderate wages advantageously to themselves, for you, and for the country, if they enter into your employment at a premature age, and are afterwards compelled to exhaust their physical powers, by unreasonable labour, without proper relaxation and leisure. – By such short-sighted practices you cut up your prosperity by the root, and most effectually kill the goose from which you would otherwise daily receive the golden egg.

I can have no motive to deceive you. My whole pecuniary interest is embarked in the same cause with you. I am one of yourselves, and should suffer more than the majority by any measure that really injured the manufacturing system. I have taken much pains not to be misled on this subject; and my view of it has been, I think, unbiassed. I have no inclination towards any particular principle or practice but what an honest love of truth directs. Under these circumstances, allow me to assure you, that my firm conviction is, that our present practices are destructive of every thing which deserves the name of comfort or happiness among our work-people, and, therefore, inconsistent with common humanity towards them; – that they are most ruinous to the best interests of our country, and ten times more powerful opponents to our success as manufacturers, than all the competition which it is possible for foreign nations to create against us.

We complain of the wretchedness of our work-people, – and yet we work them, from infancy to old age, in such a manner, and under such circumstances, that, whatever wages they receive, the mass of them must be wretched.

We complain that all markets are over stocked with our manufactures, – and yet we compel our young children, and millions of adults, to labour almost day and night, to urge forward perpetually increasing mechanical powers, that those markets may be still more over stocked.

We complain that numbers of our strong, healthy, and active labourers are unemployed, – and yet we prematurely employ children – infants almost – and greatly overwork a large part of our population; as if it were purposely to keep those out of employment who ought to work, and to whom employment would be of the greatest individual and national advantage.

We complain that the Poor Rates are become an evil so alarming, that if they continue to go on unchecked they threaten to shake the foundation of civil society; – and yet we leave the mass of our population in ignorance, suffer their health and morals to be undermined in childhood – destroyed in manhood – and subject them to premature helpless old age; thereby taking the most effectual means to compel our working classes to resort to the Poor Laws, as their sole inheritance, and thus accelerate the most formidable evil, that ever yet, from within, assailed a civilized community.

We complain that foreign raw materials are extravagantly high, yielding the cultivator an enormous profit, and that the articles we manufacture from them, by the over-wrought exertions of our men, women, and children, under every deprivation of natural comfort, and aided by unrivalled and almost perpetually moving mechanism, will not enable us to give a bare subsistence to these wretched beings, – and yet by our long hours of labour, we take every means in our power to increase the price of the foreign raw material, and to diminish the profit on the articles we manufacture.

Such is the blind ignorance of our conduct, that I am compelled to ask, where is the boasted intellect of the British Isles?

To those who can comprehend and steadily trace the rise, progress, and consequences of the manufacturing system, it is evident that it has given birth to circumstances, which train men to think it their proper business and duty, technically speaking, to take a *fair advantage* of all their fellows, and to sacrifice their own happiness, and the well-being of society, at the shrine of individual gain; although by such practices the most favoured of them obtain only the shadow of their wishes, while, by their over-strained exertions, in a wrong direction, the substance of their desires is removed to a greater and greater distance from their grasp.

Let us, my friends, now no longer proceed thus; let us stand still and examine the wisdom of those practices so dear to some of us – namely, the premature employment of children, and the exaction of excessive labour from a part of our adult population, while thousands are wholly unemployed, and miserable, and starving for want of occupation. A very limited share of sagacity, properly directed, will show us that, in our character of manufacturers only, it is clearly our interest to permit children to be properly educated and to possess sound and vigorous constitutions; that our operatives and all the working-classes should not be asked or permitted to labour more than 12 hours per day, with two hours' intermission, for rest, air, and meals, and that in return for their labour, they should be allowed wages sufficient to enable them to purchase wholesome food and some of the most useful articles of manufacture. View these changes in the most unfavourable light in which they can be placed for the manufacturing interest, and they will be found, each and all of them, to be beneficial to it. Should the non-employment of children under 12 years of age, and the limitation of the hours of labour to 12, inclusive of meals, occasion a small fractional addition to the prime cost of our manufactured articles by the consequent diminution of the supply, yet as the latter now exceeds the demand, the prices of the articles, will advance in a greater proportion, and the consumer, as he ought will make up the difference. But any difference that may thus arise, must be small indeed, compared to the perpetual fluctuations which are made in the prices of all articles, by a few wealthy speculators buying up at once immense quantities of the raw materials, from which the various articles of commerce are made. In the cotton business, for instance, as being now the most extended, (but the principle applies equally to all,) the ameliorations proposed will not affect the prime cost of the thread more than the fraction of a penny per pound, and in the finished cloth or muslin, not more than a fraction of that fraction per yard – while such speculations will increase the prime cost of the raw material from 1d. to 12d. or 18d. per pound, and that to benefit a very few individuals, at the expence of the Public. I find no fault with such speculations – but it does not become those who are the most active in them, and the chief gainers by them, to contend against the removal of evils which affect the well-being and vital interests of millions of the most helpless of the population, merely on the plea that a small fractional addition would thereby be made to the prime cost of an article – when for their own immediate gain they would add ten or twenty times the amount to its price.

In short, my friends, when you come to examine the subject fairly and honestly, you will certainly find that no valid reason exists for the longer continuance of the grievous and pernicious practices which now prevail in our trade; and that instead of opposing them, it is especially our interest, one and all to petition the Legislature to remove them without delay, and I trust, that when you have dispassionately and without prejudice taken all these circumstances into your consideration, you will accordingly pour petitions in from every district in which manufacturers are established.

New Lanark, March 30th, 1819 ROBERT OWEN

AN ADDRESS TO THE WORKING CLASSES[a]
1819

The truly intelligent in Europe and America, by their silence when publicly called upon, now admit the truth of those principles which I have advocated as preliminary to the introduction of a New System for the government of mankind, Hitherto, no individual, either in this country or abroad, who possesses any knowledge of the theory and practice of governing men or of forming their character, has attempted to prove error in any one of the principles developed in the 'New View of Society.' On close examination they are all found to be nature's laws, and therefore unassailable.

Yet all men have from infancy been *forced* to think and act as if other notions were true; and, as they have never seen any part of mankind placed under circumstances in which they could act on those principles which, they are now obliged to admit, are true in theory, they very naturally from past experience conclude that although the principles of the 'New System' are capable of the most evident demonstration, they cannot be applied to practice. All this however means no more than that they who come to this conclusion are incompetent to reduce erected principles into beneficial practice: and the persons who thus hastily decide, without having sufficient data on which to form any accurate judgment, would have made the same random assertions respecting any of the great improvements in science, prior to their introduction. Such individuals forget that it is a modern invention to enable one man, with the aid of a little steam, to perform the labour of 1000 men. What would these unbelievers in human improvement say, if the truths of the Copernican System were now for the first time to be introduced to their notice?

But we will leave them to brood over their melancholy fancied wisdom until facts shall overcome their disbelief; for the time is at hand when they will behold with astonishment the simplicity and beautiful order of those movements, the combination of which they now deem to be impossible.

Yet before this change, so much to be desired by you and every other class, from the highest to the lowest, can be permitted to take place, one formidable

[a] First published in *The Star*, 15 April 1819, and *The Examiner*, 25 April 1819. Reprinted in *The Economist*, vol. 1, no. 29 (11 August 1821), pp. 48–51, and Owen, *Life*, vol. 1A (1858), pp. 225–33. Later reprints include 1927, 1991.

obstacle must be removed. From infancy you, like others, have been made to despise and to hate those who differ from you in manners, language, and sentiments. You have been filled with all uncharitableness, and in consequence cherish feelings of anger towards your fellow-men who have been placed in opposition to your interests. Those feelings of anger must be withdrawn before any being who has your real interest at heart can place power in your hands. You must be made to know yourselves, by which means alone you can discover what other men are. You will then distinctly perceive that no rational ground for anger exists, even against those who by the errors of the present system have been made your greatest oppressors and your most bitter enemies. An endless multiplicity of circumstances, over which you had not the smallest control, placed you where you are, and as you are. In the same manner, others of your fellow-men have been formed by circumstances, equally uncontrolable by them, to become your enemies and grievous oppressors. In strict justice they are no more to be blamed for these results than you are; nor you than they; and, splendid as their exterior may be, this state of matters often causes them to suffer even more poignantly than you. They have therefore an interest, strong as yours, in the change which is about to commence for the equal benefit of all, provided *you* do not create a more formidable counteracting interest on *their* parts; of which the result must be, to prolong the existing misery of both classes, and to retard the public good.

The existing order of things has placed some of your fellow-men in situations of power and emolument, and in the possession of privileges on which they have been taught to set a value. While you shew by your conduct any desire violently to dispossess them of this power, these emoluments, and privileges, – is it not evident that they must continue to regard you with jealous and hostile feelings, that the contention between the rich and the poor will never have an end, and that, whatever relative changes may take place among you, there will ever be the same oppression of the weak by the party who has attained to power? Before your condition can be ameliorated this irrational and useless contest must cease, and measures must be adopted in which both parties may have a substantial interest. Then will anger and opposition subside, and those arrangements which now appear impracticable to the inexperienced, be carried most easily into practice. And these changes are at hand; for a crisis has arrived, new in the history of mankind.

The experience of ages has now developed truths which demonstrate, 'That all men have been forced by the circumstances which have surrounded them from birth to become mere irrational and localized animals, and who in consequence have been compelled to think and act on data directly opposed to facts, and of course to pursue measures destructive alike of their own happiness and of the happiness of human nature.' I am well aware of the feelings which the development of this truth will at first excite in those who are now deemed rich, learned, and powerful, and in all those who have been taught to imagine that they possess some knowledge. The truth however is not thus declared to inflict unnecessary pain on a single human being. On the contrary, it is held up to the light of the world, solely to shew mankind the first step of knowledge which can lead them to rationality, and out of the ignorance and misery in which they have hitherto existed. The pain which the development of this all-important truth must create will be transient and pass away without real injury to any one; while the substantial benefits which it will produce will be perpetually experienced by the whole of human nature through all succeeding generations. It is from a thorough knowledge of this truth, and of the infinite beneficial consequences which will result to mankind from its being universally known, that I now bring it before your minds, not as an abstract theory to amuse speculative men, but to shew you the source of all the errors which afflict society, and which must be removed before your condition can be ameliorated.

There is no knowledge except this which can make human nature truly benevolent and kind to the whole of the species, and, with the certainty of a mathematical demonstration, render all men charitable, in the most enlarged and best sense of the term. It will force on the human mind the conviction that to blame and to be angry with our fellow-men for the evils which exist, is the very essence of folly and irrationality, and that notions which can give rise to such feelings never could enter into the composition of any human being that had been once made rational.

Are you then prepared to look upon all your fellow-creatures, in power and out of power, rich and poor, learned and unlearned, good and bad, as beings formed solely by the circumstances of their birth, and who have been made as they are, whatever they may be, from causes which exclude the possibility of the smallest control on their parts in the formation of those faculties and qualities they may happen to possess? If you cannot see and comprehend this truth, then is the time not yet to come for your deliverance from the depths of mental darkness and physical misery. But I trust the light is not now too strong for you to receive without injury; for I have been gradually preparing you for years for its reception, and if the experience which I have been permitted to acquire of human nature does not very much deceive me, it is not now a premature disclosure.

If you then can bear to be told that human beings possessing the most attractive form and the highest intellectual attainments which the world has yet seen, can justly claim no other appellation than that of localised animals, peculiar to some of the innumerable districts into which irrationality has divided the world; and if your minds can now comprehend the principles which place this truth among those which are capable of the easiest demonstration; then is the time of your deliverance from mental slavery come, and the period is approaching when you may acquire some title to be considered rational creatures.

If you are in this advanced mental state, so much to be desired for your happiness, then you will at once cease to blame others for the evils which you suffer; anger, revenge, and hatred, almost to the very recollection of them, will be withdrawn from your feelings; you will not longer dissipate all your energies in attempting to find the cause of your miseries among any of your fellow-men, and thus destroy your minds and happiness by creating unceasing, useless irritation.

No! In all respects your conduct will become the very reverse of this. You will regard all your fellow-men, without distinction, as beings who are soon to become your friends and active co-operaters in the attainment of the substantial happiness to which human nature is evidently destined. You will say to those who are now in possession of riches, honours, power, and privileges, which they have been taught to value, – 'Retain these in perfect security as long as you can hold them in estimation. Our whole conduct and proceedings shall be a pledge to you that we will never attempt to dispossess you of any part of them; nay, while you can derive pleasure from additional wealth, we will add to that which you now possess. The cause of contest between us will henceforth cease. We have discovered its irrationality and utter uselessness. We will not, except to acquire experience from it, recur to the past, in which all have been compelled to act an irrational part; but we will earnestly apply ourselves to the future; and having discovered the light of true knowledge, we will henceforth walk by it.'

All this you may with confidence say to the higher classes, whose supposed privileges you will soon cease to envy. For, without entering into contest with them, without infringing on any of the imaginary privileges which prior circumstances have placed in their hands, a new view of your interests shall be speedily opened to you, by which, without interfering with the rights of any class, without exciting any feeling of opposition to your proceedings, you shall be enabled to relieve yourselves and your descendents from poverty, from ignorance, and from the innumerable causes of misery to which you have hitherto been victims. When you shall thus be enabled to understand your real interests, you will have no desire for any of the fancied advantages now possessed by the higher classes.

Had those who are of this order in the civilized world been permitted to discover what human nature really is, they would have distinctly known long ago that, by being raised, as it is termed, to the privileged ranks, they are placed under circumstances which render their successors, except by some extraordinary chance, increasingly useless to themselves and to society.

They are taught from infancy to set an inordinate value on themselves because they possess what are miscalled privileges, the only real effect of which is to surround them by circumstances which must inevitably make them more helpless and dependent than other men.

They are trained from the cradle (and therefore call for our pity, not blame,) to take pride to themselves for pursuing measures which deprive the great mass of mankind of the most essential benefits that belong to human nature, in order that they, a most insignificant part in point of numbers, may be distinguished by advantages over their fellows.

The feelings which this absurd conduct generates throughout society, keep the whole population of the world in a lower degree of enjoyment and rationality than most of the animal creation. They are the very essence of ignorant selfishness.

You will now soon pass this error. You will discover that there is no comparison between the result of such conduct and the pleasure to be derived from the most active exertions to give to all your fellow-creatures the same privileges and benefits which you yourselves possess, and, by this means, so far increase the aggregate of human enjoyment, that the least gifted member of society will experience a larger share of continued and permanent happiness than has hitherto fallen to the lot of the most fortunate. The motives which lead to the former conduct are altogether irrational, and will not bear the glance of an enlightened mind; while those which will compel you to adopt the latter are in unison with every sound principle and just feeling, and defy the most rigid scrutiny to detect in them any error.

Let me however guard you against a mistake which exists to a great extent among the unprivileged orders. The privileged classes of the present day, throughout Europe, are not, as this mistake supposes, influenced so much by a desire to keep *you* down, as by an anxiety to retain the means of securing to *themselves* a comfortable and respectable enjoyment of life. Let them distinctly perceive that the ameliorations which you are about to experience are not intended or calculated to inflict any real injury on them or their posterity, but, on the contrary, that the same measures which will improve *you*, must, as they assuredly will, essentially benefit *them*, and raise them in the scale of happiness and intellectual enjoyment, – and you will speedily have their co-operation to carry the contemplated arrangements into effect. It must be satisfactory to you to learn that I have had the most evident proofs from many individuals, high in these classes, that they have now a real desire to improve your condition; but, from the unfortunate situation in which they have been placed by birth, they cannot, of themselves, devise measures by which you can be benefited and their own circumstances improved. Such changes must proceed from practical men.

What has been said is sufficient for your minds to digest at one time. When you are prepared to receive more, it shall be given to you.

Heed not what men with fanciful theories and without practical knowledge may say to you. Many of them, I have no doubt, mean well. But be assured that whatever tends to irritation and violence proceeds from the most gross ignorance of human nature, and evinces an utter inexperience in those practical measures by which alone society can be relieved from the evils which it has so long suffered.

My fixed intention has long been to develop truths which it is of the utmost importance to the well-being of mankind to make publicly known at this period; and I have been gradually preparing the public mind to receive them. Where great darkness has ever existed, a sudden admission of strong light would destroy the infant powers of vision. Unless the most salutary truths, when they are opposed to centuries of prejudice, are introduced with due care to those whose minds have wandered in a labyrinth of error from their birth, the tender germ of rationality would likewise perish, and ignorance and misery must continue to prevail over knowledge and happiness.

As you become acquainted with these truths, one after the other, your long injured minds will acquire strength, and your rational powers gradually expand, until the knowledge of human nature, which now appears so incomprehensible to you, will discover itself to be as simple as any of the other facts which surround you, and with which you are now the most familiar.

What I have now stated is intended to prepare the public mind for the following conclusions:-

1st. That the rich and the poor, the governors and the governed, have really but one interest.

2nd. That the notions and arrangements which at present prevail throughout society are necessarily destructive of the happiness of all ranks.

3rd. That a correct knowledge of human nature will destroy all animosity and anger among men, and will prepare the way for new arrangements, which will be introduced without violence and without injury to any party, and which will effectually remove the cause from which all the errors and evils of society now proceed.

4th. That the higher classes in general no longer wish to degrade you, but in any change that may be proposed for *your* benefit, they demand only that advantages should be secured to *them*, at least equal to those which they now possess: and this feeling is quite natural; it would be yours if you were in their situation.

5th. That you now possess all the means which are necessary to relieve yourselves and your descendants to the latest period from the sufferings which you have hitherto experienced, – except the knowledge how to direct those means.

6th. That this knowledge is withheld from you only until the violence of your irritation against your fellow-men shall cease; that is, until you thoroughly understand and are influenced in all your conduct by the principle, 'That it is the circumstances of birth, with subsequent surrounding circumstances, all formed *for* the individual, (and over which society has now a complete control,) that have hitherto made the past generations of mankind into the irrational creatures exhibited in history, and fashioned them, up to the present hour, into those localised beings of country, sect, class, and party, who now compose the population of the earth.'

7th and last. That the past ages of the world present the history of human irrationality only, and that we are but now advancing towards the dawn of reason, and to the period when the mind of man shall be born again.

ROBERT OWEN

New Lanark, March 29, 1819

[a][The *Examiner* of Sunday, April 25th, 1819, contained in a leading article the following remarks upon the preceding address:-

'We lay before our readers (for though it is addressed to a particular class, it is interesting to all,) another paper by Mr OWEN of Lanark. We are glad to find from an intelligent and amiable writer on this subject, ("Remarks on the Practicability of Mr OWEN's Plan,") that "the Benevolent Society lately established in Holland, and now in active operation, has for its object the formation of colonies in the northern provinces upon a principle closely resembling that of Mr OWEN's plan." By an extract which follows from a Dutch paper of November last, it appears that land had been purchased near the Overyssel, and materials collected for building fifty houses, twenty of which indeed were in a state of forwardness. Sub-committees had been appointed in eighty different towns; and the society already consisted of 17,000 members.

'Those who think Mr OWEN's plans calculated to cramp and formalise human nature will perhaps smile to see them imitated by the *Dutch*. But not to mention that the Dutch are not the cold people they were before their late intimacy with the French, there is M. FELLENBERG's Establishment at Hofwyl, of which an account was given in the last *Edinburgh Review*,[b] and Mr OWEN's own place at Lanark, both of which, though not in the same manner, serve to show the difference between forming and formalising. Mr OWEN's *projects in particular tend to make people too well acquainted with their own nature, to run a chance of rendering them stiff and narrow-minded.* His catechism is self-knowledge. Now knowledge of every species is power; and knowledge of our own natures and wants is the power of all others that cannot be contented with the evils here anticipated. If Mr OWEN's plans were found to be too formal in their operation, they would alter themselves of their own accord. This is the inevitable nature of the elements with which they set out; and this is a sufficient answer to all the objections on such a score. The only actual objection we ever heard against New Lanark from those who had visited it was one certainly of no cramping nature. Some persons thought that the *esprit du corps* was a little too social. But it may be said that New Lanark, by Mr OWEN's own confession, is not altogether what he should wish it to be. He had not the complete forming of the materials. Granted. How far this deficiency points to

[a] Note to the 1858 edn.

[b] See *Edinburgh Review*, 31 (1818–19), pp. 150–64.

a more or less social plan, we know not; but the great outcry against his villages, such as they are drawn upon paper, is – "Why they are all squares! So the people are to live in squares! are they? – like barracks or workhouses!" Aye, or suppose we say like Portman Square; for, as far as mere shape goes, one square is as good as another, only Portman Square, with the idea of its trees, and its music, and its young ladies, is a pleasurable one; and that of a barrack or a workhouse, which has nothing of all these, a painful one. Now, as to the young women, it depends upon the conditions of those who might choose to live in one of Mr OWEN's squares, whether they were ladies or not; but there are both trees and music, and these help to make very charming girls.'

(Very charming girls! Good GOD, Mr Examiner, what words for a politician and a philosopher!

Why, Madam, your titles flatter me; but I should be still less of either than I am if I ran counter in these matters to such men as LYCURGUS, and PLATO, and Sir THOMAS MORE.

But, Sir, the phrase!

The phrase, Madam, cannot be better, I think. It is sincere, and expresses what it means, and what it means cannot possibly be better.

But, Sir, how are the trees and the music to make us charming?

You could best explain that, Madam, if you would tell me how it is you look so smiling and good-tempered even in your objections. Trees are the best representatives of solitary nature, and music is one of the greatest links of social; and the habitual taste for these two things tends, even unconsciously, to that union of the thinking and enjoying faculties, which reflects upon each its greatest charm, and renders them both irresistible.)

'Mr OWEN should get some plans sketched of his villages in a completer style than those he has printed. The squares, filled up as he designs them, with trees and turf, would then never be mistaken for barracks. And after all, these squares, of course, will not always be necessary. They are proposed in the first instance out of economy; and be this as it may, to fancy that every body must have a tendency to grow formal who looks out of front windows upon a rural square, and out of the back upon fields, is to suppose a geometrical consciousness of a very extraordinary nature. Mr OWEN's plan is mutual co-operation; and if this brings people into closer contact, it brings them also into a more mutual system of enjoyment; for it is neighbourhood *without* co-operation that produces all those unneighbourly vices which Christians profess to hate at the very moment they practice them most. People get uneasy, and dissatisfied with themselves, and then they want the excitement of discovering others to be as bad and uneasy as themselves. Those make the worst neighbours who have the least self-knowledge. To know one's own nature, is to know every body's in its elements; and then the next thing is to assist and to teach every body to enjoy, as well as ourselves; for all become so many reflections of the same idea, not in its selfishness, but in its identity; and being identified, and, as it were, one, we wish it to realise the largest possible sum of happiness. Thus sociality has become another word for enjoyment. Let it also become, for the same purpose, another word for utility.

'We shall return to this subject.']

REPORT
TO THE COUNTY OF LANARK[a]
1820

To the County of Lanark, of a Plan for relieving Public Distress and Removing Discontent, by giving permanent, productive Employment to the Poor and Working Classes, under Arrangements which will essentially improve their Character, and ameliorate their Condition, diminish the Expenses of Production and Consumption, and create Markets co-extensive with Production. By Robert Owen, May 1, 1820.

The following Report was submitted, at the request of Committee of Gentlemen of the Upper Ward of Lanarkshire, to a General Meeting of the County, held at Lanark on the 1st May, 1820, and was ordered to be referred to the consideration of a Committee, composed of the following gentlemen:

Norman Lockhart, Esq., Convener of the Committee; Robert Hamilton, Esq., Sheriff Depute of Lanarkshire; Sir James Stewart Denham of Coltness, Bart; Sir William Honyman of Armadale, Bart; Sir Henry Steuart of Allanton, Bart; Colonel Gordon of Harperfield; Hugh Mosman of Auchtyfardle, Esq.[b]

---

[a] An MS copy of pts 2–3 is in the University of London Library (MS 692). The full title of the first edn is: *Report to the County of Lanark, of a Plan for Relieving Public Distress, and Removing Discontent, By Giving Permanent, Productive Employment, to the Poor and Working Classes; Under Arrangements Which Will Essentially Improve Their Character, and Ameliorate Their Condition; Diminish the Expenses of Production and Consumption, and Create Markets Co-extensive with Production.* Another edn 1832, Reprinted in *New Moral World*, vol. 11, nos 38–43, 45–6 (1843), pp. 301–2, 209–10, 317–18, 325–6, 334–5, 343, 357–8, 365–6, vol. 12, no. 1 (1 July 1843), pp. 1–2. *The New Existence of Man Upon the Earth* (1854), pt 3, pp. i–xlii, Owen, *Life*, vol. 1A (1858), pp. 263–320. Later reprints include 1927, 1963, 1970, 1991.

[b] Norman Lockhart (1802–49), 3rd baronet from 1832.

Robert Hamilton (?1750–1831), who fought at Bunker Hill and other battles against the Americans; legal writer and genealogist.

General Sir James Steuart Denham (1744–1839), best-known for his role in suppressing the 1798 Irish rebellion.

Sir William Honyman (1756–1825), Lord Armadale: judge.

Sir Henry Steuart (1759–1836): author of *The Planter's Guide*.

Lt-Col. Thomas Gordon (d. 1832).

Hugh Mosman (1754–1828).

PART I

Introduction

The evil for which your Reporter has been required to provide a remedy, is the general want of employment, at wages sufficient to support the family of a working man beneficially for the community.

After the most earnest consideration of the subject he has been compelled to conclude that such employment cannot be procured through the medium of trade, commerce, or manufactures, or even of agriculture, until the Government and the Legislature, cordially supported by the country, shall previously adopt measures to remove obstacles, which, without their interference, will now permanently keep the working classes in poverty and discontent, and gradually deterioriate all the resources of the empire.

Your Reporter has been impressed with the truth of this conclusion by the following considerations: –

1st. – That manual labour, properly directed, is the source of all wealth, and of national prosperity.

2nd. – That, when properly directed, labour is of far more value to the community than the expense necessary to maintain the labourer in considerable comfort.

3rd. – That manual labour, properly directed, may be made to continue of this value in all parts of the world, under any supposable increase of its population, for many centuries to come.

4th. – That, under a proper direction of manual labour, Great Britain and its dependencies may be made to support an incalculable increase of population, most advantageously for all its inhabitants.

5th. – That when manual labour shall be so directed, it will be found that population cannot, for many years, be stimulated to advance as rapidly as society might be benefited by its increase.

These considerations, deduced from the first and most obvious principles of the science of political economy, convinced your Reporter that some formidable artificial obstacle intervened to obstruct the natural improvement and progress of society.

It is well known that, during the last half century in particular, Great Britain, beyond any other nation, has progressively increased its powers of production, by a rapid advancement in scientific improvements and arrangements, introduced, more or less, into all the departments of productive industry throughout the empire.

The amount of this new productive power cannot, for want of proper data, be very accurately estimated; but your Reporter has ascertained from facts which none will dispute, that its increase has been enormous; – that, compared with the manual labour of the whole population of Great Britain and Ireland, it is, at least, as *forty to one*, and may be easily made as 100 *to one*; and that this increase may be extended to other countries; that it is already sufficient to saturate the world with wealth, and that the power of creating wealth may be made to advance perpetually in an accelerating ratio.

It appeared to your Reporter that the natural effect of the aid thus obtained from knowledge and science should be to add to the wealth and happiness of society in proportion as the new power increased and was judiciously directed; and that, in consequence, all parties would thereby be substantially benefited. All know, however, that these beneficial effects do not exist. On the contrary, it must be acknowledged that the working classes, which form so large a proportion of the population, cannot obtain even the comforts which their labour formerly procured for them, and that no party appears to gain, but all to suffer, by their distress.

Having taken this view of the subject, your Reporter was induced to conclude that the want of beneficial employment for the working classes, and the consequent public distress, were owing to the rapid increase of the new productive power, for the advantageous application of which, society had neglected to make the proper arrangements. Could these arrangements be formed, he entertained the most confident expectation that productive employment might again be found for all who required it; and that the national distress, of which all now so loudly complain, might be gradually converted into a much higher degree of prosperity than was attainable prior to the extraordinary accession lately made to the productive powers of society.

Cheered by such a prospect, your Reporter directed his attention to the consideration of the possibility of devising arrangements by means of which the whole population might participate in the benefits derivable from the increase of scientific productive power; and he has the satisfaction to state to the meeting, that he has strong grounds to believe that such arrangements are practicable.

His opinion on this important part of the subject is founded on the following considerations:

1st. – It must be admitted that scientific or artificial aid to man increases his productive powers, his natural wants remaining the same; and in proportion as his productive powers increase he becomes less dependent on his physical strength and on the many contingencies connected with it.

2nd. – That the direct effect of every addition to scientific, or mechanical and chemical power, is to increase wealth; and it is found, accordingly, that the immediate cause of the present want of employment for the working classes is an excess of production of all kinds of wealth, by which, under the existing arrangements of commerce, all the markets of the world are overstocked.

3rd. – That, could markets be found, an incalculable addition might yet be made to the wealth of society, as is most evident from the number of persons who seek employment, and the far greater number who, from ignorance, are inefficiently employed, but still more from the means we possess of increasing, to an unlimited extent, our scientific powers of production.

4th. – That the deficiency of employment for the working classes cannot proceed from a want of wealth or capital, or of the means of greatly adding to that which now exists, but from some defect in the mode of distributing this extraordinary addition of new capital throughout society, or, to speak commercially, from the want of a market, or means of exchange, co-extensive with the means of production.

Were effective measures devised to facilitate the distribution of wealth after it was created, your Reporter could have no difficulty in suggesting the means of beneficial occupation for all who are unemployed, and for a considerable increase to their number.

Your Reporter is aware that mankind are naturally averse to the commencement of any material alteration in long-established practices, and that, in many cases, such an innovation, however beneficial its tendency, cannot take place unless forced on society by strong necessity.

It is urgent necessity alone that will effect the changes which our present situation demands; one of which respects the mode of distributing the enormous supply of new wealth or capital which has been lately created, and which may be now indefinitely increased. To the ignorance which prevails on this and other subjects connected with the science of political economy may be attributed the present general stagnation of commerce, and the consequent distress of the country.

Your Reporter, undismayed by any opposition he may excite, is determined to perform his duty, and to use his utmost exertions to induce the Public to take into calm consideration those practical measures which to him appear the only remedy adequate to remove this distress.

One of the measures which he thus ventures to propose, *to let prosperity loose on the country*, (if he may be allowed the expression,) is *a change in the standard of value*.

It is true that in the civilised parts of the world gold and silver have been long used for this purpose; but these metals have been a mere artificial standard, and they have performed the office very imperfectly and inconveniently.

Their introduction as a standard of value altered the *intrinsic* values of all things into *artificial* values; and, in consequence, they have materially retarded the general improvement of society. So much so, indeed that, in this sense, it may well be said, 'Money is the root of all evil.'[a] It is fortunate for society that

[a] See 1 Timothy 6:10.

these metals cannot longer perform the task which ignorance assigned to them. The rapid increase of wealth, which extraordinary scientific improvements had been the means of producing in this country prior to 1797, imposed upon the Legislature in that year an overwhelming necessity to declare virtually by Act of Parliament that gold ceased to be the British standard of value.[a] Experience then proved that gold and silver could no longer practically represent the increased wealth created by British industry aided by its scientific improvements.

A temporary expedient was thought of and adopted, and Bank of England paper became the British legal standard of value; – a convincing proof that society may make any artificial substance, whether possessing intrinsic worth or not, a legal standard of value.

It soon appeared, however, that the adoption of this new artificial standard was attended with extreme danger, because it placed the prosperity and well-being of the community at the mercy of a trading company, which, although highly respectable in that capacity, was itself, in a great degree, ignorant of the nature of the mighty machine which it wielded. The Legislature, with almost one voice, demanded that this monopoly of the standard of value should cease. But it was wholly unprepared with a remedy. The expedient adopted was to make preparations for an attempt to return to the former artificial standard, which, in 1797, was proved by experience to be inadequate to represent the then existing wealth of British empire, and which was, of course, still more inadequate to the purpose when that wealth and the means of adding to it had been in the interim increased to an incalculable extent. This impolitic measure involved the Government in the most formidable difficulties, and plunged the country into poverty, discontent, and danger.

Seeing the distress which a slight progress towards the fulfilment of this measure has already occasioned, by the unparalleled depression of agriculture, commerce, and manufactures, and the consequent almost total annihilation of the value of labour, it is to be hoped that the Government and the Legislature, and the enlightened and reasonable part of society, will pause while they are yet only on the brink of the frightful abyss into which they are about to precipitate the prosperity and safety of themselves and the country.

The meeting may now justly ask of the Reporter, what remedy he has to offer, and what standard of value he proposes to substitute for gold and silver?

Before proceeding to this part of the subject he begs to claim the indulgence of the meeting for occupying so much of its time, trusting that the intricacy, difficulty, and importance of the question, added to the daily increasing poverty and distress of the working classes, (going on apparently without limitation,) and the consequent alarming and dangerous state of the country, will be accepted as some apology for him; and more especially when it is considered that

[b] Redemption of banknotes in gold was suspended by the Bank Restriction Act in 1797 and reintroduced in 1819, causing deflation.

he is not advocating any private interest, but simply stating a case in which the prosperity and well-being of all ranks in the community are deeply concerned.

To understand the subject on which your Reporter is now about to enter requires much profound study of the whole circle of political economy. A knowledge of some of its parts, with ignorance of the remainder, will be found to be most injurious to the practical statesman; and it is owing to this cause, perhaps, more than to any other, that the world has been so wretchedly governed; for the object of this science is to direct how the whole faculties of men may be most advantageously applied; whereas those powers have been combined, hitherto, chiefly to retard the improvements of society.

Your Reporter, then, after deeply studying these subjects, practically and theoretically, for a period exceeding thirty years, and during which his practice without a single exception has confirmed the theory which practice first suggested, now ventures to state, as one of the results of this study and experience,

THAT THE NATURAL STANDARD OF VALUE IS, IN PRINCIPLE, HUMAN LABOUR, OR THE COMBINED MANUAL AND MENTAL POWERS OF MEN CALLED INTO ACTION.

And that it would be highly beneficial, and has now become absolutely necessary, to reduce this principle into immediate practice.

It will be said, by those who have taken a superficial or mere partial view of the question, that human labour or power is so unequal in individuals, that its average amount cannot be estimated.

Already, however, the average physical power of men as well as of horses, (equally varied in the individuals,) has been calculated for scientific purposes, and both now serve to measure inanimate powers.

On the same principle the average of human labour or power may be ascertained; and as it forms the essence of all wealth, its value in every article of produce may also be ascertained, and its exchangeable value with all other values fixed accordingly; the whole to be permanent for a given period.

Human labour would thus acquire its natural or intrinsic value, which would increase as science advanced; and this is, in fact, the only really useful object of science.

The demand for human labour would be no longer subject to caprice, nor would the support of human life be made, as at present, a perpetually varying article of commerce, and the working classes made the slaves of an artificial system of wages, more cruel in its effects than any slavery ever practised by society, either barbarous or civilised.

This change in the standard of value would immediately open the most advantageous domestic markets, until the wants of all were amply supplied; nor while this standard continued could any evil arise in future from the want of markets.

It would secure the means for the most unlimited and advantageous intercourse and exchange with other nations, without compromising national interests, and enable all governments to withdraw every existing injurious commercial restriction.

It would render unnecessary and entirely useless the present demoralising system of bargaining between individuals; and no practice perhaps tends more than this to deteriorate and degrade the human character.

It would speedily remove pauperism and ignorance from society, by furnishing time and means for the adequate instruction of the working classes, who might be rendered of far more commercial value to themselves and to society than they have yet been at any period of the world.

It would supply the means of gradually improving the condition of all ranks, to an extent not yet to be estimated.

And, as it would materially improve human nature, and raise all in the scale of well-being and happiness, none could be injured or oppressed.

These are some of the important advantages which would arise (when due preparation shall be made for the change,) from introducing the natural standard of value, and abandoning an artificial one, which can no longer serve the purpose.

It now remains to be considered how this change can be effected without creating temporary confusion.

To accomplish this desirable object, several legislative measures will be necessary.

The first, as an intermediate and temporary one, to put a stop to the increasing pecuniary distress of the working classes, will be to relieve the country from the ruinous effects which have been produced by the various attempts to compel a return to cash payments; a longer perseverance in which is calculated to derange the whole of the existing social system. The attempt will prove as vain as to try to restore a full-grown bird to the shell in which it was hatched, or to make the clothes of an infant cover a giant; for the improvements of society have equally outgrown the late system of cash payments. Should the attempt be persevered in, no more wealth will be created, and much of that which is now considered wealth will be destroyed. A perseverance in such a course will compel the working classes to starve or emigrate, while the present higher orders will be left an easy prey to their enemies and to poverty. No real benefit could arise to any party from a return to cash payments, if such a measure were practicable.

The next step is to adopt such measures as will permit the labouring unoccupied poor to be employed to raise their own subsistence, and as large a surplus for the infant, the aged, and the incapacitated poor, as their labour can be made to yield; the labourer to receive an equitable remuneration for the surplus he may create.

But the industry of the poor, thus applied, will tend still further to overstock the markets of the world with agricultural and manufactured produce, and, in the same proportion to decrease the *nominal or monied prices* of both, and of course add to the public distress.

It is this view of the subject that has induced your Reporter so strongly to urge those who take a lead in the affairs of this populous and distressed county to come forward at this critical juncture to recommend to the Government, and to petition the Legislature, to take into their most serious consideration such means as may be proposed to remove the existing obstructions in the way of the general prosperity of the country.

It is the want of a profitable market that alone checks the successful and otherwise beneficial industry of the working classes.

The markets of the world are created solely by the remuneration allowed for the industry of the working classes, and those markets are more or less extended and profitable in proportion as these classes are well or ill remunerated for their labour.

But the existing arrangements of society will not permit the labourer to be remunerated for his industry, and in consequence all markets fail.

To re-create and extend demand in proportion as the late scientific improvements, and others which are daily advancing to perfection, extend the means of supply, the natural standard of value is required.

It will be found equal to the important task which it has to perform.

It will at once remove the obstruction which has paralysed the industry of the country; and experience will prove that this effect cannot be accomplished by any other expedient.

Your Reporter, having given the foregoing general explanation of the principles which his experience leads him to recommend for adoption to relieve the country from its distress and danger, will now proceed to a development of all the measures necessary to put these principles into practice.

PART II

Outlines of the Plan

It is admitted that under the present system no more hands can be employed advantageously in agriculture or manufactures; and that both interests are on the eve of bankruptcy.

It is also admitted that the prosperity of the country, or rather that which ought to create prosperity, the improvement in mechanical and chemical science, has enabled the population to produce more than the present system permits to be consumed.

In consequence, new arrangements become necessary, by which *consumption* may be made to keep pace with *production* and the following are recommended:

1st. – To cultivate the soil with the spade instead of the plough.

2nd. – To make such changes as the spade cultivation requires, to render it easy and profitable to individuals, and beneficial to the country.

3rd. – To adopt a standard of value by means of which the exchange of the products of labour may proceed without check or limit, until wealth shall become so abundant that any further increase to it will be considered useless, and will not be desired.

We proceed to give the reasons for recommending these arrangements in preference to all others.

And first, those for preferring the spade to the plough for the universal cultivation of the soil.

Practical cultivators of the soil know, that the most favourable circumstance for promoting the growth of vegetation is a due supply of moisture, and that when this is provided for, a good general crop seldom, if ever, fails.

Water enters so largely into the food of all plants, that if its gradual supply can be secured, the farmer and horticulturist feel assured of a fair return for their labour. Whatever mode of cultivation, therefore, can best effect the object of drawing off from the seed or plant an excess of water, and retaining this surplus as a reservoir from which a gradual supply of moisture may be obtained as required, must possess decided advantages.

It is also known to all practical agriculturists, that to obtain the best crops, the soil ought to be well broken and separated; and that the nearer it is brought to a garden mould, the more perfect is the cultivation.

These facts no one will dispute, nor will any deny that the spade is calculated to prepare a better recipient than the plough for an excess of water in rainy seasons, and to return it to the seed or plant afterwards in a manner most favourable to vegetation.

The spade, whenever there is sufficient soil, opens it to a depth that allows the water to pass freely below the bed of the seed or plant, and to remain there until a long continuance of heat draws it forth again to replenish the crop in the ground when it most requires to be gradually supplied with moisture; and the greater the depth to which the soil is opened, the greater will be the advantage of this important operation. Hence the increased crops after deep ploughing, and after trenching, although the latter process may be also in some degree assisted by the new or rested soil which it brings into action; yet both these effects are obtained by the use of the spade.

The action of the plough upon the soil is the reverse of that of the spade in the following important particulars: –

Instead of *loosening* the subsoil, it *hardens* it; the heavy smooth surface of the plough, and the frequent trampling of the horses' feet, tend to form a surface on the subsoil, well calculated to prevent the water from penetrating below it; and in many soils, after a few years' ploughing, it is there retained to drown the seed or plant in rainy seasons, and to be speedily evaporated when it would be the most desirable to retain it. Thus the crop is injured, and often destroyed, in dry weather, for the want of that moisture which, under a different system, might have been retained in the subsoil.

It is evident, therefore, that the plough conceals from the eye its own imperfections, and deceives its employers, being in truth a *mere surface implement*, and extremely defective in principle.

The spade, on the contrary, makes a good subsoil, as well as a superior surface, and the longer it is used on the same soil, the more easily will it be worked; and by occasional trenching, where there is sufficient depth of soil, new earth will be brought into action, and the benefits to be derived from a well prepared subsoil will be increased.

These facts being incontrovertible, few perhaps will hesitate to admit them.

But it may be said that, 'admitting the statement to be true to the full extent, yet the plough, with a pair of horses and one man, performs so much work in a given time, that, with all its imperfections, it may be a more economical instrument for the purpose required.'

Such has been the almost universal impression for ages past, and, in consequence, the plough has superseded the spade, and is considered to be an improved machine for ordinary cultivation.

All this is plausible, and is sanctioned by the old prejudices of the world; but your Reporter maintains that it is not true that the plough is, or has ever been, in any stage of society, the most economical instrument for the cultivation of the soil. It has been so in appearance only, not in reality.

Cultivated as the soil has been hitherto, the direct expense of preparing it by the plough (in the manner in which the plough prepares it,) has been in many cases less per acre than it would have been by the spade. The increased crop which the latter implement would have produced, all other circumstances being the same, does not seem to have been taken into account, or to have been accurately ascertained, except by Mr Falla, of Gateshead, near Newcastle, who, for many years, has had a hundred acres under spade cultivation, chiefly for nursery purposes, and who, by his practical knowledge of the subject, has realised, as your Reporter is informed, a large fortune.[a] He has satisfactorily proved, by the experiments of four successive years, (for the particulars of which see the Appendix to this Report), that although the expense of cultivation by the spade exceeds that of the plough per acre, yet the increased value of the crop greatly overbalances the increased expense of cultivation, and that even with 'things as they are' the spade is a much better, and also a much more economical instrument with which to cultivate the soil, than the plough.

Why, then, your Reporter may be asked, is not the spade more generally used, and why is there now so much reluctance, on the part of those who cultivate the soil for profit, to its introduction?

---

[a] William Falla (1761–1830) was a Nonconformist nurseryman at Gateshead who inherited his father's business in 1804 and specialised in forest trees. Though renowned as an advocate of spade husbandry, he also approved of and adopted new machinery, like the iron plough. For his relations with Owen, see Owen, *Life*, vol. 1A (1858), pp. 314–20.

A little will explain this.

Hitherto, those who have cultivated the soil for profit have generally been men trained to be tenacious of old established practices, all their ideas have been confined within a very narrow range; they have not been taught to think about anything, till lately, except that which was in the common routine of their daily practice. Their minds were uncultivated; yet, having naturally the use of their senses, they could not fail gradually to acquire by experience a useful knowledge of their domestic animals, of pigs, sheep, cattle, and horses. These they could treat and manage well; but, taught as men have ever yet been instructed, they could acquire no knowledge of themselves, and must have consequently remained ignorant of human nature and of the means by which the powers of *men* could be applied more advantageously to the soil than the powers of *animals*. The system in which man has been hitherto trained, so far as our knowledge of history extends, has kept him in utter ignorance of himself and his fellows; and hence the best and most valuable powers of the human race could not be made available for their own well-being and happiness. And if the most enlightened disciples of this system have been incapable of governing human beings aright, and of giving a beneficial direction to their powers, much less could those be equal to the task, whose knowledge of men was necessarily more confined, as is the case with farmers of the present day. These can better direct the employment of ten horses than ten men; and yet the spade husbandry would require that each horse now in use should be superseded by eight or ten human beings; and, to succeed in the business, an economical direction of their powers, which implies a knowledge of human nature in all respects, ought to be as well understood by those who conduct the spade operations, as the nature and management of horses are by farmers of the present day. For this change the cultivators of the soil are not prepared; and however more profitable the spade husbandry may be proved to be than the plough, they are not yet competent to undertake it. Many *preparatory* changes are necessary.

They must acquire as accurate a knowledge of *human* nature as they now possess of common *animal* nature. Agriculture, instead of being, as heretofore, the occupation of the mere peasant and farmer, with minds as defective in their cultivation as their soils, will then become the delightful employment of a race of men trained in the best habits and dispositions, familiar with the most useful practice in arts and sciences, and with minds fraught with the most valuable information and extensive general knowledge, – capable of forming and conducting combined arrangements in agriculture, trade, commerce, and manufactures, far superior to those which have yet existed in any of these departments, as they have been hitherto disjointed and separately conducted.

It will be readily perceived that this is an advance in civilisation and general improvement that is to be effected solely *through the science of the influence of circumstances over human nature, and the knowledge of the means by which those circumstances may be easily controlled.*

Closet theorists and inexperienced persons suppose that to exchange the plough for the spade would be to turn back in the road of improvement, – to give up a superior for an inferior implement of cultivation. Little do they imagine that the introduction of the spade, with the scientific arrangements which it requires, will produce far greater improvements in agriculture, than the steam engine has effected in manufactures. Still less do they imagine that the change from the plough to the spade will prove to be a far more extensive and beneficial innovation than that which the invention of the spinning machine has occasioned, by the introduction of which, instead of the single wheel in a corner of a farm house, we now see thousands of spindles revolving with the noise of a waterfall in buildings palace-like for their cost, magnitude, and appearance.

Yet this extraordinary change is at hand. It will immediately take place; for the interest and well-being of all classes require it. Society cannot longer proceed another step in advance without it; and until it is adopted, civilisation must retrograde, and the working classes starve for want of employment.

The introduction of the steam engine and the spinning machine added in an extraordinary manner to the powers of human nature. In their consequences they have in half a century multiplied the productive power, or the means of creating wealth, among the population of these islands, more than twelve-fold, besides giving a great increase to the means of creating wealth in other countries.

The steam engine and spinning machines, with the endless mechanical inventions to which they have given rise, have, however, inflicted evils on society, which now greatly over-balance the benefits which are derived from them. They have created an aggregate of wealth, and placed it in the hands of a few, who, by its aid, continue to absorb the wealth produced by the industry of the many. Thus the mass of the population are become mere slaves to the ignorance and caprice of these monopolists, and are far more truly helpless and wretched than they were before the names of WATT and ARKWRIGHT were known. Yet these celebrated and ingenious men have been the instruments of preparing society for the important beneficial changes which are about to occur.

All now know and feel that the good which these inventions are calculated to impart to the community has not yet been realised. The condition of society, instead of being improved, has been deteriorated, under the new circumstances to which they have given birth; and it is now experiencing a retrograde movement.

'Something, therefore, must be done,' as the general voice exclaims, to give to our suffering population, and to society at large, the means of deriving from these inventions the advantages which all men of science expect from them.

In recommending the change from the plough to the spade cultivation your Reporter has in view such scientific arrangements, as, he is persuaded, will, on due examination, convince every intelligent mind that they offer the only means by which we can be relieved from our present overwhelming difficulties, or by which Great Britain can be enabled to maintain in future her rank among nations. They are the only effectual remedy for the evils which the steam engine and the spinning machine have, by their mis-direction, created, and are alone capable of giving a real and substantial value to these and other scientific inventions. Of all our splendid improvements in art and science the effect has hitherto been to demoralise society, through the misapplication of the new wealth created.

The arrangements to which your Reporter now calls the attention of the Public, present the certain means of renovating the moral character, and of improving, to an unlimited extent, the general condition of the population, and, while they lead to a far more rapid multiplication of wealth than the present system permits to take place, they will effectually preclude all the evils with which wealth is now accompanied.

It is estimated that in Great Britain and Ireland there are now under cultivation upwards of *sixty millions* of acres; and of these, *twenty millions* are arable, and *forty millions* in pasture; – that, under the present system of cultivation by the plough and of pasturing, about *two millions*, at most, of *actual labourers* are employed on the soil, giving immediate support to about *three times* that number, and supplying food for a population of about *eighteen millions*. *Sixty millions* of acres, under a judicious arrangement of spade cultivation, with manufactures as an appendage, might be made to give healthy advantageous employment to *sixty millions* of labourers at the least, and to support, in high comfort a population greatly exceeding *one hundred millions*. But in the present low state of population in these islands not more than *five or six millions* of acres could be properly cultivated by the spade, although all the operative manufacturers were to be chiefly employed in this mode of agriculture. Imperfect, therefore, as the plough is for the cultivation of the soil, it is probable that, in this country, for want of an adequate population, many centuries will elapse before it can be entirely superseded by the spade; yet under the plough system Great Britain and Ireland are even now supposed to be greatly over-peopled.

It follows from this statement, that we possess the means of supplying the labouring poor, however numerous they may be, with permanent beneficial employment for many centuries to come.

The spade husbandry has been proved, by well-devised and accurately conducted experiments, to be a profitable mode of cultivation. It is now become also absolutely necessary, to give relief to the working classes, and it may be safely calculated upon as the certain source of future permanent occupation for them. [See communication from Mr Falla, of Gateshead, at the end.][a]

The next consideration which demands our attention is, – what constitutes a proper system of spade husbandry? – or, in other words, *how these new cultivators*

[a] See Owen, *Life*, vol. 1A (1858), pp. 314–20.

can be placed on the soil and associated, that their exertions may have the most beneficial result for themselves and the community?

The leading principle which should direct us in the outline of this arrangement, and from which there should be no deviation in any of its parts, is the public good, or the general interest of the whole population.

To this end, the following considerations must be combined.

1st. – Where, in general, can the labourers be best placed for spade cultivation?

2nd. – What is the quantity of land which it may be the most advantageous to cultivate *in cumulo* by the spade?

3rd. – What number of workmen can be the most beneficially employed together, with a view to all the objects of their labour?

4th. – What are the best arrangements under which these men and their families can be well and economically *lodged, fed, clothed, trained, educated, employed* and *governed?*

5th. – What is the best mode of disposing of the surplus produce to be thus created by their labour?

6th. – What are the means best calculated to render the conduct and industry of these workmen beneficial to their neighbours, to their country, and to foreign nations?

These are some of the leading objects which naturally arise for our consideration in forming arrangements for the introduction of the spade as a substitute for the plough cultivation.

To substitute the spade for the plough may seem most trivial in the expression; and to inexperienced, and even to learned men, – to my respected friends the Edinburgh Reviewers,[a] for instance, who cannot be supposed to have much useful practical knowledge, – will appear to indicate a change equally simple and unimportant in practice.

It generally happens, however, that when a great calamity overwhelms a country, relief is obtained from practical men, and not from mere theorists, however acute, learned, and eloquent. In the present case, simple as at first appears to be the alteration proposed, yet, when the mind of the practical agriculturist, of the commercial man, of the man of science, of the political economist, of the statesman, and of the philosopher, shall be directed to the subject as its importance demands, the change will be found to be one of the deepest interest to society, involving consequences of much higher concernment to the well-being of mankind than the change from hunting to the pastoral state, or from the pastoral state to the plough cultivation.[b]

[a] The *Edinburgh Review* was the leading organ of the classical political economists. Founded in 1802, it was edited by Francis Jeffrey, Francis Horner, and Henry Brougham.

[b] Scottish theorists in particular commonly classified the evolution of society into hunting and gathering, pastoral, agricultural and commercial stages. See Ronald Meek, *Social Science and the Ignoble Savage* (Cambridge: Cambridge University Press, 1976).

The change comes, too, at a crisis most momentous for the safety of the civilised world, to re-unite the most jarring interests, which were on the extreme point of severing all the old connections of society.

It comes, too, at a period when the force of circumstances has trained men, even by the destructive art of war, to understand in part the extraordinary effects which may be produced by well-devised arrangements and extensive combinations.

It has occurred, too, at the first moment when experience has, in some degree, prepared men to comprehend the superior advantages which each may gain by attending to the great interests of human nature, rather than to the mistaken feeling and policy which rivet the whole attention of the individual to benefit himself, or his party, through any other medium than the public good.

Were the subject now before us to be entered upon with more confined views of its interest, magnitude, and importance, it would fail to be understood, and justice could not be done to it. Yet how few of the celebrated political economists of the day have their minds prepared for this investigation!

Having given the outline of the considerations which show the superiority in principle of the spade over the plough as a scientific and economical instrument of cultivation; – having also described briefly the objects to be attended to in forming economical arrangements for the change proposed: – it now remains that the principle should be generally explained by which an advantageous interchange and exchange may be made of the greatly increased products of labour which will be created by the spade cultivation aided by the improved arrangements now contemplated.

These incalculably increased products will render gold, the old artificial standard of value, far more unfit for the task which is to be performed, than it was in 1797, when it ceased to be the British legal standard of value, or than it is now, when wealth has so much increased.

Your Reporter is of opinion that *the natural standard of human labour*, fixed to represent its natural worth, or power of creating new wealth, will alone be found adequate to the purposes required.

To a mind coming first to this subject, innumerable and apparently insurmountable difficulties will occur; but by the steady application of that fixed and persevering attention which is alone calculated successfully to contend against and overcome difficulties, every obstacle will vanish, and the practice will prove simple and easy.

That which can create new wealth is of course worth the wealth which it creates. Human labour, whenever, common justice shall be done to human beings, can now be applied to produce, advantageously for all ranks in society, many times the amount of wealth that is necessary to support the individual in considerable comfort. Of this new wealth, so created, the labourer who produces it is justly entitled to his fair proportion; and the best interests of every community require that the producer should have a fair and fixed proportion of all the wealth which he creates. This can be assigned to him on no other principle than by forming arrangements by which the *natural* standard of value shall become the *practical* standard of value. To make labour the standard of value it is necessary to ascertain the amount of it in all articles to be bought and sold. This is, in fact, already accomplished, and is denoted by what in commerce is technically termed 'the prime cost,' or the net value of the whole labour contained in any article of value, – the material contained in or consumed by the manufacture of the article forming a part of the whole labour.

The great object of society is, to obtain wealth, and to enjoy it. The genuine principle of barter was, to exchange the supposed prime cost of, or value of labour in, one article, against the prime cost of, or amount of labour contained in any other article. This is the only equitable principle of exchange; but, as inventions increased and human desires multiplied, it was found to be inconvenient in practice. Barter was succeeded by commerce, the principle of which is, to produce or procure every article at the *lowest,* and to obtain for it, in exchange, the *highest* amount of labour. To effect this, an artificial standard of value was necessary; and metals were, by common consent among nations, permitted to perform the office.[a]

This principle, in the progress of its operation, has been productive of important advantages, and of very great evils; but, like barter, it has been suited to a certain stage of society.

It has stimulated invention; it has given industry and talent to the human character; and has secured the future exertion of those energies which otherwise might have remained dormant and unknown.

But it has made man ignorantly, individually selfish; placed him in opposition to his fellows; engendered fraud and deceit; blindly urged him forward to create, but deprived him of the wisdom to enjoy. In striving to take advantage of others he has over-reached himself. The strong hand of necessity will now force him into the path which conducts to that wisdom in which he has been so long deficient. He will discover the advantages to be derived from uniting in practice the best parts of the principles of barter and commerce, and dismissing those which experience has proved to be inconvenient and injurious.

This substantial improvement in the progress of society may be easily effected by exchanging all articles with each other at their prime cost, or with reference to the amount of labour in each, which can be equitably ascertained, and by permitting the exchange to be made through a convenient medium to represent this value, and which will thus represent a real and unchanging value, and be issued only as substantial wealth increases.

---

[a] On the emergence of exchange from barter, see for example Adam Smith, *Wealth of Nations* (1776), Bk 1, ch. 4.

The profit of production will arise, in all cases, from the value of the labour contained in the article produced, and it will be for the interest of society that this profit should be most ample. Its exact amount will depend upon what, by strict examination, shall be proved to be the present real value of a day's labour; calculated with reference to the amount of wealth, in the necessaries and comforts of life, which an average labourer may, by temperate exertions, be now made to produce.

It would require an accurate and extended consideration of the existing state of society to determine the exact value of the unit or day's labour which society ought now to fix as a standard of value: – but a more slight and general view of the subject is sufficient to show, that this unit need not represent a less value than the wealth contained in the necessaries and comforts of life which may now be purchased with five shillings.

The landholder and capitalist would be benefited by this arrangement in the same degree with the labourer; because labour is the foundation of all values, and it is only from labour, liberally remunerated, that high profits can be paid for agricultural and manufactured products.

Depressed as the value of labour now is, there is no proposition in Euclid more true, than that society would be immediately benefited, in a great variety of ways, to an incalculable extent, by making labour the standard of value.

By this expedient all the markets in the world, which are now virtually closed against offering a profit to the producers of wealth, would be opened to an unlimited extent; and in each individual exchange all the parties interested would be sure to receive ample remuneration for their labour.

Before this change can be carried into effect, various preparatory measures will be necessary; the explanatory details of which will naturally succeed the development of those arrangements which your Reporter has to propose, to give all the advantages to the spade cultivation, of which that system of husbandry is susceptible.

PART III

Details of the Plan

This part of the Report naturally divides itself under the following heads, each of which shall be considered separately, and the whole, afterwards, in connection, as forming an improved practical system for the working classes, highly beneficial, in whatever light it may be viewed, to every part of society.

1st. – The number of persons who can be associated to give the greatest advantages to themselves and to the community.

2nd. – The extent of the land to be cultivated by such association.

3rd. – The arrangements for feeding, lodging, and clothing the population, and for training and educating the children.

4th. – Those for forming and superintending the establishments.

5th. – The disposal of the surplus produce, and the relation which will subsist between the several establishments.

6th. – Their connection with the government of the country and with general society.

The first object, then, of the political economist, in forming these arrangements, must be, to consider well *under what limitation of numbers, individuals should be associated to form the first nucleus or division of society*.

All his future proceedings will be materially influenced by the decision of this point, which is one of the most difficult problems in the science of political economy. It will affect essentially the future character of individuals, and influence the general proceedings of mankind.

It is, in fact, the corner-stone of the whole fabric of human society. The consequences, immediate and remote, which depend upon it, are so numerous and important, that to do justice to this part of the arrangement alone would require a work of many volumes.

To form anything resembling a rational opinion on this subject, the mind must steadily survey the various effects which have arisen from associations which accident has hitherto combined in the history of the human species; and it should have a distinct idea of the results which other associations are capable of producing.

Thus impressed with the magnitude and importance of the subject, after many years of deep and anxious reflection, and viewing it with reference to an improved spade cultivation, and to all the purposes of society, your Reporter ventures to recommend the formation of such arrangements as will unite about 300 men, women, and children, in their natural proportions, as the *minimum*, and about 2,000 as the *maximum*, for the future associations of the cultivators of the soil, who will be employed also in such additional occupations as may be advantageously annexed to it.

In coming to this conclusion your Reporter never lost sight of that only sure guide to the political economist, the principle, *that it is the interest of all men, whatever may be their present artificial station in society, that there should be the largest amount of intrinsically valuable produce created, at the least expense of labour, and in a way the most advantageous to the producers and society*.

Whatever fanciful notions may govern the mere closet theorist, who so often leads the public mind astray from its true course, the practical economist will never come to any one conclusion that is inconsistent with the foregoing fundamental principle of his science, well knowing that where there is inconsistency there *must be* error.

It is with reference to this principle that the minimum and maximum above stated (viz. 300 and 2,000,) have been fixed upon, as will be more particularly developed under the subsequent heads.

Within this range more advantages can be given to the individuals and to society, than by the association of any greater or lesser number.

But from 800 to 1,200 will be found the most desirable number to form into agricultural villages; and unless some very strong local causes interfere, the permanent arrangements should be adapted to the complete accommodation of that amount of population only.

Villages of this extent, in the neighbourhood of others of a similar description, at due distances, will be found capable of combining within themselves all the advantages that city and country residences now afford, without any of the numerous inconveniences and evils which necessarily attach to both those modes of society.

But a very erroneous opinion will be formed of the proposed arrangements and the social advantages which they will exhibit, if it should be imagined from what has been said that they will in any respect resemble any of the present agricultural villages of Europe, or the associated communities in America, except in so far as the latter may be founded *on the principle of united labour, expenditure, and property, and equal privileges.*

Recommending, then, from 300 to 2,000 according to the localities of the farm or village, as the number of persons who should compose the associations for the new system of spade husbandry, we now proceed to consider –

2nd. – *The extent of land to be cultivated by such association.* This will depend upon the quality of soil and other local considerations.

Great Britain and Ireland, however, do not possess a population nearly sufficient to cultivate our *best* soils in the most advantageous manner. It would therefore be nationally impolitic to place these associations upon *inferior* lands, which, in consequence, may be dismissed from present consideration.

Society, ever misled by closet theorists, has committed almost every kind of error in practice, and in no instance perhaps a greater, than in separating the workman from his food, and making his existence depend upon the labour and uncertain supplies of others, as is the case under our present manufacturing system; and it is a vulgar error to suppose that a single individual more can be supported by means of such a system than without it; on the contrary, a whole population engaged in agriculture, with manufactures as an appendage, will, in a given district, support many more, and in a much higher degree of comfort, than the same district could do with its agricultural separate from its manufacturing population.

Improved arrangements for the working classes will, in almost all cases, place the workman in the midst of his food, which it will be as beneficial for him to create as to consume.

Sufficient land, therefore, will be allotted to these cultivators to enable them to raise an abundant supply of food and the necessaries of life for themselves, and as much additional agricultural produce as the public demands may require from such a portion of the population.

Under a well devised arrangement for the working classes they will all procure for themselves the necessaries and comforts of life in so short a time, and so easily and pleasantly, that the occupation will be experienced to be little more than a recreation, sufficient to keep them in the best health and spirits for rational enjoyment of life.

The surplus produce from the soil will be required only for the higher classes, those who live without manual labour, and those whose nice manual operations will not permit them at any time to be employed in agriculture and gardening.

Of the latter, very few, if any, will be necessary, as mechanism may be made to supersede such operations, which are almost always injurious to health.

Under this view of the subject, the quantity of land which it would be the most beneficial for these associations to cultivate, with reference to their own well-being and the interests of society, will probably be from half an acre to an acre and a half for each individual.

An association, therefore, of 1,200 persons, would require from 600 to 1,800 statute acres, according as it may be intended to be more or less agricultural.

Thus, when it should be thought expedient that the chief surplus products should consist in manufactured commodities, the lesser quantity of land would be sufficient; if a large surplus from the produce of the soil were deemed desirable, the greater quantity would be allotted; and when the localities of the situation should render it expedient for the association to create an equal surplus quantity of each, the medium quantity, or 1,200 acres, would be the most suitable.

It follows that land under the proposed system of husbandry would be divided into farms of from 150 to 3,000 acres, but generally perhaps from 800 to 1,500 acres. This division of the land will be found to be productive of incalculable benefits in practice; it will give all the advantages, without any of the disadvantages of small and large farms.

The next head for consideration is –

3rd. – *The arrangement for feeding, lodging, and clothing the population, and for training and educating the children.*

It being always most convenient for the workman to reside near to his employment, the site for the dwellings of the cultivators will be chosen as near to the centre of the land, as water, proper levels, dry situation, etc, may admit; and as courts, alleys, lanes, and streets create many unnecessary inconveniences, are injurious to health, and destructive to almost all the natural comforts of human life, they will be excluded, and a disposition of the buildings free from these objections and greatly more economical will be adopted.

As it will afterwards appear that the food for the whole population can be provided better and cheaper under one general arrangement of cooking,[a] and that the children can be better trained and educated together under the eye of their parents than under any other circumstances, a large square, or rather parallelogram, will be found to combine the greatest advantages in its form for the domestic arrangements of the association.

This form, indeed, affords so many advantages for the comfort of human life, that if great ignorance respecting the means necessary to secure good conduct and happiness among the working classes had not prevailed in all ranks, it must long ago have become universal.

It admits of a most simple, easy, convenient, and economical arrangement for all the purposes required.

The four sides of this figure may be adapted to contain all the private apartments or sleeping and sitting rooms for the adult part of the population; general sleeping apartments for the children while under tuition; store-rooms, or warehouses in which to deposit various products; an inn, or house for the accommodation of strangers; an infirmary, etc, etc.

In a line across the centre of the parallelogram, leaving free space for air and light and easy communication, might be erected the church, or places for worship; the schools; kitchen and apartments for eating; all in the most convenient situation for the whole population, and under the best possible public superintendence, without trouble, expense, or inconvenience to any party.

The advantages of this general domestic arrangement can only be known and appreciated by those who have had great experience in the beneficial results of extensive combinations in improving the condition of the working classes, and whose minds, advancing beyond the petty range of individual party interests, have been calmly directed to consider what may now be attained by a well-devised association of human powers for the benefit of all ranks. It is such individuals only who can detect the present total want of foresight in the conduct of society, and its gross misapplication of the most valuable and abundant means of securing prosperity. They can distinctly perceive that the blind are leading the blind from difficulties to dangers, which they feel to increase at every step.

The parallelogram being found to be the best form in which to dispose the dwelling and chief domestic arrangements for the proposed associations of cultivators, it will be useful now to explain the principles on which those arrangements have been formed.

The first in order, and the most necessary, are those respecting food.

It has been, and still is, a received opinion among theorists in political

---

[a] For Owen's attempt to introduce common kitchens at New Lanark, see *infra*, vol. 1, p. xx.

economy, that man can provide better for himself, and more advantageously for the public, when left to his own individual exertions, opposed to and in competition with his fellows, than when aided by any social arrangement which shall unite his interests individually and generally with society.[a]

This principle of individual interest, opposed as it is perpetually to the public good, is considered, by the most celebrated political economists, to be the corner-stone to the social system, and without which, society could not subsist.

Yet when they shall know themselves, and discover the wonderful effects which combination and union can produce, they will acknowledge that the present arrangement of society is the most anti-social, impolitic, and irrational, that can be devised; that under its influence all the superior and valuable qualities of human nature are repressed from infancy, and that the most unnatural means are used to bring out the most injurious propensities; in short, that the utmost pains are taken to make that which by nature is the most delightful compound for producing excellence and happiness, absurd, imbecile, and wretched.

Such is the conduct now pursued by those who are called the best and wisest of the present generation, although there is not one rational object to be gained by it.

From this principle of individual interest have arisen all the divisions of mankind, the endless errors and mischiefs of class, sect, party, and of national antipathies, creating the angry and malevolent passions, and all the crimes and misery with which the human race have been hitherto afflicted.

In short, if there be one closet doctrine more contrary to truth than another, it is the notion that individual interest, as that term is now understood, is a more advantageous principle on which to found the social system, for the benefit of all, or of any, than the principle of union and mutual co-operation.

The former acts like an immense weight to repress the most valuable faculties and dispositions, and to give a wrong direction to all human powers. It is one of those magnificent errors, (if the expression may be allowed,) that when enforced in practice brings ten thousand evils in its train. The principle on which these economists proceed, instead of adding to the wealth of nations or of individuals, is itself the sole cause of poverty; and but for its operation wealth would long ago have ceased to be a subject of contention in any part of the world. If, it may be asked, experience has proved that union, combination, and extensive arrangement among mankind, are a thousand times more powerful to destroy, than the efforts of an unconnected multitude, where each acts individually for himself, – would not a similar increased effect be produced by

[a] See for example Adam Smith, *Wealth of Nations* (1776), Bk 5, ch. 2: 'It is not from the benevolence of the butcher, the brewer, or the baker that we expect our dinner, but from their regard to their own interest'.

union, combination, and extensive arrangement, to *create and conserve?* Why should not the result be the same in the one case as in the other? But it is well known that a combination of men and of interests can effect that which it would be futile to attempt, and impossible to accomplish, by individual exertions and separate interests. Then why, it may be inquired, have men so long acted individually, and in opposition to each other? This is an important question, and merits the most serious attention.

Men have not yet been trained in principles that will permit them *to act in union*, except to defend themselves or to destroy others. For self-preservation they were early compelled to unite for these purposes in war. A necessity, however, equally powerful, will now compel men to be trained to act together to *create and conserve*, that, in like manner, they may preserve life in peace. Fortunately for mankind the system of individual opposing interests has now reached the extreme point of error and inconsistency; – in the midst of the most ample means to create wealth, all are in poverty, or in imminent danger from the effects of poverty upon others.

The reflecting part of mankind have admitted, in theory, that the characters of men are formed chiefly by the circumstances in which they are placed; yet the science of the influence of circumstances, which is the most important of all the sciences, remains unknown for the great practical business of life. When it shall be fully developed it will be discovered that to unite the mental faculties of men for the attainment of pacific and civil objects will be a far more easy task than it has been to combine their physical powers to carry on extensive war-like preparations.

The discovery of the distance and movements of the heavenly bodies, – of the time-piece, – of a vessel to navigate the most distant parts of the ocean, – of the steam-engine, which performs under the easy control of one man the labour of many thousands, – and of the press, by which knowledge and improvement may be speedily given to the most ignorant in all parts of the earth, – these have, indeed, been discoveries of high import to mankind; but, important as these and others have been in their effects on the condition of human society, their combined benefits in practice will fall far short of those which will be speedily attained by the new intellectual power which men will acquire through the knowledge of 'the science of the influence of circumstances over the whole conduct, character, and proceedings of the human race.' By this latter discovery, more will be accomplished in one year, for the well-being of human nature, including, without any exceptions, all ranks and descriptions of men, than has ever yet been effected in one or in many centuries. Strange as this language may seem to those whose minds have not yet had a glimpse of the real state in which society now is, it will prove to be not more strange than true.

Are not the mental energies of the world at this moment in a state of high effervescence? – Is not society at a stand, incompetent to proceed in its present course? – And do not all men cry out that 'something must be done?' – That 'something' to produce the effect desired, must be a complete renovation of the whole social compact; one not forced on prematurely, by confusion and violence; not one to be brought about by the futile measures of the Radicals, Whigs, or Tories, of Britain, – the Liberals or Royalists of France, – the Illuminati[a] of Germany, or the mere party proceedings of any little local portion of human beings, trained as they have hitherto been in almost every kind of error, and without any true knowledge of themselves.

No! The change sought for must be preceded by the clear development of a great and universal principle which shall unite in one all the petty jarring interests, by which, till now, human nature has been made a most inveterate enemy to itself.

No! Extensive, – nay, rather, universal, – as the re-arrangement of society must be, to relieve it from the difficulties with which it is now overwhelmed, it will be effected in peace and quietness, with the goodwill and hearty concurrence of all parties, and of every people. It will necessarily commence by common consent, on account of its advantage, almost simultaneously among all civilised nations; and, once begun, will daily advance with an accelerating ratio, unopposed, and bearing down before it the existing systems of the world. The only astonishment then will be that such systems could so long have existed.

Under the new arrangements which will succeed them, no complaints of any kind will be heard in society. The causes of the evils that exist will become evident to every one, as well as the natural means of easily withdrawing those causes. These, by common consent, will be removed, and the evils, of course, will permanently cease, soon to be known only by description. Should any of the causes of evil be irremovable by the new powers which men are about to acquire, they will then know that they are necessary and unavoidable evils; and childish unavailing complaints will cease to be made. But your Reporter has yet failed to discover any which do not proceed from the errors of the existing system, or which, under the contemplated arrangements, are not easily removable.

Of the natural effects of this language and these sentiments upon mankind in general, your Reporter is, perhaps, as fully aware as any individual can be; but he knows that the full development of these truths is absolutely necessary to prepare the public to receive and understand the practical details which he is about to explain, and to comprehend those enlarged measures for the amelioration of society, which the distress of the times, arising from the errors of the present arrangements, now renders unavoidable. He is not now,

[a] Supposed late-eighteenth-century secret society of Enlightenment rationalists whom conservatives accused of fomenting the French Revolution, principally by undermining the authority of the Church.

however, addressing the common public, but those whose minds have had all the benefit of the knowledge which society at present affords; and it is from such individuals that he hopes to derive the assistance requisite to effect the practical good which he has devoted all the powers and faculties of his mind to obtain for his fellow-creatures.

Your Reporter has stated that this happy change will be effected through the knowledge which will be derived from the science of the influence of circumstances over human nature.

Through this science, new mental powers will be created, which will place all those circumstances that determine the misery or happiness of men under the immediate control and direction of the present population of the world, and will entirely supersede all necessity for *the present truly irrational system of individual rewards and punishments*: – a system which has ever been opposed to the most obvious dictates of common sense and of humanity, and which will be no longer permitted than while men continue unenlightened and barbarous.

The first rays of knowledge will show, to the meanest capacity, that all the tendencies of this system are to degrade men below the ordinary state of animals, and to render them more miserable and irrational.

The science of the influence of circumstances over human nature will dispel this ignorance, and will prove how much more easily men may be trained by other means to become, without exception, active, kind and intelligent, – devoid of those unpleasant and irrational feelings which for ages have tormented the whole human race.

This science may be truly called one whereby ignorance, poverty, crime and misery, may be prevented; and will indeed open a new era to the human race; one in which real happiness will commence, and perpetually go on increasing through every succeeding generation.

And although the characters of all have been formed under the existing circumstances, which are together unfavourable to their habits, dispositions, mental acquirements, and happiness, – yet, by the attainment of this new science those of the present day will be enabled to place themselves, and more especially the rising generation, under circumstances so agreeable to human nature, and so well adapted to all the acknowledged ends of human life, that those objects of anxious desire so ardently sought for through past ages will be secured to every one with the certainty of a mathematical procedure.

Improbable as this statement must seem to those who have necessarily been formed, by existing circumstances, into the creatures of the place in which they happen to live; which circumstances, to speak correctly, and with the sincerity and honesty which the subject now demands, could not form them into anything but mere local animals; still, even they must be conscious that the time is not long passed when their forefathers would have deemed it far more improbable that the light cloudy mist which they saw arise from boiling water could be so applied, by human agency, that under the easy control of one of themselves it should be made to execute the labour of thousands. Yet, by the aid of mechanical and chemical science, this and many other supposed impossibilities have been made familiar certainties. In like manner, fearful as men may now be to allow themselves to hope that the accumulated evils of ages are not permanent in their nature, probably many now live who will see the science introduced, that, in their days, will rapidly diminish, and, in the latter days of their children, will entirely remove these evils.

It is now time to return to the consideration of the preparatory means by which these important results are to be accomplished.

Your Reporter now uses the term 'preparatory,' because the present state of society, *governed by circumstances*, is so different, in its several parts and entire combination, from that which will arise when society shall be taught to *govern circumstances*, that some temporary intermediate arrangements, to serve as a step whereby we may advance from the one to the other, will be necessary.

The long experience which he has had in the practice of the science now about to be introduced has convinced him of the utility, nay, of the absolute necessity, of forming arrangements for a temporary intermediate stage of existence, in which we, who have acquired the wretched habits of the old system, may be permitted, without inconvenience, gradually to part with them, and exchange them for those requisite for the new and improved state of society. Thus will the means be prepared, by which, silently and without contest, all the local errors and prejudices which have kept men and nations strangers to each other and to themselves, will be removed. The habits, dispositions, notions, and consequent feelings, engendered by old society, will be thus allowed, without disturbance of any kind, to die a natural death; but as the character, conduct, and enjoyment of individuals formed under the new system will speedily become living examples of the vast superiority of the one state over the other, the natural death of old society and all that appertains to it although gradual, will not be lingering. Simple inspection, when both can be seen together, will produce motives sufficiently strong to carry the new arrangements as speedily into execution as practice will admit. The change, even in those who are now the most tenacious supporters of 'things as they are,' though left entirely to the influence of their own inclinations, will be so rapid, that they will wonder at themselves.

This intermediate change is the one, the details of which your Reporter has in part explained, and to which he now again begs to direct your attention.

Under the present system there is the most minute division of mental power and manual labour in the individuals of the working classes; private interests are placed perpetually at variance with the public good; and in every nation men are purposely trained from infancy to suppose that their well-being is incompatible with the progress and prosperity of other nations. Such are the means by which old society seeks to obtain the desired objects of life. The details now to be submitted have been devised upon principles which will lead to an opposite practice; to the combination of extensive mental and manual powers in the individuals of the working classes; to a complete identity of private and public interest; and to the training of nations to comprehend that their power and happiness cannot attain their full and natural development but through an equal increase of the power and happiness of all other states. These, therefore, are the real points at variance between that which *is* and that which *ought to be*.

It is upon these principles that arrangements are now proposed for the new agricultural villages, by which the food of the inhabitants may be prepared in one establishment, where they will eat together as one family.

Various objections have been urged against this practice; but they have come from those only, who, whatever may be their pretensions in other respects, are mere children in the knowledge of the principles and economy of social life.

By such arrangements the members of these new associations may be supplied with food at far less expense and with much more comfort than by any individual or family arrangements; and when the parties have been once trained and accustomed, as they easily may be, to the former mode, they will never afterwards feel any inclination to return to the latter.

If a saving in the quantity of food, – the obtaining of a superior quality of prepared provisions from the same materials, – and the operation of preparing them being effected in much less time, with far less fuel, and with greater ease, comfort, and health, to all the parties employed, – be advantages, these will be obtained in a remarkable manner by the new arrangements proposed.

And if to partake of viands so prepared, served up with every regard to comfort, in clean, spacious, well-lighted, and pleasantly ventilated apartments, and in the society of well-dressed, well-trained, well-educated, and well-informed associates, possessing the most benevolent dispositions and desirable habits, can give zest and proper enjoyment to meals, then will the inhabitants of the proposed villages experience all this in an eminent degree.

When the new arrangements shall become familiar to the parties, this superior mode of living may be enjoyed at far less expense and with much less trouble than are necessary to procure such meals as the poor are now compelled to eat, surrounded by every object of discomfort and disgust, in the cellars and garrets of the most unhealthy courts, alleys, and lanes, in London, Dublin, and Edinburgh, or Glasgow, Manchester, Leeds, and Birmingham.

Striking, however as the contrast is in this description, and although the actual practice will far exceed what words can convey, yet there are many closet theorists and inexperienced persons, probably, who will still contend for individual arrangements and interests, in preference to that which they cannot comprehend.

These individuals must be left to be convinced by the facts themselves.

We now proceed to describe the interior accommodations of the private lodging-houses, which will occupy three sides of the parallelogram.

As it is of essential importance that there should be abundance of space within the line of the private dwellings, the parallelogram, in all cases, whether the association is intended to be near the maximum or the minimum in numbers, should be of large dimensions; and to accommodate a greater or less population, the private dwellings should be of one, two, three, or four stories, and the interior arrangements formed accordingly.

These will be very simple.

No kitchen will be necessary, as the public arrangements for cooking will supersede the necessity for any.

The apartments will be always well-ventilated, and, when necessary, heated or cooled on the improved principles lately introduced in the Derby Infirmary.[a]

The expense and trouble, to say nothing of the superior health and comforts which these improvements will give, will be very greatly less than attach to the present practice.

To heat, cool, and ventilate their apartments, the parties will have no further trouble than to open or shut two slides, or valves, in each room, the atmosphere of which, by this simple contrivance, may always be kept temperate and pure.

One stove of proper dimensions, judiciously placed, will supply the apartments of several dwellings, with little trouble and at a very little expense, when the buildings are originally adapted for this arrangement.

Thus will all the inconveniences and expense of separate fires and fireplaces, and their appendages, be avoided, as well as the trouble and disagreeable effects of mending fires and removing ashes, etc, etc.

Good sleeping apartments looking over the gardens in the country, and sitting-rooms of proper dimensions fronting the square, will afford as much lodging-accommodation, as, with the other public arrangements, can be useful to, or desired by, these associated cultivators.

Food and lodging being thus provided for, the next consideration regards dress.

This, too, is a subject, the utility and disadvantages of which seem to be little understood by the Public generally; and, in consequence, the most ridiculous and absurd notions and practices have prevailed respecting it.

Most persons take it for granted, without thinking on the subject, that to be warm and healthy it is necessary to cover the body with thick clothing and to exclude the air as much as possible; and first appearances favour this conclusion. Facts, however, prove, that under the same circumstances, those who

[a] See Charles Sylvester, *The Philosophy of Domestic Economy; As Exemplified in . . . the Derbyshire General Infirmary* (Nottingham, 1819), pp. 8–48. The heating system was by steam pipes built into the foundation of the building, on a design originated by William Strutt.

from infancy have been the most lightly clad, and who, by their form of dress, have been the most exposed to the atmosphere, are much stronger, more active, in better general health, warmer in cold weather, and far less incommoded by heat, than those who from constant habit have been dressed in such description of clothing as excludes the air from their bodies. The more the air is excluded by clothing, although at first the wearer feels warmer by each additional covering he puts on, yet in a few weeks, or months at most, the less capable he becomes of bearing cold than before.

The Romans and the Highlanders of Scotland appear to be the only two nations who adopted a national dress on account of its utility, without however neglecting to render it highly becoming and ornamental. The form of the dress of these nations was calculated first to give strength and manly beauty to the figure, and afterwards to display it to advantage. The time, expense, thought, and labour now employed to create a variety of dress, the effects of which are to deteriorate the physical powers, and to render the human figure an object of pity and commiseration, are a certain proof of the low state of intellect among all classes in society. The whole of this gross misapplication of the human faculties serves no one useful or rational purpose. On the contrary, it essentially weakens all the physical and mental powers, and is, in all respects, highly pernicious to society.

All other circumstances remaining the same, sexual delicacy and virtue will be found much higher in nations among whom the person, *from infancy*, is the most exposed, than among those people who exclude from sight every part of the body except the eyes.

Although your Reporter is satisfied that the principle now stated is derived from the unchanging laws of nature; and is true to the utmost extent to which it can be carried; yet mankind must be trained in different habits, dispositions, and sentiments, before they can be permitted to act rationally on this, or almost any other law of nature.

The intermediate stage of society which your Reporter now recommends, admits, however, of judicious practical approximations towards the observance of these laws.

In the present case he recommends that the male children of the new villagers should be clothed in a dress somewhat resembling the Roman and Highland garb, in order that the limbs may be free from ligatures, and the air may circulate over every part of the body, and that they may be trained to become strong, active, well-limbed, and healthy.

And the females should have a well-chosen dress to secure similar important advantages.

The inhabitants of these villages, under the arrangements which your Reporter has in view, may be better dressed, for all the acknowledged purposes of dress, at much less than the one-hundredth part of the labour, inconvenience, and expense, that are now required to clothe the same number of persons in the middle ranks of life; while the form and material of the new dress will be acknowledged to be superior to any of the old.

If your Reporter should be told that all this waste of thought, time, labour, and capital is useful, inasmuch as it affords employment for the working classes; he replies, that no waste of any of these valuable means can be of the slightest benefit to any class; and that it would be far better, if superior occupations cannot be found for human beings, to resort to a Noble Lord's expedient, and direct them to make holes in the earth and fill them up again, repeating the operation without limit, rather than suffer a very large proportion of the working classes to be immured all their lives in unhealthy atmospheres, and toil at wretched employments, merely to render their fellow-creatures weak and absurd, both in body and mind.

The new villagers having adopted the best form and material of dress, permanent arrangements will be made to produce it with little trouble or expense to any party; and all further considerations respecting it will give them neither care, thought, nor trouble, for many years, or perhaps centuries.

The advantages of this part of the Plan will prove to be so great in practice, that fashions will exist but for a very short period, and then only among the most weak and silly part of the creation.

Your Reporter has now to enter upon the most interesting portion of this division of the subject, and, he may add, the most important part of the economy of human life, with reference to the science of the influence of circumstances over the well-being and happiness of mankind, and to the full power and control which men may now acquire over those circumstances, and by which they may direct them to produce among the human race, with ease and certainty, either universal good or evil.

No one can mistake the application of these terms to the training and education of the children.

Since men began to think and write, much has been thought and written on this subject; and yet all that has been thought and written has failed to make the subject understood, or to disclose the principles on which we should proceed. Even now, the minds of the most enlightened are scarcely prepared to being to think rationally respecting it. The circumstances of the times, however, require that a substantial advance should now be made in this part of the economy of human life.

Before any rational plan can be devised for the proper training and education of children, it should be distinctly known what capabilities and qualities infants and children possess, or, in fact, what they really are by nature.

If this knowledge is to be attained, as all human knowledge has been acquired, through the evidence of our senses, then is it evident that infants receive from a source and power over which they have no control, all the natural qualities they possess, and that from birth they are continually subjected to impressions derived from the circumstances around them; which impressions, combined with their natural qualities, (whatever fanciful speculative men say to the contrary), do truly determine the character of the individual through every period of life.

The knowledge thus acquired will give to men the same kind of control over the combination of the natural powers and faculties of infants, as they now possess over the formation of animals: and although, from the nature of the subject, it must be slow in its progress and limited in extent, yet the time is not perhaps far distant when it may be applied to an important rational purpose, that is, to improve the breed of men, more than men have yet improved the breed of domestic animals.

But, whatever knowledge may be attained to enable man to improve the breed of his progeny at birth, facts exist in endless profusion to prove to every mind capable of reflection, that men may now possess a most extensive control over those circumstances which affect the infant after birth; and that, as far as such circumstances can influence the human character, the day has arrived when the existing generation may so far control them, that the rising generations may become in character, without any individual exceptions, whatever men can now desire them to be, that is not contrary to human nature.

It is with reference to this important consideration that your Reporter, in the forming of these new arrangements, has taken so much pains to exclude every circumstance that could make an evil impression on the infants and children of this new generation.

And he is prepared, when others can follow him, so to combine new circumstances, that real vice, or that conduct which creates evil and misery in society, shall be utterly unknown in these villages, to whatever number they may extend.

Proceeding on these principles, your Reporter recommends arrangements by which the children shall be trained together as though they were literally all of one family.

For this purpose two schools will be required within the interior of the square, with spacious play and exercise grounds.

The schools may be conveniently placed in the line of buildings to be erected across the centre of the parallelograms, in connection with the church and places of worship.

The first School will be for the infants from two to six years of age. The second for children from six to twelve.

It may be stated, without fear of contradiction from any party who is master of the subject, that the whole success of these arrangements will depend upon the manner in which the infants and children shall be trained and educated in these schools. Men are, and ever will be, what they are and shall be made in infancy and childhood. The apparent exceptions to this law are the effects of the same causes, combined with subsequent impressions, arising from the new circumstances in which the individuals showing these exceptions have been placed.

One of the most general sources of error and of evil to the world is the notion *that infants, children, and men, are agents governed by a will formed by themselves and fashioned after their own choice.*

It is, however, as evident as any fact can be made to man, that he does not possess the smallest control over the formation of any of his own faculties or powers, or over the peculiar and ever-varying manner in which those powers and faculties, physical and mental, are combined in each individual.

Such being the case, it follows that human nature up to this period has been misunderstood, vilified, and savagely ill-treated; and that, in consequence, the language and conduct of mankind respecting it form a compound of all that is inconsistent and incongruous and most injurious to themselves, from the greatest to the least. All at this moment suffer grievously in consequence of this fundamental error.

To those who possess any knowledge on this subject it is known, that 'man is the creature of circumstances,' and that he really is, at every moment of his existence, precisely what the circumstances in which he has been placed, combined with his natural qualities, make him.

Does it then, your Reporter would ask, exhibit any sign of real wisdom to train him as if he were a being who created himself, formed his individual will, and was the author of his own inclinations and propensities?

Surely if men ever become wise – if they ever acquire knowledge enough to know themselves and enjoy a happy existence, it must be from discovering that they are not subjects for praise or blame, reward, or punishment; but are beings capable, by proper treatment, of receiving unlimited improvement and knowledge; and, in consequence, of experiencing such uninterrupted enjoyment through this life as will best prepare them for an after-existence.

This view of human nature rests upon facts which no one can disprove. Your Reporter now challenges all those who, from imagined interest, or from the notions which they have been taught to suppose true, are disposed to question its solidity, to point out one of his deductions on this subject which does not immediately follow from a self evident truth. He is satisfied that the united wisdom of old society will fail in the attempt.

Why, then, may your Reporter be permitted to ask, should any parties tenaciously defend these notions? Are they, although false, in any manner beneficial to man? Does any party, or does a single individual, derive any real advantage from them?

Could your Reporter devise the means effectually to dispel the impressions so powerfully made on the human mind through early life, by the locality of the circumstances of birth and education, he would be enabled thoroughly to convince those who now suppose themselves the chief gainers by the present popular belief on those points and the order of things which proceeds from such belief, that they are themselves *essential* sufferers in consequence, – that they are deceived and deceive others greatly to their own cost. Superior knowledge of the subject will one day convince all, that every human being, of every rank or station in life, has suffered and is now suffering a useless and grievous yoke by reason of these fallacies of the imagination.

Your Reporter is well aware that for ages past the great mass of mankind have been so placed as to be compelled to believe that all derived incalculable benefits from them. Yet there is no truth more certain than that these same individuals might have been placed under circumstances which would have enabled them not only to discover the falsehood of these notions, but to see distinctly the innumerable positive evils which they alone have inflicted upon society. While these fallacies of the brain shall be taught and believed by any portion of mankind, *in them* charity and benevolence, in their true sense, can never exist. Such men have imbibed notions that must make them, whatever be their language, haters and opposers of those who contend for the truth in opposition to their errors; nor can men so taught bear to be told that they have been made the mere dupes of the most useless and mischievous fantasies. Their errors, having been generated by circumstances over which they had no control, and for which, consequently, they cannot be blameable, are to be removed only by other circumstances sufficiently powerful to counteract the effects of the former.

From what has been said it is obvious that to produce such a total change among men as the one now contemplated by your Reporter will require the arrangement of new circumstances, that, in each part, and in their entire combinations, shall be so consistent with the known laws of nature, that the most acute mind shall fail to discover the slightest deviation from them.

It is upon these grounds that your Reporter, in educating the rising generation within his influence, has long adopted principles different from those which are usually acted upon.

He considers all children as beings whose dispositions, habits, and sentiments are to be formed *for* them; that these can be well-formed only by excluding all notions of reward, punishment, and emulation; and that, if their characters are not such as they ought to be, the error proceeds from their instructors and the other circumstances which surround them. He knows that principles as certain as those upon which the science of mathematics is founded may be applied to the forming of any given general character, and that by the influence of other circumstances, not a few individuals only, but the whole population of the world, may in a few years be rendered a very far superior race of beings to any now upon the earth, or which has been made known to us by history.

The children in these new schools should be therefore trained systematically to acquire useful knowledge through the means of sensible signs, by which their powers of reflection and judgment may be habituated to draw accurate conclusions from the facts presented to them. This mode of instruction is founded in nature, and will supersede the present defective and tiresome system of book learning, which is ill-calculated to give either pleasure or instruction to the minds of children. When arrangements founded on these principles shall be judiciously formed and applied to practice, children will, with ease and delight to themselves, acquire more real knowledge in a day, than they have yet attained under the old system in many months. They will not only thus acquire valuable knowledge, but the best habits and dispositions will be at the same time imperceptibly created in every one; and they will be trained to fill every office and to perform every duty that the well-being of their associates and the establishments can require. It is only by education, rightly understood, that communities of men can ever be well governed, and by means of such education every object of human society will be attained with the least labour and the most satisfaction.

It is obvious that training and education must be viewed as intimately connected with the employments of the association. The latter, indeed, will form an essential part of education under these arrangements. Each association, generally speaking, should create for itself a full supply of the usual necessaries, conveniences and comforts of life.

The dwelling-houses and domestic arrangements being placed as near the centre of the land to be cultivated as circumstances will permit, it is concluded that the most convenient situation for the gardens will be adjoining the houses on the outside of the square; that these should be bounded by the principal roads; and that beyond them, at a sufficient distance to be covered by a plantation, should be placed the workshops and manufactory.

All will take their turn at *some one or more* of the occupations in this department, aided by every improvement that science can afford, alternately with employment in agriculture and gardening.

It has been a popular opinion to recommend a minute division of labour and division of interests. It will presently appear, however, that this minute division of labour and division of interests are only other terms for poverty, ignorance, waste of every kind, universal opposition throughout society, crime, misery, and great bodily and mental imbecility.

To avoid these evils, which, while they continue, must keep mankind in a most degraded state, each child will receive a general education, early in life, that will fit him for the proper purposes of society, make him the most useful to it, and the most capable of enjoying it.

Before he is twelve years old he may with ease be trained to acquire a correct view of the outline of all the knowledge which men have yet attained.

By this means he will early learn what he is in relation to past ages, to the period in which he lives, to the circumstances in which he is placed, to the individuals around him, and to future events. *He will then only have any pretensions to the name of a rational being.*

His physical powers may be equally enlarged, in a manner as beneficial to himself as to those around him. As his strength increases he will be initiated in the practice of all the leading operations of his community; by which his services, at all times and under all circumstances, will afford a great gain to society beyond the expense of his subsistence; while at the same time he will be in the continual possession of more substantial comforts and real enjoyments than have ever yet appertained to any class in society.

The new wealth which one individual, by comparatively light and always healthy employment, may create under the arrangements now proposed, is indeed incalculable. They would give him giant powers compared with those which the working class or any other now possesses. There would at once be an end of all mere animal machines, who could only follow a plough, or turn a sod, or make some insignificant part of some insignificant manufacture or frivolous article which society could better spare than possess. Instead of the unhealthy pointer of a pin, – header of a nail, – piecer of a thread – or clodhopper, senselessly gazing at the soil or around him, without understanding or rational reflection, there would spring up a working class full of activity and useful knowledge, with habits, information, manners, and dispositions, that would place the lowest in the scale many degrees above the best of any class which has yet been formed by the circumstances of past or present society.

Such are a few only of the advantages which a rational mode of training and education, combined with the other parts of this system, would give to all the individuals within the action of its influence.

The next object of attention is, –

4th. – *The formation and superintendence of these establishments.*

These new farming and general working arrangements may be formed by one or any number of landed proprietors or large capitalists; by established companies having large funds to expend for benevolent and public objects; by parishes and counties, to relieve themselves from paupers and poor's rates; and by associations of the middle and working classes of farmers, mechanics, and tradesmen, to relieve themselves from the evils of the present system.

As land, capital, and labour, may be applied *to far greater pecuniary advantage* under the proposed arrangements than under any other at present known to the public, all parties will readily unite in carrying them into execution as soon as they shall be so plainly developed in principle as to be generally understood, and as parties who possess sufficient knowledge of the practical details to direct them advantageously can be found or trained to superintend them.

The chief difficulty lies in the latter part of the business. The principles may be made plain to every capacity. They are simple principles of nature, in strict unison with all we see or know from facts to be true. But the practice of everything new, however trifling, requires time and experience to perfect it. It cannot be expected that arrangements which comprehend the whole business of life, and reduce to practice the entire science of political economy, can at once be combined and executed in the best manner. Many errors will be at first committed; and, as in every other attempt by human means to unite a great variety of parts to produce one grand general result, many partial failures may be anticipated.

In all probability in the first experiment many of the parts will be out of due proportion to the whole; and experience will suggest a thousand improvements. No union of minds previously to actual practice can correctly adjust such a multiplicity of movements as will be combined in this new machine, which is to perform so many important offices for society.

A machine it truly is, that will simplify and facilitate, in a very remarkable manner, all the operations of human life, and multiply rational and permanently desirable enjoyments to an extent that cannot be yet calmly contemplated by ordinary minds.

If the invention of various machines has multiplied the power of labour, in several instances, to the apparent advantage of particular individuals, while it has deteriorated the condition of many others, THIS is an invention which will at once multiply the physical and mental powers of the whole society to an incalculable extent, without injuring any one by its introduction or its most rapid diffusion.

Surely when the power of this extraordinary machine shall be estimated, and the amount of the work shall be ascertained which it will perform for society, some exertions may be made to acquire a knowledge of its practice.

The same class of minds that can be trained to direct any of the usual complicated businesses of life, may be with ease rendered competent to take a part in the management and superintendence of these new establishments.

The principal difficulty will be to set the first establishment in motion; and much care and circumspection will be requisite in bringing each part into action at the proper time, and with the guards and checks which a change from one set of habits to another renders necessary.

Yet, the principles being understood, a man of fair ordinary capacity would superintend such arrangements with more ease than most large commercial or manufacturing establishments are now conducted.

In these there is a continual opposition of various interests and feelings, and extensive principles of counteraction, among the parties themselves, and between the parties and the public.

On the contrary, in the new arrangements each part will give facility to all the others, and unity of interest and design will be seen and felt in every one of the operations. The mental, manual, and scientific movements will all harmonise, and produce with ease results which must appear inexplicable to those who remain ignorant of the principles which govern the proceedings.

In the first instance men must be sought who, in addition to a practical knowledge of gardening, agriculture, manufactures, the ordinary trades, etc, etc, can comprehend the principles on which these associations are formed, and, comprehending them, can feel an interest and a pleasure in putting them into execution. Such individuals may be found; for there is nothing new in the separate parts of the proposed practice – the arrangement alone can be considered new.

When one establishment shall have been formed, there will be no great difficulty in providing superintendents for many other establishments. All the children will be trained to be equal to the care of any of the departments, more particularly as there will be no counteraction between those who direct and those who perform the various operations.

Let the business be at once set about in good earnest, and the obstacles which now seem so formidable will speedily disappear.

The peculiar mode of governing these establishments will depend on the parties who form them.

Those founded by landowners and capitalists, public companies, parishes, or counties, will be under the direction of the individuals whom these powers may appoint to superintend them, and will of course be subject to the rules and regulations laid down by their founders.

Those formed by the middle and working classes, upon a complete reciprocity of interests, should be governed by themselves, upon principles that will *prevent* divisions, opposition of interests, jealousies, or any of the common and vulgar passions which a contention for power is certain to generate. Their affairs should be conducted by a committee, composed of all the members of the association between certain ages – for instance, of those between thirty-five and forty-five, or between forty and fifty. Perhaps the former will unite more of the activity of youth with the experience of age than the latter; but it is of little moment which period of life may be fixed upon. In a short time the ease with which these associations will proceed in all their operations will be such as to render the business of governing a mere recreation; and as the parties who govern will in a few years again become the governed, they must always be conscious that at a future period they will experience the good or evil effects of the measures of their administration.

By this equitable and natural arrangement all the numberless evils of election and electioneering will be avoided.

As all are to be trained and educated together and without distinction, they will be delightful companions and associates, intimately acquainted with each other's inmost thoughts. There will be no foundation for disguise or deceit of any kind; all will be as open as the hearts and feelings of young children before they are trained (as they necessarily are under the present system,) in complicated arts of deception. At the same time their whole conduct will be regulated by a sound and rational discretion and intelligence, such as human beings trained and placed as they have hitherto been will deem it visionary to expect, and impossible to attain, in every-day practice.

The superior advantages which these associations will speedily possess, and the still greater superiority of knowledge which they will readily acquire, will preclude on their parts the smallest desire for what are now called honours and peculiar privileges.

They will have minds so well informed – their power of accurately tracing cause and effect will be so much increased, that they must clearly perceive that to be raised to one of the privileged orders would be to themselves a serious evil, and to their posterity would certainly occasion an incalculable loss of intellect and enjoyment, equally injurious to themselves and to society.

They will therefore have every motive not to interfere with the honours and privileges of the existing higher orders, but to remain well satisfied with their own station in life.

The only distinction which can be found of the least utility in these associations is that of age or experience. It is the only just and natural distinction; and any other would be inconsistent with the enlarged and superior acquirements of the individuals who would compose these associations. The deference to age or experience will be natural, and readily given; and many advantageous regulations may be formed in consequence, for apportioning the proper employments to the period of life best calculated for them, and diminishing the labour of the individual as age advances beyond the term when the period of governing is concluded.

5th. – *The disposal of the surplus produce, and the connection which will subsist between the several establishments.*

Under the proposed system the facilities of production, the absence of all the counteracting circumstances which so abundantly exist in common society, with the saving of time and waste in all the domestic arrangements, will secure, other circumstances being equal, *a much larger amount of wealth at a greatly reduced expenditure*. The next question is, in what manner is this produce to be disposed of?

Society has been hitherto so constituted that all parties are afraid of being over-reached by others, and, without great care to secure their individual interests, of being deprived of the means of existence. This feeling has created a universal selfishness of the most ignorant nature, for it almost *ensures* the evils which it means to prevent.

These new associations can scarcely be formed before it will be discovered that by the most simple and easy regulations all the natural wants of human nature may be abundantly supplied; and the principle of selfishness (in the sense in which that term is here used,) will cease to exist, for want of an adequate motive to produce it.

It will be quite evident to all, that wealth of that kind which will alone be held in any estimation amongst them, may be so easily created to exceed all their wants, that every desire for individual accumulation will be extinguished. To them individual accumulation of wealth will appear as irrational as to bottle up or store water in situations where there is more of this invaluable fluid than all can consume.

With this knowledge, and the feelings which will arise from it, the existing thousand counteractions to the creation of new wealth will also cease, as well as those innumerable motives to deception which now pervade all ranks in society. A principle of equity and justice, openness and fairness, will influence the whole proceedings of these societies. There will, consequently, be no difficulty whatever in the exchange of the products of labour, mental or manual, among themselves. The amount of labour in all products, calculated on the present principle of estimating the prime cost of commodities, will be readily ascertained, and the exchange made accordingly. There will be no inducement to raise or manufacture an inferior article, or to deteriorate by deceptious practices, any of the necessaries, comforts, or luxuries of life. Every one will distinctly see it to be the immediate interest of all, that none of these irrational proceedings shall take place; and the best security against their occurrence will be the entire absence of all motives to have recourse to them. As the easy, regular, healthy, rational employment of the individuals forming these societies will create a very large surplus of their own products, beyond what they will have any desire to consume, each may be freely permitted to receive from the general store of the community whatever they may require. This, in practice, will prove to be the greatest economy, and will at once remove all those preconceived insurmountable difficulties that now haunt the minds of those who have been trained in common society, and who necessarily view all things through the distorted medium of their own little circle of local prejudices.

It may be safely predicted that one of these new associations cannot be formed without creating a general desire throughout society to establish others, and that they will rapidly multiply. The same knowledge and principles which unite the interest of the individuals within each establishment, will as effectually lead to the same kind of enlightened union between the different establishments. They will each render to the others the same benefits as are now given, or rather much greater benefits than are now given to each other by the members of the most closely united and affectionate families.

In their original formation they will be established so as to yield the greatest reciprocity of benefits.

The peculiar produce to be raised in each establishment, beyond the general supply of the necessaries and comforts of life, which, if possible, will be abundantly created in each, will be adapted to afford the greatest variety of intrinsically valuable objects to exchange with each other; and the particular surplus products which will serve to give energy and pleasure to the industry of the members of each association will be regulated by the nature of the soil and climate and other local capabilities of the situation of each establishment. In all these labour will be the standard of value, and as there will always be a progressive advance in the amount of labour, manual, mental, and scientific, if we suppose population to increase under these arrangements, there will be in the same proportion a perpetually extending market or demand for all the industry of society, whatever may be its extent. Under such arrangements what are technically called 'bad times' can never occur.

These establishments will be provided with granaries and warehouses, which will always contain a supply sufficient to protect the population against the occurrence even of more unfavourable seasons than have ever yet been experienced since agriculture has been general in society. In these granaries and storehouses proper persons will be appointed to receive, examine, deposit, and deliver out again, the wealth of these communities.

Arrangements will be formed to distribute this wealth among the members of the association which created it, and to exchange the surplus for the surplus of the other communities, by general regulations that will render these transactions most simple and easy, to whatever distance these communities may extend.

A paper representative of the value of labour, manufactured on the principle of the new notes of the Bank of England, will serve for every purpose of their domestic commerce or exchanges, and will be issued only for intrinsic value received and in store. It has been mentioned already that all motives to deception will be effectually removed from the minds of the inhabitants of these new villages, and of course forgeries, though not guarded against by this new improvement, would not have any existence among them; and as this representative would be of no use in old society, no injury could come from that quarter.

But these associations must contribute their fair quota to the exigencies of the state. This consideration leads your Reporter to the next general head, or, 6th. – *The connection of the new establishments with the government of the country and with old society.*

Under this head are to be noticed, the amount and collection of the revenue, and the public or legal duties of the associations in peace and war.

Your Reporter concludes that whatever taxes are paid from land, capital, and labour, under the existing arrangements of society, the same amount for the same proportion of each may be collected with far more ease under those now proposed. The government would of course require its revenue to be paid in the legal circulating medium, to obtain which, the associations would have to dispose of as much of their surplus produce to common society for the legal coin or paper of the realm, as would discharge the demands of government.

In time of peace these associations would give no trouble to government; their internal regulations being founded on principles of prevention, not only with reference to public crimes, but to the private evils and errors which so fatally abound in common society. Courts of law, prisons, and punishments, would not be required. These are requisite only where human nature is greatly misunderstood; where society rests on the demoralising system of individual competition, rewards, and punishments; – they are necessary only in a stage of existence previous to the discovery of the science of the certain and overwhelming influence of circumstances over the whole character and conduct of mankind. Whatever courts of law, prisons, and punishments have yet effected for society, the influence of other circumstances, which may now be easily introduced, will accomplish infinitely more; for they will effectually prevent the growth of those evils of which our present institutions do not take cognizance till they are already full-formed and in baneful activity. In time of peace, therefore, these associations will save much charge and trouble to government.

In reference to war also, they will be equally beneficial. Bodily exercises, adapted to improve the dispositions and increase the health and strength of the individual, will form part of the training and education of the children. In these exercises they may be instructed to acquire facility in the execution of combined movements, a habit which is calculated to produce regularity and order in time of peace, as well as to aid defensive and offensive operations in war. The children, therefore, at an early age, will acquire, *through their amusements,* those habits which will render them capable of becoming, in a short time, at any future period of life, the best defenders of their country, if necessity should again arise to defend it; since they would, in all probability, be far more to be depended upon than those whose physical, intellectual, and moral training had been less carefully conducted. In furnishing their quotas for the militia or common army they would probably adopt the pecuniary alternative; by which means they would form a reserve, that, in proportion to their numbers, would be a great security for the nation's safety. They would prefer this alternative, to avoid the demoralising effects of recruiting.

But the knowledge of the science of the influence of circumstances over mankind will speedily enable all nations to discover, not only the evils of war, but the folly of it. Of all modes of conduct adopted by mankind to obtain advantages in the present stage of society, this is the most certain to defeat its object. It is, in truth, a system of direct demoralisation and of destruction; while it is the highest interest of all individuals and of all countries to *remoralise and conserve.* Men surely cannot with truth be termed rational beings until they shall discover and put in practice the principles which shall enable them to conduct their affairs without war. The arrangements we are considering would speedily show how easily these principles and practices may be introduced into general society.

From what has been stated it is evident that these associations would not subject the government to the same proportion of trouble and expense that an equal population would do in old society; on the contrary, they would relieve the government of the whole burthen; and by the certain and decisive influence of these arrangements upon the character and conduct of the parties, would materially add to the political strength, power, and resources of the country into which they shall be introduced.

Your Reporter having now explained as much of the separate details of the measures which he recommends, to give permanent beneficial employment to the poor, and, consequently, relief to all classes, as this mode of communication in its present stage will admit, now proceeds to take a general view of these parts thus combined into an entire whole; as a practical system purposely devised, from the beginning to the end, to ameliorate materially the condition of human life.

He concludes that the subject thus developed is new both to theorists and to practical men. The former, being ignorant of the means by which extensive arrangements, when founded on correct principles, can be easily carried into execution, will at once, with their usual decision when any new measures at variance with their own theories are proposed, pronounce the whole to be impracticable and undeserving of notice. The others, accustomed to view everything within the limits of some particular pursuit, – of agriculture, or trade, or commerce, or manufactures, or some of the professions, – have their minds so warped in consequence, that they are for the most part incapable of comprehending any general measures in which their peculiar trade or calling constitutes but a small part of the whole. With them the particular art or employment in which each is engaged becomes so magnified to the individual, that, like Aaron's rod,[a] it swallows up all the others; and thus the most petty minds only are formed. This lamentable compression of the human intellect is the certain and necessary consequence of the present division of labour, and of the existing general arrangements of society.

So far, however, from the measures now proposed being impracticable, a longer continuance of the existing arrangements of society will speedily appear to be so; one and all now reiterate the cry that *something must be done*.

Your Reporter begs leave to ask if this 'something' to be effectual for the general relief of all classes, is expected to come from the mere agriculturist, or the tradesman, or the manufacturer, or the merchant, or the lawyer, or the physician, or the divine, or the literary man; – or from radicals, whigs, or tories; – or from any particular religious sect? Have we not before us, as upon an accurately drawn map, most distinctly defined, all the ideas and the utmost bounds within which this exclusive devotion to particular sects, parties, or pursuits, necessarily confines each mind? Can we reasonably expect anything resembling a rational 'something' to relieve the widely extending distress of society, from the microscopic views which the most enlarged of these circles afford? Or, rather, does it not argue the most childish weakness to entertain such futile expectations? It can never be that the universal division of men's pursuits can create any cordial union of interests among mankind. It can never be that a notion which necessarily separates, in a greater or less degree, every

[a] See Exodus 7:12.

human being from his fellows, can ever be productive of practical benefit to society. This notion, as far as our knowledge extends, has ever been forced on the mind of every child, up to this period. Peace, good will, charity, and benevolence, have been preached for centuries past – nay, for thousands of years, yet they nowhere exist; on the contrary, qualities the reverse of these have at all times constituted the character and influenced the conduct of individuals and of nations, and must continue to do so *while the system of individual rewards, punishments, and competition, is permitted to constitute the basis of human society.*

The conduct of mankind may, not unaptly, be compared to that of an individual who, possessing an excellent soil for the purpose, desired to raise grapes, but was ignorant of the plant. Having imbibed a notion, which had taken deep root in his mind, that the thorn was the vine, he planted the former, watered, and cultivated it; but it produced only prickles. He again planted the thorn, varying his mode of cultivation, yet the result was still the same. A third time he planted it, applying now abundance of manure, and bestowing increased care on its cultivation; but, in return, his thorns only produced him prickles stronger and sharper than before. Thus baffled, he blamed the sterility of the ground, and became convinced that human agency alone could never raise grapes from such a soil; – but he had no other. He therefore sought for supernatural assistance, and prayed that the soil might be fertilised.

His hopes being now revived, he again planted the thorn, applied himself with redoubled industry to its culture, and anxiously watched the hourly growth of his plants. He varied their training in every conceivable manner; some he bent in one direction, and some in another; he exposed some to the full light of day, and others he hid in the shade; some were continually watered, and their growth encouraged by richly manured soil. The harvest, looked for with so much interest, at length arrived, but it was again prickles of varied forms and dimensions; and his most sanguine hopes were disappointed.

He now turned his thoughts to other supernatural powers, and from each change he anticipated at least some approximation of the prickle towards the grape. Seeing, however, after every trial, that the thorns which he planted yielded him no fruit, he felt his utmost hope and expectation exhausted. He concluded that the power which created the soil had ordained that it should produce only prickles, and that the grape would one day or other, and in some way or other, be an after production from the seed of the thorn.

Thus, with a perpetual longing for the grape, and with a soil admirably adapted for the cultivation of vines that would produce the most delicious fruit with a thousandth part of the anxiety, expense, and trouble which he had bestowed upon the thorn, he now in a dissatisfied mood endeavoured to calm his feelings, and, if possible, to console himself for the want of present enjoyment, with the contemplation of that distant better fortune which he hoped awaited him.

This is an accurate picture of what human life has hitherto been. Possessing in human nature, a soil capable of yielding abundantly the product which man most desires, we have, in our ignorance, planted the thorn instead of the vine. The evil principle which has been instilled into all minds from infancy, 'that the character is formed *by* the individual,' has produced, and so long as it shall continue to be cherished will ever produce, the same unwelcome harvest of evil passions, – hatred, revenge, and all uncharitableness, and the innumerable crimes and miseries to which they have given birth; for these are the certain and necessary effects of the institutions which have arisen among mankind in consequence of the universally received and long coerced belief in this erroneous principle.

'That the character is formed *for* and not *by* the individual,' is a truth to which every fact connected with man's history bears testimony, and of which the evidence of our senses affords us daily and hourly proof. It is also a truth which, when its practical application shall be fully understood, will be of inestimable value to mankind. Let us not, therefore, continue to act as if the reverse of this proposition were true. Let us cease to do violence to human nature; and, having at length discovered the vine, or the good principle, let us henceforward substitute it for the thorn. The knowledge of this principle will necessarily lead to the gradual and peaceful introduction of other institutions and improved arrangements, which will preclude all the existing evils, and permanently secure the well-being and happiness of mankind.

The system, the separate parts of which have been explained in this Report, will lead to this improved condition of society by the least circuitous route that the present degraded state of the human mind and character will admit. But to understand the nature and objects of these several parts the whole attention and powers of the mind must be called in to action.

Can the use or value of a time-piece be ascertained from a knowledge only of the spring, or of some of the separate wheels, or even of all its parts with the exception of one essential to its movements?

If, then, a knowledge of the whole is absolutely requisite before a simple piece of mechanism to mark time can be comprehended, surely it is far more necessary that a system which promises to impart the greatest benefits ever yet offered to mankind should be so thoroughly examined, in its several parts and entire combination, as to be well understood, before any party ventures to decide whether or not it is competent to produce the effects intended.

The result of such an examination will show, *that each part has been devised with reference to a simple general principle;* and that there is a necessary connection between the several parts, which cannot be disturbed without destroying the use and value of this new mental and physical combination.

It may be further opposed, as every other very great beneficial change in society has been: but what avail the puny efforts which the united ignorance of the world can now make to resist its introduction in this and other countries, when it may be easily proved, by experiment, to be fraught, with the highest benefits to every individual of the human race? Even the strong natural prejudices in favour of all old established customs will contend against it but for a time.

There does not exist an individual who, when he shall understand the nature and purport of this system, will anticipate from it the slightest degree of injury to himself, – or rather, who will not perceive that he must derive immediate and incalculable advantages from its introduction. Circumstances far beyond the knowledge or control of those whose minds are confined within the narrow prejudices of class, sect, party or country, now render this change inevitable; silence will not retard its progress, and opposition will give increased celerity to its movements.

What, then, to sum up the whole in a few words, does your Reporter now propose to his fellow-creatures?

After a life spent in the investigation of the causes of the evils with which society is afflicted, and of the means of removing them, – and being now in possession of facts demonstrating the practicability and the efficacy of the arrangements now exhibited, which have been the fruit of that investigation, aided by a long course of actual experiments, – he offers to exchange their poverty for wealth, their ignorance for knowledge, their anger for kindness, their divisions for union. He offers to effect this change without subjecting a single individual even to temporary inconvenience. No one shall suffer by it for an hour; all shall be essentially benefited within a short period from its introduction; and yet not any part of the existing system shall be prematurely disturbed.

His practical operations will commence with those who are now a burthen to the country for want of employment. He will enable these persons to support themselves and families, and pay the interest of the capital requisite to put their labour in activity. From the effects which will be thus produced on the character and circumstances of this oppressed class, the public will soon see and acknowledge that he has promised far less than will be realised; and when, by these arrangements, the vicious, the idle, and the pauper, shall be made virtuous, industrious, and independent, those who shall be still the lowest in the scale of old society may place themselves under the new arrangements, when they have evidence before them that these offer greater advantages than the old.

Upon this principle the change from the old system to the new will be checked in its progress whenever the latter ceases to afford decided inducements to embrace it; for long established habits and prejudices will continue to have a powerful influence over those who have been trained in them. The change, then, beyond the beneficial employment of those who now cannot obtain work, will proceed solely from proof, in practice, of the very great superiority of the new arrangements over the old. Unlike, therefore, all former great changes, this may be effected without a single evil or inconvenience. It calls for no sacrifice of principle or property to any individual in any rank or condition; through every step of its progress it effects unmixed good only.

Acting on principles merely *approximating* to those of the new system, and at the same time powerfully counteracted by innumerable errors of the old system, he has succeeded in giving to a population originally of the most wretched description, and placed under the most unfavourable circumstances, such habits, feelings, and dispositions, as enable them to enjoy more happiness than is to be found among any other population of the same extent in any part of the world; a degree of happiness, indeed, which it is utterly impossible for the old system to create among any class of persons placed under the most favourable circumstances.

Seeing, therefore, on the one hand, the sufferings which are now experienced, and the increasing discontent which prevails, especially among the most numerous and most useful class of our population, and, on the other, the relief and the extensive benefits which are offered to society on the authority of facts open to inspection, – can the public any longer with decency decline investigation? Can those who profess a sincere desire to improve the condition of the poor and working classes longer refuse to examine a proposal, which, on the most rational grounds, promises them ample relief, accompanied with unmixed good to every other part of society?

Your Reporter solicits no favour from any party; he belongs to none. He merely calls upon those who are the most competent to the task, honestly, as men valuing their own interests and the interests of society, to investigate, without favour or affection, a 'Plan (derived from thirty years' study and practical experience,) for relieving public distress and removing discontent, by giving permanent productive employment to the poor and working classes, under arrangements which will essentially improve their character and ameliorate their condition, diminish the expenses of production and consumption, and create markets co-extensive with production.'

AN ATTEMPT TO EXPLAIN THE CAUSE OF COMMERCIAL AND OTHER DIFFICULTIES WHICH ARE NOW EXPERIENCED IN THE CIVILIZED PARTS OF THE WORLD AND TO DEVELOPE THE MEANS BY WHICH THEY MAY BE REMOVED[a]

1821

The legitimate object of society is to improve the physical, moral, and intellectual characters of men, and in the most convenient manner to supply all their wants, in order that they may experience the least suffering and the greatest enjoyment.

Society, as it is now constituted, is not calculated to produce these results. The physical, moral, and intellectual powers of the general part of men are neglected; while their natural wants are supplied without foresight or science, and in a manner most detrimental to the interests and well-being of every individual of which society is composed.

In consequence, the great mass of mankind can scarcely obtain the common necessaries of life, by severe and oftentimes unhealthy and disagreeable labour; while comparatively very few procure a superfluity of luxuries, which are perhaps still more injurious to them.

By this system, *wealth* and not *happiness* is made the chief aim of society. It is in truth a system founded on error, and all its results are, and must be, misery. In consequence, the states most advanced in this system, and which ought to be the most prosperous, are now overwhelmed with *poverty*, *distress*, and *crime*; from which they know not how to extricate themselves. Yet these nations superabound in all the materials requisite to place their well-being and

---

[a] The full title of the original work was A *Report of the Holkham Sheep Shearing, on Monday, Tuesday, Wednesday, and Thursday, July 2, 3, 4, and 5, Being the Forty-Third Anniversary of That Meeting*, edited by Richard N. Bacon (Norwich, 1821). The preamble reads: 'On Thursday morning (the day after the general duration of the meeting) Mr Owen consented to explain to such of Mr Coke's visitors as remained at Holkham, and who were principally of the highest rank, the outlines of his plan for the amelioration of the condition of the industrious classes. His very interesting paper is subjoined, and concludes the transactions of this important meeting.'

prosperity on a foundation from which none of the past occurrences of human affairs could remove them.

The wants of the world have been long supplied through a commerce founded on *a profit upon cost price – a minute division of labour – and a competition of individual interests.* The various systems founded on these principles, have been necessary and useful for a particular period of human affairs; but that period is now passed – these systems cannot longer proceed – and profit upon price cannot henceforth be generally obtained.

The minute division of labour has materially weakened the physical and mental powers of man; and a competition of individual interests now destroys the real interests of society, and of every individual of which it is composed.

In the rude ages of the world, before mechanical and other scientific inventions were known, the natural wants of men exceeded the productions of their industry; for much labour was necessary even to create their ordinary food, clothing, and a few simple conveniences. When by mechanical and other inventions and improvements, the natural wants of men came to be more easily supplied, artificial wants were then excited, and a new æra commenced; a commerce was established, founded on a profit upon price, and individual gain became the ruling passion throughout society; a profit upon price, for individual gain, brought into action the lower faculties of human nature; cunning and deception usurped the place of wisdom and sincerity; and in consequence, all parties, whether successful or not in their pursuits, have been disappointed.

A minute division of labour, and a competition of individual interests, have been found to degrade the human character, materially to weaken the social system, and involve society in its most advanced stages in every kind of difficulty. The impossibility of proceeding further in this course is felt by every one; and among all classes it is now perpetually reiterated that something must be done, for the present arrangements of society cannot much longer continue. The truth is, that a profit upon price can be obtained only when the demand of society *is equal to or exceeds the supply.* In the present advanced state of science, this period is not likely again to occur; for a small number of men, with the aid of science, can easily produce more than a large number can advantageously for themselves consume. At the period when peace was last proclaimed,[a] the powers of supply which had been called into action by the previous extraordinary demand for the materials of war, were found to be far too abundant for the former peace arrangements of society, and from that day to this a profit on price upon the average of all British productions has not been obtained; nor is it likely that a profit upon price can be again procured, except through some great public calamity.

[a] Peace between Britain and France was agreed in 1815, after twenty-two years of war.

Some measures are therefore necessary to relieve civilized society from the difficulties created by an excess of the new powers of supply, or of the means by which, when properly directed, society is to obtain the highest state of prosperity. All parties agree in thinking that something may be done, without perhaps having any defined notion of what that something must be. It is now evident that that something, by whatever means it may be attained in practice, must bring the consumption and production of society into a due proportion to each other.

Since the war has ceased, production has greatly exceeded consumption, although production has been exceedingly restricted in almost all civilized states. It is not, however, the interest of any portion of society, that production should be restrained until the wants of all parties shall be fully supplied. The existing arrangements of society permit production and consumption to proceed only through *profit upon price*, and it has been already stated, that society has arrived at the period when profit upon price can be no longer generally obtained.

Productions can be now easily created to an unlimited extent, even to over-supply the wants of all; but it is impracticable to permit those who are now in want to supply themselves, *except through their own labour*, and also without the means being secured by which *there shall be at all times an excess of supply over consumption*. This can be alone effected by scientific arrangements, founded on extensive foresight, produced by experience; which shall permit the producers, advantageously for all ranks, not only to produce with facility, but also to *consume a larger portion than heretofore of that which they produce*. This may now be done, and yet the producers shall create for the higher ranks in society, *a much larger surplus than they have ever yet received from the working classes*. But it assuredly cannot be effected by a profit upon price, which the advanced state of society and of the sciences will no longer admit, but *through the advantages of unlimited productions, and the unrestrained exchange of them*: the details of which are given in the writer's Report to the County of Lanark. This change will be effected by arrangements that shall enable the parties engaged in them to create produce either from the soil or by the manufactures, cheaper and with more health and comfort to themselves than can be done by any parties under the existing system; *and the change must commence with those who are now in the lowest rank of society*.

The arrangements alluded to, are in consequence made for those who are now paupers, who subsist on the industry and wealth of others, and who are not only a burden to all classes, but a fertile source of crime, and from whom much of the evil and misery of life proceed. The first object intended to be attained by these arrangements, is to improve the character and condition of this class, and to apply their powers for the benefit of themselves and society. It has been said, that the proposed change may be made by means of the existing commercial system; indeed no other mode of relieving society from its present difficulties appears practicable, and by these means the change becomes not only natural, but irresistible.

To accomplish the change in this manner, it is necessary to create labour of a superior quality and cheaper than it can be now brought to market; for all cost resolves itself into labour, and it is evident that those arrangements which can produce the most skilful labour at the least expence, and at the same time support the labourer in the best health and most comfort, will upon common commercial principles put all other methods out of the market.

The inferior plans will be replaced by the superior, as human labour has been by the steam engine – as the single thread-spinning wheel has been by Arkwright's superior mechanism, and as the common hand printing press is now being replaced by the new power-printing machinery.

From these and a thousand other instances which may be easily adduced of the extensive and rapid application of the sciences to manufactures, commerce, agriculture, and the common purposes of life, a necessity has arisen for other corresponding changes among the working classes, in order to permit society to benefit by the scientific improvements which have been so liberally introduced.

The changes proposed for this purpose consist of new arrangements derived from science:

1st. *To* ERECT, HEAT and VENTILATE LODGING APARTMENTS for the working classes *better and cheaper* than can be effected by any of the plans now in practice.

2d. *To* FEED *them better and cheaper.*

3d. *To* CLOTHE *them better and cheaper.*

4th. *To* TRAIN *and* EDUCATE *them better and cheaper.*

5th. *To secure to them* BETTER HEALTH *than they now enjoy.*

6th. *To apply* THEIR LABOUR *to Agriculture, Manufactures, and all the purposes of society* MORE ADVANTAGEOUSLY *than has hitherto been practiced.*

And lastly – *To make them in* ALL RESPECTS *more valuable members of society.*

All must acknowledge that these will prove important improvements if they can be obtained.

It is now to be shown that they are easily attainable, and that all the means to give them permanence now superabound.

The most difficult problem to solve was, 'to ascertain what number of persons could be associated together so as to give to each the most advantage with the least inconvenience.'

The second, 'to discover on what principle the new association could be formed so as to avoid the evils which have hitherto kept society in a state of poverty, degradation, imbecility, and misery.'

The third, 'to find out how all their wants could be permanently and amply supplied, without a collision of individual interests, and at the same time to secure a progressive improvement in all knowledge, so as to give a continued zest and enjoyment to human existence.'

The arrangements best adapted for the improvement and enjoyment of the working classes, and which must at the same time render their labour superior to, and cheaper than that of all other labourers, are as follows: –

From about 500 to 1500 individuals, or (supposing 4 to a family) about 300 families are to reside in habitations in the country, on which the utmost foresight and science have been exercised in devising both their erection and combination. Every domestic advantage and comfort of which the dwellings of the working classes are susceptible, is to be found in these buildings. They comprise spacious sitting and bed rooms, extensive public kitchens and eating rooms, schools for different ages, church, places of worship for dissenters, infirmary, lecture room, and inn for the accommodation of friends or visitors of the inhabitants.

These buildings are to enclose an extensive play-ground for the younger children, space for gymnastic exercises for the elder children, and of recreation for adults. They will be surrounded by gardens, which are to be chiefly cultivated by the females and elder children, and to be placed in the midst of about 600 acres of land, the principal part of which will be principally cultivated by the spade.

All the buildings have been accurately designed, working plans for the builders are prepared, and every expence attending their erection has been estimated with great care, at the present cost price of materials and labour in the city of Glasgow, being nearest the proposed establishment, and 10 per cent on the whole has been added for contingencies. The whole cost of these erections has been found to be about £34,260.

For furnishing the apartments of 300 families	3,600
Fitting up school-room and places of worship for dissenters	200
Do. church	400
Do. infirmary	200
Do. lecture-room	300
Do. inn	500
Do. library	500
Making the entire cost about	£40,000

£40,000, at 7½ per cent interest per ann. is	3000
600 acres of land, at 30s. per acre	900
Annual interest and rent to pay	£3900

The buildings, as before remarked, will accommodate, in a more commodious and comfortable manner than any now in use, a population of 1,200 persons, or (supposing four to each family) 300 families. By dividing the above-mentioned annual interest and rent (£3,900) by 300, being the number of families accommodated, will give £13 to be paid by each family of four persons for the use of the spacious private furnished apartment, public buildings, and two acres of land; and by an accurate calculation, made on the expenditure of the working class at New Lanark, whose population is well known to be amply supplied, it is found that the average expenditure of each family does not exceed £45* per annum, including rent. However, to prevent the possibility of over-stating the argument, each family is here supposed to cost £50 per annum, including rent and interest. – This for 300 families will amount to £15,000 per annum. Now in a working population of 1200 individuals, there appears, from the more accurate data that can be obtained, an average of

248	individuals	under 10 years of age,	which we will call	first class
178	do.	from 10 to 15	do.	second class
719	do.	from 15 to 60	do.	third class
55	do.	from 60 and upwards	....	fourth class.

The labour of the children in the first class is not taken to account, although the occasional employment of those from 7 to 10 in weeding the gardens, and other light occupations, will be of value to the establishment. The labour of both

						per annum.
Sexes of the 2d class,	consisting of	165	individuals,	4s.	per wk. is	£1,716
Do. 3d class,	do.	680	do.	10s.	....	17,680
Do. 4th class,	do.	40	do.	5s.	....	520
						£19,916
Total expenditure, taken at a high rate, including rent and interest						15,000
					Surplus	£4,916

In this calculation the labour of 8 of the 2d class – 19 of the 3d class – 5 of the 4th class, is not taken to account, as they would be employed in various domestic purposes and superintendance – and also the labour of 5 of the 2d class – 20 of the 3d – and 10 of the 4th class, are supposed to be at all times ineffective, either from indisposition or other causes.†

* The expenditure of the new establishment will in fact be greatly diminished, even compared with that of New Lanark, as the former is to be supplied with all the necessaries of life by its own inhabitants, and by this means the various profits which are paid to the dealers in these articles will be saved to the establishment, as well as a considerable sum in fuel, cooking, etc.

† All these calculations are derived from a census which has been carefully kept at New Lanark for many years.

Thus in return for their services, estimated at the common prices of manual labour, will these working classes attain solid advantages which many of the middle classes do not possess at an expenditure of several hundreds per annum.

The advantages of these new arrangements to the physical, moral, and intellectual character of the working classes are so great, that when they can be once fairly placed before the public, they will plainly show the extravagance, loss, and absurdity of the present occupation and expenditure of the working classes.

The general advantages of these new arrangements are, (to state them in few words) that they will *prevent* the rising generation from being subject to poverty or the fear of poverty, from ignorance, from acquiring any bad habits or dispositions, from being angry with their fellow creatures, or from being in any degree intolerant to them, in consequence of any sentiments, habits, or dispositions which they may have been taught. The particular advantages are, that they will exist amidst a superfluity of whatever can be necessary to their well-being and happiness; that they will be made active and intelligent, and trained to possess the kindest and best dispositions, and that through their example all classes, sects and parties, will be induced to adopt whatever experience shall prove to be advantageous in these establishments.

ROBERT OWEN

PERMANENT RELIEF FOR THE BRITISH AGRICULTURAL AND MANUFACTURING LABOURERS, AND THE IRISH PEASANTRY[a] 1822

My present journey to this part of the kingdom,[b] commenced with a view of collecting information with regard to the real state of the public mind, respecting the singular situation in which this country has been since the termination of the late war, exhibiting the same privations and distress among its inhabitants from peace and plenty, as usually attend war and famine; and also to discover if means existed, by which a union could be effected between the great opposing interests which now retard the prosperity of all classes.

With these intentions, I attended several of the most popular public meetings which are held in the metropolis at this season, and I have freely mixed with all parties in private, to acquire a knowledge of the real, as well as of the more popular sentiments expressed in public, which are sometimes at variance with each other.

The result of this proceeding has convinced me, there is a large amount of good feeling throughout society, and that nothing more is now required to relieve, effectually, the general distress which pressed so severely on the lower classes, and particularly on the Irish, than to give to that feeling a sound practical direction.

Several individuals, who saw this subject in the same light, sent a delegation to request I would call a public meeting for the purpose of stating these sentiments, and of explaining the means by which a union of all parties may be now formed, with a view to effect a great and necessary public benefit, without the sacrifice of any conscientious principle. At this time I was preparing to return to Scotland, but the delegates urged their request with so much earnestness, as to induce me to yield to their solicitations, and in consequence this meeting was called.

---

[a] A Dublin edition appeared in 1823.

[b] Owen spent a number of months in Ireland in the autumn of 1822, and returned in 1823. A Hibernian Philanthropic Society was founded to further his proposals, but did not progress far. The full details of his chief public meetings were published in the *Report of the Proceedings at the Several Public Meetings Held in Dublin* (Dublin, 1823).

A union of the leading parties in the state, may at first sight appear to be of difficult attainment, but when the *necessity* which now exists, to effect a great public benefit, shall be fully understood, and the extent of good feeling which now pervades all classes shall be duly considered, it ought not, perhaps, to be deemed impracticable. And if this first attempt should fail, it may suggest to others the means by which they may afterwards secure success.

The union formed by the British and Foreign Bible Society;[a] a union at one time much more improbable than that about to be proposed, and the effects which in so short a period have been produced, in practice, by this Society acting on a single principle, while so many opposing sentiments and feelings are still retained by its members, is a convincing proof, when no sacrifice of opinion is required, both of the practicability of obtaining a very extended co-operation, and of the important effects which such a combination may be made to produce.

With this example then for your guide, measures are about to be proposed for your consideration by which a union, even more extended than that of the British and Foreign Bible Society, and more efficacious in its practical results, may be formed; a union by which Christians may unite with all men in good and conciliating offices, and by which all men may as cordially, and without any sacrifice of opinion, unite with Christians; and men must be brought to act together in some useful practical purpose before they can be induced to unite as brethren of one family, an event for which many Christians are now looking.

It is not therefore the union of the different sects of one religion only, that is now contemplated but the cordial unity in genuine charity, of the reflecting, intelligent, and truly benevolent of all classes, of all countries, and of all religions.

All these, as it appears to me, may now unite, and by so doing obtain the most important object, that is, the gradual but certain improvement and elevation of the most vicious and helpless of their fellow-creatures.

When the effects which can be produced by the power of extended union shall be understood, and the ease with which it may accomplish the most important purposes shall be known, it is not likely that any removable obstacles will be allowed to remain, to retard this great work which in consequence of the rapid extension of mechanism, is now absolutely necessary to prevent the destruction of a large portion of the most industrious classes.

The principle of union about to be proposed, is not only practicable, but so simple, that, with a little attention, it may be understood by every one.

All will admit that some individuals are placed from birth amidst demoralizing circumstances, such, for example, as are experienced by some of our fellow-

[a] Missionary society founded 1804.

creatures, who are born in the worst part of St Giles's, or similar situations in this metropolis; while others are surrounded from infancy withal most everything favourable to the forming of good moral habits and principles, such, for instance, as the children of parents, whose character and station in life may by comparison be said to be strictly moral.

All the past experience of the world prove, that these different situations do materially influence the character and conduct of children.

And in consequence it will be found to be of great permanent benefit to every one, that the best practical arrangements should be devised to prevent the existence, if possible, of any demoralizing circumstances among the lower classes of society; and to surround them with those which have the most moral tendency.

This is a practical conclusion to which intelligent minds of all ranks and classes, and sects and parties, in all countries, cannot refuse their assent; on which all may act, at all times, with a certainty that they are proceeding in a right course; that in so doing they cannot fail to accomplish a lasting benefit to humanity, and on this basis, without any sacrifice of opinion or injury to any, a union of the well disposed of all descriptions and denominations may now be formed to effect the most beneficial changes throughout society.

Here then is a base on which men of the most opposite opinions, whether in religion or politics, or political economy, may cordially unite. The only difference which can arise is in the degree of good which may be accomplished by the judicious arrangement of moral circumstances, some will contend for it to one extent and some to another; but as no attempt is to be made to define the exact point where this benefit terminates, no difference of sentiment can exist respecting the truth of the great fundamental principle on which this union is proposed to be formed, which is 'that circumstances have a material influence in forming the human character.'

And as little difference can arise in applying this principle to practice, because there are certain circumstances which all parties will admit to have a decided moral, and others which have as evidently a demoral tendency. And the past experience of society is now abundantly sufficient to mark distinctly the character of the one and of the other.

Every one will admit, that among the lower classes, ignorance, poverty, and idleness, have a strong general tendency to produce bad habits, and to demoralize the character; while a judicious early training, good example, and the absence of temptation, are the most likely means by which, in general, a useful and valuable character may be formed; with the few exceptions that appear to occur, it is not necessary to occupy the time of the meeting; our main object is now to explain the means by which the character and condition of the poor unoccupied peasant, and the working classes generally, may be permanently improved, and those frequent calls to avert the appalling effects of famine, by instant and immediate relief, after half the evils have been actually experienced, may hereafter be rendered unnecessary.

To prepare the practical detail of measures for the permanent removal of ignorance, idleness, bad habits, and poverty, is a task which has required from me much time, patience, and forbearance; and to enable you and the public at large to acquire a useful knowledge of this subject, I fear I must *now* trespass on *your* time and patience, and solicit *your* forbearance.

When first I addressed you in this place, I declared it as my fixed opinion, that none of the various remedies proposed by any party, would be found of any efficacy in relieving the national distress. Since that period many years have passed but not one without witnessing some fruitless attempt to restore prosperity to the country; and at this moment the distress, and consequent demoralization and disorders of Society, are rapidly advancing. Five years, since the public mind was not sufficiently prepared for the adoption of the Plans of Relief which were then brought forward. I therefore patiently waited the progress of time and circumstances; and now, after the experience you have had of the unsuccessful attempts which have been made, I again submit Proposals for uniting the present conflicting interests of Society.

To secure permanent relief to the working classes, it is necessary –

1. That they shall be usefully trained and educated.
2. That they shall be rendered industrious, and be usefully employed.
3. That the objects on which their industry shall be exerted shall be readily exchanged with advantage; and, that the demoralizing circumstances with which they are now surrounded, shall be removed, and be replaced by others having a more moral tendency.

Until these measures become the common practice of Great Britain and Ireland, it is vain to expect permanent relief can be given either to the Irish peasant, or to any of the working classes. New arrangements are now about to be explained to you, that will secure all these important advantages to those who may be placed within them.

To these arrangements when they shall be understood, neither the religious world, the politician, the mercantile world, or the political economist, the man of science, the man of the world, or the real lover of rational liberty, can consistently refuse their support, because by these arrangements the primary objects of each will be sooner and more effectually attained than under the existing customs and practices of society. The religious of all sects will have each child, within these arrangements, trained from infancy with good habits and dispositions, and prepared with a sound well formed intellect, yet with humility of mind, to receive the most valuable truths that can be placed before him, and to estimate them according to their real value, both for time and eternity.

The politician will, by these means, have the population trained to be the most useful and valuable members of the State, and to be the most competent to appreciate the benefits of a paternal and wise government, and to give it essential aid.

The mercantile world will thus be enabled to obtain a superfluity of wealth, and to enjoy it rationally, without the fear of bankruptcies, or of any of the miserable, degrading, and demoralizing effects which are now necessary appendages to the manufacturing, mercantile, and trading agricultural system.

The political economist will find these arrangements to contain well devised measures to enable all the active members of society to create the most valuable products in the best manner, that is, with the least labour and most comfort to the producers and consumers; and the means by which the products of labour shall be always conveniently distributed, and a beneficial supply be provided for all. By these arrangements also, when necessary, the most powerful moral restraints on an injurious increase of population may be obtained, and by which, when the interests of society shall require it, the powers of production and consumption can be the most advantageously economised, in order that the creation of capital shall be made to keep pace with the increase of population.

The men of science will by these means attain their utmost wishes; because, under the arrangements to be proposed, every child will receive an education that will draw forth scientific talent wherever it exists; and when discovered, it will be cultivated in the best manner for the benefit of the individual and of society. Science will be thus greatly extended, and every encouragement will be given to its general introduction into the whole business of life, and in consequence the most rapid and extensive improvements may be confidently anticipated; to their progress under such circumstances there can be no assurable limit. It will also be soon perceived, that it will be for the general interest of society that the knowledge of every invention, improvement, and discovery, should be freely communicated even to the most distant countries.

The men of the world will be gratified to the utmost extent of every rational wish and desire. All things of intrinsic value will be abundantly created, and a new population will arise, improved in all respects, both physically and mentally; and the real enjoyment of life to all must be thus essentially increased.

And lastly, the real lovers of liberty will discover that it is by these means only that rational liberty can ever be acquired or permanently enjoyed. In the exact proportion in which individuals shall be well trained from infancy, and placed under circumstances in which they can well govern themselves, may the restraints of general government be safely withdrawn; and as real knowledge and improvements advance among the mass of the population of the world, these restraints will be withdrawn, because no arbitrary power will then be able to restrain them.

It is now for me to explain, on the base of the principle stated, the means by which the Irish Peasantry, and the poor and working classes in general, may be permanently relieved. To those who have had much experience among these classes, it will be at once obvious, that while they remain in ungovernable masses, or live scattered in single families, apart from their species, that even at a great expense of time, labour and money, very little comparative benefit can be effected for them.

To proceed the most speedily, economically, and effectually, to improve these who have been hitherto neglected, it is absolutely necessary that they should be combined into convenient masses for training, education, and employment: for a ready permanent distribution of the products of their labour, and for the most easy mode of governing them for their own benefit.

The numbers in each of these associations should be confined within certain limits; if too large, the evils of towns and cities, crowded dwellings, and unwholesome atmosphere, unhealthy occupations, defective training and education, and other inconveniences, could not be avoided. If on the other hand the number were below a certain amount, the full benefits of combination would not be attained, and the children could not be well educated. – As the result of much consideration of this subject, it is proposed that each Association shall consist of from 500 to 2000 persons, according to circumstances. The form of a large square seems to present the most eligible disposition for the domestic accommodation of such Society, the dwelling houses occupying the sides of the square, and the public buildings being placed in the centre. This plan combines all the advantages of a town and country residence, without the inconveniences of either, and admits of the best and most simple economical arrangements, for securing the health of the whole population, for training, instruction, and recreation, for ventilating, lighting and cleaning, for cooking, and eating, and for every domestic object.

The engravings (annexed to this work)[a] will explain the general outlines and the detail of the most essential parts of the plan, and from which, workmen in any part of the world may form similar arrangements, and add to them any scientific or other improvements, that experience may suggest. Around the establishment there must be a sufficient quantity of land to supply its members with a surplus of the best or most wholesome food. Accurate experiments continued for a series of years, have satisfactorily proved, that a comparatively small extent of land (when the powers of the soil shall be adequately called forth under a proper system of spade culture,) will amply satisfy the wants of such a population. At a short distance from the gardens, which will surround the square, may be placed the workshops and manufactories, washing and drying houses, granaries and store rooms; with the aid of the embellishments which trees properly disposed afford, the whole of this combination may, in almost any situation, be made to present an animated and cheerful scene of great rural beauty.

These arrangements are intended to comprehend all the facilities which modern science can afford to the every day business of life, in order to render it healthy and agreeable, that intelligent and superior minds may no longer regard it as irksome and incompatible with intellectual pursuits, and that no necessity may exist for the longer continuance of the present ignorant and degraded class.

[a] No longer extant.

Mechanism and chemistry will be made essentially to aid these domestic operations.

To secure many important advantages that cannot be otherwise obtained (in society,) all will possess equal advantages; there will, therefore, be an equality in their houses, food, clothing, instruction, and treatment; except that those who at birth are the least favoured by nature, shall experience from infancy, increased kindness and attention, in proportion to their natural inferiority.

Individuals thus circumstanced, having but one and the same interest, to the promotion of which, their whole concentrated powers of body and mind will be steadily directed, will command the means of producing much more than they can require or desire to consume. They will always have in store a surplus of the necessaries of life to protect them against unfavourable seasons, and an excess of some kind of useful products, in return for which they can obtain from their neighbours, such commodities as their own territory may not yield, or which their localities may not permit them to create advantageously.

All the powers of production which can be derived from science, may be beneficially called into action; the introduction of a machine for the abridgement of human labour, will not, as at present, have the miserable effect of wringing from the labourer an *increased* amount of exertion in return for diminished means of decent subsistence; but, on the contrary, will give him increased advantages for *less* labour.

The gifts of science will no longer be perverted and rendered a curse to the great mass of society. Under the arrangements proposed, the discoveries and inventions of the last half century, will afford to these Associations the most effectual aid.

Manual labour will thus be converted into healthy, pleasant, and desirable occupation; while each individual will possess leisure for mental improvement and social enjoyment.

The evils which necessarily arise from the practice of commerce, in the present advanced state of the sciences, are incalculable. Since the termination of the last war, the period when its profitable continuance to the producers expired, it has annually destroyed many millions of their capital, and the process of destruction is still going on. As manufactures, trade, and commerce can yield a profit only as long as the demand exceeds the supply, or is barely equal to it, the present commercial system cannot admit of the supply exceeding the demand; although it is the interest of all that it should do so: but society has now acquired the means of producing far more than the population of the world can advantageously consume. To render the existing system profitable, therefore, it would be necessary to destroy so much of the power of production as should reduce the supply within the demand, and continually restrain that power; but it is directly contrary to the interests of every one that this power should be checked or restrained.

Various circumstances connected with the late war, gave a peculiar impetus to the powers of production in Great Britain, of which the developement was commensurate with the wants occasioned by the gigantic armies of the contending powers; but at the termination of this widespread contest, when so formidable a demon of waste and destruction ceased its active operations, and the world was allowed to be at peace, peace could not be enjoyed, because a general stop was put to trading and commercial prosperity, by the excess of supply beyond the demand.

So deep-rooted are the notions which make men cling to the present commercial system, as the only means by which the wants of the world can be supplied, that they will resort to every expedient to uphold it, notwithstanding the frightful sacrifices of capital, and the extreme distress in which the attempt is hourly involving them; nor will they cease their efforts until their ingenuity, again and again baffled, shall at length be exhausted. They will then perhaps ask themselves this simple question; – Why should we wish to reduce the supply within the demand?

When the mind can be divested of the prevailing prejudices on this subject, the true interests of society will be found to consist, 1st. In the discovery of what those things are which are necessary to give the greatest advantages to human nature; and 2dly. In the adoption of the best means by which a *redundant* supply of them may be produced and be accessible to all, that no cause may remain for opposition of interests. At this moment all parties are suffering grievously from the effects of the error of the commercial system; and none more than the individuals immediately engaged in it; millions of whom, for the sake of a bare subsistence, are subjected to every kind of degradation and wretchedness; while by the proposed arrangements, each individual will be enabled to possess much comfort, and many advantages, through every period of his life. In consequence of their number and union, the members of the new Associations, even at first, will have to sell and purchase far less than individuals under the existing system, and in the same proportion will the risk and expense of their commercial transactions be diminished.

To prevent loss and law-suits, as well as the evils arising from a system of credit, these transactions should always be in money, and be finally settled in the shortest time, that circumstances will admit. As the number of these Communities increases, the exchange of products with each other will gradually supersede the necessity of having recourse to common society for the supply of their wants. This exchange in the earlier stages of their progress, may be advantageously effected on the principle of estimating the value of commodities by the quantity of labour required for their production; the quantity, with reference to each article, being previously ascertained and mutually agreed upon and fixed for defined periods; and for convenience, this labour may be represented by notes, or Community bank paper, bearing the value of one, or any number of days labour. But after a sufficient number of Communities, within a moderate distance of each other, shall be in action to create a full supply of all the articles required by each; any such medium of exchange will be found neither necessary nor desirable.

The connection subsisting between the several Associations, being founded on the same common interest by which the members of each are united together, they will cordially cooperate in forming arrangements, which shall place the production and consumption of the whole confederation on the most permanent basis. All that can be necessary, in order to attain this object, will be first to regulate the production of each Community according to its localities and to the general wants; and, secondly, (as each Community will produce a surplus of certain products beyond its own possible wants,) to establish periodical conveyances, by means of which, these various surplus products may be regularly interchanged. In this manner will the public stores of each Community always contain an overflowing stock of all those things which can minister to the comfort or gratification of rational beings; and in these associations, poverty, or the fear of poverty will have no existence.

Men placed in these associations, will soon realize abundance of the necessaries and comforts of life, and little inducement will exist for individual accumulation; nor, as a Society, can they be influenced by any desire to amass wealth beyond what may be amply sufficient to protect them against every contingency.

It cannot fail to be perceived, that the harmony and stability of the new institutions will mainly depend upon the training and education of the young. In regard to this subject of paramount importance, the principles which have been developed in the first part of this work, will guide us with unerring certainty to sound conclusions and correct practice. We have shown that man is naturally influenced by circumstances, and it is easy to prove, that it depends in a great degree upon the influence of these circumstances, whether the individual shall become a civilized man or a cannibal, a charitable or a ferocious being, enlightened or ignorant, happy or miserable.

It is the distinguishing feature of the new arrangements, that being throughout consistent with the principles just stated, they at once place the rising Generation beyond the influence of all those circumstances which in every existing state of Society are continually operating to produce Vice and Misery. – By the very act of introducing a Child into one of these associations, constituted in the manner we have described, we shall have surmounted all the great obstacles which are at present interposed to his right training and education and to his future well-being. The course which remains to be pursued is simple and straight forward.

His instructors will regard him as a Being upon whose plastic nature, education, as it is well or ill directed, may stamp the best or worst impression; in whom under one system of treatment, may be implanted in his earliest years the seeds of jealousy, hatred, revenge, and every evil passion, while under another, these feelings may be greatly diminished if not entirely excluded.

Rewards and punishments, emulation and partialities are the characteristics of the present system, while the proposed will accomplish every thing by kindness alone.

The former system with the utmost difficulty and labour to all concerned, effects very inferior results; the system of kindness on the other hand, when commenced systematically from infancy, is calculated to produce only the best result, with little labour or difficulty of any kind; and it will be found to be beneficial that no other should be hereafter applied. Is it rational to punish a child because Nature has endowed him with inferior powers, or because circumstances over which he could have no control have impressed upon him a character which is displeasing to us? or is it more rational to reward another to whom nature has been more liberal and circumstances more propitious? Is punishment a likely method of improving and reforming the one, or can reward have any other effect upon the latter, than to pervert his good qualities, the possession of which in no degree depended upon himself? to render him a vain and conceited being and to lead him to despise his less fortunate fellow-creatures? Can charity be expected in men, when the elements of all uncharitableness are thus effectually instilled into the minds of children?

Such are the views which will be uniformly acted up to, in regard to education in the new state of society. The children of each Community will be brought up together, and literally be as one family, in which partialities and distinctions will have no place. They will eat at the same table, wear the same dress, enjoy the same means of amusement, receive the same instruction, and be treated in all respects with the same undeviating kindness. No circumstances will exist around them, which can excite in their young minds a single antisocial thought, which can possibly lead them to imagine that the happiness of each does not consist in the happiness of the whole. Long before verbal instruction can be intelligent to them, they will act instinctively, as it were, in the very spirit of the precept, 'Love thy Neighbour;'[a] and why will they act thus? because under the system in which they are trained no motives will be infused in to their minds which can give rise to any other conduct. But this result cannot depend upon the children themselves, for we might place them under such circumstances as should with equal certainty force them to hate each other.

The system of instruction which will be adopted, under the new arrangements, will differ essentially from that which prevails at present. It is a mistake to suppose that there exists in children any repugnance to acquire knowledge, or to imagine that the business of tuition is necessarily an irksome task, and that which is proper for them to learn must needs be forced upon them. The truth is, that at no age is the desire of knowledge, stronger than in childhood,

[a] See Leviticus 19:18.

at this period of life all the objects which surround the human being, possess the charm of novelty, and the feeling of curiosity is intense. That the office of instructor may be rendered agreeable, and his services efficient and acceptable, and that none but the best feeling may be created between him and his pupils, it is necessary to present to them the objects of their instruction, in the order which corresponds with the natural developement of their faculties; and instead of disgusting them with confused notions, by endeavouring in early life to give them ideas of things through the medium of written language only; to convey to their minds clear and distinct perceptions, and correct knowledge, by the aid of sensible signs, with oral explanations. More especially is it necessary to withhold from their young minds any disputed opinions, regarding the truth or consistency of which their previous attainments do not enable them to form a rational opinion; for to act otherwise tends directly to weaken and destroy the most valuable of their intellectual powers.

We shall not however do justice to human nature, if we cultivate the Intellectual at the expense of the physical powers. That the individual may enjoy the highest degree of happiness of which he is susceptible, a sound mind must reside in a sound body. The powers of the body and of the mind will, in every individual under the proposed arrangements, be cultivated with equal care; a due proportion of time being allotted to the exercise and improvement of each.

Political Economists have hitherto totally misunderstood their subject. They have in all cases supposed, that the sole object of Society, was the accumulation of Riches, and that Men would necessarily obtain all they required in proportion as their wealth increased. They have always reasoned as though man were an inanimate machine, without the capacity of *suffering, understanding,* or *enjoying,* and have consequently recommended those Measures which were calculated to reduce the mass of Mankind, into mere implements of production, and to deteriorate the general powers, physical and mental, of each individual, that some small part of his faculties might be unnaturally and most injuriously cultivated. Thus have they led the public step by step, from one error to another, until, at length, they can proceed no farther, for the fact has become too evident, that Men can easily produce more than they know how to distribute or consume advantageously. At this moment the chief suffering of mankind arises from an excess of wealth, which cannot be rendered available for the great Mass of the People, who in several districts are suffering many severe privations – The science of Political Economy is, or ought to be, only another term for the science of Human Happiness, for if it does not promote this, it is of no value whatever.

As it has hitherto been taught, however, it is directly opposed to human happiness, nor is it calculated to attain, even the inferior object of wealth, which it professes to have in view.

It recommends as its fundamental principles the most minute division of labour, and separate or individual interests, among the whole human race; while the first dawn of real knowledge respecting the means of creating riches, and of promoting the well being and happiness of mankind will make it evident that these principles are at once opposed, 1st. to the most advantageous creation, distribution, and preservation, of wealth, and 2dly to the best formation of the human character, physically, mentally, and morally.

No one can doubt that it is for the interest of mankind, that abundance of the most useful and intrinsically valuable products, should be created, with the least labour and the greatest benefit to the producer and consumer; that this wealth should be distributed in the best manner throughout Society, in order that each may have a full supply; that that which remains for future consumption and reproduction, should be the most easily preserved; and that every individual should be trained to be capable of enjoying in the highest degree the use of these productions. – But not one of these essential objects can be attained under a system of which the characteristics are, a minute division of labour, and separate or individual interests.

The effect of the first of these erroneous principles, is to form man into a creature far inferior to an inanimate Machine; to deprive him (except in a single point of little comparative value) of all excellence as an intelligent, rational being; and to render him an unequal competitor with the harder material, of wood, brass, and iron, to effect often the most useless result. The second of these principles destroys all the supposed advantages arising from the first, by preventing to an incalculable extent the adoption of the best means, for distributing and preserving wealth, after it has been created, and together they render it impossible that the population of the World, can ever become under their influence, either rich, healthy, intelligent, moral or happy.

Political Economists have hitherto been entirely ignorant of human nature, and consequently of the very elementary principles on which the science of Political Economy (in any rational signification of the term) is founded.

'How to create the largest supply of the most valuable productions with the least expense of labour, and with the greatest amount of benefits to all,' is the problem which this science is required to solve.

A correct knowledge of human nature is all that is now necessary for the attainment of each of these objects in a high degree of perfection, and if that knowledge be acted upon poverty or the fear of it, will no longer counteract the happiness of Society. But instead of pushing the division of labour so far as to mutilate,[a] if we may so speak, the character of man – to reduce him in fact to a small fraction of an intelligent being, it will be the great object of all our arrangements to place him under circumstances in which all his valuable

[a] Adam Smith had written of 'that sort of mental mutilation, deformity, and wretchedness' which a narrow division of labour might bring to the working classes. See *Wealth of Nations*, Bk 5, ch. 1.

powers both physical and mental, will be so well and equally trained from infancy, that he will possess the abilities and inclination to create abundantly whatever can be necessary to his comfortable existence.

At this hour, with great industry and application, and much good intention, the modern Economists from wholly mistaking their subject are producing throughout civilized Society, the greatest suffering and evil.

They have assumed it as an incontrovertible position, that wealth is created of a superior kind and more abundantly, is more wisely distributed, better preserved for future consumption or reproduced and more advantageously used, under the present System of separate and opposing interests, than it would be under one of mutual Aid and Co-operation, or of united interests. And although the reverse were the case, they have also supposed, that it is impossible to unite mankind to act cordially and beneficially for the general good; in short, that human beings could not be stimulated to exertion, except through the influence of individual, separate, and opposing interests. – No greater proof than these conclusions afford, could be exhibited of the utter ignorance respecting human nature and the elementary principles of their Science, in which the Economists are involved.

Every one at once admits the superiority of an army well organized, and abundantly supplied with all the materials of war, over the same number of individuals unconnected, untrained, unsupplied with arms and necessaries for the contest, and each being obliged to think, act and provide for himself, not only unaided but opposed by his Comrades. The different effects to be produced by the same number, under these opposite circumstances, scarcely admit of a comparison. Union in war obviously increases the power of the individual a thousand fold. Is there the shadow of a reason why it should not produce equal effects in peace? Why the principle of co-operation should not give to men the same superior powers and advantages in the creation, preservation, distribution and enjoyment of wealth? but it may be urged, that men cannot be made to unite for the purposes of creating, preserving, distributing and enjoying wealth and happiness, in the same manner as they have been associated to prevent the creation of wealth, to destroy it when created, to overwhelm their fellow creatures with poverty and ignorance, and to inflict upon them every species of suffering, and to render them destitute and miserable.

These and all such notions are surely a libel on human nature, and have arisen solely from a misconception of what it really is. The experience of the writer has removed all doubts from his mind on this subject; and he hesitates not to say, that the time is now arrived when it will be far more easy (as much more so as it will be more beneficial) to unite men heartily in measures for promoting and securing their interests, than it has been through the past ages of the world, to induce them to act in numbers, as one body and one mind, for the purpose of inflicting misery and destruction on each other. Men can be impelled to co-operate for the latter purpose, only so long as they are made irrational, and kept in that state.

To produce a union of the working classes for the attainment of all the objects of life, nothing more is necessary than to train men from their infancy in good habits, and to be rational, and this will be easily accomplished under the proposed arrangements.

It remains to be explained, in order to complete the outline of these arrangements, in what manner the local government of the new Communities, may be the most advantageously conducted.

The administration of affairs, in the first instance, must be delegated to a select Committee, composed of such persons as the knowledge of the parties concerned may point out as being the best qualified to superintend the different departments; or appointed by the persons who furnish the capital. Such individuals should be appointed by the management of these associations as may be the most competent. When the members of the association shall have received the advantages of the system of training and education to which we have referred, each will be fully competent to undertake the charge of some of the departments. And a very simple mode suggests itself by which every individual may then, advantageously for all, participate equally in the business of management.

The future Committee accordingly will be composed of all the members of the Society, between certain ages of these, for instance between 40 and 50. From what has been said it is easy to foresee, that in such a state of Society the business of the association will be easily managed.

If any evils in practice should be found to arise at first, from inexperience, immediate measures will be adopted to discover the cause from which they originated, and it may be safely predicted, that they will be easily removed.

While each association will in its internal affairs be independent of all others, there will exist for general purposes a cordial union among them.

The same spirit which unites the members of each will, necessarily, lead to the most amicable alliance between one association and every other.

As these institutions multiply, in the same proportion will an increase of benefits accrue to all who are placed within the sphere of their influence. National distinction and prejudices will gradually subside and cease to form a barrier to the establishment of a friendly intercourse and a free communication and interchange of inventions, discoveries, and improvements, among the great families of mankind. The happiness of one portion of the human species will not be founded upon the sacrifice and miseries of another.

Thus, if I am right, will the object of every great party in the state be obtained in the shortest time, at the least expense, with the least inconvenience to any one, and the most effectually.